THE CIVILIZATION

OF

BABYLONIA AND ASSYRIA

LECTURES DELIVERED

UNDER THE

RICHARD B. WESTBROOK LECTURESHIP FOUNDATION

AT THE

WAGNER FREE INSTITUTE OF SCIENCE
PHILADELPHIA

THIRD IMPRESSION

THE CIVILIZATION
OF
BABYLONIA AND ASSYRIA

PLATE I

Sir Austen Henry Layard

Ernest de Sarzec

Georg Friedrich Grotefend

Sir Henry C. Rawlinson

Rev. Edward Hincks

Jules Oppert

George Smith

John Henry Haynes

EXPLORERS AND DECIPHERERS

THE CIVILIZATION

OF

BABYLONIA AND ASSYRIA

ITS REMAINS, LANGUAGE, HISTORY, RELIGION, COMMERCE, LAW, ART, AND LITERATURE

BY

MORRIS JASTROW, Jr., Ph.D., LL.D.

PROFESSOR IN THE UNIVERSITY OF PENNSYLVANIA

WITH MAP AND 164 ILLUSTRATIONS

PHILADELPHIA AND LONDON
J. B. LIPPINCOTT COMPANY

To
JOSEPH GEORGE ROSENGARTEN, A.M., LL.D.
SCHOLAR AND FRIEND OF SCHOLARS

PREFACE

To my knowledge this is the first time that the attempt has been made on a somewhat large scale to cover the entire subject of Babylonian-Assyrian civilization for English readers.

The aim of this work is to present a survey of the remarkable civilization which arose in the Euphrates Valley thousands of years ago and which, spreading northwards, continued to flourish till close to the threshold of the Christian era. As a result of the combined activities of explorers, decipherers and investigators of many lands during the past seventy years, we can follow the unfolding of the growth of the centres of settlement in the south which led ultimately to the formation of the Babylonian Empire, and of the offshoot of Babylonian civilization which resulted in the rise of a rival empire to the north, known as Assyria. While much still remains to be done before we can be said to have solved the problems—historical, linguistic, archæological and ethnological—raised by the discoveries made beneath the mounds which concealed the remains of forgotten Babylonian and Assyrian cities for so many centuries, we have learned to know the customs and manners, the religion, the law, the commerce and art of both Babylonia and Assyria quite intimately. We know how these peoples lived and how they died, the arrangement of their houses, palaces and temples, as well as of their tombs; their daily life and their religious aspirations. The various occupations of the people are revealed in thousands upon thousands of clay documents, found in the mounds, which tell of business activities, of commercial intercourse, of legal disputes, of the growing complications of social life, and of judicial decisions affecting all classes of the population. The beliefs and practises prevailing in Babylonia and Assyria are illustrated by abundant literary material, dating from the oldest period down to the fall of Babylonia and beyond that into the era of Persian and Greek control. A considerable amount of literature in the stricter sense of the term has also come down to us on the clay tablets; and finally monuments, the remains of temples and palaces, with wall sculptures, statues, votive offerings, cult objects and ornaments enable us to trace the course of art development along the centuries that span the existence of the Babylonian and Assyrian Empires.

The moment seems, therefore, opportune for grouping together the large amount of material at our disposal, with a view of presenting a general picture of Babylonian-Assyrian civilization. In this endeavor I have utilized the results of the researches of many others, besides embodying those of my own, for the field of investigation embracing Babylonia and Assyria is now too large to be cultivated in its entirety by any single investigator. It has been my aim throughout to present only such results as may safely be regarded as definite, and to abstain from mere haphazard and conjectural views. Naturally, in a work of a general character and intended for the larger public, some details had to be passed over for fear of crowding the picture. In such a selection personal judgment must inevitably be the guiding factor, but I trust that I have, on the whole, succeeded in picking out what is

most important for a general view of the civilization
and also most characteristic.

I hope that the liberal use which has been made
of illustrations will be looked upon as contributing to
the clearer setting forth of the results. Here, too, a
selection was called for, and I have had in mind to
place at the disposal of the reader reproductions of
all the more important monuments, as well as of many
less known objects, so as to furnish a series that may
form a tolerably complete companion to the text. I
have included specimens also of cuneiform documents
so as to show the kind of material from which Assyriologists obtain their results. Special attention may
also be called to the attempt to illustrate the course
of decipherment of the cuneiform inscriptions with
the aid of reproduction and selection of cuneiform
signs and combinations of such signs into words. The
decipherment of an unknown script is a fascinating
theme even to the layman, and I feel that I owe no
apology for taking the space necessary to make clear
to the general reader how it was possible to find a
key to the reading of the puzzling combinations of
wedges that became the medium of written expression
in the Euphrates Valley. Equally interesting is the
story of the way in which the ancient cities of Babylonia and Assyria were dug up by explorers, undaunted
by difficulties that at times seemed insurmountable. I
have tried to tell the story without belaboring the general reader with too many details, but with due regard
to setting forth the merits of each one of the pioneers
to whom the world owes a lasting debt. To emphasize
this debt I have united in one plate the portraits of
Layard, Rawlinson, Grotefend, Hincks, Oppert, George

Smith, de Sarzec, and Haynes, whose names are indissolubly linked with the recovery of our knowledge of the long-forgotten civilization of Babylonia and Assyria. Three of these men, George Smith, Ernest de Sarzec and John Henry Haynes, went to premature graves as the result of their arduous labors in the interest of science, which claims its martyrs no less than religion. But for circumstances beyond my control, I would have included the portrait of P. E. Botta,[1] the pioneer among the explorers of Assyrian mounds, as well as those of two scholars still with us, of Robert Koldewey, the leader of the German expedition which has conducted excavations in Babylonia for upwards of fourteen years, and of Friedrich Delitzsch, the distinguished Professor of Assyriology at the University of Berlin, who has done more than any other living scholar to stimulate the study of Assyriology through the training of scholars, now scattered in various parts of the world, and through his own contributions in advancing our knowledge of the Babylonian and Assyrian language and literature. Besides these, there is a long honor roll among living scholars, who, in this country, in England, France, Germany, Italy, Austria, Russia, Holland and the Scandinavian countries, are devoting their careers to the further elucidation of the subject, and through whom contributions to the sum of human knowledge are being constantly made. To all of these, from whose researches I have derived help, I wish to make a hearty acknowledgment.

In the closing chapter I have added specimens from the various branches of the literature of Babylonia and

---

[1] There is a portrait of Botta in the Louvre Museum, but unfortunately, on account of the war, no photograph of it could be taken.

Assyria, which are intended to serve in part as amplifying the references to such literary products in the body of the book, and partly to give the reader a view at closer range of literary composition as developed in the Euphrates Valley, and as further carried on in Assyria. The translations, it may be added, aim at being literal, with due regard, however, to reproducing in English the effect of the original.

A sense of deepest gratitude leads me to express, as on former occasions, my indebtedness to my dear wife for her aid in preparing this work, an aid ever generously and lovingly given. In addition to other services she has read a proof of the entire work and if, as a result, the pages are comparatively free from those slips which are so difficult to avoid, and which one likes to ascribe to the pranks of devilish imps by whom in proof-reading one is surrounded, it is due to the care which she has bestowed on her task.

The index is the work of my pupil and colleague, Dr. B. B. Charles, Instructor in Semitic Languages at the University of Pennsylvania, whose co-operation has, as on former occasions, been most cheerfully given. To the publishers my thanks are due for the interest that they have displayed in the progress of the work, for their patience in waiting for the completion of the manuscript, prepared under many inevitable interruptions, and for the handsome form that they have given to the text and to the illustrations.

My thanks are due also to the authorities of the British Museum, of the Musée de Louvre, of the Berlin Museum, to Dr. G. B. Gordon, the director of the University of Pennsylvania Archaeological Museum, to Mr. J. Pierpont Morgan Jr. and to Miss Belle Da Costa

Greene, the efficient Librarian and custodian of the
Morgan collection, and to the Deutsche Orient Gesellschaft, for permission to use illustrations from publications, and reproductions from antiquities and monuments in their possession; likewise, for similar permission, most generously given, to a number of publishers in
this country and abroad, namely, Behrend & Co. Berlin;
Chapman and Hall, London; Chatto & Windus, London; J. C. Hinrichs, Leipzig; Curts and Jennings, Cin-
cinnati; Ernest Leroux, Paris; Luzac & Company, London; Macmillan & Company, New York; W. A. Mansell
and Co., London; John Murray, London; Martinus
Nijhoff, The Hague; G. P. Putnam's Sons, New York;
Georg Reimer, Berlin; The Society of Biblical Archæology, London; W. Speman, Berlin; *Sunday School
Times,* Philadelphia; Alfred Toepelmann, Giessen; and
thirdly to a large number of colleagues, who either
placed photographs at my disposal or have allowed me to
reproduce illustrations from books published by them.
It gives me particular pleasure to acknowledge in this
way the kindness of such friends of many years' standing as Prof. Paul Haupt of Johns Hopkins University;
Dr. W. Hayes Ward; Prof. A. T. Clay of Yale University, Prof. A. V. Williams Jackson of Columbia University; Prof. Carl Bezold of the University of Heidelberg; Mr. L. W. King of the British Museum, Mr. R. C.
Thompson, M. Salomon Reinach of Paris; Dr. T. G.
Pinches of London; Prof. R. W. Rogers of Drew Theological Seminary; Rev. Dr. John P. Peters of New
York; Dr. E. J. Banks; Prof. Friedrich Delitzsch of the
University of Berlin; Prof. Eduard Meyer of the Uni-
versity of Berlin, and M. François Thureau-Dangin of
Paris.

Lastly, I wish to record here the debt of gratitude that I owe to the friend of so many years to whom it is a pleasure and a great privilege to be permitted to dedicate this work. What I owe to the friendship of Joseph George Rosengarten and to my association with him cannot be adequately expressed in words. Himself a scholar, active and fruitful in many fields, he has been the guide and friend of many scholars connected with the institution in whose service I have now spent thirty years. Keenly appreciative of scholarly efforts in every field, he has done much to promote by his example and by his aid researches among the members of the faculty of the University of Pennsylvania, which more than anything else redound to the honor and glory of an institution of learning. In dedicating this book to him I feel that I am also acknowledging, though in poor coin, the debt of my colleagues as well as my own.

MORRIS JASTROW, JR.

UNIVERSITY OF PENNSYLVANIA
SEPTEMBER, 1915

CONTENTS

ILLUSTRATIONS

ILLUSTRATIONS xxiii

THE CIVILIZATION OF BABYLONIA AND ASSYRIA

CHAPTER I

EXCAVATIONS AT BABYLONIAN AND ASSYRIAN SITES

I

THE land to which we are led in the exposition of this subject lies thousands of miles away and the time with which we are concerned lies thousands of years behind us. The question may, therefore, properly be asked, what is our interest in the civilization that flourished in the Euphrates Valley as early, at least, as 3500 years before our era, and that spread northwards into the region lying along the banks of the Tigris as early as 2500 B.C., if not earlier.[1]

In the case of Babylonia and Assyria, the very remoteness of the theme, of the place, and of the time constitute three reasons why its history, culture, and religion should be of real interest to us, for the past, and

---

[1] See the accompanying map. Babylonia is the name given to the southern portion, Assyria to the northern portion. For the oldest period, Sumer and Akkad may be used as designations of the southern and northern sections of the Euphrates Valley, while Chaldea represents an early name for a part of the southern section which, owing to the accidental circumstance that the latest dynasty of Babylonia—the so-called neo-Babylonian period (625 to the advent of Cyrus in 539 B.C.)—came from Chaldea, led Roman writers to use this term for the whole region, *i.e.*, for Babylonia and Assyria. Mesopotamia, the land "between the rivers," properly applies only to the section included between the Euphrates and Tigris from their junction northwards. It is, therefore, an inaccurate designation for Babylonia and Assyria, since it does not include the Euphrates Valley.

1

more particularly the remote past, exercises an intense fascination upon us—a fascination due to the conviction, deep-seated within us, that whereas we belong to the present, the past belongs to us. The history of mankind is a continuous series of links, forming, as Herder phrased it, the "golden chain of culture." Each civilization as it arises is the heir of the ages that have gone before, every phase of human culture stands in some connection with the preceding phase. Our American civilization is an offshoot of European culture to which we have made some contributions. The culture of Western and Northern Europe represents the extension of Roman civilization. Rome owes its intellectual stimulus to Greece, whose heir she became, and Greek culture, as we know, rests on a substratum of Asiatic influence and embodies elements derived from Egypt and Babylonia as well as from Asia Minor; and even when we pass to the distant East, the chain is not broken. Persia looks back to India, as Japan to China. Through Buddhism the connection is established between Chinese and Hindu civilization, and there are good reasons for believing that a direct cultural influence came to China from India at a period even earlier than the introduction of Buddhism, while the evidence, though not yet complete, is increasing which indicates that both the Chinese and Hindu civilizations lie within the sphere of influences emanating from such far older cultural centres as the Valley of the Euphrates and the Valley of the Nile.

In studying the past we are, therefore, in reality studying ourselves, we are concerned with something that is not remote, but on the contrary with something that is quite close to us—with flesh of our flesh and bone of our bone. It is this direct interest in the past as a part of ourselves that underlies the remarkable activity unfolded in Europe and in our own country in the task of recovering the remains of the past, so long hidden under the soil. Everywhere—in Greece and Italy, in Asia Minor and India, in Palestine and Syria, in Egypt and

Babylonia the spade of the explorer has been busy[2] revealing the vestiges of ancient civilizations—revealing in many cases the entirely forgotten annals of mankind and enabling us to replace dimmed traditions by clearly ascertained facts, to sift legend and myths from actual historical occurrence, to reconstruct, in short, the earlier periods of that endeavor of mankind to rise superior to its surroundings which we call intellectual, social and religious progress.

But apart from the antiquity of Babylonia and Assyria, there are certain circumstances which invest the region of the Euphrates and Tigris with a special kind of interest. Time-honored tradition places here not only the beginnings of civilization but also the cradle of the human race. The Garden of Eden is a section of Babylonia, as is sufficiently attested by the express mention of the Tigris and Euphrates as two of the rivers which flowed through the primeval habitation of mankind; and though the story of Adam and Eve is devoid of any historical value, yet the tradition which assigns the first human pair to Babylonia is of great significance for the prominence which Babylonia must have acquired in the minds of the Hebrews, whose religious traditions are thus indissolubly bound up with Babylonia. Again, even when driven out of the mythical paradise, man does not leave Babylonia. The Valley of Shinar in which all of mankind is represented as being settled at the time of the building of the great tower that should reach to heaven, is merely a designation for the southern portion of the Euphrates Valley,[3] while the tower itself was suggested by the *zikkurats* or stage-towers, which were a

[2] See Michaelis, *A Century of Archeological Discoveries* (Translated by Bettina Kahnweiler, N. Y., 1908).

[3] Shinar is identical with Sumer—the original force of which appears to have been " the land " *par excellence*. It came in time to be the specific designation of the southern part of the Valley in contrast to Akkad as the designation of the northern portion. See King, *History of Sumer and Akkad*, pp. 13–15.

characteristic feature of the religious architecture of Babylonia.[4] In this story, or rather in the two stories intertwined in the 11th chapter of Genesis,—one the building of the city which is given the name of Babylon, and the other the building of the tower[5]—the significant feature is the tradition which thus ascribed to the Euphrates Valley the distinction of once harboring all mankind in addition to being the cradle of the human race. Where the cradle of the human race stood is still a problem of Ethnology in our days, and is perhaps incapable of solution by scientific methods, but the fact that even to the ancient Hebrews, the region of the Euphrates and Tigris appeared as the one which had been settled from time immemorial favors the hypothesis for which we have other evidence, albeit not conclusive, that a high order of civilization first developed in that region. Its only possible rival is Egypt, and the indications at present are that while the actual beginnings of Egyptian civilization may lie further back than the Euphratean culture, yet Babylonia takes precedence in the unfolding of an *advanced* form of cultural achievements.

Leaving this question aside for the present and returning to Biblical traditions, it is also of moment to note that the Hebrews traced their wanderings prior to their entrance into Palestine to Babylonia, for Ur of the Chaldees, whence Terah the father of Abram sets out, is a well-known city in Babylonia, and Harran where he sojourned is another city farther to the north. There is no reason to question the correctness of the tradition which traces the Hebrews, or at least one of the groups that afterwards formed the combination known by this designation, back to Babylonia. As a matter of fact we come across traces of the Euphratean civilization at almost every period of Hebrew history. We encounter it

---

[4] See Jastrow, *Aspects of Religious Belief and Practice in Babylonia and Assyria*, p. 289 seq.

[5] See an article by the writer on ''The Tower of Babel'' in the *Independent*, vol. 57 (1905), pp. 822–826.

PLATE II

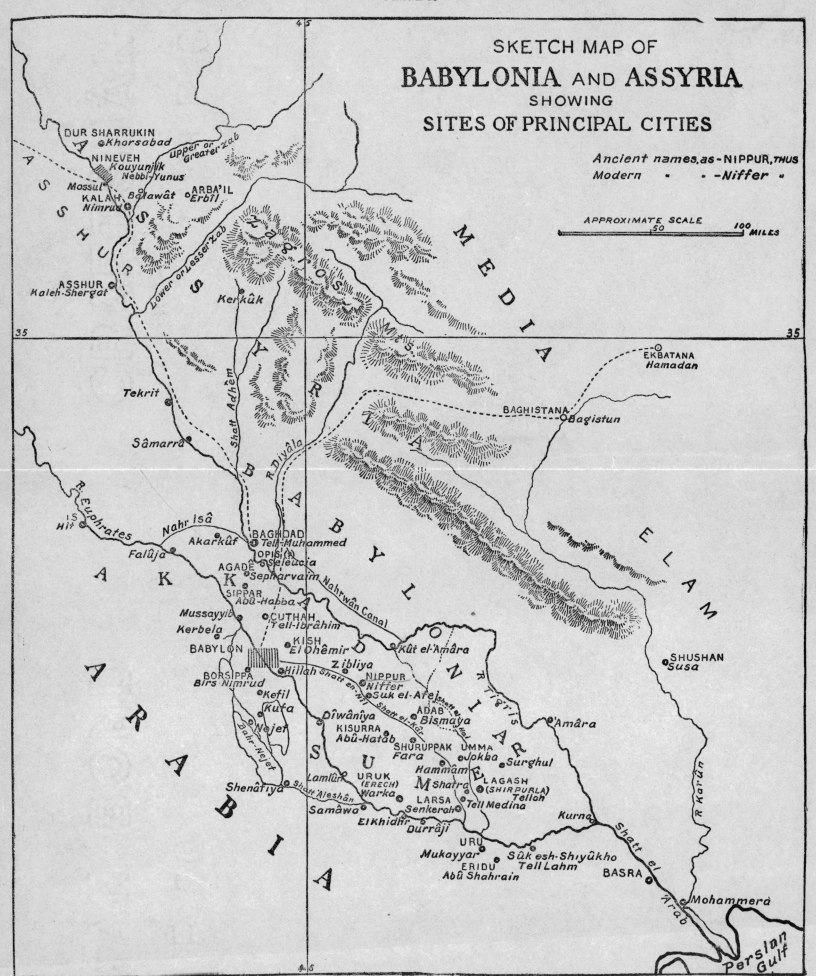

SKETCH MAP OF
BABYLONIA AND ASSYRIA
SHOWING
SITES OF PRINCIPAL CITIES

Ancient names, as - NIPPUR, THUS
Modern " " -Niffer "

APPROXIMATE SCALE
50   100 MILES

DUR SHARRUKIN
Khorsabad
NINEVEH
Kouyunjik
Nebbi-Yunus
Mossul
KALAH
Nimrud
Balawât
ARBA'IL
Erbîl

ASSHUR
A S S H U R
Kaleh-Shergat
Upper or Greater Zab
Lower or Lesser Zab
Z A G R O S
M E D I A
Kerkûk

35   35
EKBATANA
Hamadan
Tekrit
Shatt Adhêm
BAGHISTANA
Bagistun
Sâmarra
A S S Y R I A
R. Divâla

R. Euphrates
Hit
IS
Nahr Isâ
Falûja
Akarkûf
BAGHDAD
Tell-Muhammed
OPIS
Seleucia
AGADE
Sepharvaim
Nahrwân Canal
SIPPAR
Abû-Habba
A K K A D
Mussayyib
CUTHAH
Kerbela
Tell-Ibrâhim
BABYLON
KISH
El Ohêmir
Kût el-Amâra
SHUSHAN
Susa
Zibliya
BORSIPPA
Hillah
Birs Nimrud
Shatt en-Nîl
NIPPUR
Niffer
Suk el-Afej
Kefil
Kufa
Nejef
Dîwânîya
ADAB
Bismaya
Amâra
R. Tigris
KISURRA
Abû-Hatab
SHURUPPAK
Fara
UMMA
Jokha
Surghul
Bahr-Nejef
Hammâm
LAGASH
(SHIRPURLA)
Telloh
Lamlûn
URUK
(ERECH)
Shatra
Warka
E L A M
LARSA
Senkerah
Tell Medina
Shenâfîya
Shatt 'Aleshân
Samâwa
Kurna
Shatt el Arab
R. Karûn
Elkhidhr
Durrâji
URU
Mukayyar
Sûk esh-Shıyûkho
Tell Lahm
BASRA
ERIDU
Abû Shahrain
Mohammera
A R A B I A
B A B Y L O N I A
S U M E R
Persian Gulf

From "Aspects of Religious Belief and Practice in Babylonia and Assyria" by Morris Jastrow, Jr., by courtesy of G. P. Putnam's Sons, New York and London, 1910

in the language of the Hebrews, in the codes that grew
up among them, in their art and architecture, in their
social life, in their political organization, and to a very
considerable extent in their religious rites and earlier beliefs.[6] The Old Testament is fairly saturated with Babylonian culture, and even when we reach the time and
days of the New Testament we have not yet passed beyond the sphere of Babylonian influence.

II

A glance at the map will show some of the reasons
why civilization developed at so early a period in the Euphrates Valley. The main feature of the region is formed
by the two streams that water it—the Euphrates and
Tigris—and bring about the high degree of fertility
which Herodotus emphasizes.[7] Of these rivers, the Euphrates—the correct form of which is Purattu and described in texts as "the great river"—is the stream that
properly belongs to the southern district or Babylonia,
while the Tigris or more properly Idiklat, pictured
as " the rapid " stream, is the river of the northern district or Assyria. Both rivers start in the mountain regions of Armenia,[8] but they are quite diverse in character. The Euphrates is on the whole a quiet and, in parts,
a sluggish stream. It flows along in majestic dignity,
and receiving many tributaries on its way while still in
the mountains, proceeds first in a westerly direction as
though making directly for the Mediterranean Sea but
veers suddenly to the southeast, after which it receives
only a few tributaries until it is joined by the Tigris in
the extreme south. Of its entire length of 1780 miles it

---

[6] This subject is fully set forth in the writer's *Hebrew and
Babylonian Traditions* (New York, 1914).

[7] Book I, § 193.

[8] See Lehmann-Haupt, *Die historische Semiramis und ihre Zeit.*,
(Tübingen 1910), p. 16 seq.

is navigable for a short distance only, cataracts forming a hinderance in the north and, owing to the increasing sluggishness of the stream, sand banks in the south. As a consequence, it never became at any time an important avenue for commerce, rafts and wicker baskets, coated within and without with bitumen, being the only method of transportation which was possible under such circumstances.

The Tigris, though only 1146 miles long, is quite a different stream. After leaving its source in the mountains, it gains steadily in power, forcing its way through rugged clefts. It is joined by numerous tributaries before it reaches the plain, its volume being continually increased so that even when it reaches the alluvial soil of the south, its rapid course is not checked. It flows in a slightly fluctuating southerly direction, advances towards the Euphrates and recedes from it again until at last the two rivers join at Kurna and together pour their waters as the Shatt el-Arab or "Arabic River" into the Persian Gulf. The Tigris is navigable from Diarbekr in the north to its junction with the Euphrates. Large rafts can be floated down to Baghdad and small steamers can ascend almost up to Mosul. The Tigris is, therefore, the avenue of commerce for Mesopotamia—to use the conventional designation for the country—and forms the link that connects Babylonia and Assyria through the Persian Gulf with India on the one hand, and Egypt and the Red Sea and the Mediterranean districts on the other. The contrast presented by the two streams is paralleled by the diverse features distinguishing Assyria, the northern section, from Babylonia, the southern section. Assyria, with a length of about 350 miles and a width ranging from 190 to 300 miles,[9] is shut off to the north, northeast, and northwest by mountain ranges and retains for a considerable portion of its extent, and particularly towards the east, a

---

[9] A total area of some 75,000 square miles, or somewhat smaller than the state of Nebraska.

rugged aspect. The Kurdish Mountains run close to the Tigris for some distance below Mosul, though after that the region changes its character. Plains without any break succeed the hills, the soil becomes alluvial and the Tigris and its tributaries, swollen by the rains of winter, regularly overflow their banks and submerge entire districts. As a consequence of this overflow, to which also the united rivers were subject, and which until a canal system was perfected was also a source of danger to life and brought about much destruction, the southern region or Babylonia, with a length of about 300 miles and a maximum breadth of almost 125 miles,[10] developed an astounding fertility. According to the statement of Herodotus,[11] grain yielded a return of "two hundred fold and even up to three hundred fold," while "the blade of the wheat plant and the barley plant is often four fingers in breadth, and the stalks of the millet and sesame are surprisingly tall." It would appear, indeed, that Babylonia was the home of cultivated cereals whence wheat and barley were disseminated throughout the ancient world.

The richness of the soil in Babylonia is due to its being a deposit made by the rivers after the overflowing waters during the rainy season have receded. This deposit which is still going on at the average rate of 90 feet per year may in ancient times have proceeded more rapidly, but, at all events, in this increase we have a fairly definite standard by means of which to determine the age of Babylonian settlements through the distance at present separating cities from the Persian Gulf that once lay on or near that great body of water. So, e.g., a city, Eridu, which we know once lay on the Persian Gulf, is now some 130 miles away. Taking 90 feet as the average yearly increase, this would take us back some 7000 years for the period

[10] A total area of about 23,000 square miles, or about the size of West Virginia.

[11] Book I, § 193.

when Eridu still lay on the Persian Gulf. Since it is also known that at one time the Euphrates and Tigris entered the Persian Gulf independently, it follows that the entire district below their present juncture at Kurna is land made during the historical period. The natural conditions, therefore, such as the presence of two rivers that bring about unusual fertility, the fact that one of them is an avenue of commerce from the extreme north to the Persian Gulf, and that this gulf again constitutes a means of access to distant lands, explain why this region should have been at so early a period the seat of a population which took up agriculture as a pursuit and under conditions which with a minimum of effort yielded a maximum of sustenance.

To these conditions there is to be added as a third factor the climate, which, although according to our views intolerable, is not unhealthy and is precisely of the kind suitable for a population that cannot adequately protect itself against cold and inclemency. There are two seasons in Babylonia—a rainy season, which sets in in November and lasts until March or April, when the overflow of the rivers begins, which reaches its height in May and ceases about the middle of June, and a dry season, which lasts from March to November. The heat during this season becomes excessive according to European ideas, but it is regarded as pleasant by the natives, to whom even the moderate cold of the rainy season is decidedly more vexatious. The greater part of the year one can thus live in the open air—an important item to a people in a primitive state of culture.

III

Next to the antiquity of the civilization of the Euphrates Valley, perhaps the most astonishing fact about it is the disappearance of practically all material traces of this civilization and the loss of detailed knowledge of a period of history extending over a stretch of

several thousand years. Until a few generations ago
our knowledge of the history and culture of Babylonia
and Assyria was limited to references in the Old Testament, and to the accounts in Herodotus, to statements
in Josephus and to Ctesias, and to scattered notices
in the writings of various Greek and Latin writers.
Comparatively extensive as this material was,[12] it was
yet entirely inadequate for forming an estimate of the
civilization and for furnishing a historical survey.
In contrast to Egypt, no picturesque remains survived to recall to the wanderer the glory of the past.
To be sure, the profound impression made upon
the ancient world by the achievements of Babylonian
and Assyrian rulers, the great military power that they
developed, their extensive and remarkable building
operations—their temples, palaces and gardens—as well
as the wisdom for which the priests became famous—all
this never faded out of the memory of the people, but it
remained to a large extent an impression unsupported
by sufficient details to enable us to do more than draw a
very general picture, vague in its outlines and deficient
in details, of the civilization unfolded thousands of
years ago. Fanciful exaggerations and uncertain traditions took the place of accurate knowledge.

A country that is favorably situated for the early
development of culture is also apt to show features that
lead to rapid decline—when the decline has once set in.
The overflow of the two rivers as it conditioned and pro-
moted the remarkable fertility of the region was also, as
has already been intimated, an annual menace and until
the introduction of an elaborate canal system, loss of
property and life accompanied the overflow, which sub-
merged entire districts for weeks and even months. The

---

[12] Put together by Niebuhr, *Geschichte Assur's und Babel's*
(Berlin, 1857). See also Cory, *Ancient Fragments* (London, 1832),
for a collection of accounts of Babylonia and Assyria from Greek
and Latin writers, in part based on a lost work of a "Chaldean"
priest Berosus—a contemporary of Alexander the Great.

picture unfolded in the first chapter of Genesis, which represents the primeval chaos before the appearance of dry land as a state in which the waters covered everything, was suggested by the phenomenon which was annually witnessed throughout a considerable portion of Babylonia; and similarly, the thought that all mankind was once annihilated in consequence of a deluge lay near to the minds of a people who witnessed such a destructive event on a small scale every spring.

The neglect into which the canal system naturally fell after the downfall of Assyria and Babylonia brought about an even more lamentable state of affairs than that which existed before its institution, for in a short time the work which generations had been busy in constructing was doomed to destruction. The cities of Babylonia and Assyria fell into decay, the process being hastened by the material that was used in the construction of the buildings. Here again, the existence of so admirable a building material as the clay soil of Babylonia, enabling even untrained workmen to rear huge constructions of burnt and unburnt bricks, facilitated on the one hand the unfolding of culture in the Euphrates Valley, but on the other hand also conduced to the rapid destruction of the buildings. The clay structures had to be constantly repaired and we learn from the cuneiform records of Nebuchadnezzar II, that 45 years of neglect sufficed to reduce a temple to a condition bordering on complete decay. Clay being the only building material for houses, palaces and temples in the south, and the prevailing one in the north (though here stone was also employed in the case of large constructions), it is easy to imagine what must have happened during the two thousand years that elapsed between the desertion of the Babylonian and Assyrian cities and the effort to recover their remains. The buildings tumbled into shapeless ruins, and the winds sweeping the sands across the plains completed the destruction, and hid even the debris from view. Of the once flourishing cities, one saw

only huge shapeless mounds [13]—and yet nature, in thus
covering up the work of man, proved to be a merciful
destroyer. But for the mounds which formed over the
sites of ancient cities, the records of the past would have
been entirely swept away or ruthlessly destroyed. Beneath these mounds were safely preserved, as afterwards turned out—priceless documents, inscribed clay
tablets and cylinders, monuments and sculptures, by
means of which we are now enabled to rewrite the history of Babylonia and Assyria. Monuments and records
without number that would long ago have fallen a prey
to marauding Arabs who infested the deserted districts
were thus kept from certain destruction by the protecting mounds.

The recovery of those remains and the reconstruction of the history, art, the religion and social life, of
ancient Babylonia and Assyria, through the study and
interpretation of this material was the work largely of
the 19th century, which will always be known as the
golden age of epochal discoveries in many directions—
discoveries that have on the one hand profoundly altered
our views of the universe and modified present conditions of life, and that have on the other hand enlarged
our knowledge of the past by the recovery of so many
pages of the lost annals of mankind.

IV

That the mounds scattered along the Tigris and in
the valley of the Euphrates contained ancient remains

---

[13] Only two ruins in all the district that suggested outlines of
buildings peered out above these mounds—one at a place called Birs
Nimrud, and which proved to be the site of the city of Borsippa,
near Babylon; the other, still further to the south at Akerkuf—
both representing the remains of a stage tower. Both towers were
associated by native tradition with the " Tower of Babel," which
story, it will be recalled (see p. 4), was suggested by the high
stage-towers that formed a characteristic feature of the sacred architecture of Babylonia and Assyria.

could be concluded from the potsherds and fragments of bricks and stones with which the surface was in many cases strewn, or which came to view on penetrating a short distance beneath the surface, but the question as to the identification of the settlements that once flourished on the site of those vast rubbish heaps could not be answered by such surface examinations. Tradition that invariably survives after accurate knowledge has disappeared had connected a series of mounds opposite Mosul with the site of Nineveh. One of these mounds bore the name of Nebbi Yunus, i.e., "the prophet Jonah," and a little chapel surmounting it is revered by the natives as the tomb of the prophet who announced the destruction of Nineveh. The tomb is fictitious, but the association of Jonah with Nineveh embodies the recollection of the fact—as was established by excavations—that Nebbi Yunus indeed concealed a portion of the great capital of Assyria. In the south, some 40 miles from Baghdad, there was another series of mounds, one of which bore the name of Babil—a recollection of the fact that the great capital of the southern empire once stood there. Such were the clues on which the early travellers and explorers had to work.

In the 16th and 17th centuries these and other mounds in the region began to attract the attention of numerous travellers. Indeed, several centuries previous a famous traveller, Rabbi Benjamin of Tudela (1160 A.D.) made a brief reference in his itinerary [14] to the ruins of both Babylon and Nineveh. Passing by a number of English travellers, who visited the region during the latter part of the 16th century, we come to the Italian Pietro della Valle who early in the 17th century made extensive travels in the east, and besides furnishing a detailed account of the famous ruins at Persepolis and copying a specimen of the cuneiform

---

[14] First published in 1543 in Constantinople. See M. N. Adler, "The Itinerary of Benjamin of Tudela" (*Jewish Quarterly Review*, vol. xviii.)

inscriptions there, examined the mounds of Babylon and Mugheir—the site of Ur—in the Euphrates Valley. He was the first to bring back to Europe a few of the inscribed bricks.[15] Among the travellers of the following century whose curiosity was aroused by the mounds along the Tigris, and in the Euphrates Valley, it is sufficient for our purposes to mention two, (1) the famous Danish scholar Carsten Niebuhr,[16] to whom we owe the definite identification of the site of ancient Babylon at the mounds near Hillah, and (2) the Abbé de Beauchamp, who at the close of the 18th century specified in a more detailed fashion than any of his predecessors had done, the large extent of the mounds covering the remains of the city of Babylon. He also speaks of finding within the rubbish heaps enamelled bricks, pieces of cylinders covered with writing, and bits of statuettes.

The desire to put a spade into these mounds after it had been definitely ascertained that they contained remains of antiquity must have burned strong in the breast of the traveller who allowed his fancy to speculate on the nature of the treasures hidden for two millenniums.

Attempts on a very small scale were made by an Englishman, Claudius James Rich, who utilized a residence of about thirteen years in the region as the resident agent of the East India Company, with his head-quarters at Baghdad, to make a thorough study of the mounds of Babylon and Nineveh as well as of the topography of the entire region from Baghdad to Mosul. This investigation far surpassed in its results anything that had previously been done. Rich's death in 1821 at the early age of thirty-four cut short an activity that included the collection of such specimens as he was able to secure from

---

[15] In his "Viaggi" (Rome, 1650), Pietro della Valle reproduces some of these inscriptions and gives his reasons why they should be read from left to right, in which supposition he was correct.

[16] Niebuhr gave a detailed account of his travels in his *Reisebeschreibung nach Arabien und andern umligenden Ländern* (Copenhagen, 1774–1837), 3 vols.

scratchings in the mounds and through purchase from
natives who had rummaged them more successfully.
Rich's collections of Babylonian and Assyrian antiquities, though not large in comparison with what was soon
to be secured, were valuable by virtue of their variety—
revealing the various kinds of objects buried beneath
the mounds. He published accounts of his researches,[17]
and after his untimely death, the antiquities gathered
by him, as well as a large collection of oriental
manuscripts and coins, were purchased by the British
Museum. In 1827–28 another Englishman, Robert
Magnan, also in the employ of the East India Company,
in the course of a careful study of many of the mounds
in the south, cut trenches into a number of them, chiefly
with a view of ascertaining their age and character.
Quite a number of antiquities were discovered, but such
sporadic attempts counted for little. In 1835–37 an important survey of the region of the Euphrates and Tigris
was undertaken by the English government, but the
credit of having organized the first excavating expedition belongs to France.

V

The story of how the palaces and temples of Assyria
and Babylonia with their rich and varied contents were
brought to view through the untiring energy of a long
series of explorers, is a most fascinating one. Beginning in 1842 with the work of P. E. Botta at the mounds
opposite Mosul and continuing to our own days the great
museums of Europe and this country—more particularly the British Museum, the Louvre, the Berlin
Museum, and the Archæological Museum of the University of Pennsylvania, bear witness to the vast mate-

---

[17] His two *Memoirs on the Ruins of Babylon* (London, 1816–1818)
were republished in 1839 by his widow, together with Rich's diaries
and an account of a journey to Persepolis a few years previous
under the title *Narrative of a Residence in Koordistan and on the
Site of Ancient Nineveh* (London, 1836), 2 vols.

PLATE III

FIG. I, MOUND AND VILLAGE OF KHORSABAD

FIG. 2, BIRS NIMRUD, THE SITE OF BORSIPPA

rial that has been brought together in the space of seventy years and of which so large a part has now, through publications, been placed at the disposal of students.[18]

Botta, appointed consular agent of France at Mosul, in 1842, began work late that year on a large mound Kouyunjik on the Tigris opposite Mosul, and which, like the neighboring heap, Nebbi Yunus, covered a portion of the ancient city of Nineveh. In beginning excavations at these large mounds it was at first largely guesswork where to dig the first trenches, and it depended upon chance whether one's efforts were rewarded with tangible results. Botta worked at Kouyunjik for some months with only moderate success. Inscriptions and bas-reliefs were found, but in a fragmentary condition and nothing that appeared to be particularly striking. He accordingly, in March, 1843, transferred the scene of his operations to a mound Khorsabad, a short distance to the north of Kouyunjik, where he was almost immediately successful in coming upon two mutilated walls covered with sculptured bas-reliefs, accompanied by inscriptions in the ordinary cuneiform character. There could be no question that he had actually come across a portion of an Assyrian building and ere long a whole series of rooms had been unearthed filled with monuments of the past. The announcement of these discoveries created tremendous excitement, and soon sufficient funds were placed at Botta's disposal to enable him to carry on his work on a large scale. An artist, E. Flandin, was dispatched to sketch the monuments that could not be removed and to draw plans of the excavations. By October, 1844, a large portion of the palace— for such the edifice turned out to be—had been excavated, revealing an almost endless succession of rooms, the

[18] For detailed accounts of excavations at Babylonia and Assyrian mounds, the reader is referred to Rogers' *History of Babylonia and Assyria* (New York, 1900), vol. i, pp. 1–174; to Hilprecht, *Exploration in Bible Lands*, (Phila., 1903), pp. 1–577; and to Fossey, *Manuel d'Assyriologie*, vol. i (Paris, 1904).

walls of which were covered with sculptured bas-reliefs. These sculptures were of the most various character. Long processions of marching soldiers alternated with scenes illustrative of life in military camps—showing the horses, chariots and tents and the method of attack upon the enemy—the approach to the walls, the actual conflict, the capture of a town, and the carrying away of captives. Hunting scenes were represented in equally elaborate fashion, showing the king in his chariot, surrounded by his attendants.

Lions were depicted in the act of being let out of their enclosures, or attacked by the royal hunter. There followed a procession of servants carrying the dead lions, as well as game of a smaller character. A notable feature of the excavations were the huge winged bulls with human heads that were found at the entrances leading to the great halls. The bodies of these bulls were covered with cuneiform inscriptions which when they came to be deciphered told in general outlines of the achievements of the monarch who had erected this large palace for himself, namely, Sargon II, who ruled over Assyria from 725 to 706 B.C. As much of the vast material as possible was placed on rafts and floated down the Tigris to Basra whence it was safely carried by a French man-of-war to Havre. The antiquities were brought to the Louvre, while the detailed results of the expedition were set forth in five large folio volumes containing the drawings of Flandin, no less than 400 plates, with detailed descriptions by Botta.[19]

The great value of the remarkable discoveries stimulated further interest in France; in 1851 a second expedition was fitted out by a vote of the French Assembly. This expedition, which extended its labors to mounds in the south, was placed under the leadership of Victor Place, a trained architect, who had been appointed Botta's successor as consular agent in Mosul.

[19] P. E. Botta et E. Flandin, *Monument de Ninive* (Paris, 1849–1850), 5 vols.

PLATE IV

FIG. I, HUNTING SCENE (KHORSABAD)

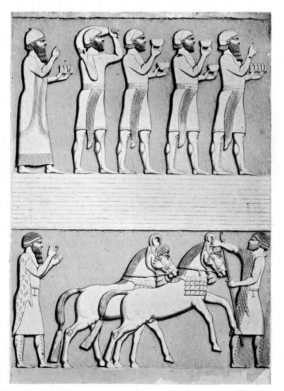

FIG. 2, PROCESSION OF CAPTIVES, BEARING TRIBUTE (KHORSABAD)

Place's architectural skill enabled him to carry on the work more systematically, and demonstrated the advantage of having an architect to conduct excavations of ancient buildings. He unearthed many more rooms of the palace, and passing beyond this building, came across a number of large gates, decorated with enamelled tiles in brilliant colors forming ornamental designs, and pictures of fantastic animals. The large courts of the palace were laid bare and several smaller buildings which, as was subsequently ascertained, represented temples. Large quantities of pottery and objects of stone, of glass and metals were found, as well as iron implements in an excellent state of preservation, and even the magazine in which the colored tiles were stored. In an elaborate publication,[20] Place embodied the results of his successful labors, on the basis of which he attempted to reconstruct the greater portion of the edifices he had unearthed. The mounds at Khorsabad, it thus resulted, represented a fortified town erected by Sargon II, and which was known as Dur-Sharrukin, *i.e.,* "Fort Sargon," as we may render the term. Surrounded by walls with eight gates, the site covered an area of some 750 acres. The central building was the royal residence, erected on a high terrace and surrounded by a number of smaller buildings for the use of the royal court. The building material was stone for the exterior walls, and in part for the floors, but for the greater part of the structure baked and unbaked bricks, which constituted the ordinary material used in the buildings of Babylonia and Assyria, were employed.

Place also extended his excavations to other mounds not far from Mosul, such as Kaleh-Shergat (the site of the ancient city of Ashur) and Nimrud (the site of Calah) besides carefully examining many other mounds, but without the same success that attended his

[20] Victor Place, *Ninive et l'Assyrie, avec des Essais de Restauration* par Félix Thomas (Paris, 1867–1870), 3 vols.

and Botta's efforts at Khorsabad. Unfortunately the antiquities selected by Place for shipment to Paris were lost through the sinking of the two boats on which they were placed. Drawings and copies had, however, been made of all of them, so that the loss to science was not as great as it might have been. At the same time another French expedition under the leadership of Fresnel was busy conducting excavations in the south on one of the mounds that covered the city of Babylon, and which lasted until 1855. Before, however, taking up an account of the excavations on mounds in Babylonia, we must consider work done simultaneously with Place's excavations at Khorsabad by an English explorer who was destined·to acquire even greater renown than either Botta, Flandin, or Place.

VI

This was Sir Austen Henry Layard, who was knighted for his services to archæology and to diplomacy.[21] During a prolonged series of travels in the east, Layard had, as early as 1840, visited the mounds near Mosul and indulged the hope of some day carrying on excavations in that region. It was not, however, until the autumn of 1845 that, with the help of a small fund placed at his disposal by Sir Stratford Canning, the British ambassador at Constantinople, he was enabled to begin excavations on a small scale at the mound Nimrud, which he selected because it was sufficiently removed from Mosul to enable him to carry on his work without attracting too much attention. All that he had hoped to do with the small sum at his disposal was to furnish the proof of the existence of buildings and antiquities beneath the mound, and then to rely upon the interest aroused to secure further grants as well as an official firman from the Turkish

---

[21] See his autobiographical narrative, *Early Adventures in Persia, Susiana and Babylonia* (2d ed., London, 1894), 2 vols.

PLATE V

FIG. I, WINGED BULL WITH HUMAN FACE FROM SARGON'S PALACE (KHORSABAD)

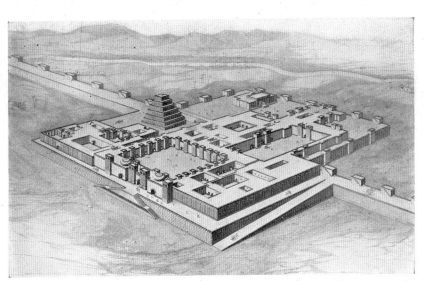

FIG. 2, ATTEMPTED RESTORATION OF SARGON'S PALACE

Government. On the very first day of the excavations
a fortunate chance revealed two rooms lined with limestone slabs, one in the southwest corner of the mound,
the other near the middle of the west side. The rooms,
therefore, belonged to two different buildings, both, as
it subsequently turned out, royal palaces. Gradually
increasing his force of laborers, he carried on his work
amidst many difficulties, owing to the opposition of
the pasha of Mosul and lack of sufficient financial support. Through funds granted him by the authorities
of the British Museum, he was, however, enabled to
carry on his work energetically until the summer of
1847. By that time he had not only unearthed many
of the rooms in no less than five palaces at Nimrud,
but he had been equally successful in the extensive
mound Kouyunjik, opposite Mosul, where he unearthed
a palace of enormous dimensions, erected by King
Sennacherib (705–681 B.C.).

At Nimrud the chief work was done on the so-called
north-west palace which was the joint work of Ashurnasirpal III (883–859 B.C.) and of Sargon II (721–706
B.C.). As at Khorsabad, so the palaces at Nimrud and
subsequently at Kouyunjik yielded an astonishingly
large number of rooms covered with bas-reliefs, besides the huge winged bulls or winged lions with human
heads that stood at the entrances to the halls. The bas-
reliefs showed the same large variety of scenes as those
found at Khorsabad. In the palace of King Ashurnasirpal at Nimrud, or to give the ancient name Calah,
the monarch had his artists picture his military expeditions in detail. Most vividly the army is portrayed
crossing a river, or in the midst of the fray and on the
victorious return march. The hunting expeditions of
the monarch were likewise represented in a long series
of sculptures. In a palace occupying the central part
of the mound, erected by Shalmaneser III (858–824
B.C.) and Tiglathpileser IV (745–727 B.C.) a particularly striking monument was discovered, which still

forms one of the show pieces of the British Museum. This was a completely preserved obelisk of hard, black stone, covered with five rows of sculptures, running around the four sides of the stone, while the balance of the monument was covered with closely written cuneiform inscriptions. The monument was set up by King Shalmaneser III in commemoration of his exploits during thirty-one years of his reign—prepared, therefore by the king himself a few years before his death, and perhaps in realization of the fact that his reign was approaching its close. The scenes portrayed represent the king receiving tribute from the nations conquered by him. Each of the five sections represents a different people as indicated by the inscription over the heads of the groups.

It can well be imagined how deeply the general interest in Assyrian discoveries was aroused when a large selection of the monuments, including two of the colossal winged figures, arrived at the British Museum. This interest was still further increased by the publication of Layard's fascinating narrative [22] in which, despite the fact that he was unable to read the inscriptions discovered by him, he succeeded, by virtue of his ingenuity, in piecing together an interpretation of the bas-reliefs, and aided by Sir Henry Rawlinson's readings, of the names of the royal builders of the palaces, could convey some idea of the historical facts revealed by the monuments. Though obliged to cover up again many of the monuments and inscriptions which he could not transport, he made drawings of the sculptures [23] as best he could and copied the inscriptions,[24] and in this

---

[22] *Nineveh and its Remains* (London, 1849).

[23] He published, in 1849, a first series of *Monuments of Nineveh from Drawings Made on the Spot* (100 plates).

[24] In 1851 there appeared a volume by him of *Inscriptions in the Cuneiform Character from Assyrian Monuments*, consisting of 98 plates. Considering that he was unable to read the inscriptions, his copies are remarkably good—a monument to his skill and patience.

PLATE VI

OBELISK OF KING SHALMANESER III OF ASSYRIA (858–824 B. C.)

way placed a large amount of valuable material, which would otherwise have been hopelessly lost, at the disposal of students. The direct result of the great interest awakened by Layard's marvellous discoveries was the organization of a far better equipped second expedition, enabling him to spend the years 1849–1851 at Nimrud and Kouyunjik. Already in his first expedition he had chosen a native Christian, Hormuzd Rassam, whose brother was the English vice-consul at Mosul, as his companion. Rassam, who was destined to win considerable renown by his own work as an explorer, accompanied Layard, on his second expedition likewise, and on Layard's departure in 1852, continued the excavations till 1854. A skilful artist, F. Cooper, was also appointed a member of the party, for the purpose of making careful drawings of everything that could not be removed. Work was undertaken simultaneously at the two mounds, Kouyunjik and Nimrud. The more important discoveries this time were made at the former site. The palace of Sennacherib was thoroughly explored, revealing some hundreds of sculptured bas-reliefs, illustrating the campaigns and hunting expeditions of this ruler. A still more extensive palace, built by the greatest of all Assyrian rulers, Ashurbanapal (668–626 B.C.), whose name was distorted by Greek writers to Sardanapalus and who appears in the Old Testament as Asnapper (Ezra 4, 10). Apart from the usual bas-reliefs and huge winged bulls and a large number of inscriptions, including cylinders furnishing the details of his many campaigns, Layard found in this palace two rooms filled with many thousand fragments of clay tablets which proved to be a royal library collected by the king with the avowed purpose of storing in his palace the literary productions of Babylonia, as well as the official archives—letters and reports—of the Assyrian empire. Subsequent supplementary excavations increased the number of tablets to about 30,000, which now constitute one of the most valuable treasures of the British Museum. These clay tablets form our main source of Babylonian literature, since a large proportion of the texts represent copies made by Ashurbanapal's scribes of originals from the temple archives of the great centres in the south, notably Babylon and Borsippa. The most extensive branch of literature represented in the collection was formed by the divination compends of the Babylonian priests— covering handbooks of divination in connection with the examination of livers of sacrificial sheep as a means of forecasting the future, astrological handbooks, collections of birth-omens, of animal omens, of dreams, and of miscellaneous divination texts based on phenomena observed in rivers, occurrences in houses, streets and cities. Another large division of the collection is formed by the incantation texts, detailing the formulæ, the symbolical rites and medicinal prescriptions to drive the demons of disease out of the bodies of victims or to counteract the influence of witches and sorcerers. Incantations lead on the one hand to medical texts of a purer type, more or less divorced from sacred formulæ, and on the other hand to prayers, hymns, and penitential rituals. Myths and legends are represented, including creation stories, as well as an extensive epic recounting the achievements of a national hero, Gilgamesh, whose exploits are brought into connection with all kinds of tales that had an independent origin. Partly of Babylonian origin, and partly representing additions made by Assyrian scribes is the text-book literature,[25] consisting of elaborate sign lists of various kinds, compiled as a means of instruction for the young aspirants to the priesthood, grammatical paradigms, exercises in the legal formula used in commercial and legal documents, commentaries to texts, and school editions of literary productions. Though the great importance of this find was immediately recognized by

[25] See Jastrow, "The Textbook Literature of Babylonia" (*Biblical World,* vol. ix, pp. 248–268).

PLATE VII

FIG. I, KING SENNACHERIB (705–681 B. C.) IN HIS CHARIOT (KOUYUNJIK)

FIG. 2, CARRYING MATERIAL ACROSS A STREAM (KOUYUNJIK)

Layard, it was only when Sir Henry Rawlinson, Edwin Norris, and George Smith, the latter an assistant in the British Museum, began to classify, edit and study the texts of the library that its real character was determined. To-day, some sixty years after the finding of the library, its study is still far from being exhausted.[26]

At Nimrud, Layard's chief discoveries consisted in unearthing the remains of a stage tower and of two small temples erected by Ashurnasirpal III (883–859 B.C.) built of sun-dried bricks, covered with plaster. In both temples, clay images of deities, bas-reliefs and inscribed slabs, were found. One of these slabs measured almost twenty-two feet, and was covered with closely written cuneiform characters. Through this inscription and through a large monolith of Ashurnasirpal found in the second temple, we have an almost exhaustive record of the exploits of this ruler—which means a history of the times in which he lived. A large statue of the king was also found in one of the temples. Continuing the excavations in the palace of this king at Nimrud, Layard was fortunate enough, in the course of the second expedition, to come across a large number of objects in copper and bronze, shields, helmets, swords, daggers, twelve large cauldrons filled with smaller vessels and miscellaneous objects, a variety of iron instruments, hammers, saws, spears, a number of beautifully embossed bronze plates, and more the like. The epigraphical material was also considerably enriched by the accompanying inscriptions on the sculptured bas-reliefs, on slabs, cylinders and on tablets which, when they came to be deciphered, added largely to our knowledge of the events of the last three centuries

[26] A most valuable publication is Bezold's monumental *Catalogue of the Cuneiform Tablets in the Kouyunjik Collection of the British Museum* (London, 1889–1899) in five large volumes, the introduction to which furnishes an excellent general account of the royal library.

before the fall of Nineveh in 606 B.C., and which were the most glorious in the eventful history of Assyria.

Over one hundred boxes of antiquities were shipped, in 1851, to England, and arrived safely at the British Museum. In a second popular volume,[27] Layard gave a fascinating account of his discoveries, and to the first series of illustrations from the monuments he added a second set of drawings which were made by F. Cooper.[28] The decipherment of cuneiform inscriptions had by this time made sufficient progress to enable Layard, by utilizing the results obtained, chiefly through Sir Henry Rawlinson and Edward Hincks, to give some account of the historical data to be gleaned from the monuments. He could also, as a result of his more thorough study of the numerous buildings unearthed by him at Nimrud and Kouyunjik, illustrate the relationship of the various royal builders to one another, showing how portions of one edifice were restored or enlarged by some successor, and how, in some cases, material used in the construction of one palace was transferred and made to do service in building the walls or forming supports for another.

The amount of work achieved by Layard during his second expedition, which lasted only two years, was enormous. Numerous other mounds, both in the north and south, were superficially searched for antiquities which definitely established the ancient origin of the cities buried beneath them. At some places, indeed, such as Kaleh-Shergat—the site of the ancient city of Ashur—Arban and Sherif Khan, most striking antiquities and inscribed monuments were discovered, while the work done by him at Niffer, in the south— the site of ancient Nippur—yielded sufficient results to furnish a clue to the American explorers who were to

---

[27] *Discoveries among the Ruins of Nineveh and Babylon* (London, 1853).

[28] *The Monuments of Nineveh*, 2d series, 71 plates (London, 1853).

PLATE VIII

FIG. I, LION HUNT—FROM THE PALACE OF KING ASHURBANAPAL (668–626 B.C.)

FIG. 2, HUNTING WILD HORSES

undertake the more thorough excavation of the mounds at that place some thirty years later.

The excavations so far had been conducted on Assyrian soil, and as a result the three chief cities of Assyria were partially unearthed, the old capital, Ashur (on the site of Kaleh-Shergat), Calah (on the site of Nimrud), originally founded by Shalmaneser I (c. 1300 B.C.) and which Ashurnasirpal III (883–859 B.C.) again made the capital, and Nineveh (on the site of Kouyunjik), which had been made the capital in the reign of Ashur-bel-kala (c. 1100 B.C.), and again became the official seat of government when Shalmaneser III (858–824 B.C.) occupied the throne, and remained so until the fall of the Assyrian Empire in 606 B.C. To these there is to be added Dur Sharrukin (on the site of Khorsabad), a creation of Sargon II (721–706 B.C.), and which served as an outpost for Nineveh. In addition, a number of other Assyrian towns were definitely identified and shown to contain treasures which warranted more systematic excavations.

Turning now to the mounds of the south, the credit of having been the first to conduct excavations for a continuous period, albeit a short one, on a site of an ancient Babylonian city belongs to the Englishman William Kennett Loftus, who, in 1850, and again in 1853–1854, spent some time in opening trenches in a series of extensive mounds at Warka, which proved to be the site of ancient Uruk (or Erech), one of the oldest as well as one of the most important political and religious centres in the Euphrates Valley. At first, as was to be expected, the latter period of the city was revealed, the chief finds being a number of slipper-shaped coffins covered with an enamel glaze, which belonged to the Persian period,[29] i.e., to the fifth and fourth centuries B.C. The city was still in existence though it had lost much of its importance, and through the odor

[29] See Plate XV for specimens of such coffins from Nippur, and Plate XL, Fig. 1, for coffins of older periods.

of its time-honored sanctity had become a favorite place of burial. Loftus, however, succeeded in penetrating to the earlier layers which revealed the existence of a temple of large dimensions to which as at other sites a stage-tower, or zikkurat, was, as was usual, attached. In another portion of one of the mounds an extensive edifice was found which had all the characteristic features of a royal palace, with wall decorations of glazed tiles, pointing to a work of the neo-Babylonian period, while the inscriptions, chiefly business documents on small clay tablets, likewise indicated the continued existence of the city until the overthrow of the neo-Babylonian dynasty through Cyrus in 539 B.C.

By a curious chance, this first Babylonian mound, or rather series of mounds, for there are several distinct ones, also happens to be the scene of the most recent excavations, for in November, 1912, the German Oriental Society, some sixty years after Loftus' arrival at Warka, began systematic excavations which have revealed details of the great temple E-anna, " the heavenly house," in honor of the goddess Nanâ (or Ishtar) whose seat of worship was in ancient Uruk.

Besides some surface scratchings at Babylon, Niffer, Tell Sifr and other mounds, Loftus also spent some time at a mound Senkereh, about fifteen miles to the south of Warka where he almost immediately came upon remains of a temple and of a stage-tower which belonged to a high antiquity, as was subsequently ascertained from the inscriptions of various kinds,—barrel-shaped clay cylinders with historical data, inscribed bricks used in the construction of the edifices, and large numbers of clay tablets representing business and legal documents. Senkereh stands on the site of an ancient city, Larsa, identical with the Biblical Ellasar (Gen. 14, 1) and the seat of the worship of the sun-god, whose temple and stage-tower at the place were objects of veneration through all periods of Babylonian history.

At Tell Sifr, still further to the south, although ex-

PLATE IX

FIG. 1, OMEN TABLET FROM ASHURBANAPAL'S
LIBRARY

FIG. 2, SYLLABARY FROM ASHURBANAPAL'S
LIBRARY

cavations were carried on by Loftus for a few days only, large quantities of inscribed tablets and a collection of miscellaneous bronze and copper utensils, such as daggers, hatchets, knives, vases, cauldrons and mirrors were found and together with many other antiquities sent to England to still further enrich the British Museum.[30]

At the same time that the second French expedition was engaged in continuing Botta's work at Khorsabad and Kouyunjik,[31] Fulgence Fresnel was placed by the French government in charge of excavations to be carried on at the site of the ancient city of Babylon. Fresnel was accompanied by Jules Oppert, a young scholar destined soon to become one of the leading Assyriologists of his day, and Félix Thomas, an architect, who was to study the construction of the buildings and to make all the drawings in connection with the excavations. In the middle of July, 1852, work was begun at one of the large mounds, known as Kasr, which was afterwards extended to two other mounds, Babil and Amran Ibn'Ali, forming part of the complex beneath which Babylon lay buried.[32] The results, owing to the enormous mass of rubbish of which these mounds consisted, were rather disappointing. Numerous brick stamps were found containing the name of Nebuchadnezzar II (604–561 B.C.), and which showed that the large edifice beneath Kasr[33] was the famous palace of that ruler. Quantities of fragments of glazed tiles with animals and decorative designs were also unearthed, but nothing that could compare in interest or sensational importance to what was being found at the same

---

[30] The results of his labors were embodied by Loftus in his *Travels and Researches in Chaldaea and Susiana* (London, 1857).

[31] Above p. 15, *seq.*

[32] The fourth mound, Djumdjuma, was not touched by this expedition.

[33] The name signifies "castle," and thus embodies a tradition of the royal residence which stood there.

time by Place and Layard at the mounds in the north. Nor were the results more striking at the other mounds, to which Fresnel and Oppert directed themselves. Some progress was made in our knowledge of the topography of Babylon, though some of the theories brought forward by Oppert [34] turned out to be erroneous. Other mounds near Babylon, such as Birs Nimrud (the site of ancient Borsippa) and el-Ohêmir (the site of Kish), were explored by this expedition which appears to have been pursued by ill luck, for even the antiquities gathered during the almost two years of continuous work were lost on the rafts that were to carry them to Basra.

An Englishman, J. E. Taylor, who was the Vice-Consul at Basra was more successful in excavations conducted by him for a short period at Mugheir,[35] considerably to the south of Babylon and which proved to be the site of the famous Ur, whence, according to Biblical tradition, Abraham set out on his wanderings which brought him to Palestine. In contrast to the massive character of the mounds at Warka, where large portions of walls are still visible, and to Birs Nimrud and Akerkuf, where the ruins of the old stage-towers rise above the rubbish, those at Mugheir are comparatively low which made the work of excavation much easier. It was not long, therefore, before Taylor had penetrated into the interior of a massive building which proved to be the great temple to Sin, the moon-god, the centre of whose cult was at Ur. He could trace the character of the edifice and follow the course of its walls for a considerable portion. The most prominent feature was as usual the stage-tower of which two stories, one

[34] *Expédition Scientifique en Mesopotamie* (Paris, 1859–1863), 2 vols. The first volume contains the reports of the journey and its results; the second, by Oppert, is devoted to setting forth the method of the decipherment of the cuneiform inscriptions.

[35] More properly Mukayyar, meaning the mound "covered with bitumen."

placed above the other, could be traced. In a corner of
the tower Taylor found a perfectly preserved clay
cylinder of which duplicates were found in the other
three corners, a plan that proved to have been commonly
followed in the case of other edifices in Babylonia as
well as Assyria. The construction of the temple could
be traced back through the inscribed bricks found at
various levels to the Ur dynasty, which flourished in
the third millennium before this era. Taylor was also
the first to come across graves of the early Babylonian
period when the coffins were much smaller in shape
than the slipper-shaped receptacles for the corpse in
the Neo-Babylonian and Persian periods.[36] The shapes
varied from a narrow but deep bath-tub variety into
which the body must have been forced in a semi-
upright position, to large dish covers beneath which the
body was placed, alternating again with two large jars,
holding the body and cemented at the place of contact.
Such discoveries threw a new and important light upon
the customs of the people, as did also the many specimens of pottery and all kinds of utensils which Taylor
unearthed besides a considerable number of the usual
business and legal documents belonging to both the
earlier and the later periods of Babylonian history.
Despite the comparatively short time spent at Mugheir, Taylor largely enriched our knowledge of early
Babylonian history; and he was equally successful in
determining the great antiquity of the city buried under
a mound, Abû Shahrain, still further to the south and in
identifying the mounds that rise more abruptly from
the plains than elsewhere as the site of the city of Eridu
which, as is now known, once lay at or very near the
head of the Persian Gulf. He was soon able to determine
the location of the conventional stage-tower at the
northern end of the mound and which still rose in parts
to a height of about seventy feet. As at Mugheir, the

---

[36] Above, p. 25, note 29.

tower appeared to consist of only two stages, one superimposed on the other, with an inclined plane leading
from one to the other; and he was furthermore able to
conclude with tolerable certainty that the tower was
crowned by a small chapel or chamber in which presumably the statue of the deity, Ea, the patron deity of
Eridu, or some symbol of the god stood. This would be
in accord with Herodotus,[37] from whose description of
the stage-tower at Babylon we may conclude that at the
top of these towers there was a shrine with a symbol
or image of the god or goddess to whom the tower was
dedicated. In contrast to all other edifices discovered
beneath the mounds of the south before and since
Taylor's days, which are built of baked or unbaked
bricks, the structures at Abu Shahrain showed the employment of a considerable amount of sandstone,
granite and marble which, since the Euphrates Valley
is entirely devoid of stone, must have been brought to
Eridu by way of the Persian Gulf. Taylor also used
his sojourn in this most southern district to examine
other mounds and make tentative excavations there so
that until the advent of the French explorer, de Sarzec,
some twenty years later, it was to Taylor that we owed
the most valuable part of our knowledge of the mounds
in the south.

Before taking up the account of de Sarzec's extraordinary activity, a few words need to be said of Sir
Henry Rawlinson's brief but successful investigations
at Birs Nimrud, the site of the ancient city of Borsippa.
The striking appearance of the ruin of a stage-tower
rising high above the mounds at that place[38] was no

_____

[37] Book I, § 181.

[38] See p. 23 and Plate XXXIX. The name of the stage-tower at
Borsippa was E-ur-imin-an-ki, "House of the seven divisions of
heaven and earth"; that at Babylon was E-temen-an-ki, "House of
foundation of heaven and earth." In both names there is evidence
of a close association of earth with heaven, implied also in the Biblical tale that is intended as a protest against these religious "sky
scrapers."

doubt a factor in giving rise to the current tradition
in the region that this ruin was the Tower of Babel.
The tradition was correct in so far as the Biblical legend
was based on the general custom, as we have seen, of
erecting high towers in connection with the temples of
Babylonia and Assyria. Borsippa, moreover, lay close
to Babylon, so close, indeed, that the two cities at times
appeared to form a single complex. Rawlinson, whose
many-sided activity as decipherer, explorer and editor
of cuneiform texts makes him on the whole the most
prominent figure in the history of Assyriology, was
most anxious to try his luck at Birs Nimrud, especially
after the rather negative results of the French expedition to Babylon and surrounding sites, and which had
dampened the enthusiasm aroused by the discoveries
of Botta, Place and Layard. While arranging as
British resident and consul general at Baghdad for the
expeditions of Loftus and Taylor and for the continuation of the work in the north under Hormuzd Rassam,
who, after Layard's departure in 1852, was placed in
charge, Rawlinson himself was given the opportunity
of spending two months, in the fall of 1854, at the
mounds of Babylon and Borsippa. Profiting by the
experience and knowledge gained through the course of
the excavations, he first made a careful study of the
exposed portions of the tower at Birs Nimrud with a
view to determine its general construction and extent,
the number of its stages and an estimate of the depth
of the lowest layer. Assuming that at the four corners
of the huge construction, foundation clay cylinders with
dedicatory inscriptions would be found *in situ,* he on
the basis of his measurements began to remove the
bricks at one of the exposed angles of the third stage
and within an hour a perfect cylinder was brought out
by one of the workmen at the very spot where Rawlinson had told the workmen to search for it. A second
one was found at another corner, and subsequently the

fragments of a third.[39] The inscription proved that
Rawlinson had discovered the famous tower of Borsippa which bore the name of E-ur-imin-an-ki,
"House of the seven divisions of heaven and earth,"
indicating that the tower symbolized the entire universe, connecting the earth, as it were, with the heavens.
Rawlinson also determined that the tower at least in
the form given to it by the restoration through
Nebuchadnezzar II, at the beginning of the sixth
century, B.C., consisted of seven stages, as symbolized
in the name, one superimposed upon the other and
receding in circumference as one proceeded from stage
to stage. The lowest stage, according to Rawlinson's
measurements, was 272 feet square and about 26 feet
high. Many fragments of the bricks showed remains
of glazing in different colors, black, blue and red being
recognizable. The number of stages varies in the case
of the towers so far excavated, from two to seven, the
number in earliest days being usually four, with the
tendency to increase the height as we pass down the
centuries. The main purpose was to build a high
mass in imitation of a mountain, with a winding
balustrade as a means of reaching the top, where the
shrine of the deity to whom the tower was dedicated,
stood.

It will be seen that as a result of the work done at
the mounds in the north and south from the year 1842
to 1855 by the splendid series of explorers, Botta, Place,
Layard, Rassam, Fresnel, Oppert, Loftus, Taylor, and
Rawlinson, an enormous mass of material had been
unearthed, many edifices, chiefly temples, towers and
palaces, had been discovered, and in some cases quite
thoroughly excavated. The general character of these
constructions had been determined and in the case of

---

[39] Rawlinson's account of his work will be found in an article *On
the Birs Nimrûd or the Great Temple of Borsippa* (*Journal of the
Royal Asiatic Society*, vol. xviii (1861), pp. 1–34).

Assyrian palaces, many of the details had also been
ascertained. The art of the time was illustrated by
numerous monuments, dating from various periods,
valuable historical and votive inscriptions, clay tablets
representing business and legal documents of various
periods and, above all, the extensive library archives
gathered in his palace by the greatest of Assyrian kings
had been brought to light.

VII

For about twenty years after Rawlinson's departure
from Baghdad, no excavations were carried on either
in the north or the south, and it was perhaps just as well
that a period elapsed before excavations were resumed
so as to afford the scholars of Europe, devoting themselves to cuneiform research, opportunity to study the
material which had been gathered and which both the
British Museum and the Louvre, with commendable
zeal, were planning to make accessible to scholars.[40]
By the year 1870 a large amount of the material had
been published, besides many detailed studies on the
language of the inscriptions to which the name Assyrian
was currently given. The decipherment was thus placed
on a securer basis, and translations of some of the
more important historical and dedicatory texts on
cylinders and on inscribed slabs and monuments were
made, which, however deficient in details, left no doubt
in the minds of impartial judges that the main facts
had been correctly determined.

Interest in continuing the excavations was aroused

---

[40] See pp. 16, 17 and 28, for Botta's, Place's and Oppert's
publications. In 1861 the British Museum began, under the editor-
ship of Sir Henry Rawlinson, the publication of the cuneiform texts
in the British Museum. Five large folio volumes under the title *The
Cuneiform Inscriptions of Western Asia,* were issued (1861–1880),
and this series was followed by a second, *Cuneiform Texts from
Babylonian Tablets, etc., in the British Museum* (1900 to date), of
which, up to the present, 34 parts, each containing about 50 plates,
have been issued.

3

anew through the discoveries made among the tablets of Ashurbanapal's library, by George Smith, first engaged as an engraver in the British Museum, and then as an Assistant in the Department of Assyrian Antiquities. In the fall of 1872 he came across a large fragment on which, as he found by patient study, there was related the story of a great Deluge. Upon proceeding further he ascertained that the cuneiform record bore striking points of resemblance with the Biblical account. At a meeting of the Society of Biblical Archæology, held on December third of that year, he presented the results of his studies which showed that the Assyrian account of the Deluge formed part of a large composition recounting the adventures of a hero whose name was provisionally read Izdubar, but who, as we now know, was called Gilgamesh. The resemblance between the Biblical and the cuneiform tale of a great catastrophe which destroyed all mankind was the chief reason for the profound sensation aroused by Smith's discoveries. The London "Daily Telegraph" at once came forward with an offer to defray the cost of an expedition to Kouyunjik to search for further portions of the royal library. The offer was accepted by the trustees of the British Museum, and early in 1873 George Smith left for the mounds of Assyria and Babylonia, which he was to visit again in 1874 and 1876, only to meet his death at Aleppo on the occasion of his third trip, stricken down with a malarial fever that was sweeping through the region. His death, on the nineteenth of August, 1876, at the early age of forty-seven years, was a severe loss to science, for his past work had given promise of still greater usefulness in the future. As a result of his two sojourns at Kouyunjik several hundred fragments of the library tablets were added to the collections of the British Museum, besides numerous inscribed cylinders, slabs and other objects which he obtained as a result of further search in the mounds at Nimrud, Kaleh-Shergat and elsewhere. Previous to this Rassam, during his excavations at Kouyunjik after Layard's departure, had also found many hundreds of fragments and a last gleaning was secured many years afterwards through a further search of the ruins of the palace made by E. A. Wallis-Budge and by L. W. King of the British Museum.

George Smith's sojourn at the mounds was too brief to allow him to undertake systematic or even extensive excavations. All that he could do was to rummage through the ruins uncovered by his predecessors, chiefly at Kouyunjik, Nimrud and Kaleh-Shergat, to open some further trenches and hunt in a more or less desultory manner for further inscriptions and monuments. The same general remark holds good for the labors of Hormuzd Rassam at mounds both in the north and the south during the years following upon Smith's death. For a period of five years, 1878–1882, he spent several months each year at the mounds. His energy was indefatigable, and with added experience he was able frequently to achieve remarkable success in a comparatively short time. He gathered, during his prolonged sojourn, a large number of most important antiquities, and definitely identified many mounds as covering ancient remains. Among his discoveries perhaps the most remarkable was the finding of a large number of strips of bronze embossed with ornaments, figures and inscriptions that proved to be parts of huge bronze plates covering the cedar gates of a palace of Shalmaneser III.[41] This discovery was made at a site, Balawat, about fifteen miles to the east of Mosul, the ancient name of which was Imgur-Enlil. The scenes represented on the bronze panels were illustrative of the campaigns of Shalmaneser III. With remarkable

---

[41] See the superb publication, *Bronze Ornaments of the Palace Gates of Balawat*, by Samuel Birch and T. G. Pinches (London, 1881), and Billerbeck and Delitzsch, *die Palasttore Salmanassars II von Balawat* (*Beiträge zur Assyriologie*, vi, 1). See Plates LXVIII and LXIX.

attention to details, the camp scenes, the marching Assyrian armies, the attacks on the enemy, the capture of forts, the taking of booty and captives, as well as sacrificial rites in connection with the campaigns were depicted. Through such illustrations the costumes of the various divisions of the army, the trappings of the horses, the arrangement of the camps, the utensils and customs of daily life and many details of the ritual were revealed. These data were supplemented and further illustrated by the inscriptions accompanying the designs. Still greater success awaited Rassam in his excavations at a number of the southern mounds, which were also more systematically conducted. Attacking several of the mounds that cover the site of Babylon, he was far more successful than his predecessors in securing rich returns in epigraphical material. Significant among the historical records was a clay cylinder giving the account by Cyrus himself of his conquest of Babylonia in 539 B.C.,[42] that event of world-wide import which was destined to bring to an end the history of Babylonia and Assyria. A large collection of business documents covering the Neo-Babylonian period (625–539 B.C.)[43] was also found which, together with several thousand similar tablets from the mounds at Babylon secured by George Smith shortly before his death, greatly increased the material for studying the legal procedure and the many-sided business activity of Babylonia. Through these tablets we obtain an insight into the life, the occupations, the business methods and the commercial activity of the people which supplemented the view of the intellectual life obtained through the literary documents and the picture of the political and military energies and ambitions resulting from a study of the historical records. The business documents covered every phase of every-day occurrences, sale and hire

[42] See Plate XXV, Fig. 2.
[43] See Chapter VI for specimens of such documents.

PLATE X

SHAMASH, THE SUN-GOD, IN HIS SHRINE AT SIPPAR

of fields, rent and sale of houses, loans and receipts, contracts for work, reports of business agents, marriage and divorce, last testaments and terms of adoption, suits of all kinds and the decisions of judges, and so on through the entire gamut of the records one might find in the legal archives of any municipality of the present day.[44] Besides the archive of Babylon, Rassam also discovered an extensive business archive in the temple area of Abû Habba, a new site which Rassam's excavations definitely identified as the ancient city Sippar, a centre of the cult of Shamash, the sun-god, which played a most notable part in Babylonian history. The mounds at Abû Habba cover an enormous extent, no less than 250 acres, according to recent calculations,[45] of which the temple area—including, as in all of the large cities of Babylonia, numerous edifices, smaller temples and chapels, besides houses for the temple administration and for the housing of the priests—alone covered about 40 acres. He opened up a large number of rooms and was rewarded by finding no less than 60,000 clay tablets in the temple archives, most of them business documents, but also quite a sprinkling of literary documents, such as those in Ashurbanapal's library,—hymns, reports, omen texts, grammatical exercises, mathematical lists, etc. Numerous historical documents were also found at Abû Habba by Rassam, most valuable among these being a superb stone tablet containing at the head a design representing Shamash seated in his shrine, with his two attendants, holding ropes attached to a wheel as the symbol of the sun, while into the presence of the sun-god a king is being led preceded by a priest and followed by the goddess A, the consort of Shamash, in the attitude of interceding with her divine husband on behalf of the king. A long inscription covering both sides of the tablet recounts the history of the temple, relating how in consequence of

---

[44] See, for details, Chapter VI.
[45] Hilprecht, *Explorations in Bible Lands*, p. 268.

disasters to Sippar, the cult of Shamash had been neglected, and the old image of the god had disappeared, but Nebopaliddin, the king of Babylonia (c. 888–854 B.C.), determined on restoring the grandeur of the old temple, had been fortunate in finding a terra-cotta relief of the image, from which as a model a new image was made. The inscription, full of interesting historical details and of regulations of the cult, closes with a list of gifts and offerings ordered by Nebopaliddin to be set aside regularly on six festive occasions during the year.[46] He also found some remarkable boundary-stones, recording grants of land to royal officials and decorated with symbols of the gods, who were invoked as witnesses to the transaction and whose curses are called down upon any one defacing or destroying the monument or altering any of its specifications. Twelve years later, in 1894, supplemental excavations were carried on at Abû Habba by Prof. Vincent Scheil, of Paris, under the auspices of the Turkish government, which resulted in adding many hundreds of literary documents from the temple archives, terra-cotta figurines and bas-reliefs, some representing Shamash and his consort, others models of animals, deposited as votive offerings, utensils and weapons in bronze, numerous seal-cylinders with various designs and used to roll over the soft clay of the business documents as signatures of the parties interested, numerous inscribed bricks and pieces of pottery.[47] Scheil was also able, despite the shortness of his stay at Abû Habba, more accurately to determine the various

---

[46] For a summary of the inscription see Harper, *Assyrian and Babylonian Literature*, pp. 30–33; it is fully treated by Johannes Jeremias, "Die Cultustafel von Sippar" (*Beiträge zur Assyriologie I*, pp. 268–292).

[47] A full account of Scheil's excavations will be found in his volume, *Une Saison de Fouilles à Sippar* (Mémoires de l'Institut Français d'Archéologie Orientale du Caire, (1902) vol. i., fax. 1).

PLATE XI

FIG. I, BABYLONIAN BOUNDARY STONE

FIG. 2, STONE PEDESTAL (STEATITE) FROM EXCAVATIONS AT TELLOH

divisions of the temple and something of its interior arrangement, including the site of the temple school.

Rassam, during the five years covered by his firman, searched many other mounds in the north and south, conducting hurried excavations at some of them with varying results. Notably at Birs Nimrud [48] he laid bare no less than eighty rooms in the huge temple E-zida, "the legitimate house," dedicated to Nabu, the chief deity of Borsippa. Among the documents found here, special mention should be made of a terra-cotta cylinder containing in cuneiform an account of the restoration of the temple by the Greek governor of Babylonia, Antiochus Soter, in the year 270 B.C., a most interesting proof of the continued sanctity which the temple continued to enjoy almost three centuries after the fall of Babylon. The mounds at Tell Ibrahîm, about fifteen miles to the north-east of Hillah, and those at Daillum, about ten miles to the south of Hillah, were among those included in his tours through the region with, however, indifferent results. In an interesting volume [49] he gives an account of his entire career as an explorer which, beginning in the days of Layard, extended to the threshold of the latest epoch in Babylonian and Assyrian excavations. With Rassam a second period in excavations on the Tigris and Euphrates closes. The third, which begins about the time that Rassam started on his last series of campaigns, is marked by systematic excavations concentrated on a single series of mounds.

VIII

In 1877 the French Vice-consul at Basra, Ernest de Sarzec, began a series of excavations in a series of mounds at Telloh, in the extreme southern section of the Euphrates Valley, selected by him after a reconnoitering tour as a most promising locality. With

[48] See above, p. 31 *seq.*
[49] *Asshur and the Land of Nimrod* (N. Y., 1897).

short interruptions these excavations were continued
by de Sarzec until his death, in 1901, and since that
time under the guidance of Gaston Cros.

Of the series of mounds at Telloh there were two
which attracted particular attention, each rising about
fifty to sixty feet above the plain. De Sarzec began his
work at the smaller of the two and soon came upon the
remains of an extensive palace which, however, turned
out to be a late construction [50] belonging to about the
beginning of the third century B.C. Along with evidence of a late construction, indications of a very early
edifice were found, and the interesting problem thus
raised was finally solved by the definite proof that the
palace, dating from Parthian times, and following in
its general construction the model of Assyrian palaces,
was erected on the site of an ancient Babylonian temple,
the material of which was partly used in the late construction. The substratum was erected, in accordance
with a practice that was thus shown to be a trait of the
architecture of the region from the earliest to the
latest period on an immense terrace, about forty feet
high, while the expanse itself covered some 600 feet
square. The older building, which alone interests us
proves to be a temple of large proportions and dedicated
to Ningirsu, the patron deity of Shirpurla (or Lagash),
which was thus identified as the city covered by the
mound Telloh.[51] The foundation of the temple can be
traced back to Urukagina (c. 2700 B.C.), and may be
several centuries older even than this ruler. It was
an object of veneration to all rulers of the city and
acquired a significance that prompted rulers of other
centres to leave traces of their devotion to Ningirsu,
through enlarging the dimensions of the temple or

[50] Shown by inscribed bricks bearing the name of Hadad-
nadin-akhê in Aramæan and Greek characters.

[51] Telloh means the "mound of tablets," and thus preserves the
tradition of the temple archive which was discovered by de Sarzec
and which formed one of the features of the temple area.

PLATE XII

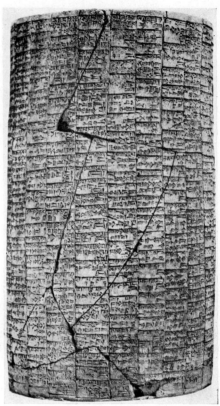

FIGS. I AND 2, EXCAVATIONS AT TELLOH   FIG. 3, INSCRIBED TERRA-COTTA CYLINDER FROM
TELLOH

through repairs of portions that had fallen into decay. Little was left, however, of the old temple beyond a wall at the east corner, which formed part of the work done by Ur-Bau (c. 2450 B.C.), and a tower and gate constructed by Gudea about a century later, and some layers of bricks in various sections. In the course of the excavations, however, a large number of remarkable monuments were found, and a truly astonishing array of miscellaneous objects, inscribed vases, seal cylinders, bas-reliefs, bronze votive offerings, pottery, iron utensils, terra-cotta cylinders, and inscribed cones. Chief among these were nine magnificent diorite statues of Gudea, in whose days Shirpurla, although no longer forming an independent state, enjoyed a second period of grandeur. These statues, representing the ruler in sitting posture or standing, were covered with inscriptions indicating that they were set up as votive offerings. Gudea in thus placing statues of himself in the sacred edifice followed the example of Ur-Bau, of whom likewise an inscribed statue was found. The stone, as Gudea tells us in his inscriptions, was brought from a distant land, as he brought copper and gold and precious woods from various parts of Arabia and cedars from northern Syria. Such intercourse with distant lands is an illustration of the commercial activity prevailing at that early period.

The interest aroused in France through the arrival of the statues at the Louvre was sufficient to ensure further grants from the French government to continue the excavations. The inscriptions proved to be couched in the old Sumerian language spoken by the non-Semitic inhabitants who in the earliest period were in control of the region. When they came to be deciphered, they threw a new light on early political conditions in the Euphrates Valley, and our knowledge of those conditions was still further increased through the inter-containing about 2000 lines, which furnished us with pretation of the two large terra-cotta cylinders, each detailed information regarding Gudea's plans in the construction of E-ninnu, how he was prompted to undertake this work at the direct instance of Ningirsu, who appeared to him in a dream and gave him instructions how to proceed. The picture of the earliest culture in the south now grew more distinct and it became evident that Assyrian culture was only an extension of the civilization that arose in the south. It was therefore in the southern mounds that the origin of the civilization of the region was to be sought, and as a consequence the activity of exploring expeditions since de Sarzec's days was largely directed to the mounds in the south. The work at Telloh was by no means limited to the illustration of the days of Gudea. Monuments were found taking us back far beyond this period, as, *e.g.,* the fragments of an elaborate sculptured votive offering, showing on the one side the god Ningirsu with the double-headed eagle, the standard of Shirpurla, in one hand and a great net in the other, in which he has gathered the heads of the enemy.[52] The accompanying inscription told the story of the conflict against the people of Umma, the triumph of Eannatum (c. 2900 B.C.) and the agreement made between the contesting parties.[53] Another monument, likewise a votive offering, dating from the days of Eannatum's grandfather Ur-Ninâ, who placed a tablet of sandstone in the great temple of Ningirsu, inscribed with his name and titles and exhibiting a lion-headed eagle clutching a lion with each of its talons.[54] Other votive offerings were of bronze and represented a kneel-

---

[52] See the comprehensive work by Ernest de Larzec et Léon Heuzey, *Découvertes en Chaldée* (Paris, 1884–1912) followed by Gaston Cros, Léon Heuzey et François Thureau-Dangin, *Nouvelles Fouilles de Tello* (Paris, 1910).

[53] See the recent publication of Léon Heuzey et F. Thureau-Dangin, *Restitution Matérielle de la Stèle des Vautours* (Paris, 1909). See Plates XLVII and XLVIII.

[54] See Plate XLIX, Fig. 1.

PLATE XIII

FIG. 1, DIORITE STATUE OF GUDEA (C. 2450 B. C.)   FIG. 2, STANDING STATUE OF GUDEA

ing deity holding a pointed cone, others again crouching bulls surmounting a pointed cone, female or male
figures bearing baskets on their heads and covered with
dedicatory inscriptions, or statuettes terminating in a
point.

In the second of the two larger mounds de Sarzec
was no less successful. Remains of buildings of various
dates were unearthed, all of which seemed to have
served some purpose connected with the great temple,
such as smaller shrines for the deities worshipped at
Lagash, forming the court around Ningirsu, store-
rooms, granaries and perhaps archive chambers, as well
as dwellings for some of the many officials connected
with the constantly growing temple administration.
Many valuable monuments were likewise found in this
mound. Prominent among these was a superb silver
vase, delicately incised with representations, running
around the vase, of lion-headed eagles clutching lions,
ibexes and deers, while the upper portion depicts a
series of crouching bulls. The accompanying inscription tells us that the vase, which is one of the finest
specimens of Babylonian art and reveals the high development reached in very early days, was an offering
made by Entemena, a ruler of Shirpurla, whose date
is about 2850 B.C., and who was a son of Eannatum, to
whom we owe the monument above described, which is
commonly known among archæologists as the "Stele
of Vultures." A series of three limestone votive tablets
showing Ur-Ninâ, a ruler of Shirpurla (c. 3000 B.C.),
accompanied by his children, is of special interest in
revealing to us an array of Sumerian types and further
details of the Sumerian mode of dress.[55]

Our knowledge of the remarkable art of the earliest
period was further enriched through the discovery of
such objects as an elaborately sculptured pedestal in

---

[55] Plate XLVI, Fig. 1; Plates LXIII and LXIV for votive
statuettes, above referred to; and Plate LXXI, Fig. 1, for the silver
vase of Entemena.

dark green steatite, forming the support to some large piece and showing seven small squatting figures distributed around the pedestal, a mace-head elaborately carved, dedicated by a King Mesilim of the city of Kish (c. 3100 B.C.), a large spear-head of copper about two and a half feet long and dedicated to Ningirsu by another ruler of Kish, superb lion heads carved in limestone and serving a decorative purpose, libation bowls and sculptured placques of various kinds, round trays in veined onyx, furnishing additional names of rulers of Lagash, an unusually large bas-relief in limestone, over four feet high and representing priests and a musician playing a harp of eleven strings, the whole being again a votive offering for the ancient temple.[56] Through such objects as well as through the various designs on seal cylinders,[57] of a religious character or illustrating episodes in myths and popular tales, a further insight into the religious life and beliefs was afforded, the forms and features given to the various gods and goddesses, their symbols, the style of their altars, the kind of sacrifices offered to them, and the various phases of symbolism in the cult. Supplemental to the monuments, to the works of art, and to the votive and historical inscriptions, de Sarzec was fortunate enough to discover in another section of the mounds the extensive temple archive of clay tablets, dealing with the administration of the temple property and the commercial affairs of the temple officials. The tablets were arranged in layers, evidently according to some system so that any particular one could readily be picked out. In all, some 30,000 tablets were found, but the greater portion were stolen by the natives during de Sarzec's absence and falling into the hands of dealers are now scattered throughout the museums of Europe and this country, and in private hands. Many thousands have now been published, from which we

---

[56] See Plate XLV, Fig. 2, and Plate LIII for the lion heads.
[57] See at the close of Chapter VII, and Plate LXXV–LXXVII.

PLATE XIV

FIG. I, SPECIMENS OF TABLETS AND INSCRIBED CONES FROM TELLOH

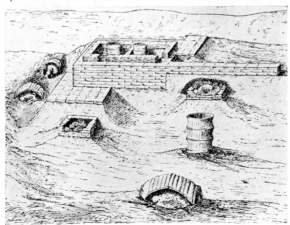

FIG. 2, NECROPOLIS AT TELLOH

have secured a detailed view of the extent of temple activity and the methods of temple administration in early Babylonian days. The new series of excavations also resulted in discovering the section of the ancient city in which the dead were buried. A considerable portion of the necropolis has been laid bare, showing for the first time the arrangement of an ancient Babylonian cemetery, and incidentally settling a hitherto disputed point whether burial constituted the oldest form of disposing of the dead in the Euphrates Valley. No traces of cremation were found, but the methods of burial were not uniform. Some of the graves were square vaults into which the bodies were sunk, others were shaped somewhat like barrels, within which the bodies were placed.

IX

It is time, however, to turn to other excavations conducted during the past thirty years at southern mounds. Early in 1889, an expedition fitted out by the University of Pennsylvania, under the leadership of Dr. John P. Peters (now of New York), began work at a large series of mounds at Niffer, the site of ancient Nippur, at which Layard, it will be recalled,[58] had made some tentative explorations. With some interruptions the excavations were continued till the summer of 1900, Dr. Peters being replaced, after 1888, by the late John H. Haynes, who was the first to demonstrate the possibility of continuing work at the mounds throughout the year and not merely during the dry season, though the hardships endured no doubt drained his vitality and hastened his early death. In 1889, the late Prof. R. F. Harper, of the University of Chicago, and Prof. H. V. Hilprecht, of the University of Pennsylvania, also accompanied the expedition as Assyriologists during the two and a half months of active work, and the latter paid another short visit to the mounds in 1900,

[58] Above, p. 24. The more accurate native form is Nuffar.

in his capacity as Scientific Director. The chief work was in a portion of the mounds that covered the extensive temple area of ancient Nippur. A sanctuary of large proportions dedicated to Enlil, the chief deity of Nippur, was unearthed together with remains of smaller temples, shrines, store-rooms and dwellings of the priests grouped around the central sanctuary. Attached to the temple was a large stage-tower which was thoroughly explored and yielded important results for the construction of these adjuncts to the temple proper. Dr. Peters was fortunate enough to come across remains of the temple archive during the period that he was in charge, but it was left for Haynes, in 1900, to determine the extensive character of these archives, which have yielded upwards of 20,000 tablets. Unlike the archive at Telloh, however, that at Nippur also contained a considerable number of tablets other than mere temple documents and business records. It yielded hundreds of tablets forming part of the equipment of the school attached to the temple for the education of the young priests—just as was the case at Sippar.[59] The publication of this portion of the archive has only recently begun,[60] but from the specimens it is evident that the temple school contained besides syllabaries, grammatical paradigms and other divisions of the school paraphernalia, also the hymns, incantations, and ritual texts used in connection with the cult at Nippur. One should also expect to find many omen tablets in the collection. On the other hand, it is doubtful whether any ruler of Nippur conceived the idea of collecting for

---

[59] Several volumes of lists of proper names from the Temple School are in preparation by Dr. Edward Chiera, and a volume of Letters from the Archives by Prof. Arthur Ungnad.

[60] A volume of mathematical exercise tablets was published by Prof. Hilprecht in 1906, a number of hymns and prayers, by Dr. D. W. Myhrman and by Dr. Hugo Radau, and three volumes of miscellaneous *Grammatical and Historical Texts from Nippur*, by Dr. Arno Poebel, in 1914.

the temple of Nippur the extant literature originating
in the various centres of the Euphrates Valley and
which would have expanded the temple archive into a
real library, such as Ashurbanapal gathered in his
palace at Nineveh. In addition to the discovery of
tablets within the temple area, documents of a legal and
business nature were found elsewhere in the mounds,—
so in one section which appeared to have been the residential portion of the city in the later Neo-Babylonian
and Persian periods and where among other things the
private business archive of one of the banking concerns
of the day was unearthed. Several hundred tablets of
this archive have been published by Prof. A. T. Clay
(now of Yale University), whose researches have shown
that the Murashu family conducted business affairs of
all kinds in Nippur during the fifth century. They
loaned money and farmed out lands, they acted as
agents in drawing up all kinds of contracts and dealt
in various commodities. These documents showed that
Nippur was still an important settlement after the fall
of the Neo-Babylonian dynasty when the Persians came
into control. This was also indicated by the discovery
of numerous slipper-shaped coffins of the Persian
period found in the upper layers, as by the remains
of a Parthian fortress built on the site of the old *zikkurat* of Enlil, just as at Telloh. It was with the greatest difficulty and only after long and patient work done,
chiefly by Haynes, that the extent and nature of the
original stage-tower was determined, which had been
frequently rebuilt and submitted to frequent alterations
ever since its foundation at a period considerably
earlier than Sargon of Akkad, whose stamped bricks
were found in the ruins. Testimony to the large number of rulers who had left traces of their presence in
Nippur was forthcoming in votive inscriptions which
carry us down to the days of Ashurbanapal, the king
of Assyria (668–626 B.C.), who was the last to undertake building operations at the tower, which consisted

at that time of four—possibly five—stages, rising to a
height of over 150 feet. Within the temple area, covering a large extent and surrounded by two walls, an
inner and an outer one, traces of numerous shrines besides the main temple were discovered, and, in the case
of some of these, the definite outlines could be determined. The main temple, known as E-kur, or " mountain house," was the special sanctuary of Enlil, whom
the Sumerians, as it would appear, brought with them
from their mountain homes. Nippur became, as early
at least as 3000 B.C., the chief religious centre of
Sumerian settlements, which carried with it the undisputed position of Enlil as the head of the pantheon.
We have seen that Nippur, like Telloh, continued to
be a stronghold in Persian days. The coming of the
Greeks made no change in its status, as Greek inscriptions and Greek figurines attest; and when finally Nippur was abandoned as a settlement of the living, its old-
time sanctity made it a favorite place of burial. Hundreds of clay bowls, containing magical inscriptions in
Aramaic and Syriac as a protection of the dead against
evil demons, and dating from about the sixth century
of our era were found in graves [61] of the uppermost
layers in certain sections of the mound as a proof that
Nippur continued to be a sacred necropolis for Jews
and Christians many centuries after it had ceased to
be occupied and at a time when all traces and even the
recollection of its one-time grandeur had disappeared.[62]

---

[61] See Prof. J. A. Montgomery's valuable publication of the portion of the collection that came to the University of Pennsylvania,
under the title of *Aramaic Incantation Texts from Nippur* (Philadelphia, 1913).

[62] To this day southern Babylonia is a favorite burial place for
Mohammedans who bring the bodies of their relatives from a long
distance to lie in the sacred cities of Kerbela and Nedjef, associated
with the deeds and martyrdom of the two sons of Ali. It is a
question worth investigating, whether the sanctity of such places
as Kerbela and Nedjef may not revert to the ancient Babylonian

PLATE XV

FIG. I, COFFINS OF THE LATER PERIOD FOUND AT NIPPUR

FIG. 2, INCANTATION BOWLS WITH ARAMAIC INSCRIPTIONS (NIPPUR)

Through the work of Peters and Haynes,[63] scholars were enabled for the first time to obtain a more definite view of the religious architecture of early Babylonia, which was closely followed in Assyria, though with some modifications. The temple proper was divided into two courts, an outer and an inner one. In the outer one stood the altar to which the sacrifices were brought.[64] It was here that the people assembled, while the inner court leading to the holy of holies, in which the statue of the deity stood, was accessible to the priests only. Attached to the temple, either behind it or to one side was the stage-tower, the stories of which, as already pointed out, varied from two to seven stages, one set upon the other, and each succeeding stage being somewhat smaller until the top was reached.

Mention should be made of the large number of votive inscriptions found in the Nippur mounds, which, by nature of the historical data contained in them, added much to our knowledge of political events and conditions in the third millennium B.C., and revealed the names of rulers of whom nothing or little was known ere this.[65] Thus many fragments of stone vases were

---

period, in which case the Mohammedan traditions in regard to these places may simply be the adaptation of the pre-Islamic sanctity to later conditions. In a private communication, Prof. Nöldeke (June 13, 1913) calls my attention to the fact that a village by the name of Nineveh in southern Babylonia is frequently mentioned in Arabic literature (Yakût and Tabari)—an indication of the continuance of Babylonian and Assyrian traditions far into the Islamic period.

[63] Great credit is also due to Mr. C. S. Fisher, now associated with Harvard University and the Boston Museum of Fine Arts, who accompanied the expedition in 1899–1900 as architect and through whom many of the architectural problems suggested by the mounds were solved. In a large publication, *Nippur,* unfortunately not yet completed, Mr. Fisher has set forth the results of his careful and important investigations.

[64] See Chapter VII and the temple plan there given.

[65] Published by H. V. Hilprecht in Vol. I, Parts 1 and 2, of the *Babylonian Expedition of the University of Pennsylvania* and in Poebel's volumes above, p. 46, note 60, referred to.

found which, upon being pieced together, furnished a large inscription of Lugalzaggisi (c. 2675 B.C.), the king of Erech or Uruk, who extended his dominions until he could lay claim to the title also of King of Sumer, and who tells us in the inscription accompanying his votive offerings of his various campaigns and conquests. In the lowest strata of the mounds a large number of vases and jars—some of them of unusually large size—were found, and among other interesting discoveries, a series of drain pipes laid in vaulted tunnels showed that at an early period a system for drainage had been devised. The monuments unearthed up to the present at Nippur are not as numerous as those found by de Sarzec and Cros at Telloh, but include such interesting specimens as a large votive tablet of Ur-Enlil (c. 3000 B.C.), showing the ruler in the act of offering a libation to Enlil. The great antiquity of the plaque, perforated in the centre so that it could be fastened to a wall, is proved not merely by the characters used in the inscription but by the representation of the ruler in a naked state before his god. The lower part of the tablet shows a goat and a sheep followed by two attendants who are presumably leading the animals, as sacrifices, into the presence of the god.[66]

Another expedition fitted out by an American insti-

[66] A detailed account of the work during 1888–1890 was given by Dr. Peters in his work, *Nippur* (2 vols., New York, 1890), and an account of the entire series of excavations from 1888–1900 by Prof. H. V. Hilprecht in *Explorations in Bible Lands,* pp. 289–568, though this account is unfortunately marred by belittling of Peters' and Haynes' work, and by some statements which give one an erroneous impression, both of the conditions under which finds were made and of the finds themselves. The publication of texts found at Nippur has proceeded steadily since 1891. Apart from the volumes above (p. 46 and p. 49), instanced, Prof. Clay has issued seven volumes of business and legal documents from the Cassite, neo-Babylonian and Persian periods, Drs. H. Ranke, A. Poebel and D. W. Myhrman, similar documents of the First Dynasty of Babylon and of the Ur dynasty, and Dr. H. Radau a selection of official

tution conducted excavations for some months in 1903–
1904, at Bismya, with Dr. E. J. Banks as director, who
was acting for the University of Chicago. In some
respects this work of Dr. Banks was the most remarkable of the many undertakings at the mounds, both because of the rich results obtained in a comparatively
short time and because of the conditions under which
these results were obtained. Bismya lies in the very
heart of the desert region of southern Babylonia, difficult of access owing to the desperate character of the
Arab tribes in the vicinity.

Alone and unaided Banks proceeded to Bismya,
organized his corps of workmen and began his excavations on Christmas Day, 1903. He kept up the work
until well into May of the following year, when the
excessive heat and the wretched sanitary conditions
forced an abandonment till fall. Proceeding as methodically as the difficult circumstances could allow, he
soon determined that Bismya covered the remains of an
ancient city that was abandoned long before the Babylonian empire came to an end. A little below the surface,
remains of ancient buildings came to view, and it soon
became evident also that the city had been destroyed by
an invasion. Banks traced the outlines of the royal
palace, of the temple and its stage-tower, and uncovered a large portion of the residential district. The
palace fronting on the canal contained a large number
of rooms grouped around a central court, and Banks
ascertained that the same general plan was followed
in the case of the private houses, only that the number
of rooms was of course much smaller, and that the
palace probably contained, besides the large court, a
second one around which the apartments reserved for
the harem were distributed. Vertical drains leading

---

reports and administrative documents, and a monograph on fragments of a Ninib myth found among the tablets of the literary section
of the temple archive. See Plate XLIII, Fig. 2, for the native tablet
of Ur-Enlil.

down to the foundations were found in several rooms, suggesting their use as bath rooms and indicative of at least some attempts at sanitation in very early days. Pottery of various shapes, animals modelled in clay, suggesting their use as toys, statuettes of deities serving as household gods, and several hundred tablets were among the finds of the palace, but far richer were the objects discovered in the temple area. Chief among these were remains of various statues of stone, revealing a high order of work in the modelling of the face and in the arrangement of the garments. One of these statues, though found in several pieces, could be almost entirely restored, and constitutes one of the most valuable specimens of the art of early Babylonia. It proved to be that of an ancient ruler whose name is probably to be read Lugal-daudu (Plate XXIV, Fig. 1) and the inscription on the right arm of the statue also revealed the name of the temple as E-sar, and that of the city as Adab. Most of the heads found show the ordinary Sumerian type, with shaven head, but there was one with distinctly Semitic features with a full beard, proving that at an early period the population consisted of the two elements which we encounter everywhere in the remains of the ancient cities of the Euphrates region. Sinking a shaft some fifty feet through the mound down to the pure sand of the desert level, Banks was able to determine that below the temple, erected on a platform of plano-convex bricks there was an older structure. Inscribed bricks and vases found at the higher level furnished the names of Dungi and Ur-Engur, of the Ur dynasty (c. 2450 B.C.), and of Sargon and Narâm-Sin, of Akkad, belonging to c. 2650 B.C. For the older temple we may thus go back to at least 3000 B.C. and perhaps to a still earlier date. On a fragment of a blue-stone vase found in the temple, a drawing occurs of a stage-tower which is of inestimable value in illustrating the ancient shape of these adjuncts to the temple proper. The drawing shows four stories or stages of

PLATE XVI

FIG. 1, STATUE OF THE GODDESS NINLIL (FOUND AT BISMYA)

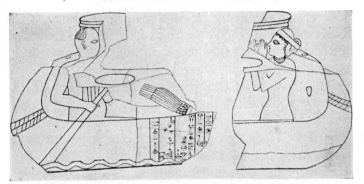

FIG. 2, DESIGN ON AN INSCRIBED BOAT-SHAPED VASE (BISMYA)

FIG. 3, DESIGN ON AN INLAID VASE (BISMYA)

receding size, one placed on the other, and we may conclude that four stories represented the number in the
case of the *zikkurat* in ancient Adab.

Numerous inscribed vases, placed as votive offerings
in the temple, confirmed E-sar as the name of the sacred
edifice and that it was sacred to the goddess Nin-
kharsag, " the lady of the mountain." Statuettes of the
goddess seated on a throne were discovered, and also a
statue of white stone, which enables us to see at closer
range the features given by the Babylonians to the
divine patron of the place, who seems to be identical
with Ninlil, the consort of Enlil, of Nippur, and whose
cult may have been transferred from the latter place.
Banks was also fortunate enough to come across hundreds of fragments of vases of almost every conceivable
shape and of such various materials as onyx, porphyry,
sandstone, limestone and alabaster. Many of them contained inscriptions and curious designs, such as
dragons, religious processions, deities in a boat, and
so forth. Numerous objects of ivory and mother-of-
pearl—fishes, cats, rosettes—partly to be regarded as
votive offerings and partly merely ornaments alternated
with inscribed copper tablets, copper spikes terminating in little lions, engraved marble slabs and fragments
of splendidly moulded alabaster cows.

In a portion of the mounds not far from the temple,
several thousand clay tablets with inscriptions of the
oldest period were unearthed which presumably formed
part of the temple archives. Lastly, the excavations
also threw further light on the ancient mode of burial
in Babylonia. Vaulted brick tombs having the appearance of small houses, on an average six feet long and
three feet high, were built to receive the dead, who
were placed on the floor, while along the back wall a
series of clay pots of various sizes were arranged.
Beads and copper rings and seal cylinders were also
found in the graves, showing that the dead were buried
with their ornaments, while some of the pots may have

contained food. Banks remarks that these little houses
of the dead dating, as tablets found in the mound
proved, from the Hammurapi period, *i.e.*, c. 2000 B.C.,
were not unlike the mounds built over graves in modern
Mesopotamia. A large number of these vaulted tombs
were found in close proximity to one another, indicating that a portion of the ancient city had been set aside
as a cemetery.

In his account [67] he gives some specimens of the
historical material unearthed by him. Even these few
specimens furnish names of rulers hitherto unknown,
and we may therefore look forward to a considerable
enrichment of our knowledge of the earliest history
of the Euphrates Valley with the more complete publication of the rich finds made by him.

X

The last comer on the field of excavations is the
German Orient Society, which, organized in 1900, has
the distinction of having conducted its work more thoroughly and more systematically than any of its predecessors, not even excepting de Sarzec's labors at
Telloh. The organization of the Society was due largely
to the distinguished Prof. Friedrich Delitzsch, who has
done more than any other single individual in training
a large body of Assyriologists and in arousing popular
interest in the civilizations that once flourished in the
Euphrates Valley. Among those whose interest he secured was the German Emperor, who has been a gen-
erous supporter of excavations in Babylonia and
Assyria. The German Orient Society [68] has not limited

---

[67] *Bismya or the Lost City of Adab* (New York, 1912).

[68] Accounts of the work are published in the *Mitteilungen der
Deutschen Orientgesellschaft*, published at intervals of every two or
three months, while texts and more detailed reports and investigations are given in an important series known as the *Wissenschaft-
liche Veröffentlichungen der Deutschen Orientgesellschaft*, of which,
up to the present, eighteen substantial volumes have been issued.

its activity to the region of the Euphrates. It has carried on work regularly in Egypt, notably at Abusir and at El-Amarna, and has also carried on some important explorations in Galilee. Until recently the work in Mesopotamia was concentrated on two sites—Kaleh-Shergat in the north, representing Ashur, the earliest capital of Assyria, and the mounds in the south that cover the remains of ancient Babylon. Some work has, however, also been done at Fara and Abû Hatab, the sites of Shuruppak and Kisurra respectively, and late in 1912 work was begun on one of the most important ruins of the south, Warka, the name of which still preserves the recollection of the city of Erech or Uruk, the seat of the cult of the goddess Nanâ which once flourished there.

The result of fourteen years of steady and uninterrupted excavations has been to reveal in the case of Ashur the history of the city from the earliest period, c. 2000 B.C., to which it can now be traced back, down to the time when it ceased to be the capital of the northern empire and even beyond this period, while in the case of Babylon the excavations have shown that King Sennacherib, of Assyria, did not exaggerate when, in his inscriptions, he told us that weary of the frequent uprisings in the south against Assyrian control, he decided to set an example by completely destroying the city of Babylon—razing its large structures to the ground and placing the city under water in order to make the work of destruction complete. This happened in the year 689 B.C. While some remains of the older Babylon, chiefly through the discovery of clay tablets belonging to earlier periods, have come to light, the city unearthed by the German Orient Society is the new city, the creation chiefly of Nebopolassar (625–604 B.C.), the founder of the neo-Babylonian dynasty, and of his famous son, the great Nebuchadnezzar II (604–561 B.C.).

At Ashur the walls, quays and fortifications of the

ancient city have been most carefully and methodically excavated and traced on all sides. Already in the earliest days (c. 2000 B.C.) the rulers of the city made it their concern to strongly fortify their stronghold, and as time went on these fortifications grew in massiveness and in strength until, in the days of Shalmaneser III (858–824 B.C.), they reached their highest point of perfection through a series of double walls— an inner and an outer one—both solidly built with turreted tops and eight huge gates forming the entrances to the city.[69]

Within the city, the remains of various palaces dating from earlier and later periods and of the chief temples of the place as well as considerable portions of the residential section of the city and many graves of the earliest period were thoroughly explored. The method employed by the German explorers, with Walter Andrae and Robert Koldewey as the leaders in the northern and southern fields of activity respectively, was to dig trenches at a distance of a few hundred feet apart, and in carrying them down to the lowest stratum, carefully to follow any leads furnished in doing so. Under such conditions it was hardly possible for any noteworthy contents of the mounds to escape detection. The moment an important structure was struck, work was carried on at that portion of the mound until all that remained of it had been thoroughly explored, after which the combined architectural, archæological and engineering skill of the exploring party would be brought to bear on the study of the remains and in the efforts at reconstruction.

The huge stage-tower attached to the oldest temple in Ashur, known as E-kharsag-gal-kurra, "great mountain house of all lands," and sacred to the chief deity,

---

[69] See W. Andrae's magnificent work, *Die Festungswerke von Assur* (Leipzig, 1913), 2 vols., with several hundred illustrations and plates.

PLATE XVII

FIG. I, EXCAVATIONS AT KALEH-SHERGAT, THE SITE OF ASHUR

FIG. 2, ASSYRIAN MEMORIAL STELES

Ashur, whose name is derived from that of the place,[70] was uncovered and the foundations of the temple itself traced back to a ruler, Ushpia, who still combined in his person priestly and civic functions. This temple stood near the royal palace, while at some distance away was another sanctuary hardly less famous, and which is constantly referred to in the annals of the Assyrian rulers. It bore a double name—"the temple of Anu and Adad" and proved to be a double construction with a common exterior court.[71]

With the help of a large number of inscribed bricks and clay cylinders found within the temple enclosure, we can trace the work done on the structures by the many rulers anxious to show their devotion to Anu and Adad through additions to the temple or through repairs. An interesting feature of the cult at Ashur in later days as revealed through the excavations,[72] has been the finding of a "festival house" referred to in the inscriptions of Sennacherib to accommodate the multitude that made a pilgrimage annually to the sacred city to celebrate the New Year's festival—occurring in the spring—under the shadow of the temples.

Besides unearthing various temples and palaces, the German expedition has also uncovered a portion of the residential quarter of the city and has given us, for the first time, a closer view of the manner in which the people lived. Entire rows of private houses have been dug out; they were on the whole of a very simple brick construction, consisting of one story, and a series of rooms grouped around a central court, which was open to the sky. Ordinarily the houses were quite small, but larger ones have also been found consisting of a large

---

[70] He is the god of the city of Ashur and then becomes simply Ashur. See the writer's article, "The God Ashur," in the *Journal of the Am. Or. Soc.*, 1903, pp. 283–311.

[71] See the detailed account in Andrae's *Der Anu-Adad Tempel* (Leipzig, 1909), and see Plate XXXIX, Fig. 1.

[72] See *Mitteilungen der Deutschen Orientgesellschaft*, Nr. 33.

outer court, leading into a long room, at the end of
which there was a passageway, giving access to an
inner court around which a large series of rooms, varying in size, were grouped, while the back part of the
house again consisted of a long room like the corresponding one at the end of the outer court.

A notable discovery made in the space between the
outer and inner walls of the city and with which we
must close our account was that of a large series of
steles of various material—alabaster, basalt, limestone,
sandstone and composite material—containing commemorative inscriptions of rulers and their consorts
and of high officials.[73] No less than 140 of such steles
were found, many in a fragmentary condition, but
enough in a sufficiently preserved state to enable us to
say that these monuments varied in height from about
six to seven feet. They were generally rounded at the
top and some contained, in addition to the commemorative inscription, a sculptured image of the individual in
whose honor the monument was erected. The names
of no less than twenty-five rulers of Assyria are revealed through these steles. Besides these twenty-five
rulers, we have steles of three "ladies of the palace,"
including the famous Semiramis, who turns out to be
the "palace lady" of Shamshi-Adad IV (or V), who
ruled from 823 to 811, and further designated in the
accompanying inscription as the mother of King Adad-
nirari IV (810–782) and the daughter-in-law of Shalmaneser III (858–824 B.C.). Of officials represented
by monuments, the names of forty-four are preserved
in whole or in part. The monuments of the kings and
their consorts were found near the inner wall, those of
the officials near the outer wall. The steles range from
c. 1400 B.C. to the days of Ashurbanapal (668–626 B.C.),
that is to say within twenty years of the fall of the
Assyrian Empire. It is evident that these monuments

---

[72] See the publication of the German Orient Society, by Andrae,
Die Stelenreihen in Assur (Leipzig. 1913).

were erected by the rulers themselves and set up in a place of honor, and it is a reasonable conjecture that those of the officials were erected by their royal masters in recognition of their services to the state or to the royal house. There has thus been revealed the custom in ancient Assyria of erecting monuments in public places.

In Babylon, where the work was conducted chiefly under the superintendence of Dr. Robert Koldewey [74] for an equally long period as at Ashur, the chief efforts of the German explorers were directed to the mound Kasr, the name of which, viz.: "fortress," preserved the tradition of the royal palace built by Nebopolassar and considerably enlarged by Nebuchadnezzar, that once stood there, and to the mount Amran, the southern of the three mounds which covered the ancient city and which proved to be the site of the famous temple, E-sagila, "the lofty house," sacred to the chief god of Babylon and the head of the Babylonian pantheon after the days of Hammurapi, the supreme Marduk. The entire foundations of the palace were uncovered, the hundreds of rooms that it comprised, traced, and a most careful study made of every detail that was brought to light. Of great importance were the discoveries made in the space between the palace and the chief temple. A sacred procession street was laid bare, a *via sacra* built high above the low houses of the city and along which the images of the numerous gods and goddesses, who formed a court around Marduk, were carried in procession on festive occasions, and more particularly on the New Year's day, which was the most solemn occasion of the year. The walls along this street were lined with glazed tiles representing a series of lions, surmounted by rows of rosettes and other ornamental

---

[74] See the summary of the results by Koldewey, *Das Wieder-Erstehende Babylon* (Leipzig, 1913). English translation by Agnes S. Johns, under the title, *The Excavations at Babylon* (London, 1914).

designs. The street was paved with large blocks of a composite material and contained at frequent intervals a dedicatory inscription indicating the name of the street as " Aibur-shabu," "may the enemy not wax strong," and the name of the builder as the great Nebuchadnezzar.[75] A magnificent gateway, known as the Ishtar gate and consisting of an outer and inner gate, formed the approach to the street. The six square towers of the gateway contained on all sides a series of glazed tiles with alternate representations of horned dragons and unicorns, so arranged that a group of dragons running as a pattern around the four sides of the tower was succeeded by a group of unicorns similarly arranged. It was found that there were eighteen such alternate groups, one above another. The effect of these brilliantly illuminated high facings of the towers must have been superb (see Plate XXXVII).

Surrounding the chief temple to Marduk that was uncovered beneath the mound Amran, stood numerous smaller temples and shrines in honor of the many gods and goddesses who were worshipped at Babylon and whose relationship to Marduk was that of members of the royal family, ministers and courtiers to the king, as the supreme chief. Nebuchadnezzar, in his inscriptions, enumerates some forty such structures within the sacred precinct which, from the name of Marduk's temple, was known as E-sagila. Unfortunately the condition in which these temples were found was most lamentable, so that little of their decoration and of their varied contents could be determined. Lastly, as at Ashur, a great part of the efforts of the expedition was directed to tracing the walls—the outer and inner walls —and the extensive fortifications of the city as begun by the founder of the Neo-Babylonian dynasty and con-

---

[75] See Koldewey, *Die Pflastersteine von Aiburschabu* (Leipzig, 1901).

PLATE XVIII

FIG. I, THE LION OF BABYLON

FIG. 2, ARCHWAY OF COLORED, GLAZED TILES (KHORSABAD)

tinued by his great son.[76]   Quite a number of inscriptions have been found in connection with the temples, and also several hundred business documents, chiefly of the Persian period, but there is every reason to believe that the soil still holds quantities of literary treasures from the archives of the great Marduk temple, which even in the neo-Babylonian period must have been extensive.

Extending their activities to Borsippa—close to Babylon, but on the other side of the Euphrates—the German expedition has been successful in coming across the chief temple, E-zida, "the legitimate house," sacred to Nabu, the son of Marduk, and in tracing the outlines and interior arrangement of that edifice which played a part only second in importance to that of E-sagila, in Babylon.

Here we may rest our survey of the work done at the mounds. The seventy years intervening between the first larger efforts inaugurated by Botta and the present date have been marked, as we have seen, by a truly astonishing activity on the part of English, French, American and German explorers, as a result of which many of the most important sites of Babylonia and Assyria have been laid bare, and a large number of others, though only partially excavated, have been identified. Palaces and temples, towers and archives, private houses and graves, walls and fortifications have been dug up from beneath the mounds so that we are in a position to reconstruct the appearance that the ancient cities of the south and north must have presented. An enormous amount of archæological material in the form of sculptured reliefs, statues, pottery of all kinds, jewelry, instruments, thousands of seal cylinders with designs representing adoration scenes, sacrificial scenes, illustrations from myths, etc., works of art of all kinds have been secured through which we

---

[76] See Koldewey, *Die Tempel von Babylon und Borsippa* (Leipzig, 1911).

are enabled to fill out the picture of the civilization of the Euphrates and Tigris with innumerable details. We can follow their methods of warfare, their daily life, the construction of their public and private buildings, their ideals of art and their religious beliefs. Still more extensive and even more valuable as furnishing the key to an understanding and full appreciation of those ancient civilizations is the yield through the excavations of inscribed material—inscriptions on bas-reliefs, statues, votive offerings and other monuments —and of the tens of thousands of clay tablets of all periods from the earliest to the latest, forming the business and legal records of the temple administration, and of private transactions of all kinds, and lastly the literary collection of some thirty thousand tablets or fragments of tablets, found in the royal palace at Nineveh, supplemented by thousands of tablets, likewise with literary contents, discovered among the remains of archives of the temples of the south. These invaluable treasures scattered throughout the public and private museums of Europe and America have for the greater part been made accessible through publications, and as new material is found it is published as speedily as possible. Through the interpretation of this inscribed material—the oldest portion written in characters approaching the picture stage of writing, but soon yielding to a cursive style in which the original pictures assume the form of wedges—the work of recovering the lost story of Babylonia and Assyria has been supplemented and completed.

CHAPTER II

THE DECIPHERMENT OF CUNEIFORM SCRIPTS

I

THE question may now be asked, how was it made possible to read the wedge-shaped characters found on the monuments, votive offerings and the tablets? When Pietro della Valle [1] brought specimens of the writing to Europe, it was the first time that such characters which did not resemble any known alphabet were seen by European scholars. They seemed so strange that it is scarcely surprising that some scholars [2] questioned whether they stood for real writing or were not merely ornamental decorations. The excavations in the mounds of Babylonia and Assyria proved conclusively that cuneiform or wedge-shaped writing was the general and only script used in the region. The strange script, however, was not limited to Babylonia and Assyria. In fact, the first specimens to reach Europe, copied, as we have seen,[3] by Pietro della Valle, came from a place that lay outside of the Euphrates Valley, and it was on cuneiform inscriptions of this type that the first attempts at decipherment were made. Della Valle, as well as other travellers, had passed in their travels the chief sites of the old Persian Empire and were particularly impressed by the tombs and the remains of great structures still standing at Persepolis, the name of which ("Persian city") preserved the tradition that it was one of the political centres in the days of the great Persian kings. Here at least there was a definite starting-point. If cuneiform inscriptions were found on

---

[1] Above, p. 12, *seq.*

[2] Among them the famous Thomas Hyde, *Historia Religionis veterum Persarum, etc.*, (Oxford, 1700), p. 527, S. S. Witte, Professor at Rostock University as late as 1799.

[3] Above, p. 12. See Plate XIX, Fig. 1.

monuments erected by Persian rulers, the conclusion
was obvious that the characters represented the ancient
Persian language which was the official speech of the
empire. At Persepolis it was not necessary to dig below
the surface to come across remains of Persian days.
The ruins of a great palace were still standing.[4] A large
number of high and beautiful columns were still in
place, and by their help one could trace the general
divisions of the structure of which they formed a part.
Besides the columns and portions of walls, sculptured
monuments of various kinds were scattered about, besides magnificently decorated tombs cut in the rocks
that surrounded the city. These well preserved monuments were covered with the wedge-shaped characters.
An English traveller, Herbert,[5] was among the first,
towards the close of the seventeenth century, to give an
account of the strange writing which he (like della
Valle) correctly conjectured was to be read from left
to right, and he also concluded that the writing represented the language spoken by the Persians. He de-
spaired, however, of the hope of the writing ever being
deciphered unless (as he says) by another Daniel who
was able to read the mystic writing on the wall of
Belshazzar's palace.

In 1711 the first complete inscription from Persepolis
was reproduced by a French traveller, the Chevalier
Chardin,[6] from which it should have been evident that
although the characters always had the form of wedges,
still the combinations varied considerably and that
there were in reality three quite distinct styles of cuneiform writing on the rocks and monuments of Persepolis. Although a number of intrepid travellers and

---

[4] See the illustrations in Stolze, *Persepolis* (Berlin, 1882).

[5] In his *Some Years' Travels into Divers Parts of Africa and
Asia the Great* (London, 1677), p. 141, *seq.*

[6] *Voyages de Monsieur le Chevalier Chardin, en Perse et autres
Lieux de l'Orient* (Amsterdam, 1711), 3 vols.

PLATE XIX

FIG. I, RUINS AT PERSEPOLIS

FIG. 2, THE PROPYLÆA OF THE PALACE OF XERXES I (486–465 B. C.) AT PERSEPOLIS

careful observers like Engelbert Kaempfer[7] and
Cornelis de Bruin[8] examined the inscriptions, it was
not, however, until the second half of the eighteenth
century that Carsten Niebuhr, whom we have already
come across[9] and who copied more of the inscriptions
than any of his predecessors, recognized the fact of
three distinct varieties of the cuneiform characters at
Persepolis, varying in the complexity of the combinations of the wedges. Though distinguishing these three
varieties as Classes I, II and III, Niebuhr did not draw
the further conclusion that the varieties represented
three distinct languages, but supposed all three to be
the same language, written in a threefold form. He
even correctly analyzed the characters in Class I as
consisting of forty-two signs and concluded that this
form represented an alphabetic method of writing.[10]
On the basis of Niebuhr's work, two scholars who were
trained philologists proceeded to make the first attempts at decipherment. Tychsen[11] drew the correct
conclusion that the three varieties represented three
distinct languages. He furnished a tentative translation of one of the smaller inscriptions of Class I which,

[7] He embodied the results of his travels in a Latin work published in 1712, with a long title, *Amœnitatum exoticarum politico-
physico-medicarum fasciculi quinti,* (Lemgo). Kempfer was the
first to apply the term cuneiform ("wedge-shaped") to the
characters.

[8] *Voyages de Corneille le Brun par la Moscovie, en Perse et aux
Indes Orientales* (Amsterdam, 1718), 2 vols. [French translation
from the Dutch edition of 1714.]

[9] See above, p. 13.

[10] In Vol. II of Carsten Niebuhr's *Reisebeschreibung nach Arabien und andern umliegenden Ländern,* completed after his death
by his son (1774–1837, Copenhagen, 3 vols.), will be found his
account of his investigations of the monuments of Persepolis.

[11] Olav Gerhard Tychsen, *De cuneatis inscriptionibus Persepolitanis lucubratio* (Rostock, 1798).

5

however, was pure guesswork, and turned out to be entirely erroneous, except for the fact that he correctly assumed a certain character to represent the vowel *a*. Tychsen proceeded on the erroneous assumption that the buildings and inscriptions at Persepolis dated from the late Persian dynasty, known as the Parthian, in the third century of our era. But for this error, he might have made further progress in the decipherment. The correct identification of the remains at Persepolis with the Achæmenian kings of Persia in the sixth and fifth centuries before our era was made by a contemporary of Tychsen, Prof. Friedrich Münter of Copenhagen, who instituted a comparison between the monuments at Persepolis and those at Naksh-i-Rustam, which the researches of a famous orientalist, Sylvestre de Sacy, had shown to be the tombs of kings of the Arsacidian dynasty. The result was to establish the identity of the art at Persepolis and Naksh-i-Rustam, further reinforced by the occurrence of the same fabulous animals or symbols on the monuments of both places. The art was distinctly Persian, as were the costumes and ornaments on the figures at Persepolis. Münter made some further progress also in unraveling the mystery of the inscriptions. He recognized that a diagonal wedge occurring constantly in the inscriptions of Class I was a word separator, a clue that proved to be of the greatest possible value, since it enabled scholars to definitely fix the beginning and end of each word. Another suggestion thrown out by Münter, that a series of seven characters occurring in all inscriptions stood for the word king, was finally rejected by him, though the conjecture proved to be correct.

Fortunately, not long before the time that Tychsen and Münter were groping their way in the dark, a French scholar, Anquetil-Duperron, was busy in the East collecting manuscripts of the Avesta, the sacred writings of Zoroastrianism, and through native Parsi priests was learning how to read the characters and to interpret the contents of the sacred books.[12]

Through the publication of his material, scholars had before them specimens of the language employed in the days of the Persian rulers. The characters used in the Avestan manuscripts were, however, totally different from those found on the Persepolitan inscriptions; they represented a cursive alphabet that probably had its origin in India and was adapted to the old Persian language. To be sure it subsequently turned out that the Avestan books represented a compilation covering a long period of gradual growth and that even the oldest portion could not be earlier than the fourth century, while the introduction of the Avestan alphabet could not have taken place before the third century. We were, therefore, still some distance from the time of the earliest Achæmenian rulers, but close enough to warrant the assumption that the language of the Avesta was practically identical with that spoken by Cyrus and his successors. The task of scholars, therefore, lay in attempts to recognize in the wedge-shaped characters the consonants and vowels corresponding to the signs for these in the Avestan alphabet. There was, of course, no possible connection between the forms of the Avestan and the cuneiform alphabet, but the same sounds must be represented in both, and the words spelled out in the Persepolitan inscriptions must be close enough to such as were furnished by the Avestan writings to show that they were genuine Persian words. The problem, therefore, resolved itself into a species of rebus, somewhat as though one were to write English with Sanskrit characters and then to determine by patient endeavor the value of the Sanskrit characters so as to furnish good English words, and above all, a sequence of thought. Simple as this may sound, it

---

[12] See the account of the beginnings of the history of Avestan studies in Darmesteter's Introduction to his monumental work, *Le Zend-Avesta* (Paris, 1892–1893), 3 vols.

involved great difficulties because of the imperfect knowledge, at the end of the eighteenth century, of the Avestan language, the study of which was still in its infancy, and because of the puzzling circumstance that Class I of the Persepolitan inscriptions showed forty-two characters—too many if each combination of wedges represented a single sound, too few if the method of writing was syllabic,[13] and not alphabetical.

Now in many of the inscriptions from Persepolis it was observed that certain words occurred frequently in all of them. It could furthermore be concluded on the assumption that Class I represented the Persian of the days of the Achæmenian kings that the names of the rulers should be found on them, and with the names also the titles. The next step seemed simple enough— to try to fit the sounds composing the names of the Persian kings which were known to us from the Old Testament, from Herodotus and from other sources to the series of characters in the Persepolitan inscriptions that might represent proper names. Had Münter not rejected his conjecture that a certain series of characters stood for the word "king,"[14] he might have been the one to take the next step and to become the decipherer of the inscriptions. Münter was led to seek for the word for king in the Persepolitan inscriptions by the analogy which they presented to those on the royal tombs at Naksh-i-Rustam. Greek inscriptions at this place by the side of those in the Pehlevi script furnished de Sacy, whom we have already mentioned,[15] with the clue both to the historical character of the monuments and to the decipherment of the Pehlevi script, which

---

[13] By syllabic is meant the use of a sign to indicate an entire syllable; thus ra-shun-al would be syllabic writing, whereas r-a-t-i-o-n-a-l is alphabetic, while if some picture or a sign derived from a picture were used to convey the idea of rational, the writing would be ideographic. The sign for dollar is ideographic writing.

[14] See above, p. 66.

[15] *Mémoires sur diverses Antiquités de la Perse* (Paris, 1793).

turned out to be a variety introduced into Persia during the rule of the Sassanian kings (227–641 A.D.). The Greek inscriptions based on Pehlevi models, of which they were in fact translations, revealed a stereotyped order of phrases and titles on these monuments. The beginning was made with the name of a ruler followed by his titles, and these in turn by the name of his father with his titles. This gave a form as follows:

> N, great king, king of kings, king of Iran and Aniran, son of N, great king, king of kings, king of Iran and Aniran.

With the help of several bilinguals—Greek and Pehlevi —de Sacy, through fitting the proper names on to the characters, the position of which could be determined by the place occupied by proper names in the Greek translation, succeeded in determining the characters of the Pehlevi alphabet, while as soon as he was able to read words, the practical identity with the older Persian, now revealed through the researches of Anquetil-Duperron, furnished an unfailing aid in recognizing the meaning of the words written in the Pehlevi script. Here then a rebus was correctly solved —the characters fitted on to the sounds which, since the words thus put together were Persian and gave a connected sense, were shown to be the correct ones.

Münter availed himself of de Sacy's results as a support for his thesis that the Persepolitan inscriptions were those of the early Persian kings, but he stopped short at this point. Had he clung to his guess regarding the combination of signs representing the word for king, it would no doubt have occurred to him to apply the stereotyped form of the Pehlevi inscriptions also to the Persepolitan monuments. This step was taken by the man who was destined to achieve immortal fame as the decipherer of the Persian cuneiform inscriptions—Georg Friedrich Grotefend (born 1775), a teacher of Greek in the gymnasium at Göttingen, who, on the fourth of September, 1802, read a paper before the Göttingen Academy in which he claimed to have found the key to the reading of the inscriptions of Class I. The paper,[16] consisting of three parts, began with a general consideration of the three varieties of script on the monuments of Persepolis. Grotefend showed the definite basis for assuming that the three varieties represented three different languages, that the variety which occupied the first place when the three scripts were written one under the other, or which was above the head of a figure—the most prominent place, —while the two others were grouped to either side, represented the old Persian language spoken in the days of the Achæmenian kings (539–331 B.C.). If, therefore, the first class could be deciphered, it would be possible to use the inscriptions of this class as a basis for deciphering the other two classes which must represent translations of the old Persian into two languages that were spoken by the subjects of the Persian Empire. A parallel to such a procedure exists to-day in the decrees of Austro-Hungary which are issued in German and Hungarian.[17] Class I would serve as the key to Classes II and III, just as de Sacy used the Greek inscriptions at Naksh-i-Rustam to decipher the accompanying Pehlevi inscriptions—the Greek being a translation of the Pehlevi; and as in the decipherment of the Egyptian inscriptions, the Greek translation of the hieroglyphic inscription on the stone found at Rosetta served as a key to François Champollion.[18] Grotefend also confirmed the results reached by his predecessors that the order of the writing in all three varieties was

---

[16] The title was *Prævia de cuneatis quas vocant inscriptionibus Persepolitanis legendis et explicandis relatio.*

[17] Some of the decrees of the Turkish Empire are similarly issued in two languages, Turkish and Arabic.

[18] See Steindorff in Hilprecht's *Explorations in Bible Lands,* p. 629 seq. The Rosetta stone also contained a version in the late demotic script of Egypt.

PLATE XX

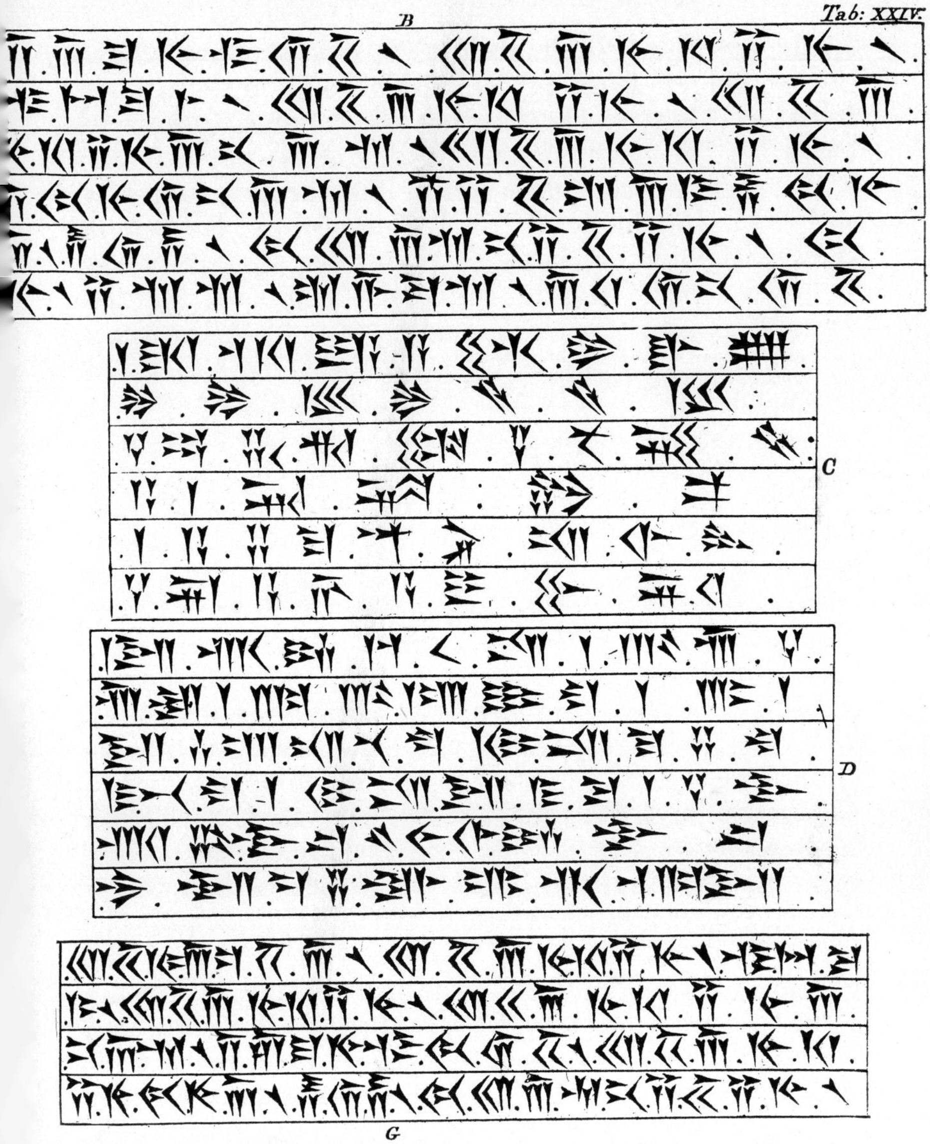

SPECIMEN OF THE THREE CLASSES OF CUNEIFORM CHARACTERS. *B* AND *G*—OLD
PERSIAN (CLASS I); *C*—BABYLONIAN-ASSYRIAN (CLASS III); *D*—NEO-ELAMITIC (CLASS II)

from left to right and that the lines followed horizontally and not vertically,[19] or in boustrophedon fashion,[20] as some scholars had maintained. In one deduction Grotefend erred, though fortunately it did not affect his key which he applied merely to Class I. He maintained that all three varieties of cuneiform writing represented an alphabetical script, not therefore ideographic like the Chinese, nor syllabic like the Japanese. He was right so far as Class I was concerned, but wrong as to the other two classes which turned out to be partly ideographic and partly syllabic.

Coming in the second part of his paper to the inscriptions of Class I, he picked out of the forty-two characters comprising the script, eight which occurred with great frequency (and two or more of which appeared in every word) and concluded that they were vowels. Availing himself at this point of the stereotyped form of the Pehlevi inscriptions of Naksh-i-Rustam and concluding that the Sassanian rulers followed in this respect the model of the old Persian kings whose realm they had taken over, he proceeded to pick out the proper names in the Persepolitan inscriptions of which one ought therefore to be found at the beginning and another somewhat further on—the name with which the inscription began being that of the one who is commemorated by the monument, and the other the name of the father.

In the third part of his paper he took up two of the short inscriptions that had been copied and published by Niebuhr and which, in his publication, were numbered B and G, the former consisting of six lines, the latter of four lines. The analogy with the Pehlevi inscriptions led him to look for the word king, which ought to follow the name at the beginning of the inscription, and should appear several times even in a

---

[19] Like the Chinese.

[20] One line from left to right, the next from right to left, and so alternately, as in the case of Hittite inscriptions.

short inscription. The diagonal wedge which Münter
had conjectured to be a word separator, made it easy
to pick out a series of characters constituting a word,
and it was not long before Grotefend hit upon seven
characters occurring just where one would expect the
word for king. These signs were

《॥.⫽.⫸.⋉.⋈.ḃ.⋉

From the dictionary which Anquetil-Duperron had
compiled for his Avestan texts, the word for king was
given as Khsheiô.[21] Now some of the seven characters
composing the word for king occurred in the series of
characters that constituted the first word in each of the
two inscriptions, and which, on the analogy of the
Pehlevi, ought to be a proper name. Grotefend's next
task, therefore, was to study the characters composing
these two names carefully. They must, of course,
conceal the names of old Persian rulers, known to us,
as has been indicated,[22] from various sources. Grotefend observed that in the inscriptions of Persepolis at
his disposal, there were only two varying series of characters constituting the beginning of the inscriptions,
which meant that all the inscriptions proceeded from
two rulers or, at all events, from rulers whose names
alternated between X and Y. Taking up now the two
inscriptions—B and G—selected by him, he found the
proper name in B to consist of seven characters as
follows:

⫲ ⫼.ꓱ. ⋉. ⋅⊨ ⟨⫼.⫽·

and in G also of seven characters

《॥.⫽.⋉⫼ꓱ.⫽ ⫼

---

[21] Be it noted once for all that kh and sh in the transliteration
of oriental languages represent a single sound and in a scientific
transliteration are given as ḫ and š. For the sake of convenience I
retain kh and sh.

[22] Above, p. 68.

He further noted in G the occurrence of the same name with which B begins, forming, to wit, the second series of characters in the third line.[23] The analogy with the Pehlevi inscriptions made it certain that the king represented by this series of characters was the father of the one whose name appeared at the beginning of G. In other words, if we designate the proper name with which inscription B begins as X, and the one with which G begins as Y, we would have the relationship

Y is the son of X.

Both X in inscription B, as well as Y and X in inscription G, were followed by the same series of characters that had been conjectured to represent the word for king. Grotefend could therefore go a step further and read in G

Y king...........son of X king.

The three characters following the group X king in the fourth line of G (after the word separator) Grotefend, after the analogy of the Pehlevi inscriptions, assumed to be the word for son. Searching for these signs in inscription B, he found them in line five immediately after the word separator, which closed the word running over from line four.[24] Hence he concluded that the name of X's father should be found before these signs for son. It was at this juncture that his keen ingenuity showed itself. In G the name of X, the father of Y, was followed by the characters for king. He could not find these characters in line four of inscription B and therefore concluded that the ten characters

---

[23] There was, to be sure, one character—the sixth—not found in the series at the beginning of B, but Grotefend at once concluded that this variation was due to the fact that the name in G stood in the genitive, whereas in B in the nominative.

[24] The Persian scribes, depending upon the diagonal wedge as the word separator, did not hesitate to allow a word to run over from one line to the other.

preceding the series "son" in B (beginning in line four
and running over into line five) represented the name
of X's father, and that this personage was not a king.
This could only mean that X was the founder of a
dynasty—not, therefore, himself of royal descent. If
we call this group of ten characters Z, we would therefore have two series:

In inscription B: X king....son of Z.
In inscription G: Y king....son of X king,

which gives us the order

Z, X, Y = grandfather, father, son.

Now in the lists of the rulers of Persia [25] there were
during the first period two dynasties, (1) the one
founded by Cyrus who was succeeded by his son
Cambyses (539–522 B.C.), (2) a second founded by
Darius I, succeeded by his son Xerxes I and grandson
Artaxerxes I (522–424 B.C.). Then came an usurper,
Xerxes II, who ruled for forty-five days, followed by
Darius II, whose son, grandson and great-grandson
followed one another, Artaxerxes II, Artaxerxes III
and Arses (424–336 B.C.), after which came Darius III
(336–331 B.C.), who succumbed in 331 B.C. to Alexander
the Great. Grotefend thus had a choice for Z, X, Y
between

(a) the father of Cyrus, Cyrus himself and Cambyses, or (b) Hystaspes (the father of Darius),
Darius himself and Xerxes, or (c) the father of
Darius II, Darius II and Artaxerxes II. The first
case was ruled out by the circumstance that the
names of Cyrus and Cambyses began with the same
letter, whereas X and Y began with different characters. X and Y would therefore turn out to be either
Darius and Xerxes, or Darius II and Artaxerxes II.
The latter alternative, if correct, would involve that

[25] See the list in Jastrow, *Aspects of Belief and Practice in
Babylonia and Assyria*, p. 448.

the name Y as the son of X should be longer than X. Both X and Y, however, consisted of the same number of characters, namely seven. Grotefend was thus thrown back on the second of the three possibilities, Darius and Xerxes, as the one fitting the required conditions. Taking up his three names once more, he observed that the first two characters of Y corresponded to the first two characters in the series that represented the word "king," which being, as we have seen, Khsheiô, showed that these two characters must stand for the sound kh and sh respectively. King Y therefore bore a name beginning with kh.sh. The fourth and the seventh character in this name was the one which, because of its frequency, Grotefend assumed to represent the vowel a or e, while the sixth sign was again the sign sh. He thus could read the name partially as

KH. SH. . . E . . SH. E

Completing the word for king in the series of seven characters, he assigned values tentatively as follows:

KH. SH. E.[26] H.[27] I.[28] O. H

which was certainly close enough to the form *Khsheio* to justify Grotefend's confidence in his method. Proceeding to compare the signs composing the name of King X with those in the word for king, he could read three of the seven characters as follows:

. . A . . H. .. . . SH.

---

[26] Grotefend, as occasion required, assigned the value *â* or *ê* to this sign. It turned out that the value was always *a*.

[27] This was subsequently shown to be *ya*.

[28] Subsequently shown to be *t*.

Now the Old Testament form of the name Darius (occurring in the Book of Daniel), which would be nearer to the original pronunciation of it than the Græcized form Dareios, was Daryawesh. It was, therefore, like fitting on a rebus to assign the value *d* to the first sign and *r* to the third, which gave him

d.a.r.h....sh

All that was needed was to assume the value e and u for the fifth and sixth characters to obtain the full name

𒀭 𒈪 𒂍 𒆜 𒂖 𒄡 𒌍

D   A   R   H   E   U   SH

The assigning of the value *r* to the third character was confirmed by the occurrence of the same character as the fifth in the name Y, while the value *h* occurring as the fourth character in the series for "king" and in the name X also fitted in with Y, though it ultimately proved to be erroneous. He thus could read Y as

𒋼 𒌍 𒆜 𒈪 𒄡 𒈪

KH. SH. H. E.[29] R. SH.   E

which could very well be the original form of a Persian name distorted by the Greeks to Xerxes.[30]

Passing to the name of the father of Darius, his decipherment of Darius and Xerxes gave him the values of the third, fifth, ninth and tenth characters as

𒄡 𒁹 𒌍 𒂍 𒈪 𒆜 𒄡 𒆜 𒈪

SH.   ..   A.   (..   H.   E)

The eighth because of its frequent occurrence he as-

---

[29] Or *a*. Note that in this name the third sign has an additional horizontal stroke and that the fifth sign lacks a third horizontal stroke—due to slight defects in Niebuhr's copies which were easily recognized as such by scholars.

[30] In Babylonian inscriptions the name appears as Khishiarshi, which is quite close to the correct Persian form Khshayarsha.

sumed to be also the vowel a.[31] The Greek form of Darius' father was Hystaspis, but several other forms were known from various sources, including Goshtasp or Gushtasp and Vishtaspo. Grotefend assumed the original consonant to have been g [32] and, accordingly, he supplied the values for the remaining characters as g for the first, o for the second, t for the fourth, s for the sixth, p for the seventh, and thus obtained the reading

G.   O.   SH.   T.   A.   S.   P.   (A.   H.   E)

He had thus succeeded in puzzling out three proper names and the word for king; he could feel tolerably certain that he had correctly identified the two kings, Darius and his son, Xerxes, as the authors of the two inscriptions. It was subsequently shown that he had erred in a number of the values assigned by him to the fourteen signs, but the way had been opened for further progress.

Taking up the two inscriptions B and G for further comparison, he noticed that the third word in both was the same. The analogy with the stereotyped form of the Pehlevi inscriptions suggested that this word was an adjective like "great," descriptive of the preceding word king. The fourth and fifth words likewise agreed in both B and G. The former was again the word for king, while the latter was king, plus four signs, which indicated some form of this word. The stereotyped form of the Pehlevi inscriptions read: X king great, king of kings. Grotefend assumed the same model for

---

[31] It turned out to be h.

[32] It turned out to be v, the form Vishtaspo, found in Zend literature, being closer to the original than the late form Gushtasp or Goshtasp. The three additional signs (8, 9, 10) a, h, e, Grotefend regarded as an attached ending.

the Persepolitan inscriptions, which enabled him to read B as

Darius, great king, king of kings

and G as

Xerxes, great king, king of kings.

Then followed in G the name Darius with the word king, and thirdly, the series of signs which, occurring in both inscriptions, he had assumed to be the word for son, with the preceding name in the genitive.[33]   He thus could read all of G except the last word, as

Xerxes, great king, king of kings,
son of Darius king,[34] . . . . .

In B there were five words which he could not determine by this process.

Darius, great king, king of kings,
king [35] . . . . . . son of Goshtaspa (*i.e.,* Hystaspis)
. . . . [36]

As for the values of the word for son and the plural of the word for kings, some of the signs had already occurred in the proper names.   So in the three signs

B   U   N

which he had identified as son, the middle one was the character to which, in the name of Darius, he had given the value *u*.   Prompted by the existence of a word "bun" in Pehlevi in the sense of offspring, his guess of *b* or *p* for the first sign of the word for son was correct,[37] his conjecture for the third as *n* was far off,

---

[33] Indicated by the three additional signs a, h, e, as in the case of Goshtasp.

[34] Of the last word consisting of nine signs he could read a . kh . a . . o . sh . o . h.—*i.e.*, all except the fourth and fifth.

[35] G did not have the signs for king at this point.

[36] Four words of which the first was identical with the last word in G.

[37] The same as the seventh sign in Goshtasp.   The correct reading of the word for son was *putra,* identical with the Zend word.

since the correct reading was shown by Sir Henry Rawlinson, in 1847, to be *tr*. Similarly his supposition for the second and fourth signs of the ending added to king —indicating the plural—as *s* and *o* were both wrong. A Danish scholar, Rask, in 1826, correctly determined the values as *n* and *m* respectively. Nor did Grotefend have more success in his attempt to read the additional words in B or the last word in G. There was thus still much left to do before it could be said that a firm basis had been secured for the decipherment of the Persepolitan inscriptions.

Grotefend's method had been successful in determining with tolerable certainty the reading of the three proper names, but when he attempted to read other words, he floundered about and generally went wrong. The errors made by Grotefend were seized upon as a basis of attack, and only scant acknowledgment was made of his success in identifying the three proper names. The Göttingen Academy published merely an extract of his attempt at decipherment in 1802,[38] and it was not until three years later that a fuller account of his decipherment appeared as an appendix to Heeren's work on the "Politics, Intercourse and Trade of the Principal Nations of Antiquity,"[39] Meantime Grotefend had profited by some of the criticism passed on his efforts and had succeeded in reading the last word in inscription G, identical with the second in line five of B as Achæmenian, so that he could read this inscription completely as

> Xerxes, great king, king of kings, son of
> Darius, king, the Achæmenian.

---

[38] Ninety years later Grotefend's paper, because of its historic interest, was published in full by the Göttingen Academy, together with three others subsequently presented by him. See *Nachrichten d. Kgl. Gesells. d. Wiss.* 1893, No. 14, pp. 573–616.

[39] *Ideen über die Politik, den Verkehr und den Handel der vornehmsten Völker der alten Welt*, 2d ed. (Göttingen, 1805). [English translation, London, 1854.]

To have thus determined the ancient designation of Achæmenian by which all the Persian rulers from Cyrus down were known was a considerable step in advance.

A striking confirmation of Grotefend's identification of the name of Xerxes was furnished by Saint-Martin, in 1823, who took up the fourfold inscription on an alabaster vase, published as far back as 1762,[40] and which, as now was apparent, contained an inscription in the three classes of cuneiform script, besides an Egyptian inscription enclosed in a cartouche. The Egyptian name had been read by Champollion as "Xerxes, great king," and Saint-Martin showed that the cuneiform inscription in Class I tallied completely with the signs read in inscription G by Grotefend as Xerxes, followed by the words for "king" and "great." In this way there was established a mutual confirmation of the key to the reading of both the hieroglyphic and the old Persian inscriptions. Other Oriental philologists now took up the task. A Danish scholar, Rask, in a study on the Zend language,[41] showed its affiliation to Sanskrit, though a separate language and quite as old as Sanskrit, and that it was closely related to the language of the Persepolitan inscriptions, as Grotefend had indeed assumed. He was able to correct Grotefend's reading of the genitive plural attached to the word for "king," and thus at one stroke definitely determined the correct value of two signs (m and n) that had not occurred in proper names. His philological training also enabled him to prove that each sign in Class I could have only a single value and not, as Grotefend supposed, more than one. The establishment of this principle marked a forward step in determining

---

[40] By A. de Caylus in his *Recueil d'Antiquités Egyptiennes*, etc., vol. v., (Paris, 1762), p. 79, *seq.*, and Plate XXX.

[41] *Observations sur les alphabets Zend et Pehlevi* (*Journal Asiatique*, 1823, vol. ii, pp. 143–150), followed by a more elaborate work in 1826.

the signs in this class that stood for vowels. Further progress in the study of old Persian, or Zend as it was at that time called, was made by the most eminent Persian scholar of his day, Eugène Bournouf, of Paris. As a result [42] he could correct Grotefend's reading of the word for "great" following that of king and he determined the values of two more signs, k and z, while Saint-Martin, whose name has already been mentioned, correctly assumed that Vishtaspa was an older form than Goshtasp for Hystaspis, and correctly read the initial sign of the cuneiform form of the name as v instead of g. A further advance was signalled by the appearance of a comprehensive work, in 1836, on the old Persian inscriptions (as the monuments of Class I were henceforth to be called), by a German Orientalist, Christian Lassen.[43] Examining anew the basis of the decipherment so far as it had proceeded, he confirmed the identification of the proper names as made by Grotefend, but showed that the word for "king" and for the plural, while correctly guessed by Grotefend, had been incorrectly read.[44] In all, seven signs were correctly determined by Lassen's researches, so that next to Grotefend, of whose identifications eleven were definitely accepted, he has a larger share to his credit than any other of the early decipherers.

A result, however, of Bournouf's and Lassen's accurate studies was to show that, while it was true, as Rask had maintained, that each sign had only one value, the reverse of the proposition that a single letter was represented by one sign was not true. Thus, three signs having the value d had been found, two for g,

---

[42] *Commentaire sur le Yaçna*, (Paris, 1833) and *Mémoire sur deux Inscriptions Cunéiformes* (Paris, 1836).

[43] *Die Altpersischen Keilinschriften von Persepolis* (Bonn, 1836).

[44] Instead of Kh.sh.e.h.i.o.h, it should be read Kh.sh.a.ia. t.i.ia—the fifth sign being *t* and the sixth *i*, besides *ia* instead of *h* for the fourth and seventh signs.

6

two for k, three for m and two for n, r and t. If the
cuneiform script of Class I was an alphabetic form of
writing, what could this mean? The solution of the
problem was due to the combined efforts of three
scholars, Edward Hincks, Sir Henry Rawlinson and
Jules Oppert,[45] who definitely established the fact that
the use of signs having the same consonantal value
differed according to the vowel that followed. So the
one form of d, g, k, m, n occurred only in case the following sign was the vowel a, whereas the other sign for d
and m was used before the vowel i, the third sign for d
and m and the alternate one for g, k, n, r before the
vowel u, while in the case of the two signs for t, one was
used before a or i and the other before u.

Before leaving the subject a few words must be said
of Sir Henry C. Rawlinson, who in many respects was
the most remarkable of the early decipherers, not even
excluding Grotefend. While in the service of the
English army [46] in Persia, his attention was directed
to the cuneiform inscriptions scattered throughout the
country.[47] He copied some of them and began to study
the strange looking characters. He prepared a list of
the signs used and without even knowing of the work
of Grotefend, de Sacy, Saint-Martin, Rask, Bournouf
and Lassen, started in the year 1835 to decipher the
proper names in the shorter inscriptions. Uncon-
sciously he followed exactly the same method as Grote-

---

[45] The papers of Hincks on the subject were published in the
Transactions of the Royal Irish Academy for 1846–1847; those of
Rawlinson in the Journal of the Royal Asiatic Society for 1846–
1851; while Oppert's work on *Das Lautsystem des Altpersischen*
appeared in Berlin in 1847.

[46] See *A Memoir of Major-General Sir Henry Creswicke Rawlinson*, (London, 1898) by his brother, George Rawlinson.

[47] Besides Persepolis, trilingual inscriptions showing the same
three classes of cuneiform script had been discovered at Elvend,
Hamadan, Murgab, Mesdjid, Mader-i-Suleiman, Naksh-i-Rustam,
in addition to the large one on the rock at Behistun. See page 83.

PLATE XXI

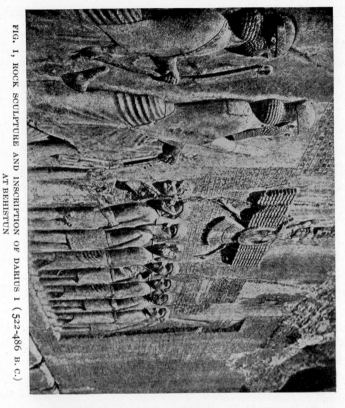

FIG. 1, ROCK SCULPTURE AND INSCRIPTION OF DARIUS I (522–486 B. C.)
AT BEHISTUN

FIG. 2, VASE OF XERXES I (486–
465 B.C.)

fend, and by a strange coincidence the first three names read by him were Darius, Xerxes and Hystaspis. The key to the decipherment of Class I was thus actually found twice, though the credit as the pioneer belongs to Grotefend. Rawlinson realized that in order to determine the full syllabary, that is to identify all of the forty-two characters used in Class I, a study of a large number of proper names was required. He, therefore, devoted his special attention to a long inscription cut into a rock at Behistun on the high road leading from Persepolis westwards into the Euphrates Valley. While the inscriptions found elsewhere were brief, consisting of from 4 to 7 or 8 lines, this one contained some 400 lines in each of the three varieties of the cuneiform script. The task of copying this remarkable document, on a rock that rose several hundred feet above the road, was in itself a testimony to Rawlinson's skill and endurance. The inscription proved to have been placed there by King Darius, who recorded on it in an impressive manner his suppression of rebellions, his conquests of numerous peoples and other achievements of his reign.[48] There were indications that the king had erected some kind of an ascent to the rock so that passers-by might mount to see it, but all traces of such an approach had disappeared. Rawlinson had to construct a scaffold to reach the inscription and at certain portions of the rock was suspended by a rope so as to obtain as complete a copy as possible.

Here he had an inscription with several hundred

---

[48] In 1907, Messrs. King and Thompson published the standard edition of *Sculptures and Inscription of Darius the Great on the Rock of Behistûn, in Persia,* with the complete text of all three classes of the inscription, together with transliteration, translation and commentary. At the head of the inscription, the king has portrayed himself, surmounted by the symbol of his god, Ahura Mazda, in the act of receiving as prisoners a series of nine usurpers to the throne, whom he had succeeded in overthrowing.

names of places that could be picked out. By dint of
great perseverance he managed to read and identify
with the help of classical writers and mediæval geographers a number of such names, which furnished him
with the values of no less than 18 additional signs. By
the year 1839 he was able to read 200 lines of the
Persian text of the Behistun inscription. Rawlinson
thus worked out for himself the entire syllabary of the
old Persian cuneiform script through the identification
of the proper names in the Behistun inscription.[49] That
his conclusions, independently reached and without his
ever knowing of the work done by others, agreed in
almost all particulars with the results obtained through
the combined efforts of Grotefend, Saint-Martin, Rask,
Bournouf, Lassen, Hincks and Oppert was a guarantee
of their reasonableness and helped to inspire confidence
in the method pursued. After the first steps had been
taken by Rawlinson, and he learned of what the scholars
of Europe were doing, he entered into correspondence
with them, more particularly with Bournouf and

---

[49] To make the method pursued by Rawlinson clear, let me remind the reader of the illustrations given above, p. 76, of names of
persons which could be identified when a few of the letters comprising the name could be read. Similarly in the case of names of
places. When, e.g., through having deciphered the names of Darius
and Xerxes the signs for d, r, u and a had been ascertained, it was
a comparatively simple matter to complete a name written with
seven characters

..u.d.r.a....

by supplying m as the first letter and filling up the end of the line
by ya and obtain mudraya which a Byzantine writer gave as the
equivalent of Egypt and which, moreover, came close to the Arabic
designation of Miṣr for Egypt. If, now, the same character to
which Rawlinson had assigned the value m occurred in another
proper name, he could readily decide whether the supposition was
correct. In this way, as in working out a rebus, one conjecture was
either confirmed or refuted by another.

Lassen. Rawlinson availed himself of the results of Bournouf's researches which revealed the character of the Zend or old Persian language in such a manner as to be capable of being utilized in the decipherment of the Persian inscriptions. The comparison with Sanskrit was another aid that secured valuable results, for after the real relationship of Zend to Sanskrit had been determined [50] the Sanskrit could be used to settle the meaning of words where Zend failed. By such methods the guesses and conjectures of the earlier decipherments were subjected to reliable tests and were confirmed, rejected or modified as the case might be. The appearance of Rawlinson's papers in the Journal of the Royal Asiatic Society,[51] therefore, placed the decipherment on an absolutely sure foundation. The "rebus" stage had been definitely passed, and it merely remained for the successors of Rawlinson to modify some of his results in minor points. In 1862 Prof. Friedrich Spiegel's work on the old Persian inscriptions,[52] giving the text and translations of all the inscriptions of Class I and accompanied by a grammar of the language and a glossary, set the coping stone to the structure that had been so laboriously constructed through the combined efforts of some of the best scholars of the day.

---

[50] Thus, *e.g.*, it was found that *s* in Sanskrit consistently changed to *h* in Zend and old Persian, Sindhus becoming Hindu in Zend, and Hindus, *i.e.*, India, in old Persian; *dasyu*, "people" in Sanskrit, was *dahyu* in Zend and old Persian, etc. It will easily be seen how important such a law of consonantal interchange was in interpreting endings to words, as well as words themselves in the Persepolitan inscriptions.

[51] Above, p. 82, note 45.

[52] *Die Altpersischen Keilinschriften im Grundtexte mit Uebersetzung, Grammatik und Glossar.* A second edition appeared in 1881. Spiegel also embodied in his work a history of the decipherment.

II

It was by the roundabout way of the old Persian inscriptions that the approach to the decipherment of the cuneiform material, found in such abundance through the excavations conducted during the past seventy years in the mounds covering Babylonian and Assyrian cities, was made. Even before Botta's finds at Khorsabad arrived at the Louvre, it was apparent from the few specimens of cuneiform inscriptions from the Euphrates Valley brought to London by Rich early in the nineteenth century,[53] that the script was of the same style as Class III on the trilingual inscriptions from Perseopolis and neighboring districts. It was some time, however, before the obvious conclusion was drawn that Class III represented the script and language used in Babylonia and Assyria. Grotefend began, in 1814, to publish the results of his study of the writing of Class III on the few inscriptions that had come from Babylonia, but it was not until 1818 that he recognized the identity of the two and explained the variations as merely incidental—modifications of the same order as the differences in handwritings. He also recognized the much larger number of combinations of wedges forming the signs in Class III and in the inscriptions from Babylonia. Indeed, by the year 1819 he had distinguished no less than 287 signs. For all that, he assumed that the Babylonian cuneiform also represented, like the Persian variety, an alphabetic script, though with this modification, that the sign varied according to the vowel accompanying a consonant. In this way he hoped to account for the larger number of signs in Class III as against Class I.

As more and more inscriptions were brought out of the mounds at Khorsabad, at Nimrud, at Kouyunjik and Kaleh-Shergat and subsequently from the mounds in

---

[53] Above, p. 14.

the south, the identity of both the Assyrian and Babylonian varieties of cuneiform characters with Class III of the Persepolitan inscriptions was confirmed, and at the same time the nature of the variations—entirely secondary in character—came to be better understood. There was no longer any doubt that Class III represented the variety of cuneiform writing used in Babylonia and Assyria and, therefore, also the language spoken in these countries. Because of the accident that the first large finds were made at northern mounds, *i.e.,* on the site of Assyrian cities, the language of Class III was designated as Assyrian, and the science that grew up out of the discoveries in the northern and southern mounds, Assyriology. Since, however, the north owes her civilization, her literature and art largely to the south, it is more proper to speak of the language as Babylonian or as Babylonian-Assyrian.

That Persian kings should commemorate themselves and their deeds in the language of Babylonia and Assyria in addition to doing so in the official language of the kingdom was quite natural, seeing that the old realm of Babylonia and Assyria formed one of the most important of the lands conquered by Cyrus and retained by his successors, just as the third variety of cuneiform script on the monuments of Persian rulers —Class II—proved to be [54] the language of the large district of Elam within which the Persian kings had established their capital cities, Persepolis, Susa and Ecbatana.

The Babylonian on all the trilingual inscriptions from ancient Persia was evidently a translation. The inscription in old Persian as the official language of the kingdom was the original—occupying, therefore, always the first or most prominent position of the three —of which those in the two other varieties of script

---

[54] See below, p. 107 *seq.*

were translations. The decipherment of Class I, therefore, served as a vantage point for attacking Class III,
old Persian cuneiform furnishing the same aid in deciphering Babylonian cuneiform script as the Greek
translation on the Rosetta stone served in laying the
foundation for the reading of the Egyptian hieroglyphics. In both cases, as indeed in the decipherment
of any unknown script, the beginning was made with
proper names, which could be picked out through a
comparison of their relative position in inscriptions of
Class I and Class III, or in the case of the Rosetta
Stone, by a study of their relative position in the Greek
and hieroglyphic texts. When proper names occurred
more than once in any inscription or occurred in several
inscriptions, as was the case in the old Persian monuments, most of which dated from Darius and Xerxes,
there could of course be no difficulty in picking out in
Class III the series of signs corresponding to these
names in Class I. The case was somewhat more difficult
when a proper name occurred only once, since Class III
did not have the very convenient diagonal wedge
separating words from one another, but, on the other
hand, with a large number of names, both of persons
and places revealed through the large inscription at
Behistun, the constant occurrence of the same signs
in a variety of names that could be read in Class I
furnished a control in picking out the series of signs in
Class III, corresponding to any particular name in
Class I.

The early decipherers like Löwenstern,[55] Long-

---

[55] *Essai de déchiffrement de l'écriture assyrienne pour servir
à l'explication du monument de Khorsabad* (Paris, 1845). Löwenstern attempted to explain the Khorsabad inscriptions without having recourse to the Persian inscriptions, with results that were
naturally disastrous. He did guess correctly that the Assyrians
spoke a Semitic language, but this led him to make the absurd
attempt to explain the cuneiform characters as modifications of
Hebrew letters.

perier [56] and Saulcy [57] floundered about considerably. Botta, the successful explorer of Khorsabad, alone made a really valuable contribution by his careful study of the numerous inscriptions found by him and which showed a large number of words evidently identical and yet written in different ways. By making a list of these variants he paved the way for the discovery made by Hincks—that the Babylonian-Assyrian script was not alphabetical but syllabic and ideographic, that is to say, that words were written by means of signs, each having a syllabic value, or by means of a single sign standing for the word. This discovery was announced by Hincks, in 1847,[58] and threw an entirely new light on the character of the third variety of cuneiform script. With signs expressing syllables or standing for entire words, it at once became clear why there should be so many signs in this variety of script. The variant ways of writing the same word, as shown by Botta, also became clear. Not only could a word be written by a single sign used ideographically or by a series of signs, each having a syllabic value, but since syllables were of three kinds, (a) consonant and vowel, (b) vowel and consonant, (c) consonant, vowel and consonant, it was possible to write a word syllabically in various ways. Thus the word for god, *ilu,* could be written by a single sign or it could be spelled out and written by two signs *i* and *lu;* and if, *e.g.,* the syllable *lab* formed part of a word, it might be written by one sign having that value

---

[56] Several articles in the *Revue Archéologique* for 1847 in reply to Löwenstern's second work, *Exposé des éléments constitutifs du système de la troisième écriture cunéiforme de Persépolis* (Paris, 1847).

[57] *Recherches sur l'écriture cunéiforme du système Assyrien* (Paris, 1849). Both Longperier and Saulcy made some correct and ingenious guesses, by the side, however, of so many errors that their work did not mark any real progress.

[58] *On the Third Persepolitan Writing,* etc. (Transactions of the Royal Irish Academy, vol. xxi, Part II, pp. 249–256.)

or further subdivided into *la* and *ab* and written with
two signs. Until this discovery was made by Hincks
there was no certainty even as to the reading of the
proper names that could be picked out in Class III
through comparison with Class I. The signs constituting the names could be chosen, but since the number of
signs forming a name in Class III did not agree with
the number in Class I, it was evidently impossible to
determine the value of each sign. Guess followed upon
guess, conjecture upon conjecture, until Hincks definitely demonstrated the general character of the script
of Class III, which represented the same language as
that found on the monuments of Assyria and Babylonia. It was now possible by a comparison between
proper names in Classes I and III of the Persepolitan
inscriptions to read the syllabic equivalents in Class III
for the alphabetical signs in Class I. Thus, *e.g.*, the
seven signs representing the name Xerxes in Class I

Kh.sh(a).y.a.r.sh.a

corresponded to six signs in Class III, to be read

Khi-shi-'i-ar-shi-i.

Similarly the seven signs in Class I for the name Darius

D.a.r.h.e.u.sh

corresponded to five signs in Class III, the correct
reading of which turned out to be

Da-ri-'i-a-mush

but which might also be written with six signs

Da-ri-'i-a-a-mush.

The word designating these rulers as Achæmenians appeared in Class I as

H(a).kh.a.m(a).n.i.sh.i.y(a).

These nine signs were represented in Class III by seven
signs to be read

A-kha-ma-an-nish-shi-'i

or by eight signs

A-kha-ma-an-ni-ish-shi-'i

since nish could be written either by one sign or by two (ni and ish). An important result of Hincks' investigations, which greatly facilitated the picking out of proper names, both in Class III and in the unilingual inscriptions of Assyria and Babylonia, was the observation that names of persons were preceded by a vertical wedge, names of gods by a sign which signified "heaven," while names of countries and of cities also had special "determinatives," as they were called. It was thus possible to be quite certain as to the beginning of names at least, whether in the trilingual or in the unilingual inscriptions. A secure basis for determining the correct reading of signs occurring in proper names was obtained upon the recognition of the fact that the vowels alone represented the alphabetic element in the Assyrian and Babylonian cuneiform script. It was now possible also to proceed with a greater feeling of assurance to the reading of ordinary words in Class III, such as "son," "king," "country," "father," "god," "heaven," "earth," which occurred with sufficient frequency to enable scholars, by a comparison with Class I, to pick out the series of signs or the single sign with which they were written. At this juncture, in 1851,[59] Henry Rawlinson again appeared on the scene with the publication of the Babylonian section (*i.e.,* Class III) of the great Behistun inscription.[60] Accepting Hincks' principle of the syllabism of the Babylonian cuneiform, he was enabled through the comparison of the several hundred names of persons and places occurring in Class I with the corresponding manner of writing these names in Class III—now rendered comparatively simple through the observation of the determinatives preceding names of persons, cities and countries,—to settle the value of a very large number of the signs, in fact over 200 of them. This

[59] *Analysis of the Babylonian Text at Behistun* (Journal of the Royal Asiatic Society, vol. xiv, pp. i–civ).

[60] See above, p. 83.

marked a great progress indeed. Rawlinson was also enabled to add to the number of ideographic writings that could be regarded as certain, including the signs designating son, father, great, lord and more the like. Hincks followed up his own researches by preparing lists of the Assyro-Babylonian characters and by 1855 he had fixed the value of 252 combinations of wedges.

The investigations of Hincks and Rawlinson had shown beyond possible doubt another fact which at first sight seemed very strange, that a single sign could have more than one syllabic value. To this feature the name "polyphony" was given; and though the proposition encountered opposition, it was not long before it replaced the supposed "homophony," proposed by Löwenstern, according to which different signs were supposed to have the same value; and that in this way the existence of so many signs was to be accounted for. Jules Oppert, who in 1855 gave a survey of the stage reached in the decipherment of Babylonian cuneiform, came to the support of Hincks and Rawlinson and showed that even a larger number of signs than Hincks had suspected had more than one sound, and it subsequently turned out that outside of the vowels the number that had only one syllabic value was very limited.

We owe to Oppert also the utilization of an important help for determining the various syllabic values for a sign and for proving that corresponding to "polyphony" we have also the phenomenon of "polyideography" in Babylonian cuneiform, that is to say, the circumstance that the same sign may also stand for several words, though usually in some logical connection with each other. Among the tablets of Ashurbanapal's library brought to the British Museum by Layard,[61] were long lists of signs arranged in columns. Oppert went to the British Museum to study these lists and found that they formed part of a large text-book

---

[61] See above, p. 22, *seq.*

literature prepared by Babylonian and Assyrian scribes
to facilitate instruction in cuneiform writing. The
lists were of various kinds, consisting usually of three
columns with a single sign in the central column and a
series of signs in each of the two other columns. Hincks
had recognized that in some of these lists the signs in
the right hand column were intended to indicate the
syllabic value of the sign in the central column. Thus
a certain sign ⊩𝍤 was repeated three times in the central
column, while the right hand column contained different
signs, as follows:

$$\text{⊩𝍤} = \text{⊢≣𝍤 ⫡⊔}$$

$$\text{⊩𝍤} = \text{⊨𝍤 ⊩⊤}$$

$$\text{⊩𝍤} = \text{⊬⊔ ⊩⊠}$$

The value of the signs of the right hand column having
been determined from a comparison of proper names
of Class III with those of Class I of the Persepolitan
inscriptions, Hincks could interpret the lines as
follows:

The sign ⊩𝍤 has the syllabic value of *li-ib*
    "   "   "   "   "   "   "   " *da-an*
    "   "   "   "   "   "   "   " *ka-al.*

That is to say the sign in question may be read in the
composition of words as *lib, dan* or *kal,* as the case may
be. It will readily be seen how with long lists of such
signs, the principle of syllabism and polyphony was not
only definitely confirmed, but the syllabic values of the
signs were ascertained with equal definiteness. It is
one of the many merits of Oppert to have demonstrated
the full significance of these syllabaries (as the lists
were called) in the further progress of decipherment.
The right hand column in some of these syllabaries contained a series of signs which furnished in syllabic
writing the words which a sign represented, or in other

words the ideographic values, while the left hand column furnished the syllabic values. Thus in the case of a sign 𒆠 we had a series as follows:

ki-i	𒆠	*it-tu*, "side"
"	"	*ash-ru*, "place"
"	"	*ir-ṣi-tu*, "earth"

which meant that the sign in question as an ideograph could be read *ittu, ashru* or *irsitu* with the meanings "side," "place" and "earth" respectively, while when used as a syllable entering in the composition, written syllabically it had the value *ki*, so that a word *kirib* meaning "within" could be written by the sign 𒆠 (*i.e., ki*) and the sign 𒌈 which, in addition to the syllabic values above [62] pointed out, has also the value *rib*. Again, a sign 𒔉 appeared in a list as follows:

shi-ti	𒔉	*me-nu-tu*, "number"
ag	"	*it-ku*, "strong"
la-ag	"	*kir-ba-an-nu*, "offering"

i.e., the sign in question as an ideograph could be read in one of the three fashions indicated, while corresponding to the three ideographic values, there were also three syllabic values. An invaluable aid had thus been secured for the reading of the Assyrian and Babylonian inscriptions and an aid, moreover, whose authenticity could not be doubted, since we had before us the syllabic and ideographic values of the signs that the schoolmasters of ancient Mesopotamia had themselves compiled as a help towards reading the inscriptions on the monuments and with a view of initiating their pupils into the method of writing cuneiform, as well as reading it.

Now to be sure the existence of various syllabic and ideographic values for one and the same sign added to the difficulty of reading inscriptions of Class III, but it

[62] Page 93.

was not long before, through the combined efforts again
of Hincks, Rawlinson and Oppert, it was found that the
Babylonian and Assyrian scribes used certain devices
to simplify the cumbersomeness of their cuneiform
script. In case of a sign X which could be read lib, dan,
kal, rib, etc., the final consonant was frequently repeated by following up the sign in question with a sign
beginning with that consonant. Thus, if after the sign
in question, a sign Y was written which had the value
bi, it was an indication that the preceding sign was *lib;*
if the next sign, however, was *li,* it was an indication
that in that particular instance the sign X was to be
read *kal;* if the next sign was *nin,* it indicated that the
sign was to be read *dan.* Besides, when once the character of the Babylonian language was ascertained, it
was possible, in a large number of cases, to decide without difficulty which of several values attached to a sign
should be chosen in order to produce a word which could
represent either a possible verbal form or a noun
formation in the language.

This brings us to the important question as to the
language of Class III and of the Babylonian-Assyrian
inscriptions, and how it was possible, after spelling out
the words of an Assyrian or Babylonian inscription to
determine to what class of languages the words belonged. At first, scholars were entirely at the mercy
of their individual guesses. Grotefend, who was the
first to call the language Assyrian, refrained from com-
mitting himself beyond expressing his opinion that he
could find no indications that the language belonged to
the Semitic class. Gesenius, one of the most eminent
Semitic scholars of his day, declared that it belonged
to the Medo-Persian group. Philoxenus Luzatto, the
son of a distinguished Hebrew scholar, published two
monographs in 1849,[63] in which he proposed the thesis
that the Assyrian was allied to Sanskrit. There were
others, however, who, starting from the Biblical tra-

---

[63] *Le Sanscritisme de la Langue Assyrienne,* etc. (Padua, 1849).

dition,[64] which placed Ashur (or the Assyrians) among
the sons of Shem, conjectured that the language was
Semitic. The question could not be definitely decided
until it was possible to reach a degree of certainty as to
the exact way in which proper names and the most
common words of the Assyrian inscriptions could be
read. With the recognition of the syllabism of the
Babylonian-Assyrian cuneiform a beginning in this
direction was made; and when, by following the method
introduced by Hincks and his successors, such words as
a-bu ("father"), *ra-bu-u* ("great"), *shar-ru* ("king"),
a-na-ku ("I") and verbal forms like *i-zan-nan* ("he
beautifies"), *i-kash-shad* ("he conquers"), were
spelled out,—the meanings of which were settled by a
comparison with the corresponding words in inscriptions of Class I or through the context—the comparison
with the common Semitic noun *ab* for "father," with
the Semitic stem *rab* ("great"), with the Hebrew *sar*
("prince"), with the Hebrew pronoun of the first person *anôkî* and with the common Semitic verbs *zanânu*
and *kashâdu* in the sense of "adorning" and "conquer,"
the indications pointed unmistakably towards Assyrian
as one of the group of languages known as Semitic.[65]

---

[64] Gen. 10, 22. The grouping of nations in this chapter as sons
of Shem, Ham and Japhet has of course no scientific value, though
the list is remarkable as an indication of the knowledge of the day
and because of the traditions that it embodies. The division appears to be into three zones. The peoples living in the northern
zone are grouped as sons of Japhet, those in the middle as sons of
Shem and those in the south as sons of Ham. Babylonia is placed in
the southern zone, Assyria in the northern. The chapter is composite in character and full of late insertions and glosses. The
system is abandoned in the case of the Canaanites, who are placed
among the sons of Ham because of the hostile feelings of the
Hebrews towards them.

[65] It is now customary to range the Semitic languages into two
groups: (1) Northern Semitic to which Hebrew, Phœnician and
the various dialects of Aramaic and Syriac and Babylonian-Assyrian
belong, and (2) Southern—Arabic, Himyaritic, Ethiopic with their

The peculiarities of the Semitic languages are so marked that one cannot long be in doubt in the case of a new language discovered whether it belongs to the group or not. The forms or moods of the Semitic verb are also of a stereotyped character, and a Semitist can tell almost at a glance whether any given verbal form is a possible one in a Semitic language. Furthermore the agreement in vocabulary among the Semitic languages is also considerable, though this varies naturally among the subdivisions of the group. Step by step, little by little, the difficulties were overcome, one problem after the other was solved until, in 1857, a test was made which showed that the decipherment of Assyrian rested on a firm basis. At the suggestion of H. Fox Talbot, who was among the early students of Assyriology, an Assyrian historical text was chosen and four scholars —Hincks, Rawlinson, Oppert and Talbot himself— agreed to send to the Royal Asiatic Society a translation independently made. No translation of the inscription had ever been published. The plan was carried out, and the commission appointed to compare the four translations [66] found the agreement to be so complete in all essentials as to carry conviction even to those who had hitherto questioned the soundness of the method pursued. But the skeptics were not all silenced, and even when a few years later another remarkable confirmation of the correctness of the decipherment was quite accidentally furnished, many scholars—among them distinguished investigators like Ernest Renan in France and Alfred Gutschmid in Germany—continued to query the results reached. The

---

various dialects. Other scholars prefer a division into eastern and western. See on these divisions Brockelmann's *Grundriss der vergleichenden Grammatik der Semitischen Sprachen* (Leipzig, 1908–1913), I, p. 5, *seq.*

[66] Published by the Royal Asiatic Society in 1857. The text chosen was an inscription of Tiglath-pileser I, King of Assyria, who ruled c. 1130–1100 B.C.

7

reason for the doubt still existing in the minds of such
scholars as Renan and Gutschmid [67] was due largely to
the difficulty of accounting for the polyphonic character of the signs and to the puzzling complications in
the writing of native Assyrian and Babylonian names
of persons and places, in consequence of their being
written in part ideographically and in part syllabically.
It was natural to raise the question, since writing is a
medium of expressing facts and ideas, why a people
should have developed a script so confusing that each
sign might have one of several values, and furthermore
how could one ever be sure in the case of signs used
ideographically that any proposed reading was the
correct one, since a sign could stand for a number of
words, even though there was an association of ideas
between the words so represented? The answer to these
questions could not be furnished until some light had
been thrown on the origin of cuneiform writing. That
the wedge-shaped signs represented originally pictures
and were modifications of hieroglyphics was to be concluded from the fact that a sign could stand for an
entire word. In the case of some of the signs, the
pictorial origin was, moreover, quite apparent. Thus,
the sign for "god" and "heaven" which had ordinarily
the form ⊁, in older inscriptions, particularly in
those found in mounds of the south, had a form like ✳
and it was an obvious conclusion that this represented
a star. A sign 𒂷 signifying "hand" showed even in
this late form its origin from a picture of the fingers
of the hand; nor was it difficult to recognize in the form
𒂍, standing for "house", its development from the
picture of some kind of construction, especially when
one compared the late form with a more elaborate one
⊞, found in some inscriptions of an older period or

---

[67] Renan voiced his doubts in an elaborate criticism of Oppert's
Expédition scientifique en Mésopotamie, published in the *Journal
des Savants* for 1859, pp. 165–186; 244–260; 360–68; Gutschmid in
Neue Beiträge zur Geschichte des alten Orients (Leipzig, 1876).

which imitated the older forms of the script. Oppert, as far back as 1856, had shown that the sign 𝍇 signifying "fish" had been evolved from the picture of a fish, the outlines of which—head, body, tail and fins— could still be distinguished in a more archaic form 𝍆 , found on Babylonian monuments. As a means of facilitating the reading of signs used ideographically, Oppert and others had also pointed out the use of a sign intended to be read syllabically and placed after an ideograph to indicate the final syllable of the word designated. By means of this phonetic complement it was possible to feel certain, *e.g.,* that the sign for "god" and "heaven" when followed by a sign having the value *tu* was to be read *elîtu,* "upper"; a sign that could stand for *ûmu* (day), *urru* (light) and *shamshu* (sun) was to be read as *ûm* if followed by *mu,* whereas if "sun" was intended, it was accompanied by a phonetic complement *shu* or *shi* or *ash,* which indicated that it was to be read *shamshu*(nominative case), *shamshi*(gen.), or *shamash* (construct state). All this was of some help, but uncertainty still existed in very many cases, and even the explanation of the hieroglyphic origin of the wedges did not account for the many values that a sign used phonetically might have, for there seemed to be no connection between the syllabic and ideographic values.

It was again the ingenuity of Hincks that suggested the solution. In a paper read before the British Association for the Advancement of Science, in 1850,[68] Hincks threw out the hint that while the oldest cuneiform writing—that of Class III and the Assyrian-Babylonian inscriptions—was Semitic, the origin of the script was not Semitic. He based this view upon the insufficiency of the cuneiform syllabary for distinguishing between softer and harder palatals and dentals that form an ingredient of the consonantal system in

---

[68] *On the Language and the Mode of Writing of the Ancient Assyrians* (Transactions of the twentieth meeting of the British Association for the Advancement of Science, p. 140, *seq.*).

the Semitic languages, and that in other respects it
was not suitable for writing words belonging to a language of the Semitic group. He drew the inference
that the writing had been adopted by the Babylonians
and Assyrians from some Indo-European people which
had conquered the country; he expressed the further
belief that this people had relations with Egypt from
which the cuneiform script was ultimately drawn.
Rawlinson at first also accepted the Egyptian origin
of the cuneiform script, but afterwards advanced the
view that the people who conquered Babylonia and imposed their script on the country were Scythians—a
view that was modified by Oppert to the extent of designating the language of the inventors as Casdo-Scythian,
and who compared it to some of the languages of the
Turanian group of Russia. On the assumption of a
foreign origin for the cuneiform script, it was possible
to explain the circumstance that there was no agreement between the ideographic and the syllabic values
of a sign. The syllabic values represented the non-
Semitic words which were the equivalents in the language of the inventors to the ideographic values of the
sign in the Semitic idiom of Babylonia. Thus, if in the
class of three-columned syllabaries above referred to,[69]
we find the sign ⟐ in the middle column, explained as
follows:

an   ⟐   ilu

This meant that *an* was the equivalent in Casdo-
Scythian for the Semitic *ilu*, "god." The Babylonians,
when adopting the foreign script, conceived the idea
of using the non-Semitic word *an* as a syllable with
which to write words—particularly verbal forms and
inflected nouns—which could not well be expressed
ideographically. Thus the non-Semitic word *an* would
be used syllabically to write a Semitic word ending in
an like *dan-an*. The theory assumed that the inventors

---

[69] Above, p. 92, *seq.*

of the script used it as an ideographic medium, and that the borrowers took the forward step of converting it into a mixed ideographic and syllabic script. In this way the various syllabic values of a sign admitted of a reasonable explanation, while the various ideographic values could in most cases be accounted for by association of ideas. The case would be analogous if the French had adopted a form of sign-writing from the English, and at the same time used the English sounds of the signs to spell words in their own language, while the same sign when standing for a word would of course be read as a French word. Thus the French word *ciel* would be written with the sign, which would be read "heaven" in English, or it would be written syllabically *ci + el*, in which case the sign which in English designated "sea" would be used because it had the same sound as the first syllable of the French word for heaven, while the second syllable would be written by the English sign for "ell," because the sound of the English word fitted the case. In the same way, the Babylonians wrote their words in non-Semitic form but pronounced them as Semitic.

The designation Scythian or Casdo-Scythian was vehemently contested by various scholars. Rawlinson himself abandoned it in 1855 in favor of Akkadian, because of the frequency with which the name Akkadian— occurring as Akkad also in Gen. 10, 10—was mentioned in the Babylonian and Assyrian inscriptions. In 1869,[70] Oppert, basing his arguments on the occurrence of the title, "king of Sumer[71] and Akkad" in the inscriptions of very ancient rulers, proposed the term Sumerians

---

[70] *Observations sur l'origine des Chaldéens*, in the Comptes-Rendus de la Société française de Numismatique et d'Archéologie, I, pp. 73–76.

[71] Sumer is represented in the Old Testament as Shinar, *e.g.*, in Gen. 11, 2, where mankind is described as congregated in the "valley of Shinar"; in Gen. 14, 1, Amraphel, who is Hammurapi, is designated as "King of Shinar." See above, p. 4, note 3.

for the non-Semitic settlers of the Euphrates Valley,
and Akkadians for the Semitic population. This view,
after a long controversy with many changes of front
on the part of scholars, has been finally demonstrated
to be the correct one.

But who were these Sumerians? Where did they
come from? And what was the nature of the language
which they spoke? Before taking up this question a
few words need to be said about a long and animated
controversy regarding Sumerian and the Sumerians
which began in 1874, and which has continued down
to the present time. While the theory of the non-
Semitic origin and character of the cuneiform script
seemed to furnish an explanation for some of the problems involved in so complicated and comprehensive a
form of writing as the Babylonians developed and
passed on to the Assyrians, new difficulties arose as
more material was brought out of the mounds, difficulties that did not appear to be met by the Sumerian
theory as we may briefly call it. In the first place it
was observed that many of the syllabic values of the
signs were portions of a Semitic word for which the
sign stood. So a sign 𒊕 which, both in syllabaries
and in texts, stood for the word *reshu,* "head," has as
its syllabic values *sag* and *rish.* The former was the
non-Semitic word for head, according to the Sumerian
theory, but the other value, *rish,* evidently stood in
some relationship to the Semitic equivalent of the sign
used as an ideograph. Again, if among the syllabic
values of a sign which stands for the Semitic *dannu,*
"strong," we find *dan,* it was evident that this value
was an abbreviation of the Semitic word. Such instances began to multiply and when it was found that
at least one hundred syllabic values had all the appearance of representing parts of Semitic words, the conclusion was forced upon scholars that the Babylonian-
Assyrian syllabary was in part at least Semitic. To
account for this the adherents of the Sumerian theory

maintained that the Babylonians after adopting the non-Semitic mode of writing and taking the step of converting it from an ideographic to a mixed ideographic and syllabic script, continued to develop cuneiform writing and added to the Sumerian words employed as syllabic values, parts of the Semitic words for which the signs stood, but used likewise as syllabic values. Meanwhile, cuneiform texts of the older period were coming to light from mounds in the south, from which it became clear that the Assyrian civilization was merely an offshoot of the culture that arose in the south, in the Euphrates Valley. It was therefore in the south that the solution of the problem as to the origin of the culture and the script was to be sought. Now, as one proceeded backwards, the texts appeared to be more and more ideographic in character. Ere long texts were found which seemed to be entirely ideographic, and such texts increased largely in numbers with the unearthing of the ancient city of Shirpurla (or Lagash) through de Sarzec.[72] The inscriptions on the many statues and votive offerings of Gudea and of other rulers were written in the older style, which scholars now began to regard as Sumerian; and yet even on these monuments Semitic words appeared and again some of the oldest inscriptions of the south were clearly Semitic and not Sumerian.

What did all this mean? If the Sumerians originated the Sumerian culture and were the inventors of the script, we should expect to find the oldest inscriptions to be in Sumerian and, what is more, in pure Sumerian; and it ought also to be possible to reconstruct the original language of the cuneiform script in such a way as to place the language in some definite group, as the Babylonian and the Persian cuneiform had been. Various attempts of this kind to find affiliations between Sumerian and Turkish or between Sumerian and some Ural-Altaic groups failed. It was

---

[72] Above, p. 39 *seq.*

therefore natural that a doubt should have arisen whether the Sumerian represented a real language or whether the Sumerians, if they existed, were the originators of the culture and the inventors of the script. The Sumerian theory manifested at first such weaknesses that one of the most eminent Semitists of his day, Joseph Halévy, was led to put forward the thesis that what scholars regarded as the Sumerian language was nothing but an older ideographic method of writing the Semitic Akkadian or Babylonian, which, in the course of its evolution, had adopted many more or less artificial devices for expressing niceties of thought and grammatical complications. The thesis carried with it the Semitic origin of the Euphratean culture and practically eliminated the Sumerians altogether. Sumer and Akkad as they appeared on the tablets of early rulers in the Euphrates Valley were purely geographical designations of the southern and northern portions of the valley respectively.[73] Even the opponents of Halévy were obliged to admit that he had revealed weak points in the Sumerian theory and it is due to him that Assyriology was deflected from the erroneous direction into which it had turned. It is now admitted that many of the hymns and incantations which scholars had been accustomed to regard as Sumerian are comparatively late compositions, or that they have come down to us in a late revised form betraying Semitic influences. It is also generally admitted to a larger extent than was formerly the case that the Semitic settlers of Babylonia had a large share in perfecting

---

[73] It is not possible to present more than a bare outline of Halévy's thesis, which has many ramifications. He has written voluminously and always with critical acumen on the subject. For details the reader is referred to Halévy's articles in the *Revue Sémitique* edited by him. An epitome of his theory will be found in his recent work, *Précis d'Allographie Assyro-Babylonienne* (Paris, 1912). A summary of the controversy up to 1898 will be found in F. H. Weissbach's *Die Sumerische Frage* (Leipzig, 1898).

the cuneiform syllabary, that many texts which are written ideographically are in reality Semitic compositions and are to be read as such, and that even in genuine Sumerian texts Semitic influence is apparent; but for all that, evidence sufficient in both quantity and quality has been brought forward to show that the early population of the Euphrates Valley was mixed in character, that by the side of Semites we find a Turanian race clearly depicted on the monuments and demarcated by their physiognomies and by differences of costume from the Semitic population.

We owe to Eduard Meyer [74] the definite establishment of this thesis. On the linguistic side, evidence for the existence of a Sumerian language has recently been brought forward which does not rest upon guesswork or on pure conjecture, but is made conclusive by the study of the oldest texts of Babylonia. As long as Sumerian was simply to be deduced from the ideographic values of the signs, one was justified in doubting whether we were in the presence of a real language, for since ideographs could be read as Semitic as well as Sumerian, it was indeed possible to regard a "Sumerian" inscription as merely another form of writing Babylonian—a very artificial form to be sure and yet, since all writing is a more or less artificial device, a possible form. When, however, the proof was furnished from the texts that Sumerian words could be written phonetically as well as ideographically, that even in Sumerian the device existed of writing a word as in Babylonian either by a single sign representing the word or by signs representing the syllables of which it is composed, there could no longer be any question as to the genuine linguistic character of Sumerian. In addition to the evidence for phonetic writing, which became more and more abundant as scholars penetrated deeper into the study of the oldest texts from ancient

[74] *Sumerier und Semiten in Babylonien* (Berlin, 1906).

Babylonian centres,[75] the proof of a fixed grammatical structure for nouns and verbal forms was furnished in a manner to carry conviction to the minds of those who had hitherto maintained a skeptical or non-committal attitude towards the linguistic evidence.

Taking up now the question who these Sumerians were, an impartial verdict must confess that the problem still remains obscure. We know that they were not Semites; their features as depicted on the monuments reveal a Turanian type, but the term Turanian is too vague to furnish any definite clue. Various indications point to their having come from a mountainous region. They brought the worship of their native gods with them, and the nature of these deities suggests their having had their original seats on the tops of mountains. It is to the Sumerians that we owe the construction of the stage-towers of which remains have been found in all the important centres of Babylonia and Assyria. Built in imitation of mountains with an imitation of a mountain road leading to the sanctuary at the top, it is reasonable to conclude that the thought of housing the gods in this way arose in the minds of a people accustomed to the worship of gods whose seats were on mountain peaks. There is other evidence pointing in the same direction of an original mountain home whence the Sumerians came at a remote period to settle in the Euphrates Valley. Now there are mountains to the east and north-east of Babylonia, and it is

---

[75] We owe largely to F. Thureau-Dangin the progress made during the past decade in the interpretation of these texts. See especially this author's *Les Inscriptions de Sumer et d'Akkad* (Paris, 1905); also in German translation, *Die Sumerischen und Akkadischen Kœnigsinschriften* (Leipzig, 1907). See now, for an exposition of Sumerian grammar, Delitzsch's *Grundzüge der Sumerischen Grammatik* (Leipzig, 1914) and Dr. Arno Poebel's volume of Sumerian grammatical texts in the publication above referred to (page 46) and which represents a further advance on Delitzsch's investigations.

therefore possible that the Sumerians entered the Valley from this side—perhaps under pressure of other mountain hordes coming from the north. But they may also have come, as has been recently maintained, from mountainous districts to the northwest of Mesopotamia. Whether the Sumerians already found the Semites in possession of Babylonia and then conquered them, or whether the Sumerians were the earliest settlers and founded the culture in that district is another question that has not been definitely decided, with the evidence, however, in favor of the view that the Semites were the first on the ground and that they had already made some advance in culture when the Sumerians swept down on them and imposed their rule and such culture as they brought with them on the older settlers.

III

Here we may rest our survey of the decipherment of the Babylonian-Assyrian cuneiform writing, which we have followed from the successful unraveling of the old Persian inscriptions down to the time when a secure basis for the decipherment of Class III had been secured. The appearance, in 1859, of the "Expédition scientifique en Mésopotamie exécutée de 1851 à 1854,"[76] the second volume of which contained Oppert's analysis of the principles of the decipherment, may be said to mark the termination of the second period of cuneiform research, as the publication, in 1849–51, of Rawlinson's researches in the old Persian inscriptions closed the first period. The third period, marked by continuous publications of Babylonian and Assyrian texts, chiefly by French and English Assyriologists, is one of steady progress in perfecting the details of the decipherment. New ideographic and syllabic values were constantly being discovered, improved readings took the place of

---

[76] The account of the French expedition above referred to (p. 28).

earlier imperfect ones, and the beginnings were made towards a systematic treatment of the grammatical features of the Babylonian language, or Assyrian as it continued to be called. Skepticism, however, still existed in some quarters and it was not until the appearance, in 1872, of Eberhard Schrader's *Die Assyrisch-Babylonischen Keilinschriften*,[77] that what may be called the "trial" period came to an end.[78]

The fourth period of cuneiform research is marked by the participation of German scholarship, which, since the pioneer work of Grotefend, had rather held aloof in the further struggle to unravel the mysteries of the various kinds of cuneiform script.

Excepting Grotefend, the work in Assyriology was carried on by English and French scholars, unless we count Jules Oppert, who was born in Hamburg, but who, as a young man, came to Paris and settled there for the remainder of his life,[79] among German scholars. Eberhard Schrader was the first among the students of Oriental languages in Germany to take up Assyriology and when, in 1875, the University of Berlin decided to introduce the subject, Schrader was called to fill the chair and continued active till within a few years of his death, in 1908. Schrader's thoroughness and soundness of scholarship did much to gain the confidence of German scholars in general in the results of the decipherment, and after Gutschmidt's attack in 1876, all opposition practically ceased. Schrader brought to his

---

[77] Published in the *Zeits. d. Deutsch. Morgenländischen Gesellschaft*, vol. xxvi, pp. 1–392; and then as a separate volume.

[78] Gutschmid's answer to Schrader (above, p. 98) appeared in 1876, but it failed to make any deep impression.

[79] See the sketch by W. Muss-Arnolt of Oppert's life, with a complete bibliography, in the *Beiträge zur Assyriologie*, vol. ii, pp. 523–556. No adequate biography of Edward Hincks has to my knowledge as yet appeared. A brief sketch with a complete bibliography, compiled by Dr. Cyrus Adler, will be found in the Journal of the American Oriental Society, vol. xiii and xiv.

task that philological nicety for which German scholarship has so long been distinguished, and of which at that time cuneiform research stood much in need. Schrader's enthusiasm for the study attracted a number of young scholars to him, among them Friedrich Delitzsch, the son of the distinguished theologian, Franz Delitzsch. Young Delitzsch became the founder of the present German school of Assyriology. First establishing himself as *Privat-Dozent* for Assyriology at Leipzig, then called to Breslau to occupy the chair of Assyriology, and in 1906, to Berlin, he has in the course of his career trained the largest percentage of Assyriologists of Germany and a large proportion of those in other parts of the world, notably in the United States and Canada; and those of the present day who did not sit directly at his feet have imbibed inspiration from Delitzsch's fruitful researches or have been pupils of Delitzsch's pupils.[80]

The activity at the present time in all branches of Assyriology is largely due to the stimulus given to the study by Delitzsch and his pupils. The museums of London, Berlin, Paris and Philadelphia are steadily issuing new texts. Specialization within Assyriology has set in. Some scholars are devoting themselves to the extensive business and commercial literature, others to the religious texts and the development of the religious ideas and the cult, others to the study of Babylonian-Assyrian history, some to the linguistic problems, some to the further elucidation of the Sumerian texts and so forth.

Through the combined activity of scholars of many lands, supplementing the discoveries made by explor-

[80] We owe to Delitzsch the first Assyrian Chrestomathy (*Assyrische Lesestücke*, 1st ed., Leipzig, 1876; 5th ed., 1912); the first substantial grammar (*Assyrische Grammatik*, 2d ed., Leipzig, 1906, also English translation, Leipzig, 1889); and the first Assyrian Dictionary (*Assyrisches Handwörterbuch*, Leipzig, 1896) to which he is now adding a supplement.

ing expeditions, and through the interpretation of the material unearthed, which has grown, as we have seen, to such huge proportions and which is still growing, the civilization of Babylonia and Assyria stands revealed before us in all its ramifications as one of the great forces in the ancient history of mankind, the direct or indirect influence of which is to be seen in many a phase of our own modern culture.

IV

While not strictly within the limits of our subject, it will nevertheless be considered proper to close this chapter with a brief account of the decipherment of Class II of the trilingual inscriptions of Persepolis and surrounding districts. Already in his first paper on the Persepolitan inscriptions, Grotefend added some remarks on the script of Class II which he recognized as more complicated than Class I, but not so complicated as Class III. He continued his researches in this second variety from time to time and in 1837[81] was able to recognize the use of a vertical wedge (as in Class III), placed before proper names in order to distinguish them.

It was not, however, until 1844 that any decided success in deciphering the script of Class II was achieved. In that year appeared a work[82] by a Danish scholar, Westergaard, in which, through a comparison of the proper names in Class II and Class I, he succeeded in assigning correct values to 18 of the signs. This was only a small proportion of the 111 signs to

[81] *Neue Beiträge zur Erläuterung der Persepolitanischen Keilschrift* (Hanover, 1837).

[82] N. L. Westergaard, *Zur Entzifferung der Achämenidischen Keilschrift zweiter Gattung* (Zeits. für die Kunde des Morgenlandes, vol. vi, pp. 337–466); also published in English, *On the Deciphering of the Second Akhœmenian or Median Species of arrowheaded Writing* (Mémoires de la Société Royale des Antiquaires du Nord, 1840–44, pp. 271–439).

be distinguished in Class II, but it was a beginning. Progress would have been more rapid had not Westergaard fallen into some serious errors which had to be corrected by subsequent researches. He picked out correctly the signs representing the names Cyrus, Darius, Xerxes, Hystaspis, Achæmenian and Persian; and he also recognized the mixed syllabic and alphabetic character of the script, but he erred, as was quite natural, in the vowel signs and in the selection of signs representing syllables and those representing merely a consonant. For twenty-two signs he could not determine any values through the mere comparison of proper names. Hincks again came to the rescue in correcting some of Westergaard's errors. In two papers on the subject[83] he identified the three signs for the vowels, a, i, u. He recognized the determinative placed before the names of deities, added nine signs to those correctly fixed by Westergaard. The publication of the version of Class II in the great Behistun inscription by Edward Norris, in 1855,[84] to whom Rawlinson had given his copies and squeezes of this part of the great rock inscription, marked a decided advance through the recognition by Norris of the close relationship of the signs of Class II to those of Class III. By this means the value of a number of signs could be fixed by comparison with the Babylonian-Assyrian signs, and when later on the principles governing the modifications that the signs of Class III had undergone in their transformation to Class II, had been ascertained, the bulk of the syllabary of the latter class became perfectly trans-

---

[83] (a) *On the First and Second Kinds of Persepolitan Writing,* (b) *On the Three Kinds of Persepolitan Writing and On the Babylonian Lapidary Characters;* both published in the Transactions of the Royal Irish Academy, vol. xxi, Part II, pp. 114–131 and 233–248.

[84] *Memoir on the Scythic Version of the Behistun Inscription* (Journal of the Royal Asiatic Society, vol. xv, pp. 1–213). The paper was read in 1852.

parent. In this way the decipherment of Babylonian-Assyrian became of service in reading the second variety of the cuneiform script. Westergaard now took up the subject again[85] and succeeded in increasing the number of signs correctly read to sixty-seven. Steady progress was made through the efforts of various scholars, among whom M. Haig, A. D. Mordtmann, Oppert and Sayce are to be specially mentioned, so that by the year 1879, when Oppert published his work, *Le Peuple et la Langue des Mèdes,* the decipherment, so far as the reading of the signs was concerned, was practically completed. The final work on the subject, giving a full account of the course of the decipherment and detailing the results in the most exact manner, is the publication of the inscriptions of Class II by Weissbach, in 1890.[86] The question, however, as to the language of the inscriptions was a more difficult one. Scholars wavered as to the name to be given to the language. The first suggestion to call it Scythic was abandoned in favor of Median, proposed by Oppert, but this designation yielded in time to others so that at present it is generally designated from the region in which it was spoken as neo-Susian or neo-Elamitic.[87] The resemblance of the signs to those of Class III showed conclusively that the script was a derivative from the Babylonian-Assyrian cuneiform, and in view of the comparative ease in determining through this resemblance the values to be assigned to the 113 signs to be distinguished, and the existence of certain signs as in Class III, as determinatives indicating whether a word was the name of a person, a deity, a city or a country, it was possible, through the comparison with Class I and III on the

---

[85] In a paper published in the Proceedings of the Danish Academy for 1854, vol. ii, pp. 41–178.

[86] *Die Achæmenideninschriften zweiter Art,* herausgegeben und bearbeitet von F. H. Weissbach (Leipzig, 1890).

[87] The second designation is at present the one more commonly employed.

large Behistun inscription to fix the sounds of many words in the language, the meanings of which were furnished by the comparison. This extended to verbal forms as well as to nouns, to pronouns and to particles. The language turned out to be a type which was neither Semitic nor Aryan, and yet totally different from the Sumerian. Excavations conducted by the French government for several years at Susa, under the general direction of J. De Morgan, brought to the surface a large number of historical and votive inscriptions and hundreds of commercial tablets such as were found in great abundance in the Babylonian and Assyrian mounds. The material covered an extensive period; and as it was studied and interpreted by one of the most distinguished Assyriologists of the day, Vincent Scheil,[88] it was shown that the language was closely related to that of Class II. It was evident, therefore, that the inscriptions of this class represented the language spoken by the inhabitants of Elam, lying to the east and northeast of Babylonia and which, as we know from the annals of Babylonian and Assyrian rulers, was for many centuries the rival of Babylonia and at various times made inroads into the Euphrates Valley.[89] The excavations at Susa confirmed the data derived from Babylonian and Assyrian monuments as to the great age of the Elamitic kingdom, for the material unearthed carries us back beyond the third millennium before our era. The script also shows traces of having

---

[88] The results of the remarkably successful excavations at Susa are being published by the French government. Thirteen large volumes have appeared up to the present time under the title of *Délégation en Perse*, of which six are devoted to the Elamitic material, edited by Scheil. The expedition also found a magnificent series of boundary stones and the famous Hammurapi Code, all of which were captured as trophies by the Elamites during an incursion into Babylonia in the twelfth century and carried by them to their capital at Susa. See below, p. 283.

[89] See Chapter III.

8

passed through a long development, the oldest forms
representing a much closer approach to the original
pictures from which the linear wedges were derived.
The decipherment of the older Elamitic inscriptions,
successfully inaugurated by Scheil, is not, however, complete. More material will no doubt be forthcoming
which will enable scholars to clear up doubtful points.
It seems certain that the language also changed somewhat with the lapse of centuries so that scholars now
distinguish between the oldest form of Elamitic as
proto-Elamitic, and the latest form, represented by
Class II, as neo-Elamitic. The relationship of the
Elamitic and neo-Elamitic cuneiform to the Babylonian
is evident, but exactly how the proto-Elamitic characters were derived from the Babylonian script is a
question that must be left open for the present. As for
the language, we must rest content with the statement
that it is of a Turanian type and was one of the languages spoken in the districts lying to the east of
Babylonia. The Elamites at one time extended their
rule far into Asia Minor, for around the lake of Van
in Armenia inscriptions have been found which are
written in a cuneiform variety practically identical
with that of Class II.[90]

The extensive use of cuneiform script as a writing
medium for various languages and the development of
various distinct forms, all eventually to be traced back
to some early variety of picture writing, is a remarkable testimony to the profound influence exerted by the
civilization that arose in the Euphrates Valley through
the combination of the Sumerians and Semites or as
we ought to say, Sumerians and Akkadians. Even with
a consideration of these chief forms representing four
distinct languages, Sumerian, Babylonian-Assyrian,
Elamitic and Persian, we have not exhausted the scope

[90] See Sayce *The Inscription of Mal-Amir and the Language of
the Second Column of the Akhæmenian Inscriptions* (Actes du **VI.**
Congrès International des Orientalistes, Part II, pp. 639–756).

of cuneiform writing. In Cappadocia a variety derived
from the more specifically Assyrian form of cuneiform
characters was used in connection with commercial interchange. A considerable number of tablets, all of a
commercial character, have been found dating from
about the eleventh century, in which cuneiform is used
to write the current tongue of Cappadocia,[91] while at
Boghaz-Keui, a capital of a Hittite kingdom, a large
archive of clay tablets was discovered by the late Hugo
Winckler,[92] containing hundreds of tablets in cuneiform writing, but representing the Hittite language—
the same as the one found in hieroglyphic form on the
Hittite inscriptions. Among the tablets of the cuneiform archive found at Tell el-Amarna to which reference will be made,[93] there were letters in cuneiform
written by rulers of Mitanni—a district to the north-

---

[91] See Delitzsch, *Beiträge zur Entzifferung und Erklärung der
Kappadokischen Keilschrifttafeln* (Abhandlungen der Königlich-
Sächsischen Gesellschaft der Wissenschaften, Philologisch-His-
torische Classe, XIV, pp. 207–270).

[92] See *Orientalistische Literaturzeitung,* Dec. 15, 1906, and
Mitteil. d. Deutsch. Orient Gesellschaft, No. 35 (Dec., 1907), and
now, also, Delitzsch, *Sumerisch-Akkadisch-Hettitische Vokabular-
fragmente* (Berlin, 1914; Abh. d. Kgl. Preuss. Akd. d. Wiss., 1914,
Phil.-Hist. Klasse, Nr. 3), embodying a study of 26 fragments of
tablets found at Boghaz-Keui, containing in parallel columns
Sumerian and Akkadian words and phrases, together with the
Hittite equivalents (written in cuneiform characters) in the third
column. In this way a large number of words and forms can be
identified and, with the complete publication of this kind of material, promised in the near future, there will be little difficulty in
determining the exact character of the Hittite language. There is
also reason to hope that with the aid of these transliterated Hittite
texts it will be possible to find the definite key for the decipherment
for the hieroglyphic Hittite script. The publication of the important material found by the late Dr. Winckler is now announced
as ready and is expected to be published within this year by
Dr. E. F. Weidner.

[93] Below, p. 164.

east of Mesopotamia—in their own language, which is
represented again by some of the tablets found at
Boghaz-Keui. Even Greek was written in cuneiform
characters, as some tablets published a number of years
ago by Pinches showed.[94]

It is evident from this that the influence exerted by
the civilization of Babylonia and Assyria extended
throughout the ancient world, prompting the Egyptian
scribes to learn cuneiform so as to carry on a correspondence with Babylonian rulers and with the governors of Palestinian and Phœnician centres, and leading the Hittites in the north to exchange cuneiform as
a more convenient mode of writing for their own hieroglyphic script,[95] and resulting in the adoption of a
cuneiform script by the Elamites as well as by their
successors, the Persian rulers. Within Babylonia and
Assyria the script, developing from an archaic to several varieties of more modern forms, survived the fall
of the Babylonian empire through Cyrus' conquest and
even the coming of the Greeks, for cuneiform inscriptions from the days of the Greek supremacy have been
found, and it is not until almost the threshold of the
Christian era that the use of this form of writing finally
disappears. The latest cuneiform inscription dates
from the year 80 B.C.

---

[94] *Greek Transcriptions of Babylonian Tablets* (Proceedings of
the Society of Biblical Archæology, vol. xxiv [1902], pp. 118–119).
These fragments of tablets, containing transcriptions of Greek words
in cuneiform, furnished incidentally a further confirmation—
though at the time of Pinches' publication no longer necessary—
of the correctness of the method of reading the Babylonian-Assyrian
cuneiform characters.

[95] For the Hittite inscriptions see Messerschmidt, *Corpus In-
scriptionum Hettiticarum* (Mitteilungen der Vorderasiatischen
Gesellschaft, 1900, No. 4; 1902, No. 3; 1906, No. 5); Garstang, *The
Land of the Hittites* (London, 1910); Ed. Meyer, *Reich und Kultur
der Chettiter* (Berlin, 1914); and the recent attempt at decipherment by R. C. Thompson, *A New Decipherment of the Hittite
Hieroglyphics* (Archeologia, vol. lxiv, Oxford, 1913, pp. 1–144).

Lastly a word as to the origin of the cuneiform script from a pictorial form. We have carried back the forms of cuneiform writing used outside of Babylonia and Assyria to the influence exerted by these two empires, whose civilization originating in the Euphrates Valley is the result of the commingling of Sumerians and Akkadians. The oldest form of cuneiform writing, therefore, is that represented by the oldest inscriptions of Babylonia which, we have seen, are couched in Sumerian. The script, however, in these Sumerian inscriptions, while archaic, is far removed from the state in which each sign represented a picture. Moreover, we have seen that contrary to the opinion at first held by scholars, the Sumerian in the form that we have it is no longer a purely ideographic mode of writing, but has already advanced to the syllabic stage in which a sign is used to represent a sound and no longer merely the word for which it stands. A careful study, however, of the forms of the characters enables us to pass beyond the wedge-shaped variety of cuneiform to a linear type; and in many cases it is not difficult to recognize in the linear outlines the remains of a picture, representing one of the words for which the sign stands. Thus the linear form ⟩ of the sign for sun, day, light, which in the wedge-form becomes ⟨ is clearly a derivative of a picture of the sun sending forth its rays. The sign for eye, face, seeing, which in the wedge-shape takes on the form ⟨ is in the linear form ⟨ and it is not difficult to recognize in this the outlines of an eye. The sign for man ⟨ is in the linear form ⟨, which suggests a man lying on his back.

To set forth in detail how, starting with a series of pictures, the writing, passing through various stages, developed to a linear form, suitable for transferring characters to a hard material and then by further stages was transformed to a wedge-shaped variety, better adapted for writing on a soft substance like clay, would carry us too far. Nor is it necessary for our purpose, which is merely to call attention at the close of this chapter to the manner in which the cuneiform script originated, to do so. Prof. Barton, who has recently published an elaborate work on the "Origin of Cuneiform Writing," [96] in which he has embodied the results of many years of study, has added valuable tables of signs showing the changes they underwent in passing from the oldest to the latest period. He has also endeavored to reconstruct the objects represented by the signs. Thanks to the ingenious method pursued by him and to his wide and accurate scholarship, he has succeeded in a large number of instances in giving us the picture originally represented. Naturally some of his identifications are open to question. In a problem of this kind one must not expect that all phases of it can be satisfactorily solved. From a survey of the objects represented—animals, parts of the body, instruments, pictures of water, of stars, trees and plants— and making due allowance for doubtful cases, we reach the general conclusion that the script originated at a time when already a considerable advance in culture had been made, and in a land in which agricultural conditions prevailed, in which animals had been domesticated, and the gods identified with personifications of the stars, by the side of the moon and sun. There is nothing, however, to indicate more precisely where the script originated. It may have been brought by the Sumerians to the Euphrates Valley and perfected by them there, or it may have originated in the Euphrates Valley or the neighboring district of Elam. It is not impossible that the proto-Elamitic script, to which a reference has above been made,[97] may revert to the same source as the picture-writing underlying the oldest form of Sumerian inscriptions. Until we can determine more accurately whence the Sumerians came and how far

---

[96] Beiträge zur Assyriologie, vol. ix (1912–1913).
[97] Above, p. 113, *seq.*

back the Sumerian culture can be traced, it is idle to speculate further. Archæology has given us so many surprises that it is not out of the question that we should come across traces of a still earlier culture than the Sumerian or the proto-Elamitic,[98] from which both may have derived their inspiration, and with this a pictorial script further developed by each group and adapted to its purposes.[99]

From the linear form we can without difficulty trace the further development to the latest stage of wedge-writing. Variant forms continued to arise both in Assyria and Babylonia and there can be no question that the neo-Elamitic cuneiform or Class II represents a variety of the Babylonian script simplified and adapted to Elamitic about the twelfth century B.C., further modified in the course of time, while the Persian variety represents another more simplified adaptation made in the sixth or possibly as early as the seventh century B.C.

---

[98] See King's ingenious suggestion in the appendix to his *History of Sumer and Akkad* (London, 1910), in which he takes up this problem.

[99] See further on this subject besides Barton's book, Fossey's chapter on the Ideographic Origin and Evolution of Cuneiform Writing in his *Manuel d'Assyriologie,* pp. 245–268, and Delitzsch's *Entstehung des ältesten Schriftsystems oder der Ursprung der Keilschriftzeichen* (Leipzig, 1897), the first thorough discussion of the subject, full of valuable suggestions, though some of the views set forth must be modified in the light of later researches.

CHAPTER III

SURVEY OF THE HISTORY OF BABYLONIA AND ASSYRIA

I

IN any general survey of the history of Babylonia and Assyria there are two facts of fundamental importance to be borne in mind: first, that the course of civilization in the land of the Euphrates and Tigris proceeds to the north, and second, that the culture is the outcome of a mixture of two diverse elements—of a non-Semitic with a Semitic population. The obvious conclusion from the first fact is that the settlements in the south, in what is known as the Euphrates Valley, are older than those in the north—a conclusion confirmed by the excavations conducted at southern mounds, which have yielded us the documents for tracing the civilization to a very early period, though as yet insufficient for carrying us back to the small beginnings. The second fact prepares us for the distinguishing feature of the oldest period as likewise revealed by the monuments, to wit, the struggle between the non-Semites or the Sumerians, and the Semites or Akkadians for supremacy.

This struggle represents the natural process in the assimilation of two apparently incompatible elements. Civilization may be described as the spark that ensues when opposing ethnic elements come into contact. Culture up to a certain grade may develop in any centre spontaneously, but a high order of civilization is always produced through the combination of heterogeneous ethnic elements.

There is no more foolish boast than that of purity of race. A pure race, as I have it put elsewhere,[1] if it exists at all, is also a sterile race.

---

[1] *Aspects of Religious Belief and Practice in Babylonia and Assyria*, p. 5.

120

PLATE XXII

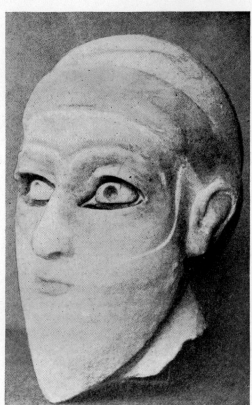

FIG. I, SUMERIAN TYPE (TELLOH)   FIG. 2, SEMITIC TYPE (BISMYA)

Whether the Semitic Akkadians were the first
settlers in the Euphrates Valley or the non-Semitic
Sumerians is a question to which, as indicated in the
last chapter,[2] no definite reply can be given in the
present state of our knowledge. My own inclination is
to side with Eduard Meyer,[3] to give the benefit of the
doubt to the Akkadians and to assume that the Sumerians, who we have every reason to believe were a
mountainous people, entered the Valley from the northeast (or northwest) as conquerors—bringing a certain
degree of culture with them, but which through the
contact with the Akkadian population was further
stimulated and modified until it acquired the traits distinguishing it when we obtain our earliest glimpse
of political, social and religious conditions in the
Euphrates Valley.

Fortunately, through the monuments of Telloh,
Sippar, Nippur and Bismya, and through the designs
on numerous seal cylinders, we are in a position to
picture to ourselves this non-Semitic race.[4] They are
portrayed in contrast to the Akkadians as beardless
and generally, though not always, with shaven heads.
The general type suggests a comparison with the Mon-
golian race. The shape of the head was inclined
towards roundness, the cheek bones were prominent
and the nose was not full and fleshy as was the case
with the Akkadians. The dress in the earliest period
consisted of a plain or fringed garment, hanging from
the waist or was formed in more elaborate fashion of
three to five flounces—yielding, however, at a later
period to a shawl or mantle, decorated with a border,
drawn over the left shoulder and falling in straight
folds. In contrast, we find the Akkadians represented

[2] Page 107.
[3] *Sumerier und Semiten in Babylonien*, p. 107, *seq.*
[4] See the accompanying illustrations, and further in Meyer,
Sumerier und Semiten in Babylonien; and in Jastrow, *Bildermappe
zur Religion Babyloniens und Assyriens*, Nos. 1–7.

with hair and beard, though it would appear that in consequence of a new wave of Semitic immigration about the time of Hammurapi or shortly before, the Bedouin custom was introduced of shaving the moustache. The features, particularly the long-shaped head and the fleshy nose, are unmistakably Semitic. In dress the Semites are represented by the loin cloth or by a plaid wrapped around the body, falling in parallel bands, with the ends thrown around the left shoulder. The Sumerians appear also to have had the custom of wearing wigs, as the Egyptians, perhaps limited to ceremonial occasions, though to what extent and during what periods the custom prevailed it is difficult to say. Curiously enough the gods, even in the oldest monuments, have abundant hair and long beards,[5] but with lips and cheeks often shaven, from which Professor Meyer has drawn the inference that the Sumerians, while retaining some of the customs that they brought with them, assimilated their gods to those worshipped in the land into which they came and therefore represented them as Semitic.

Beside some form of writing which, as pointed out, the Sumerians may have brought with them, but further developed after their conquest of the Euphrates Valley, they appear to have been skilled in sculpturing in terracotta and in stone, advancing gradually also to working in metals. Naturally, here again it is difficult to draw the line between what they brought into the country and the share of their artistic achievements due to their contact with the Semitic settlers, but since the Euphrates Valley is devoid of stone and metals, the balance is again in favor of the assumption that they brought some measure of artistic skill with them.[6]

The architecture in the earliest period is conditioned by the native soil which furnishes clay as a building material that was readily adapted for the construction

---

[5] See Meyer, l.c., p. 95, seq.

[6] Further details in Chapter VII.

of houses and temples, consisting of both unburnt and burnt bricks. The only characteristic structure that may be safely ascribed to Sumerian initiative is the stage-tower attached to the temples in all important centres.[7]

II

The change in habitat from a hilly country to a flat one was a momentous factor that brought with it an adaptation on the part of the Sumerians to the new conditions. In their mountain homes we may well suppose the Sumerians to have been hunters—of which a trace remains in the Biblical tradition that makes Nimrod, pictured as one of the founders of the Euphratean culture, a mighty hunter, whereas the conditions natural to the rich soil of southern Babylonia led to agriculture.

The political feature at the earliest period at present known to us, which may be roughly fixed on the basis of the material at our disposal at 4000 to 3500 B.C., is the existence of a number of cities under the control of Sumerians, each one of which formed a centre for a district of varying extent. These cities lay along the Euphrates or on one of the various arms into which it divides in the marshy districts. Owing, however, to the choking up of the bed of the river and of its tributaries, the direction of the Euphrates was subject to frequent changes, so that the location of the mounds beneath which cities like Nippur, Cuthah, Uruk, Sippar, Shuruppak lay buried, is at some distance to the east from the bed of the Euphrates, or from one of its branches.

We find the south itself divided into two sections, the southern part, known as Sumer, which is the main stronghold of the non-Semitic conquerors, and the northern section of the Euphrates Valley, Akkad, where the Semites gradually developed the strength neces-

---

[7] See above II, note 13; pp. 23 and 30, seq.

sary to meet the Sumerians on their own ground. A sharp boundary between Sumer and Akkad probably never existed, but in a general way Nippur may be regarded as the line of demarcation, so that Eridu, Larsa, Ur, Adab, Isin, Lagash, Shuruppak, Umma, Uruk with Nippur, constitute the chief centres in the south, and Cuthah, Opis, Akkad, Kish, Babylon and Sippar the most important cities of the north. Nor can a sharp line be drawn between the non-Semitic and Semitic settlements, beyond the general proposition that the Semites, while commingling in part with the Sumerians, were also in part driven back to the northern part of the Euphrates Valley. At all events, the south remained the chief seat of Sumerian power, though northern centres like Kish, Cuthah and Opis were for a period of indifferent extent also in the hands of the Sumerians.

We are not able as yet to trace the history of the Euphrates Valley back to the time when the Sumerians were in complete and absolute control. The oldest inscriptions so far recovered already give evidence of a decline of the south, with the tendency towards a growth of power in the northern centres. We know nothing of the earliest history of Eridu and little of such centres as Uruk and Adab; and until excavations carry us nearer to the beginnings of Sumerian supremacy, we must rest content with the testimony furnished by the material at our disposal that there was no union or, at all events, no permanent union between the cities of Sumer and that no ruler of any Sumerian centre exercised control over all of Sumer and Akkad. The relationship between the states would therefore be marked by hostilities alternating with treaties that served to keep the peace for a while, and with combinations of some of these city states against other groups. The central feature in each of these cities was the sanctuary dedicated to the local patron deity. So close was the association between the god and his city, that the former either directly gave his name to the place, or the place was known as the city of the god in question. The more precise character of these city gods we will have occasion to consider in the next chapter. The point of importance to us in an historical survey is to note that the jurisdiction of a deity was coextensive with the district controlled by his followers. The single exception to this general direction taken by the association of a deity with a city is formed by the god Enlil, who, although the god of the city of Nippur, was in this first period of Euphratean history the acknowledged head of the pantheon.[8] In part this no doubt was due to the important position occupied by Nippur when the Sumerians obtained the mastery in the Euphrates Valley, but in large part the special position acquired by Enlil is to be accounted for by the circumstance that as a storm-god having his seat on some mountain-peak, he was the chief of the gods worshipped by the conquerors before they left their mountain homes.

Curiously enough, however, we have not come across any records of a powerful dynasty established in Nippur as a centre. Instead, the earliest traditions of the Euphrates Valley, carrying us back to the mythical age, in which rulers are pictured as deities or of divine descent, ruling for as many centuries as in historical time years,[9] give Kish and Uruk as the first two dy-

---

[8] See further, p. 195, *seq.*

[9] See the publication of important lists of early mythical or semi-mythical rulers, followed by historical dynasties, in Poebel's *Historical and Grammatical Texts,* pages 73 to 96.

These lists show us, during the first two recorded dynasties of Kish and of Uruk, rulers who reign from 410 to 1200 years, and among the names of such rulers are the mythical rulers Etana and Gilgamesh, of the former of whom a story is told of an attempted flight to heaven on the back of an eagle, while the latter is the famous central figure of the great Babylonian epic.

The high figures given for the reigns or lives of these rulers are

nasties, after which we come to a series of rulers with Ur as a political centre and the length of whose reigns shows that we have reached a more definite historical tradition. Beyond names and indications of lengths of reigns, however,—and these often uncertain—we know nothing further of this earliest period until we come down to about the year 3200 B.C.

III

The accident that so much of our earliest historical material comes from the excavations on the site of the ancient city of Lagash[10] naturally places this city in the foreground of our horizon, but making due allowance for this fact, it is nevertheless certain that Lagash played a most important rôle as early at least as 3000 B.C., and exercised at one time a sway over a considerable portion of Sumer, including Nippur. Its most serious rival at the time when the outlines of this period become defined with sufficient clearness to enable us to grasp some details is the city of Kish, whose patron deity was a solar god known as Zamama. Indeed, a ruler, Mesilim, whose date can be approximately fixed at 3100 B.C., claimed Lagash as a part of his territory. This condition must have lasted for some time, for a *patesi* of Lagash, Entemena, whose date may be fixed as c. 2850 B.C., refers in a historical survey of the

---

of the same character as the ages of the antediluvian patriarchs in the fifth chapter of Genesis. Both lists are no doubt based upon some artificially constructed system, though exactly of what nature scholars have not ascertained. To discuss the bearings of these important lists, published by Poebel, in detail would carry us too far and must be left for some other occasion. Suffice it to say that the existence of such lists, which evidently form part of the school archives of ancient Babylonian centres, shows conclusively that the accounts of early Babylonian rulers given by Berosus (see Cory, *Ancient Fragments*, page 51, *seq.*) rest upon actual material which was utilized by Berosus.

[10] Above, p. 39, *seq.*

relations between Lagash and a neighboring centre, Umma, to Mesilim's intervention as arbitrator between the two hostile districts. Through his mediation a treaty was made, fixing the boundary line between Lagash and Umma.[11]

There are reasons for believing that not long before the days of Mesilim, the conditions were reversed and that Kish was in a state of dependency upon Lagash or some other centre, for a ruler, Utug,[12] who is in all probabilities older than Mesilim, calls himself *patesi* of Kish, on a vase offered as a tribute to Enlil of Nippur, in commemoration of a victory over the land of Khamazi. Under Eannatum, Kish again falls into the hands of Lagash, which, however, was not able to hold it for a long time. The Semites, perhaps originally pressed into service as mercenaries by the rulers of Kish,[13] obtain control for a time—the first indication of the coming Semitic conquest of the Euphrates Valley, but are again pushed back by Sumerians. Such a constant shift of political conditions extends over a long period, until Lugalzaggisi, of Uruk (c. 2675 B.C.), comes to the fore, puts an end to the independence of Kish, and this time in an effective manner.

The treaty between Lagash and Kish, above referred to, took place c. 3050 B.C., as nearly as we can calculate at present; and we are safe in assuming that the supremacy exercised by Kish over important centres in the south began perhaps a century earlier and lasted until c. 2975 B.C., when we find a ruler on the throne of Lagash, Ur-Ninâ, who adopts the title of king, whose reign was marked by an era of peace, during which commerce flourished and the ruler was able to devote himself to the welfare of his subjects and to honoring the gods by beautifying their temples and bringing to

---

[11] Heuzey, *Découvertes en Chaldée,* Pl. 47, and Thureau-Dangin, *Sumer. und Akkad. Königsinschriften,* p. 36.

[12] Hilprecht, *Old Babylonian Inscriptions,* I, 2, No. 108, *seq.*

[13] So Meyer, *Geschichte,* I, 2, p. 481.

their shrines evidence of his loyalty and affection in the shape of tributes and votive offerings. We have a remarkable series of limestone plaques showing Ur-Ninâ and his family in the act of taking part in the building of the temple E-Ninnu to Ningirsu—the main sacred edifice in Lagash.[14] He is also occupied with strengthening the wall of Lagash and in digging numerous canals and reservoirs, clearly intended to regulate the annual overflow of the Euphrates and to direct its waters into the fields. By the extension of this canal system, upon which the prosperity and growth of the country so largely depended, he established his claim to being a ruler devoted to the welfare of his subjects. Conditions changed soon after the death of Ur-Ninâ. His successor, Akurgal, appears to have been troubled again by the old-time rival and enemy to the north, Umma, though the crisis is not reached until the days of his son, Eannatum, c. 2920 B.C. The men of Umma removed the stele set up by Mesilim, the king of Kish, as the boundary between Lagash and Umma. This was the signal for an outbreak that ended disastrously for the district of which Umma was the centre. Eannatum appeals to his god Ningirsu for help. Ningirsu appears to Eannatum in a dream and promises victory over the enemy. Thus encouraged, Eannatum gathers his army and sets out for the encounter. The result was a total defeat of Umma, of whose warriors Eannatum assures us that he slew thirty-six hundred.[15] The victory was followed up by the pursuit of the fleeing army. Eannatum takes Umma by assault, sweeping all before him, as he tells us, "like a destructive storm." In commemoration of the engagement he sets up a monument,[16] on which he depicts in vivid form the incidents of the

---

[14] See Plate XLVI, Fig. 1.

[15] The number is under suspicion of being a round one, but nevertheless it furnishes us with an indication of the numbers that must have engaged in the struggle.

[16] See Plate XLVII and XLVIII and the description of the monument p. 387, *seq*.

battle. The old boundary stone was again set up and
a new treaty made between Eannatum and Enakalli,
the successor of Ush, who probably perished in the
encounter. The district of Gu-eddin, wrongfully ap-
propriated by Umma, was restored and a tribute imposed. A large booty was secured, and in commemoration of the event shrines were erected on the frontier
to various deities,—to Enlil and his consort, Ninkharsag, to Ningirsu and Utu (the sun-god) for their assistance. A solemn oath was sworn by the two sides. "I
have sworn the oath," says Eannatum, "and the men
of Umma have sworn the oath to Eannatum, in the
name of Enlil, the king of heaven and earth. . . . If
at any time they shall deviate from this agreement, may
the great net of Enlil, in whose name they have sworn
this oath, overwhelm them." The gods thus become
the active partners in the events of the day.

IV

The events narrated on the remarkable monument
which a fortunate chance has in part preserved for us
are typical of the political history of the Euphratean
states in this early period, marked by a frequent shifting of the particles in the political kaleidoscope, as a
consequence of which now the one, now the other of the
various rival states secures a temporary supremacy,
without, however, any permanent coalition into a united
empire. For the time being Lagash wields the baton
of authority, not only over the district of Umma, but
also over that of Kish, which appears to have sided with
Umma and whose king, Al-zu(?), was captured and
probably slain. Eannatum followed up his success by
other conquests, bringing a troublesome district, Opis,
in the north, into subjection, exercising supremacy over
Uruk, Ur, Larsa and other centres of the south and even
extending his control to Elam on the east, beyond the
bounds proper of the Euphrates Valley. The successors

9

of Eannatum, Enannatum I and Entemena, were able
to resist the attempt of Umma to throw off the yoke,
and they forced their own minions on the people as
patesis or governors of the district; they also kept Elam
in check, though not without a severe struggle. But they
seemed unable to prevent internal abuses from creeping
in, which undermined the very foundations of government. The evidence for this is found in the inscriptions of a ruler, Urukagina (c. 2700 B.C.),[17] who tells
us of his efforts to rescue the various classes of the
population—he names boatmen, shepherds, fishermen
and farmers—from the priests, into whose clutches they
had fallen. The temples had profited by the general
prosperity and become powerful commercial organizations which exercised a pressure on the land. Urukagina
goes so far as to accuse the priests of robbing the farmer
of the fruit of his labors, of imposing exorbitant taxes
on the fishermen, of taking bribes and of thwarting
justice in their capacity as the controllers of the courts
of law.

Urukagina puts an end to this shameful state of
affairs by sweeping the corrupt army of officials out
of office and by setting up a body of laws, regulating
the taxes and fees, protecting the helpless against ex-
tortion, providing against violent alienation of goods
or property. In his days divorces had been obtained
by means of bribes given to the officials, and even
divination had been carried on amidst similar abuses,
the exorbitant fee for the service being divided among
the patesi, his chief vizir and the priest. These matters
were also regulated and it is of special interest to note
that Urukagina's new code did away with polyandry.
"Women were formerly possessed by two men. Now
women in such a case will be thrown into the stream
(?)." Urukagina sums up the contrast epigrammati-

---

[17] Thureau-Dangin, *Sumerisch-Akkadische Königsinschriften*,
pp. 44–57.

cally between former and present conditions by declaring that "formerly there was slavery, now freedom has been established."

The movement for reform, however, came too late, as is often the case in history. The strength of the country had been sapped, and in a long inscription dating from Urukagina's reign, a scribe pathetically records the violent acts of the old-time enemy, Umma, in invading Lagash and destroying the sanctuaries there and elsewhere.

Urukagina suffered the fate of so many reformers in reaping the ingratitude of those whom he intended to benefit. The priests no doubt secured the coöperation of the nobles and officials in arousing opposition against the endeavor of the king to deprive them of the benefits they had so long enjoyed, and it is not impossible that they may have stood in league with the enemy in order to humiliate and overthrow their own ruler. At all events Lugalzaggisi triumphed over Lagash, reduced it to a state of subserviency so that the rulers once more became merely patesis, and succeeded in securing a supremacy over the districts of which Nippur, Uruk, Ur and Larsa were the centres. Indeed, if the statement in a long inscription of his is to be taken literally and not as a mere idle boast, he led his victorious armies to the Mediterranean, for he speaks of conquering the lands from the lower sea of the Tigris and Euphrates to the upper sea. He thus foreshadows the world-conquest which became the ambition of the later Semitic rulers of Babylonia and Assyria, and there is only one other ruler in this earlier period with whom he is to be compared, namely, Narâm-Sin, whose reign we shall take up presently.

The removal of Lugalzaggisi's capital from Umma to Uruk points to the greater importance of the latter centre, which is confirmed by the inscriptions of two rulers, Lugal-ki-gub-niddu and Lugal-kisal-si, who call

themselves kings of Uruk and kings of Ur.[18] Uruk had
accordingly succeeded in uniting the important Sumerian centre, Ur, to her dominion and Lugalzaggisi,
conquering the extreme south of the Euphrates Valley,
falls heir to the sovereignty exercised by Uruk, placing his title, "King of Uruk," before all others.

V

Had Lugalzaggisi succeeded in maintaining the extensive kingdom organized by him, the entire course
of Babylonian history might have been changed. The
factor that blocked his path was the advance of the
power of the Semites in the land. It is significant that
in the long inscription on the votive vase from which
we have quoted and in which he sums up his achievements there is no mention of Kish. We have already
encountered the influence of this centre in the conflicts
between Lagash and Umma,[19] and although Mesilim,
the king of Kish, who intervenes to fix the boundary
between these two rival states is not a Semite, there is
every reason to believe that as early as his day, c. 3100
B.C., Kish contained a considerable Semitic population,
serving perhaps as mercenaries in the army which three
centuries later had obtained the upper hand. In an
inscription [20] which belongs to a period not far removed
from the time of Lugalzaggisi, we encounter a ruler
of Kish whose name, Enbi-Ishtar, leaves no doubt of
his being a Semite. We must assume that Kish had
recovered its position, for it is through a ruler of this
centre, Sargon I, that, according to a definite statement,[21] Lugalzaggisi is overthrown after a reign of
twenty-five years, that is about 2675 B.C. With Sargon
we reach the period of a definite advance of the Semites.
The dynasty founded by him is Semitic in character,

[18] Thureau-Dangin, l.c., p. 156.
[19] See above, p. 127.
[20] Thureau-Dangin, l.c., p. 152.
[21] See Poebel, in *Orientalist. Litteraturzeitung*, XV, Sp. 481, *seq.*

as is shown by the official language of the royal inscriptions, which is Akkadian. Sargon, to be sure, comes to Kish as a conqueror. His starting-point is Agade or Akkad, somewhat to the north, but the independence of Kish is maintained, so that he calls himself interchangeably King of Kish and King of Akkad. A list recently discovered [22] assigns no less than twelve rulers to this dynasty of Akkad, but owing to the defective character of the tablet at this point, only the last six names and the beginning of the first are clearly preserved so that we are left in doubt as to the balance. Through other sources the gap can be partially filled out, with the result that by the side of Sargon, the founder, we must recognize another bearing a somewhat similar name, Sharganisharri, who in tradition became confused with Shargani or Sargon.[23] Both must have been active conquerors, extending their dominions beyond the Euphrates Valley, but it looks as though the older were the more aggressive of the two. He passes to the east and brings Elam under subjection. In the north he conquers Subartu, an extensive district later known from its capital Ashur as the land of Ashur or Assyria, and which at this time was the seat of a mixed population of Semitic tribes and of Hittite groups. Pushing on to the northwest, he checks the growing power of the Amorites—"the land of sunset in its totality"—which indicates that he reached the shores of the Mediterranean. A rebellion breaks out towards the close of Sargon's reign which, accord-

---

[22] Published by Scheil, Comptes Rendus de l'Acad. des Inscriptions, 1911, p. 606, seq., and Revue d'Assyriologie, IX, p. 69. See Meyer, Geschichte, I, 2 (3d ed.), pp. 343–347, and the same author's paper, Zur Ältesten Geschichte Babyloniens (Abhandl. d. Kgl. Preus. Akad. d. Wiss. Phil.-Hist. Klasse, 1912, p. 1062, seq.).

[23] The confusion was facilitated by the fact that the last element of the longer name, sharri, means "king," so that Shargani-sharri, meaning "Sargon is king," could easily come to be looked upon as embodying a statement of the sovereignty of the older Sargon.

ing to an official chronicle, he suppresses, but in which it is more likely to assume he must have perished, for his son tells us, at the beginning of a long inscription, of a general uprising of all lands conquered by Sargon. The name of the son is broken out, but we can definitely say that it was a ruler whose name can be read Uru-mush or Rimush, with a preference in favor of the latter.[24]   Rimush claims to have been successful in overcoming his enemies who were led by an Elamite, Abalgamash.   There is no reason to question the substantial accuracy of his narrative, but it is significant that he calls himself King of Kish and not of Akkad. The conclusion to be drawn is that Kish became the capital and remained so in the days of his son Manish-tusu, who also boasts of his conquests.   It must have been difficult, however, for Rimush and Manishtusu to maintain their position.   The former we know, from other sources, was put to death by a conspiracy hatched among the members of his court, while Manishtusu tells us of a confederation of thirty-two cities formed against him.   Such facts point to disturbed internal conditions and to frequent combinations on the part of the conquered districts of the Euphrates Valley with the help of Elam to throw off the yoke of the Semitic rulers, abetted probably by a rivalry between Akkad and Kish for the privilege of being the capital of the new kingdom.   An interesting trace of this rivalry is to be found in a most remarkable monument of the days of Manishtusu, a large obelisk of diorite, describing in detail the purchase of enormous tracts of lands in Kish and its environment on which to settle citizens of Akkad.[25]   The names of eighty-seven overseers of certain tracts acquired by the ruler are given; they are

[24] First suggested by Hrozny (Wiener Zeitschrift für die Kunde des Morgenlandes, vol. xxiii, pp. 192, seq. and xxvi, pp. 152).

[25] Published by Scheil, Délégation en Perse, Mémoires, II, pp. 1–52.   The monument is 4½ feet high and is closely inscribed on four sides.

PLATE XXIII

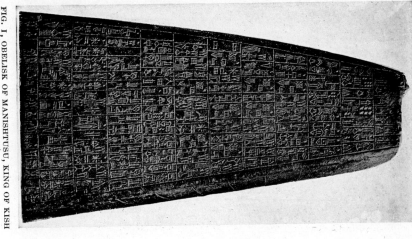

FIG. 1, OBELISK OF MANISHTUSU, KING OF KISH
(C. 2600 B.C.)

FIG. 2, BUST OF MANISHTUSU

removed by Manishtusu to other places, while in their place he appoints forty-nine new officials whom he calls "citizens of Akkad." Their followers take the place of the 1564 laborers employed by the older overseers and who are likewise sent elsewhere. Evidently Manishtusu was engaged in a deliberate policy of sending from Akkad as a disturbing centre portions of the population through offering them attractive posts in Kish and surrounding sites, where they could be kept under surveillance. We are reminded of the similar policy of deportation practised by Assyrian and Babylonian kings many centuries later, and which led to the transfer of large numbers of Hebrews, after the fall of Samaria and Jerusalem, to various sites on the Euphrates and Tigris.[26]

VI

The upshot of the activity of three rulers of unusual aggressiveness, Sargon, Rimush and Manishtusu, was a most striking advance of Semitic influence throughout the Euphrates Valley—an influence that became a permanent factor in the further development of political affairs. The Semitic rulers of Akkad and Kish took up the policy of extending in all directions their dominions left them as a legacy by Lugalzaggisi, but this ambition overvaulting itself became a source of weakness instead of strength. Manishtusu succeeds in keeping Elam under subjection and gives evidence of his control by dedicating a statue of himself to an Elamite god Naruti,[27] but under his successor, Sharganisharri, we find the Elamites strong enough to make an invasion of the Euphrates Valley, advancing as far as Opis, not far from Akkad, where they received a check. Uruk heads a coalition of Sumerian forces which was likewise repulsed. Under Narâm-Sin, the son of Sharganisharri, this disturbed condition reaches

[26] II Kings 17, 6; 24, 12–16.

[27] The bust of the statue was found at Susa. See Plate XXIII, Fig. 2.

its climax, for he speaks of combinations of nine rulers and even of seventeen kings against him. No doubt he exaggerates when he declares that he faced an army of 90,000 men drawn up against him, and yet triumphal monuments of his reign, including one found far up in the north, not far from the source of the Tigris,[28] leave no doubt of his far surpassing his father in military expeditions in all directions—against Elam in the east, against Subartu in the north, and the mountainous borders in the northeast, as well as against regions lying far to northwest and southwest. He thus merited, by his achievements, the proud title of "King of the Four Quarters," which was equivalent to "King of the Universe," borne later by the Assyrian monarchs. Narâm-Sin appears indeed to have surpassed all of his predecessors in opening up new fields of conquest, particularly to the northeast and to the southwest. His father had crossed arms with a strong mountainous group known as the Guti, and succeeded in capturing their king, Sharlak. It was left to the son, however, to follow up this movement by more systematic endeavors and on a larger scale to bring various of the groups in these distant, forbidding regions, so difficult of access, to subjection. On a monument, noteworthy also as one of the finest specimens of the older Babylonian art, Narâm-Sin gives a vivid picture of his triumph over the Lulubæans and other peoples in the Zagros range.[29] No less significant was his expedition to Magan, a distant land whence diorite was brought in large quantities for the manufacture of statues and large vessels. Occurring frequently by the side of Melucha, Magan and Melucha are probably designations of districts along the eastern coast of Arabia and the western coast

[28] At Pir Hussein. See Plate L, Fig. 2, and King, *History of Sumer and Akkad*, p. 244.

[29] See Plate L, Fig. 1. The monument was found at Susa, whither it was carried as a trophy in the eleventh century, as the others mentioned above p. 113.

of Africa. To have proceeded to such distant climes was
an achievement hitherto without parallel. We thus
obtain a view of the strength unfolded at this early
period by the Semitic settlements of the Euphrates Valley which makes the achievements of the Sumerians,
even of a Lugalzaggisi, dwindle into comparative
insignificance.

It would seem, however, that a decline began soon
after the death of Narâm-Sin, who appears to have been
succeeded by a second Sharganisharri, of whom we, to
be sure, know nothing. A period of internal disturbances sets in, marked by a succession of four rulers
within three years, so that, as the recently discovered
list of dynasties puts it, one could not tell "who was
king and who was not king." [30] It is Uruk, the Sumerian centre which Lugalzaggisi raised to its highest
glory, that succeeds in overthrowing the dynasty of
Akkad after an existence of 197 years. We may fix
this event approximately in the year 2475 B.C.

The overthrow of so powerful a dynasty as that of
Akkad must have affected the entire country; it was a
signal for the older, once independent centres, to assert
themselves. Among these centres we find Lagash profiting to a special degree by the growing weakness of
Akkad, for there must have been preliminary symptoms
of decay before the final catastrophe set in. Among the
most remarkable monuments found at Lagash are nine
diorite statues of a ruler,[31] Gudea, who, although he still
retains the title of patesi, appears to have been entirely
independent. Inscriptions in large numbers on the
statues in question, on two large clay barrels and on
votive objects confirm the power wielded by Gudea,
whose emissaries are sent to the north and south to
obtain wood and stone for his buildings and works of
art with which he embellishes his seat of residence. He

---

[30] See Poebel's ingenious interpretation of the text (Oriental.
Litteraturzeitung, XV, Sp. 481).

[31] Above, p. 41. See Plate XIII and Plate XII, Fig. 2.

does not, indeed, lay claim to the control of lands outside of his district, but it is significant that he has access to them. The only war in which he engages is a conflict against Elam which ends in victory and a large booty for Gudea. This booty is promptly dedicated to his god, Ningirsu, and deposited in the temple, E-Ninnu, at Lagash, to the enlargement of which he devoted his chief energy. Gudea's date can be approximately fixed at c. 2450 B.C. With him Lagash rises to new splendor, though the way is paved in a measure by his predecessor, Ur-Bau, from whose reign we have a number of monuments testifying to the growing power of the district ruled by Ur-Bau while still owing nominal allegiance to Akkad. Whether Uruk at the time that it became the heir of Akkad succeeded in securing control of Lagash is uncertain, but with the coming of an invasion from the north, the glory of Lagash vanishes again as suddenly as it reached its climax under Gudea.

The regions to the north and particularly those groups in the mountainous district of the upper section of the Tigris not only regained their independence as the dynasty of Akkad approached its close, but one of these groups, the Guti, took their revenge for the humiliation inflicted upon them by Sharganisharri and Narâm-Sin by making an incursion into the Euphrates Valley. For a period of about fifty years a Guti dynasty actually occupied the throne, presumably choosing Uruk as the seat of residence. Such, then, was the sad result of the conflict between Sumerians and Semites for control on the one hand and of the ambitious efforts on the other, inaugurated by Lugalzaggisi and continued by Sargon, Sharganisharri and Narâm-Sin to pass beyond the natural confines of the Euphrates Valley. The terror aroused by this northern foe, sweeping down upon the cultivated cities of the plain from their mountain homes with all the violence of an elemental force, must have been extreme. Utuche-

gal, who succeeds in driving the Guti out of the country,[32] gives us a vivid picture of the ravages committed.
He calls the Guti "the dragon of the mountains, the
enemy of the gods," and describes how they tore the
wives away from their husbands, robbing parents of
their children and spreading devastation on all sides.
Such invasions of semi-barbarous groups from the
northwest and northeast were destined to repeat themselves frequently in the course of Babylonian-Assyrian
history and inflicted a serious check to the advance of
the Euphratean culture, though on the other hand
they lead fierce tribes to take on at least a veneer of
culture through contact with a higher civilization.[33]
Tribute was no doubt exacted from the conquered
groups, and relationships were maintained with Magan
and Melucha to the extent of procuring stones and
metals from these rich districts; but the control over
such sections as Subartu and the more distant settlements of the Amorites could at most have been nominal.
The more direct result was the check given to the advance of the Semites, and another period of 250 years
elapsed before the latter were strong enough again to
risk a passage of arms with the Sumerians.

VII

With the temporary eclipse of the power of the
Semites, the old-time rivalry between the Sumerian
states, which we have seen was typical of conditions
prevailing until the days of Lugalzaggisi, again sets in.

---

[32] See the important inscription of this ruler published with a
translation and commentary by Thureau-Dangin in the *Revue
d'Assyriologie*, IX, pp. 114–120.

[33] We have an Akkadian inscription of Lasirab, King of the
Guti (Thureau-Dangin, *Sumerisch-Akkadische Königsinschriften*,
p. 170), of Erridupizir, who calls himself "King of Guti, King of
the four quarters" (Hilprecht, *Earliest Version of the Deluge*,
p. 20, *seq.*) and of Anubanini, King of the Lulubi (Thureau-
Dangin, *l.c.*, p. 172).

Ur which had been forced to play a secondary role in the combination with Uruk reasserts itself, and about thirty years after Utuchegal's accession Urengur succeeds (c. 2450 B.C.) in making Ur once more the capital of a united Sumerian kingdom. For 117 years this dynasty maintained itself and the orderly succession of its five rulers from father to son—Urengur, Dungi, Pursin, Gimilsin and Ibisin—bears witness to the tranquil conditions which these rulers established. The same testimony is borne by the large number of business documents [34] that we have of this period which give evidence of an extensive commercial activity that goes hand in hand with political stability, while the dates attached to these documents, the years being still marked in this period by important events,[35] likewise show that the rulers were able to devote themselves chiefly to works of peace, such as the rebuilding of walls or of temples to the chief deities in a variety of centres, Nippur, Eridu, Uruk, Larsa, Lagash and above all in Ur, and in otherwise improving and embellishing these and other cities and towns. Occasionally Elam to the east gives the rulers of Ur trouble, but far more serious was the menace from the distant north. Dungi, the second ruler of the dynasty, undertakes no less than nine campaigns against the land of Sumuru and Lulubi. These groups show the same resistance to a foreign yoke that formerly characterized the Guti, of whom we hear nothing during the period of the Ur dynasty and who, while unable to stand up against better disciplined forces, rebelled again and again as the opportunity offered.

We do not as yet know the circumstances as a consequence of which the Ur dynasty came to an end, through the capture of its last representative, Ibisin,

---

[34] See Legrain, *Les Temps des Rois d'Ur* (Paris, 1912).

[35] The dating of years by the reign of rulers is not introduced until the time of the Cassite dynasty in the eighteenth century. See below, pp. 156 and 351.

by the Elamites, c. 2330 B.C. Presumably, a combination of various centres was formed which did not hesitate to call in the assistance of the common enemy to the east. Between the dynasty of Akkad and that of Ur, Elam had enjoyed a short era of independence during which one of her rulers, Basha-Shushinak, actually lays claim to the control of the "four quarters." It is not impossible that the Elamites were aided by Semites, whose influence, at all events, must have been considerable in this district, for we find the rulers using Akkadian instead of their own language in official inscriptions, and for a number of centuries business documents are also couched in Akkadian, though about the middle of the second millennium before this era a reaction sets in which leads to the reintroduction of the Elamite speech. Towards the close of the Ur dynasty there are indications of a reassertion of power in Elam which led to open hostilities and the overthrow of the Ur dynasty. In place of the latter centre, we find Isin the seat of a dynasty which maintained itself for 225 years (c. 2350–2125 B.C.), though its rulers content themselves with the title of "King of Sumer and Akkad" and were unable to prevent the simultaneous rise of an independent, smaller monarchy in Larsa which outlived that of Isin and whose rulers maintained themselves till 2090 B.C., when its last representative, Rîm-Sin, was forced to yield to the great conqueror Hammurapi.[36] The kings of Larsa also exercised control over Ur, sometimes designating themselves as kings of Ur, but more frequently as patrons. These rival dynasties of Isin and Larsa must often have been in conflict with each other, but unfortunately the century and a half following the overthrow of Ur is one for which few historical documents have as yet been found. Uruk also appears to have had a number of independent rulers, until a ruler, Rîm-Sin, of Elamitic origin obtains control of Larsa, and thence as a centre both

---

[36] See below, p. 146

overthrows Uruk and puts an end to the Isin dynasty. The period was therefore one in which the centralizing tendency of former days was considerably weakened and a gradual return to the conditions prevailing before the time of Lugalzaggisi is brought about.

The rulers of Isin apart from their inability to retain control of important centres in the Euphrates Valley were menaced chiefly from two sides—from the east through the formation of a new Elamitic state in the district of Eamutbal (or Jamutbal), the borderland to the east of the Tigris, and from the north through the rise of an Amorite dynasty which established itself in the city of Babylon c. 2225 B.C., not long after the death of the usurper Amel-Ninib (c. 2256–2228 B.C.), and controlled northern Babylonia. The formation of an independent Elamitic state on the border between Babylonia and Elam proper is another indication both of the weakness of the Isin dynasty and of the inability of the central Elamitic power with its seat in the capital, Susa, to maintain the integrity of the empire.[37] From Ashurbanapal's inscriptions we know that he recaptured a statue of the goddess Nanâ, of Uruk, which he says the Elamites had carried away as a trophy 1635 years ago,[38] which brings us to the year 2280 or, according to a variant, 1535 years, which would be equivalent to 2180. He names as the Elamite ruler who plundered the temples of the Euphrates Valley, Kudurnanchundi, and since we know of a ruler of Emutbal, Kudurmabug, containing the same element, Kudur, it is quite possible that Kudurnanchundi belongs to the Emutbal dynasty rather than to one which reigned in Susa. If this be so, the lower date is probably the more correct of the two, for shortly after 2180 B.C., we find Kudurmabug as ruler of Emutbal

---

[37] See further on the relationship between this central kingdom of Elam and the rulers of Emutbal, Meyer, *Geschichte des Altertums*, I, 2, p. 601–605.

[38] Rawlinson, V, Pl. 6, 107, with parallel passages.

FIG. 1, LUGAL-DAUDU, KING OF ADAB—AS TYPE OF SUMERIAN

FIG. 2, MARDUK-NADIN-AKH, KING OF BABYLONIA

PLATE XXIV

(c. 2150 B.C.) actively interfering in the affairs of the Euphrates Valley; he rescues Larsa out of the hands of a certain Mutiabal and places his own son Aradsin in control.[39] This date is coequal with the beginning of the reign of the last ruler of the Isin dynasty and we have seen that the last sixty years of this period were marked by internal disturbances. After a reign of twelve years Aradsin is succeeded by his brother, Rîm-Sin. During the reign of these two sons of Kudurmabug, Elamitic influences must have been paramount. They no doubt kept close relations with Emutbal, which at this period exercised a sway over the old kingdom of Elam, with its capital at Susa, whose rulers became vassals of the kings of Emutbal.

VIII

The Sumerian domination of the Euphrates Valley thus comes to an end. An entirely new situation had been created by this astonishing aggressiveness of Elamitic chieftains. Instead of Sumerians and Akkadians, we have Amorites and Elamites preparing for a final test of arms.

Chronological lists at our disposal reveal a series of eleven rulers with their seat in Babylon and whose reigns can now be approximately fixed as extending from c. 2225 to 1926 B.C. The first of these rulers is Sumuabu, the form of whose name is Semitic, but of a quite different formation from the Akkadian names. The same is the case with the names of other rulers of this dynasty like Sumulailu, Sabu, Hammurapi; in fact all but two—Apil-Sin and Sin-muballit [40]—are distinctly foreign. Those bearing these names, therefore, represent part of an immigration into the Euphrates

---

[39] See his votive inscription to Nergal published by Thureau-Dangin (*Revue d'Assyriologie*, IX, pp. 121–124).

[40] Signifying "Son of the god Sin" and "Sin gives life"— genuine Akkadian names.

Valley, and there is more than sufficient evidence to
show that the new settlers came from the northwest—
the large and not sharply defined district known as
Amurru, the land of the Amorites. In fact the rulers
in question speak of themselves and of their subjects
as Amorites.[41] The Semitic character of these Amorites
is as pronounced as that of the earlier Semitic settlers
in the Euphrates Valley, if not indeed more so since
they had not been obliged to submit to an assimilating
process with Sumerians and other non-Semites. Once
in the country, however, they adopt the language, cult
and customs of the Akkadians, and only in their names
and in retaining the habit of the Semitic Bedouins of
shaving the upper lip do they reveal externally a trace
of their foreign origin. We do not know the special circumstances under which these Amorites entered Babylonia. Migrations into the Euphrates Valley on a larger
or smaller scale were probably going on at all times,
particularly from the northwest, whence Bedouin tribes
could easily pass along the course of the Euphrates into
the south.

The Akkadians themselves probably did not wel-
come these constant accessions from the north and
northwest, and conflicts ensued which must sometimes
have ended disastrously for the invaders, though they
generally led to a coalition. That appears to have been
the case with the Amorites, who, entering the country
at a time when the Akkadians were forced to submit
once more to Sumerian supremacy, were probably aided
by their fellow Semites in the endeavor to re-establish
the power of the Semites in the northern part of the
Valley, which from the time of the dynasty of Agade
becomes definitely known as Akkad, in contrast to
Sumer as the designation of the south. The Amorites
established themselves in the city of Babylon, which,
situated somewhat to the south of Agade, had already
in the days of the Akkad dynasty begun to acquire

[41] See Meyer, *Geschichte des Altertums*, I, 2, p. 615, note.

some importance. These Amorite rulers succeeded in uniting the Semitic population of the north under their banners. Sumuabu controls the old Semitic centre, Kish; his dominion reaches to Dilbat to the south of Babylon, but he makes no effort to encroach on Sumer. Indeed, he appears to have had some trouble in controlling all of Akkad, for we learn of an expedition against Kasallu to the north of Kish which refused to submit to Sumuabu's dominion and which is therefore destroyed by him. The patesi of Ashur—the old capital of Assyria—Ilushuma, also makes an attack on Sumuabu, which is significant as foreshadowing the rivalry between the two Semitic kingdoms of Mesopotamia, that of Babylonia in the south and of Assyria in the north. After a rule of eleven years, Sumuabu is succeeded by Sumulailu, whose long reign of thirty-six years (c. 2211–2176 B.C.) was largely devoted to strengthening the newly established kingdom and to overcoming rivals who appeared on various sides. It was not until near the close of his reign that Sumulailu succeeded in overcoming his foes and rivals, and in establishing himself as ruler of the entire north. He is the real founder of the dynasty of Babylon whose name is celebrated as such by his successors. His successors, to be sure, still had difficulties to contend with. Rebellions broke out here and there, but were suppressed aparently with increasingly less effort, so that the strength of the kingdom was well maintained.

The time was approaching for the supreme test of this strength in passages of arms with the Elamitie rulers who, as we have seen, had obtained the mastery of Sumer. The kings of Babylon were unable to prevent the aggressiveness of Kudurmabug and his two sons, Aradsin and Rîm-Sin, whom he had placed on the throne of Larsa. It may be, indeed, that they abetted Elam in its endeavors to crush the Sumerians. The seventeenth year of Sin-muballit's reign, corresponding to about 2126 B.C., is entered in business documents as

10

the one in which Isin was captured. This, we know, was the work of Rîm-Sin and not of Sin-muballit, but if the event is recognized in Babylon as a basis for the official dating of documents, it is tempting to suppose that Sin-muballit was in some measure involved in the overthrow of the Isin dynasty.[42] He certainly appears to have taken advantage of disturbed conditions in the south by making an attack on Ur, which was recorded as having been successful.[43] But if a coalition between Sin-muballit and Rîm-Sin existed, it must soon have become apparent that it could not last. When two aggressive kingdoms are brought face to face, it is only a question of time before hostilities between the two will break out. There was no room for both Amorites and Elamites. The one or the other had to yield.

Within two years after the end of the Isin dynasty, Sin-muballit dies and is succeeded (c. 2123 B.C.) by his son, Hammurapi, who so amply merits the title of "Great." He at once inaugurates an aggressive policy which brings city after city into his control. In 2117 he succeeds in wresting Uruk and Isin from the Elamites and follows up his advantage by moving against the Elamitic border state Emutbal in the following year. A number of years passed, however, before the great conqueror succeeded in capturing Ur and Larsa and in bringing the booty to Babylon. Emutbal became a province of the Amorite kingdom in 2090 B.C., and in another year all Sumer acknowledged Hammurapi's supremacy. During the last nine years of his reign he displayed the same energy in promoting works of peace, enlarging the canal system, and furnishing Uruk and other cities with an abundant water supply. He

---

[42] Sin-muballit did not go so far as to actually claim that he put an end to the Isin dynasty, and it is noticeable that in business documents for the seventeenth year, there is an alternative dating of a totally different character. See Schorr, *Altbabylonische Rechtsurkunden,* p. 588.

[43] See the date for the eighteenth year (Schorr, *l.c.*).

restores the temples in Larsa, Eridu, Lagash, Khallab, Cuthah, and Adab, which had suffered during the prolonged period of the wars; he is equally concerned for the old centres of the north, such as Opis and Kish. Naturally his chief concern is for his capital, Babylon, and next to this for the neighboring Borsippa and for Sippar, which remains in specially close touch with Babylon. The chief cities of Assyria, Ashur and Nineveh, included in his empire, are also the objects of his care. His aim is evidently to establish a permanent union between the Semitic and the non-Semitic elements of the population of Sumer and Akkad. The old Sumerian centres, Eridu, Nippur, Ur, Uruk and Larsa, retain their position in the religious organization, though henceforth deprived of political importance. Both languages, Sumerian and Akkadian, are recognized as official. Documents are not infrequently set up in both languages, though in the cult the Sumerian continues for some time to occupy the first place. Hammurapi crowns his career by a codification and formal promulgation of the laws which were to serve as the basis of legal decisions and according to which justice was to be dealt out. Already at the beginning of his reign he emphasizes his aim to establish justice in his dominions, so that, in a measure, his famous code—discovered at Susa in 1901, whither it had been carried as a trophy of war by the Elamites in the twelfth century [44]—is one of his earliest works, but since it was not promulgated until the close of his career, after he had finished his long series of wars and had succeeded in uniting all of Babylonia, as we may from now on designate the country brought under a single rule, it represents, as it were, his last testament —the monument of his career, which was of a more enduring character than any of his other achievements in war or in peace.[45]

[44] See above, p. 113, note 88.

[45] See an analysis of the code in Chapter VI.

IX

Hammurapi's reign thus closes an epoch in the history of the country and marks the beginning of a new age. The prolonged struggle between Sumerians and Akkadians ends in the definite supremacy of the latter, reinforced by the Amorites. Babylonia as a united empire with Semitic rulers on the throne arises out of the issue to become a dominant factor in the world's history. The Akkadian language replaces the Sumerian as the popular speech and becomes also the official medium, although for the present it did not drive the Sumerian entirely out of use.

A survey of the history such as we have attempted up to the days of Hammurapi makes it perfectly clear why the culture of Babylonia and therefore also that of Assyria is essentially a mixed product, due to the long-continued process of alternating conflict and assimilation between the Semitic and non-Semitic elements of the population. If the Semites come out of this conflict as the conquerors, they nevertheless have absorbed much of the Sumerian culture; in fact, the ability to combine these foreign elements—the script, the religious beliefs, the rites, the military organization and other features—with their own points of view and contributions to civilization is to be accounted as an important factor in leading to their ultimate triumph. From the time of Hammurapi, we may drop all distinctions of Sumer and Akkad and speak of the Sumero-Akkadian kingdom, or more briefly Babylonia, since Babylon as the political centre now assumes a fundamental importance.

A centralizing tendency in religion also sets in, as we shall have occasion to point out in the following chapter, leading to heaping on Marduk, as the god of the city of Babylon, the powers and attributes of all the chief gods, the patrons of the old centres in the south and north. Babylon and Marduk become the

dominating factors in the historical and religious fortunes of the country; and in view of the wide scope
of religion in ancient civilizations, the two factors also
that condition the further steps in the unfolding of
the culture of both Babylonia and Assyria.

X

It was no easy task for even so great a ruler such as
Hammurapi was to hold a vast empire together. The
only hope lay in bringing about an assimilation of the
population to the extent at least of creating a feeling
of national pride as the basis for the maintenance of the
political integrity of the realm. Such a policy, however, had its distinct limitations. Sumer and Akkad
could be brought together in this way. Assyria in the
north was still too weak to offer serious resistance, but
these conditions did not apply to districts beyond Assyria to the north and northeast—the land of the Guti,
Lullubi and other groups of whom, in fact, we hear
nothing during the period of the dynasty of Babylon,
while Elam to the East, chafing under the humiliat-
ing yoke, merely waited for a favorable opportunity
to again reassert herself.

The opportunity came not many years after the
death of Hammurapi, in 2081 B.C. The same Rîm-Sin
who overthrew Isin, and who was himself obliged, after
a long and desperate struggle, to yield to Hammurapi,
once more became active despite his advanced years.[46]
After his defeat by Hammurapi, he appears to have
returned into the mountain regions bordering on Elam
and there gathered recruits for a fresh attack. We
hear in the days of Samsuiluna, the son and successor
of Hammurapi, of a new group, the Cassites, who were
destined to become the controlling element in Babylonia. The origin of these Cassites is still involved in

---

[46] Assuming that he was a very young man at his conquest of
Isin in 2126 B.C., he must have been almost eighty years old when he
again makes the attempt to regain his lost prestige.

considerable doubt.[47]   They were a people of mountain-
eers, semi-barbarous, but capable of rapidly absorbing
the elements of the higher civilization with which they
came in contact in Elam and subsequently in Babylonia.
The ninth year of Samsuiluna, that is 2071 B.C., records
a conflict with the "Cassite hordes" which stands in
connection with the events of the following year, in
which Samsuiluna is at war with Emutbal, Ur, Uruk
and Isin.   In the same year we find Rîm-Sin in possession of Upi (or Opis), the old border city in the
extreme north of Babylonia, and assuming with the
consent of the chief goddess of Upi, Ninmakh, the title
of king "over the whole land."   Clearly Rîm-Sin had
succeeded in rallying to his side the districts in the
south over which he formerly ruled as well as Emutbal.   The army which he gathered must have been reinforced by the Cassite hosts, aiding him to march across
the road leading from Ecbatana to Babylon, along
which lay Upi as an important strategic point.   The
effort of Rîm-Sin and his allies, however, failed, and
Rîm-Sin appears to have perished in the flames of his
own palace.   Samsuiluna took his revenge on Ur and
Uruk by destroying the walls of these two ancient
centres.

For all that, he could not prevent frequent uprisings in various parts of Babylonia, nor the constitution
of a rival state in the marshy districts of the extreme
south, spoken of in the inscriptions as the "sea land."
Here we find Ilumailu establishing himself as king,
c. 2070 B.C., and giving considerable trouble to Samsuiluna (2080–2043 B.C.) and to his son and successor,
Abeshu (2042–2015 B.C.).   The rulers of the "sea land"
who maintained their independence during the remainder of the period of the first dynasty of Babylon
were probably not Semites, despite the Semitic formation of their names.   We may see in them the last faint
and desperate efforts of Sumerians, driven into the

---

[47] See Meyer, *Geschichte des Altertums* I, 2, p. 652, *seq.*

waste lands of the south, difficult of access, to assert
themselves. Though for the greater part obliged to
limit their jurisdiction to a small strip bordering on
the Persian Gulf—the portion of Babylonia that subsequently became known as Chaldæa—the successors of
Ilumailu, of whom we know no less than ten, made
incursions from time to time, in the hope of regaining
at least the old capital Isin—the last stronghold, as
we have seen, of the opponents of the dynasty of
Babylon. For a short time, indeed, Damikilishu II—
adopting the name of the last ruler of the Isin dynasty
—succeeds in this aim. He occupies the city and re-
builds the wall, but, about 1988 B.C., we have the record
that Ammiditana (c. 2014–1978 B.C.), the son of Abeshu,
destroyed this wall, which naturally involved the capture of the place. The two successors of Ammiditana
appear to have kept the rival kings in check, but in the
year 1926 B.C., a strange occurrence brings the dynasty
of Babylon to a sudden end. This was an invasion of
the Hittites, with whom a new and entirely unexpected
factor enters into Babylonian history. These Hittites
come from the northwest, from the Taurus range and
beyond.[48] The name Khatti given to them appears
to be one that acquired a very wide and general significance and included a variety of groups, of whom the
Mitanni in northwestern Mesopotamia represent a subdivision. The centre, however, of Hittite dominion was
in the interior of Asia Minor, stretching at an early
time up to the shores of the Caspian Sea. Here we
find a powerful kingdom established which in the fifteenth century is able to oppose an active resistance
against the attempts of Egyptian rulers to bring northern Syria under their control. The entire region from
northern Syria to Boghaz-Keui, near the Black Sea,
is covered with mounds containing remains of Hittite
palaces and forts which, while showing the decided

[48] See Garstang, *Land of the Hittites* (London, 1910), and Ed.
Meyer, *Reich und Kultur der Chetiter* (Berlin, 1914) ; also above,
p. 116.

influence of Babylonian and Assyrian models,[49] have yet
distinctive features which justify us in speaking of
the Hittites as a unit, though it must always be borne
in mind that the term is merely a convenient one for
massing together a number of groups that combined to
form powerful kingdoms in central and northern Asia
Minor, and then, pressing southwards, established a
number of independent states in northern Syria between the Euphrates and the Taurus range and probably also in the Zagros range, while offshoots proceeded
still further south and, entering Palestine proper, became an element of the very mixed population of that
region. Hittite groups thus covered an enormous area
and it is not surprising, therefore, to find a contingent,
attracted by the culture of Babylonia, passing into this
region in the hope of establishing themselves there.
The Hittites swooped down upon Babylonia and, taking advantage of weakened conditions through the constant attacks from the rival kingdom in the "sea land,"
which had to be repulsed, actually succeeded in overthrowing Samsuditana in the year 1926 B.C. The attack
was probably undertaken as a plundering raid, to which
an open country like the Euphrates Valley was frequently subject, but for the time being with the result
of actually placing a Hittite chieftain on the throne of
Babylon. How long the Hittites remained in control
we do not know, as in general our knowledge of the
closing years of the dynasty of Babylon is still very
defective, while with the downfall of this dynasty a
gap of a most serious character ensues which stretches
over the succeeding centuries.

XI

Until a short time ago it seemed possible to join a
short Hittite occupancy of Babylonia directly on to the
conquest of the land by the Cassites, whose first en-

---

[49] See Plate LIV, Fig. 1, for specimen of Hittite art, showing
Assyrian influence.

counters with the kings of Babylon, it will be recalled, took place in the reign of Samsuiluna. This is, now that a more definite basis for dating the reigns of the rulers of the Babylon dynasty has been secured,[50] not easily possible, indeed one may say out of the question. As a makeshift it is assumed that the rulers of the "sea land" availed themselves of the disturbed condition of affairs through the invasion of the Hittites and succeeded not only in gaining control of Isin and the land of Sumer in general, but also of Akkad, and ruled as kings of Sumer and Akkad for a period of about 150 years. There are some indications pointing in this direction. Until, however, further documents for this period shall be forthcoming, we cannot trace the course of events which led (c. 1760 B.C.) to the conquest of the entire country by the Cassites. All that may safely be inferred is that the interval (c. 1926–1760 B.C.) between the invasion of the Hittites and the establishment of a dynasty of Cassite rulers who maintained themselves on the throne for more than half a millennium must have been marked by unrest, by frequent shiftings of the political kaleidoscope and by internal disturbances during which there was in many respects a reversion to earlier conditions when Sumer and Akkad were hopelessly divided up into a considerable number of independent little states.

XII

The Cassites did not remain idle during this interval. While originally perhaps serving merely as mercenaries in the army of Rîm-Sin, they must soon after his death have obtained a position of mastery in the border state of Emutbal. From this point of vantage they would be apt to make incursions into the Euphrates Valley and if we were better informed regarding this period, we would probably find them hold-

---

[50] By Kugler, *Sternkunde und Sterndienst in Babel,* II, 2, Heft I, p. 257, *seq.,* on the basis of notices in astrological texts.

ing portions of the land in their control. Elam proper must also have been affected by the proximity of these warlike hordes. It does not appear to have ever actually fallen into the hands of the Cassites, though in default of documents we cannot be certain of this.

The Babylonian Chroniclers name Gandash as the first Cassite ruler who lays claim to titles emphasizing control of Babylonia. In fact he calls himself in an inscription that has been preserved in a late copy,[51] "King of the Four Regions, King of Sumer and Akkad, King of Babylon," from which we are permitted to conclude that he asserted his complete succession to the dynasty of Babylon, but it does not of course follow that he was the first Cassite who succeeded in gaining the supremacy over any portion of the Euphrates Valley. Predecessors of Gandash for many generations back may have had parts of Sumer or Akkad in their possession, dividing the authority with the rulers of the "sea land." All therefore that is to be concluded from the official recognition of Gandash as the first ruler of the Cassite dynasty is that with him the interference of the Cassites in the political fortunes of the Euphrates Valley assumes a new and more definite phase. For about forty years the rulers of the "sea land," no doubt driven back to their limited marshy district in the south, were able to maintain themselves until about 1720 B.C., when their rule was practically brought to an end by Ulamburiash, the Cassite who calls himself the brother of Kashtiliash I.

A strange issue indeed of the long continued conflicts between Sumerians and Akkadians that after such various vicissitudes in which Semitic influences steadily gained the mastery, the prize should have been snatched out of the hands of the two rivals by a foreign power, and one that represented a far lower level of culture. The Cassites indeed brought little with them that could

---

[51] Winckler, *Untersuchungen zur Altorientalischen Geschichte,* pp. 34 and 156.

be regarded as an addition to the civilization which they assimilated unless it be the horse, which appears to have been introduced by them,[52] as better adapted than the ass for purposes of war—particularly for drawing chariots across mountain regions. Indeed many centuries lapsed before it became customary to use the horse also as a riding animal as we find it on the monuments of Assyrian kings. The Cassites appear to have adopted the civilization of Babylonia in a surprisingly short time; they retain the names of the chief deities worshipped by them[53] but assimilated them to figures of the Babylonian pantheon, to whom they bore a resemblance.[54]

A civilization having reached a certain point does not stand still; it either moves forward or a period of decline, albeit temporary, sets in. The latter appears to have been the result of the coming of the Cassite hordes. The works of art of this period are few in number, which may of course be due to accidental preservation, but what we have is of a decidedly lower order. The best specimens are the so-called boundary stones, large steles of hard or soft stone or of a composite material, recording gifts of lands or special deeds illustrated with symbols and representations of the gods and occasionally of rulers in whose reigns these

---

[52] The code of Hammurapi does not mention the horse, but we find it referred to in a business document of this period. (See Ungnad, Oriental. Litteraturzeitung, X, Sp. 638, seq.); it does not become common, however, until the time of Cassite control. The horse (sisu) is written ideographically "ass of the mountain," an indication of the district whence it was brought to Babylonia. See Meyer, Geschichte des Altertums, I, 2, p. 651, seq.

[53] See Jastrow, Religion Babyloniens und Assyriens, I, p. 180 and the references there given.

[54] Shipak is identified with Marduk, Khala with the goddess Gula, Shukamuna, who appears to have been the head of the Cassite pantheon, with Nergal, Shuriash with Shamash, and Maruttash with Ninib.

monuments were set up.[55] No literary products date,
so far as can be ascertained, from the five centuries of
Cassite supremacy. The old was preserved and we do
not even find evidence of any adaptation of ancient
hymns or rituals or myths to the changed conditions,
such as happened when Babylon, with Marduk as the
chief deity, took the place of Nippur and Enlil,[56] or as
happened centuries later when the Babylonian literature
was carried over to Assyria and adapted to conditions
prevailing in the north. It may be that certain divination practises were brought to Babylonia by the
Cassites,[57] but this can certainly not be regarded as a
contribution to culture, as little as can changes in military organization and warfare which they may have
introduced. The ancient laws were retained by the
Cassite rulers, as the business documents, which from
the days of Burnaburiash (c. 1370 B.C.) become quite
numerous,[58] show. The one important innovation in
these documents is the introduction of dating according
to the years of the ruling monarch, instead of according to significant events.

While continuing to recognize Babylon as the official
residence, the Cassite rulers seemed bent on restoring
to Nippur the prestige which this centre lost in a measure through the transfer of the headship of the pantheon to Marduk as the chief deity of Babylon. We
find the Cassites displaying great zeal in restoring and

---

[55] See the illustration and also in Chapter VII. Plates LXXIII
and LXXIV.

[56] See p. 212, *seq.*

[57] Probably the divination through the play of oil bubbles in
water, for which see p. 266 and the reference there given.

[58] *E.g.,* in Nippur. See Clay, *Documents from the Temple
Archives Dated in the Reigns of Cassite Rulers* (Philadelphia, 1906,
2 vols.), and the same author's *Personal Names from Cuneiform
Inscriptions of the Cassite Period* (New Haven, 1912) ; in Babylon,
also, business documents of the time of Burnaburiash II onwards
have been found.

improving the sanctuary of Enlil at Nippur, which, however, did not hinder them from paying their homage to the chief patron deities of other centres, to Sin or Nannar at Ur, to Shamash at Larsa, to Nanâ in Uruk and naturally also to Marduk in Babylon.

XIII

We must now leave Babylonia for a while and turn our attention to the north, for before the Cassite dominion comes to an end (c. 1200 B.C.), we find the rulers of Assyria not only in a position of complete independence of the south, but inaugurating the aggressive policy which in due course, with many turns and twists, to be sure, made them the masters of a large portion of the ancient world—world-conquerors in the full sense of the term.

Despite the large advance signalled in our knowledge of the earliest period of Assyrian history as a consequence of the thorough excavations that have been conducted during the past fourteen years by the German expedition at Kaleh-Shergat,[59] the site of the ancient capital of Assyria, we are still in the dark as to the origin of the northern state or the manner of its settlement. The region offers a ready access to the northern hordes always pressing southwards from their mountain recesses, and since the names of some of the earliest personages in connection with the history of Assyria show affiliations with Mitanni names, as, for example, Ushpia, the first builder of the temple at Ashur, and Kikia who built the city wall, we are permitted to conclude that Hittite groups formed a contingent in the earliest settlements of Assyria to which the material found leads us. Waves of Amoritic migrations or invasions must also have reached Assyria at an early date, and the circumstance that one of the oldest temples in Ashur is dedicated to the god Adad, of Amoritic origin, in conjunction with Anu, the patron

[59] Above, p. 55, *seq.*

god of Uruk who becomes the god of heaven in general, is significant.[60] The natural extension northwards of the Euphratean civilization would further tend to bring a steady string of settlers from the south.

The extension of the script and language of Babylonia to Assyria forms naturally the most significant symptom of the spread of the culture produced in the south, for with the script and language went the religious beliefs and practises (adapted so far as necessary to modified conditions), as well as the laws as an inherent element of the religion, deriving their authority direct from the gods. The form in which the culture is passed on is that assumed through the gradual predominance of the Semitic or Akkadian element of the population. The earliest inscriptions recovered, which take us back to considerably beyond 2000 B.C., are couched in Akkadian, which is perhaps also to be taken as an indication that the movement to the north was largely from Akkad, the centre of the Semitic settlements, rather than from Sumer.

As already pointed out, the new documents found in considerable numbers through the excavations of Kaleh-Shergat enable us to carry back the history of Assyria to several centuries beyond the threshold of the third millennium before this era, but the facts gleaned from these documents, usually brief votive inscriptions, are meagre. We learn the names of early rulers, calling themselves at first *patesis*,[61] who record their activity in building walls or enlarging temples in the city of Ashur dedicated to various gods, as Ashur, Ishtar, Enlil, Anu and Adad and the goddess of the lower world, Ereshkigal. It is not until we reach the days of Samsi-Adad, son of Ishme-Dagan, whose date may be provisionally fixed at c. 1850 B.C., that we obtain a

---

[60] The temple is always spoken of as the ''house of Anu and Adad.''

[61] See Messerschmidt, *Keilschrifttexte Aus Assur* (Leipzig, 1911).

more definite picture of the internal state of affairs. This ruler already bestows on himself the title "king of universal reign," which the later kings of Assyria so proudly wield and with far more justification. However, Samsi-Adad would assuredly not have used the title without some claim, albeit exaggerated, as a result of conquests made by him. We find him, as a matter of fact, extending his realm far beyond the natural confines of Assyria. He speaks of subjecting to his control "the land between the Tigris and Euphrates," by which presumably he means Mesopotamia proper to the west of Assyria and which would include the Hittite settlements of Khani in that region. This is confirmed by a tablet found in Tirka, the capital of Khani, speaking of Samsi-Adad's activity in building a temple to Dagan in that centre. He passes still further to the north into the mountain districts of the Lebanon and erects monuments on "the coast of the great sea," by which he means the Mediterranean.[62] To conquer such an extensive territory was no small achievement, and it points to a remarkable advance in power that the rulers of the city of Ashur should be prepared to take up the policy of the old Sumerian kings like Lugalzaggisi and Urukagina, and of Akkadian conquerors like Sargon, Narâm-Sin and Hammurapi, to stretch their dominions to the "great sea." Samsi-Adad would not have been able to carry out such a plan but for the weakened condition of the south at the time, where, as we have seen, after the invasion of the Hittites a period of decided decline had set in.

This relationship between conditions in the south and those in the north becomes characteristic for the

---

[62] Hardly the Black Sea as Meyer, *Geschichte des Altertums,* 1, 2, p. 593. I do not hesitate to identify Lab'an with Lebanon, and since Samsi-Adad immediately thereafter (col. IV, 13–18) speaks of the "coast of the great sea," he cannot have in mind anything else than the Mediterranean—and in all probability at the point where the Dog River enters the Mediterranean.

future; and we will have occasion to see how constantly weakness in Babylonia is taken advantage of by Assyria for an aggressive policy and, vice versa, periods of decline of power in the north are marked by a renewal of strength in the south. With the triumph of the Cassites in Babylonia, a strong central power was once more established and, correspondingly, we find Assyrian rulers unable to follow up the policy of extension inaugurated by Samsi-Adad.

XIV

A problem in connection with this early history of Assyria that still awaits solution is to account for the presence of an extensive settlement in far distant Cappadocia, making use of the cuneiform script and Akkadian language (with certain modifications) for recording business transactions on clay tablets precisely like those to which we are accustomed in Babylonia and Assyria, even to the attachment of the seals of the parties concerned.[63] Through these seals furnishing names of rulers of the Ur dynasty and of early *patesis* of Ashur, we are enabled to say definitely that these Cappadocian documents, found at various places of the extensive district, revert to a period as high as about 2400 B.C., and come down to about 1900, though a definite limit at the other end has not yet been determined. The proper names in these documents are unmistakably Assyrian, as is shown by the frequent introduction of the element Ashur—generally written Ashir as in the oldest Assyrian inscriptions—in names of individuals. A further proof of the presence of Assyrians in this district at an early period is the designation Assyria given by early Greek geographers to the land on both sides of the river Halys, covering precisely the region

---

[63] See the references grouped together by Meyer, *Geschichte des Altertums*, I, 2, p. 613, *seq.*, and the note on page viii of the Introduction.

in which Cappadocian tablets have been found. Even in later times, the inhabitants of Cappadocia are spoken of as Syrians (an abbreviation of Assyrians), and by way of contrast to the Syrians south of the Taurus range are specified as "White Syrians." [64] How are we to account for this Assyrian colony in a district so remote from both Babylonia and Assyria at this early date? A plausible hypothesis which may be provisionally accepted is to assume that Assyrian garrisons were placed here to maintain some measure of control over the land and that around these garrisons, owing allegiance to rulers of Sumer and Akkad, settlements of Assyrians and perhaps also of Babylonians grew and maintained commercial and other relationships with their native land.[65]

In view of this extension of Assyrian influence in Asia Minor at so unexpectedly early a period, even though these Semitic settlements represent merely the outgrowth of military outposts, the aggressive policy of Samsi-Adad centuries later appears in a more natural light. What he did, others may have attempted before him, and indeed it is possible that he endeavored to secure for Assyria a control of lands to the northwest that had been wrested from her while her rulers were still merely *patesis,* owing allegiance to rulers of the south. At all events, the advance of the Hittites, marked by their success in overthrowing the dynasty of Babylon, must have put at least a temporary end to Assyrian control in Asia Minor, and we may perhaps bring the end of the settlements in Cappadocia in connection with this rise of the Hittites to a position of extraordinary power.

---

[64] See the references given by Nöldeke in Hermes, vol. v, pp. 443–468.

[65] A parallel in much later days would be the growth of an extensive Jewish colony in Upper Egypt out of a military frontier garrison at Elephantine. See Ed. Meyer, *Papyrusfund von Elephantine* (Leipzig, 1912).

But for the presence at this time of the strong Cassite rulers in Babylonia, one might have witnessed another Hittite invasion of the Euphrates Valley in the sixteenth century. If we place Samsi-Adad shortly before the definite control of Babylonia through the Cassites, we obtain a date for the decline of the Hittite power in Babylonia, c. 1750 B.C., which answers the required conditions—the weakened state of the south through constant uprisings of various centres, and attempts of rulers of the "sea land" to maintain or extend their power, and the advantage reaped by Assyria from this state of affairs to assert her independence and to push on to a renewed control of the regions lying to the north and northwest.

In default of historical documents of Assyrian rulers for the succeeding centuries we are left in doubt as to the further course of this extension of Assyrian power, but the existence, in the sixteenth century, of the strong, independent state of Mitanni in northwestern Mesopotamia, extending to the Taurus range, and the simultaneous establishment of a still more powerful Hittite kingdom with a centre near the Black Sea, furnish a date for the reaction which must have forced Assyria back within her proper bounds. The large admixture of Aryan elements at this time to the Hittite population, employed perhaps at first as mercenaries and then rising as successful soldiers to leading positions, is to be regarded as an important factor in bringing new vigor to the various Hittite groups throughout Asia Minor.

The supremacy of the Cassites in the south, reaching the height of their power in the seventeenth to the fifteenth centuries, would act as a further deterrent in restricting the activity of Assyrian rulers to keeping a watch on the formidable neighbor, whose natural ambition would be to re-establish the dependency of Assyria upon Babylonia which had prevailed for so many centuries. A definite point of contact between the Cassites and the Assyrians is found in a statement of a chronicler,[66] that the Cassite ruler Karaindash, whose reign may be approximately fixed in the second half of the fifteenth century, made a treaty with Ashur-rimnisheshu, the King of Assyria, agreeing by a solemn oath to respect the boundary as fixed between them. That Assyria is strong enough to compel Babylonia to make an agreement regarding the boundary between the two lands is extremely significant, pointing as it does to the failure of attempts on the part of the Cassites to secure a control of the north. The northern kingdom was thus steadily growing in strength, and it is eminently likely that after 1500 B.C. the south had given up all hope of reducing the north to the former position of subserviency. Assyria, in fact, was beginning to assume the rôle of aggressor, though some time naturally elapsed before she was ready to assume a direct interference in the affairs of the south. This was brought about through the marriage of an Assyrian princess, Muballitat-Sheru'a, the daughter of Ashur-uballit (c. 1380–1350 B.C.), with Karakhardash, the Cassite ruler of Babylonia. The offspring of this marriage, Karaindash, was murdered in a rebellion that broke out and Ashur-uballit proceeds to Babylonia to wreak vengeance for the death of his grandson. He succeeds in this to the extent of dispatching Nazibugash, an usurper and the ringleader of the uprising. In place of the latter, Kurigalzu II, another son of Burnaburiash, is placed on the throne and he rules for twenty-three years (c. 1355–1332 B.C.).

XV

We have thus reached an entirely new state of affairs. The tables are turned about. The more vigorous Assyria feels called upon to suppress internal disturbances in Babylonia and to secure the legitimate succession to the throne. There are other indications

---

[66] *Keilinschriftliche Bibliothek* (ed. Schrader), I, p. 194.

of this momentous change in the relationships between
the south and north. From this period, the middle of
the fourteenth century B.C., date the important official
archives found some twenty years ago in Tell el-
Amarna in Egypt,[67] containing a portion of the correspondence of governors and other officials of districts and cities in Palestine and Syria with the kings
of Egypt, Amenophis III and Amenophis IV, in whose
service they stood. This correspondence is carried on
in Akkadian, which, as a result of the spread of Babylonian culture, had become current beyond the borders
of Babylonia. Included in the correspondence are also
letters from Babylonian and Assyrian rulers which
throw a further light on the change in the relationship
between the two countries. The Cassite king Burnaburiash reproaches Amenophis IV for having recognized Ashur-uballit as an independent monarch, as long
as Babylonia still laid claim to a supremacy over Assyria. This complaint is a proof of the weakness to
which the south had been reduced. A foreign power is
appealed to, to make good a claim that had long since
ceased to have any warrant and that had become merely
a tradition handed down from an age that had passed
away. The Cassite ruler is not content with sending
costly gifts to Amenophis III; he adds his daughter
and his sister to be incorporated into the harem of the
Egyptian ruler, and it is indicative of the situation that
Amenophis refuses the request of the Babylonian king
for an Egyptian princess in return.

Enlil-nirari, the successor of Ashur-uballit, engages
in battle with Kurigalzu II, despite the fact that the
latter owed his throne to Assyrian interference. Assyria is victorious and apparently dictates terms in
bringing about a rearrangement of the boundary line.
From now on till towards the end of the Cassite dynasty, Assyria had a free hand in extending her power
to the north, northeast and northwest, with occasional

[67] See the Introduction to Knudtzon's standard work, *Die
El-Amarnatafeln* (Leipzig, 1908) for further details.

incursions even into Babylonia, which the latter, however, was able to resist, until, about 1290 B.C., she succumbed for a while to the authority of her northern foe.

All four rulers following upon Enlil-nirari stand
out prominently as aggressive warriors. Erik-den-ilu,
who leads his armies into the mountainous regions to
the northeast as well as to the northwest, subdues the
Guti in the Zagros range and the Hittite groups on the
western side of Assyria and drives back the Bedouins,
grouped under Akhlami and Suti, into the desert lands
to the southwest. His son, Adadnirari I, continues the
work of his father and claims control of a large region
to the east as well as to the northwest of Assyria. He
appears definitely to have put an end to the Mitanni
kingdom—an important achievement as a road, leading
again to a further extension of Assyria into and beyond
the Taurus range. Under the two successors, Shalmaneser I (c. 1300 B.C.) and Tukulti-Ninib (c. 1290
B.C.), the aggressive policy reaches the height of its
success. Chronicles record attacks on Babylonia by
Adadnirari I, by Shalmaneser I and by Tukulti-Ninib I,
corresponding to the reigns of Cassite kings from Nazi-
maruttash (c. 1332–1307 B.C.) to Kashtiliash II (c.
1261–1254 B.C.). Each attack meant not only a weak-
ening of the vitality of the Cassite rule in Babylonia,
but concessions to Assyria in the settlement of the
boundary line between the northern and southern kingdoms. Finally after several campaigns, Tukulti-ninib I
actually besieges Babylon and captures the reigning
king, Kashtiliash II. This happened about the middle
of the thirteenth century.[68] Babylonia passes entirely
into control of Assyria, as is indicated by the title,
"King of Karduniash" (*i.e.*, Babylonia [69]) and "King

---

[68] We have a definite indication for the date of Tukulti-Ninib in
a statement in one of Sennacherib's inscriptions. See King,
Records of Tukulti-Ninib, I, p. 60, *seq.*

[69] For Kar-duniash ("Fortress of the god Duniash" as the
Cassite name of Babylonia, see Meyer, *Geschichte* I, 2, p. 659, *seq.*,
and the references there given.

of Sumer and Akkad" which Tukulti-Ninib I adds to his other claims.

With Tukulti-Ninib we reach the climax in this period of Assyrian aggressiveness. Had the strength which the north unfolded at this time been maintained, Babylonia would in a short time have become merely a province of Assyria. Tukulti-Ninib, however, is killed in an uprising instituted by his own son, and the decline of Assyria now sets in with such rapidity that she not only loses her prestige but is attacked on the north by the various mountain groups, while Babylonia regains her independence and forces her favorites on the throne of Assyria. For a short time indeed, extending from the reign of Ashur-reshishi to that of Tiglathpileser I, covering the second half of the twelfth century B.C., Assyria recovers her position. The former succeeds in driving back the Lulumi and the Guti and other groups into their mountain recesses, holds the Bedouin hordes in check and successfully combats an attack from Babylonia, the purpose of which was to reduce the district recognized by previous treaties as constituting the extent of Assyria. His son, Tiglathpileser I (c. 1125–1100 B.C.), maintains the prestige recovered by his father and increases it by a series of campaigns to the northeast and northwest. He penetrates to the sources of the Euphrates, far up in the Nairi district, and erects a monument to himself there as the symbol of the extent of the dominion once more claimed by him. He forces the troublesome Hittite groups in the northwest to submission, and coming into the Taurus range makes himself master of an extensive district that stretches far into central Asia Minor. Egypt once more acknowledges the independence of Assyria; her kings send gifts to Ashur as in the days of Amenophis III and IV. Moreover, Tiglathpileser I surpasses the achievements of his predecessors on the throne of Assyria, and in imitation of the ambition of Babylonian rulers at various epochs plants his stand-

ards on the shores of the Mediterranean. At the mouth
of the Dog River he erects a statue of himself, with an
inscription recording his achievements. Tiglathpileser I crowns his achievements by two campaigns
against Babylonia, in the first of which he extends the
boundary line of Assyria, while in the second he reaches
and captures the chief cities in northern Babylonia, including the capital city, Babylon. Once more, therefore, as in the days of Tukulti-Ninib, the supremacy
of the north had to be acknowledged by the south, but
the second epoch of glory was of even shorter duration
than the first, and with Tiglathpileser's death his extensive kingdom once more crumbles to pieces. For
two centuries Assyria, restricted in her activity to
maintaining herself within her own very definite and
limited boundaries, plays little or no part in the larger
affairs of the ancient world.

It is not difficult to account for the rapid decay
after the exhibition of such great force. The burden
of military campaigns for a term of years, involving
the annual loss of thousands of men, was too large to
be borne, nor was the booty, though large, or the tribute
imposed an adequate compensation for the cost and
effort. In a summary of five years of his reign, Tiglathpileser speaks of having conquered no less than
forty-two countries, covering a territory that stretched
west to the Mediterranean, north to the Black Sea and
northeast to the lake of Van and beyond. In the case
of a single engagement,[70] the king is opposed by a force
of 20,000 men, of whom only six thousand escape. From
such a statement we can infer what enormous hosts
must have been gathered together by him to carry on
wars successfully into difficult, almost inaccessible,
regions.

Externally, indeed, everything seemed rosy for Assyria when Tiglathpileser I passed away. The old
capital of Ashur had risen to new glory in the enlarge-

[70] Rawlinson, I, Pl. 9, Col. I, 74.

ment of her temples and palaces, in the strengthening of her fortifications and in the tribute that poured in from all sides. He laid out beautiful parks about this palace, bringing trees for this purpose from distant lands. The king appears also to have been the one who introduced wild hunting sports as a royal pastime. He hunts elephants on the banks of the Chabur; he boasts of having killed almost one thousand lions and all manner of big and little game besides. In ships he sails along the Mediterranean and catches a sea monster which may have been a whale.[71] Everything that the king thus does is on a huge scale and, making due allowance for the exaggerations of his chroniclers, zealous in flattering their royal master, enough remains to show that, in peace as in war, Tiglathpileser I played the part of the *grand monarque*—with little concern, however, whether his successors would be able to keep up the grandeur and the glory.

XVI

Returning now to Babylonia, we have still to trace her history after the first serious conflicts with Assyria down to the close of the Cassite period. We have seen that the coming of the Cassites marks the beginning of a period of stagnation in the general culture, which after some time shows itself also in a political decline. Unfortunately, owing to a gap in our knowledge of the events during the two centuries that followed upon Agum II,[72] we are not in a position to indicate exactly when the decline set in and we are left to conjecture as to the specific causes which brought it about. Difficulties in keeping the native population in check, particularly in the south, may be set down as an important factor, for both Sumerians and Akkadians must have chafed

---

[71] So Haupt's view. See *Amer. Journal of Semitic Languages*, vol. xxiii, pp. 253–263. The Assyrian term is *nakhiru*.

[72] Above, p. 152.

under the humiliation of being governed by foreign invaders. The jealousy of Elam, seeking every opportunity of fomenting internal dissensions in the Euphrates Valley in the hope of profiting by the division, is a second factor, but one more fundamental was the general lowering of the *niveau* of culture through the mere presence of rulers who represented a cruder element—one that had to be assimilated to a higher civilization. In the course of such a process the more refined element suffers a temporary eclipse.

It is significant as a general symptom of the weakness of the Cassite dynasty, especially from the sixteenth century on, that Babylonia was unable to oppose the Egyptian control over Palestine and the Phœnician coast. The Hittites alone in northeastern Syria and in central Asia Minor offered resistance to the advance of Egyptian arms, while Babylonian kings seemed happy to be able to maintain friendly relations through interchange of gifts with the rulers on the Nile who were, as a matter of fact, their natural rivals and who had wrested from their control the important strip along the Mediterranean and extending inland to high table lands and to the desert region respectively. Babylonia thus seemed condemned to a policy of concentration to preserve her independence, without thought of extraterritorial extension. She is not even well prepared for this more humble rôle, for the result of the numerous conflicts with Assyria, which began, as we saw,[78] in the reign of Karaindash (c. 1430 B.C.), is a steady growth of Assyrian territory by changes in the boundary lines between the north and the south, until, about two centuries later, Babylonia is forced to accept as her rulers the candidates selected by Assyrian kings. The south profits by the decline in the power of Assyria which sets in after the murder of Tukulti-Ninib I, and through some of her rulers is able to avenge herself for the humiliation which she suffered at the hands of

[78] Above, p. 163.

Assyria. In several successful counter attacks on Assyria, Babylonia regained some of the territory that she had been obliged to yield to Assyria. At the same time, as a result of Assyrian interference in Babylonian affairs, the influence of the Semitic element of the population reasserted itself; and it is reasonable to conclude that the rivalry between Cassites and the native population, not completely assimilated despite the lapse of so many centuries of coexistence side by side, finally led to a vigorous attempt on the part of the Semites to regain complete possession of their country. A momentous change, however, was impending in the south, for within four years after the death of Marduk-paliddin (c. 1199–1187 B.C.) the native chroniclers record the rise of a new dynasty in the land.

Our knowledge of Babylonian history for the succeeding two and one-half centuries is still quite fragmentary. Of only a few rulers who flourished during this period do we possess documents of a historical character; for the rest we are dependent upon incidental references in the annals or votive inscriptions of Assyrian kings and on short notices in official chronicles. With Enlil-nadin-akhi, the second member of the new dynasty, the chroniclers close the Cassite control and again record eleven kings of the Isin dynasty covering a period of 130 years. It is no longer a question of a Sumerian uprising, for that epoch is long since past. The assimilation of Sumerians and Akkadians is an accomplished fact. To account for another Isin dynasty, we must assume that, during the closing years of the Cassite rule, native governors in some of the old centres once more made themselves independent, and that a combination of such petty states headed by Isin dealt the final blow which ended the foreign rule in the Euphrates Valley. The governors of Isin were acknowledged as the heads of the kingdom, and hence officially recognized as the basis for dating legal documents. We have boundary stones

dated in the reigns of several of these rulers from which
we glean some facts connected with their reigns. So,
for instance, Nebuchadnezzar I (c. 1140–1110 B.C.), apparently an usurper, gains some successes in expeditions against Elam. He also claims to have conquered
the Lulubi, whose seat is to be sought in the Zagros
range, and he even led his armies to the northwest,
though his achievements here could not have been of
any great moment. Nebuchadnezzar I takes the aggressive and attempts to win back Assyria, but is completely
routed by Ashurrishishi. Under Ashurrishishi's son,
the active and energetic Tiglathpileser I (c. 1125–1100
B.C.), Assyria recovered her former prestige and again
becomes the attacker of the south, threatening the very
life and independence of Babylonia. The successors of
Tiglathpileser were unable to maintain the position
won, and accordingly we find, instead of a subjection
of Babylonia to Assyria or a renewal of hostilities between the two kingdoms, an era of mutual good will
setting in. How long this period of stability lasted is
again involved in doubt, owing to a lack of historical
documents. Internal disturbances lead to the overthrow of the Isin dynasty (c. 1043 B.C.) and in its place
we once more find rulers of the "sea land" asserting
themselves and acknowledged as sovereigns over Babylonia for about twenty years. About 1020 B.C. we find
another dynasty, likewise consisting of three rulers,
ruling for about twenty years, and whose designation
Bit-Bazi is as yet a puzzle. The entire period of forty
years covered by these two dynasties must have been
marked by rivalry among the old centres of Babylonia.
The old enemy to the east, Elam, taking advantage of
the situation, overruns the Euphrates Valley in the
twelfth and again in the eleventh century, and for six
years the official chronicle records that an Elamitic sov-
ereign (c. 1000 B.C.) occupied the throne. We know
from other sources the extent to which Babylonia suffered from these incursions of Elamites, who, among

other marks of devastation, carried a large number of
the finest monuments of the country with them as
trophies to their capital, Susa, where they were found
in the course of excavations in our own days.[74]

The return of a native dynasty did not carry with
it a renewal of sufficient strength to inaugurate another
aggressive period during the succeeding centuries.
Gradually but steadily Babylonia sinks to the position
of more or less complete dependency upon Assyria. The
degree of this dependency varies somewhat, according
to the extent to which the reigning Assyrian king pursues a policy of vigorous opposition to endeavors on the
part of the south to reassert itself, or seeks to conciliate
Babylonia by allowing her as large liberties as are con-
sistent with a protection of the interests of Assyria.

About the middle of the eighth century, Assyrian
kings become *de facto* also the governors of Babylonia.
The history of Babylonia thus becomes merged with
that of Assyria, whose fortunes we must now briefly
summarize from the time of the decline which set in
again after the death of Tiglathpileser I, about 1100 B.C.

XVII

It is not until the beginning of the ninth century
that indications of a renaissance of Assyrian power
become marked. With the advent of Tukulti-Ninib II
(c. 889–884 B.C.) a new era begins, marked by a steady
growth till the climax of Assyrian glory is reached, some
two centuries later.

We find Tukulti-Ninib undertaking, after a long
interval, one of those campaigns against the moun-
taineers to the northeast which brings him up to Lake
Urmiyeh in the northeast, and Commagene in the northwest. His son, Ashurnasirpal III (885–860 B.C.), far
outdistances the father in achievements. He inaugurates his reign by a campaign against the lands to the

[74] See de Morgan, *Mémoires de la Délégation en Perse*, I, pp. 165–
182. See above, p. 113, note 88; 136, note 29, and p. 147.

northeast and northwest of a far more systematic character than the campaigns of his father, with the result
that in a few years the entire territory comes within
his control. A large booty is secured, heavy tribute
levied, and we find the king transcending all predecessors in the ruthless manner in which he burned and
pillaged settlements as he went along. All this, however, could not prevent the outbreak of rebellions in
the conquered territory which the Assyrian governors
appointed by the king were powerless to master, and
so in the reigns of Ashurnasirpal and his successors
campaign follows upon campaign with almost monotonous regularity against the same districts to the north,
northeast and northwest, varied by endeavors to force
the non-assimilated Bedouin groups, classed as Akhlami and Suti, along the Euphrates to the southwest
of Assyria, back into the desert lands beyond.

Remarkably successful in conquest by virtue of the
overwhelming force of her attack, Assyria showed herself even in her best days weak in establishing a definite
control and in maintaining order in the conquered
provinces. She failed in the organizing power which
made Rome for so long the mistress of the world.

Shalmaneser III (c. 858–824 B.C.) leads in person
annual campaigns for an uninterrupted period of
twenty-six years. The resources at the command of
the king must have been nigh inexhaustible to provide
for such a record, even if we make due allowance for
exaggerations in the number of the forces encountered
and in the enumeration of the men, horses, camels,
chariots, etc., captured.

The reign of Shalmaneser III is of special interest
because it marks the beginning of the period which
brings Syria and Palestine at the mercy of the Assyrian
power.[75] The northern Hebrew kingdom joins in a
combination with Phœnician cities, with Damascus and
Hamath and with the groups in the Taurus range to

---

[75] See the illustration above, Plate VI.

oppose the Assyrian advance. At Karkar on the Orontes a great battle was fought in 854 B.C., which ended in a victory for Assyria. This state of affairs, however, lasted for a century and more before this portion of the ancient world finally succumbed, worn out by the drain on the resources and vitality of the petty states whose rivalry with one another prevented the formation of a permanently united kingdom which might have withstood the Assyrian onslaught.

In Assyria, on the other hand, the chief stumbling block in the way of equable progress, in addition to her inability to maintain order in her widely extended dominions, were the frequent internal rebellions—precisely as in the south. Shalmaneser himself had to suffer the pain and humiliation of seeing one of his own sons, Ashurdaninapal, lead an uprising against him a few years before his death. Shamshi-Adad IV, however, succeeded in overcoming his brother and in securing an undisputed hold on the throne, though his reign was of short duration—just twelve years. Naturally, the internal disturbances had given all the provinces the desired opportunity to throw off the Assyrian yoke, and even Babylonia made attempts to regain her independence. Accordingly, we find Shamshi-Adad obliged to go over the same territory again to the north and south, to the northeast, northwest, and even to the southwest in a series of campaigns for the purpose of regaining Assyria's lost prestige.

We can pass rapidly over the next century, during which the rulers of Assyria on the whole maintained the strength of their kingdom and manifested the same weaknesses as their predecessors, and come to Tiglath-pileser IV, a usurper who in 745 B.C. inaugurates an era which gives to Assyria its most famous rulers—Shalmaneser V, Sargon, Sennacherib, Esarhaddon, and Ashurbanapal. With him Assyria enters upon the last but also the most glorious phase of her history. Profiting by the abundant experience of the past, the rulers

PLATE XXV

FIG. 1, THE ANNALS OF ASHURBANAPAL. KING OF ASSYRIA (668–626 B.C.)

FIG. 2, CLAY CYLINDER OF CYRUS WITH ACCOUNT OF THE CAPTURE OF BABYLON
(539 B.C.)

of the dynasty founded by Tiglathpileser perfected the organization of the Assyrian army to a degree which still arouses the admiration of students of military strategy of our own days.

With Tiglathpileser the last step in the subjection of Babylonia to Assyria is taken through the direct assumption in its affairs by the kings of Assyria, who, no longer trusting the government to Babylonians, appointed by them, either themselves act as the governors —"lieutenants of the god Bel" as they designate themselves—or name a son or a brother as the ruler of the southern province, as which Babylonia is from this time on reckoned. Several expeditions were needed to bring about a reassertion of Assyrian supremacy in the troublesome districts to the east and southeast. In both Babylonia and in districts to the east of Assyria, Tiglathpileser adopted on a larger scale the policy of settling colonists from parts of Assyria, and in return to transport portions of the population to other countries. In this way the rulers hoped to remove unruly elements and to secure by a mixture of the natives with loyal Assyrians, or with those who had no special interest in the district to which they were transported a more amenable populace.

Hardly less difficult was Tiglathpileser's task in the lands to the north, including the northeast and northwest. Here, after the reign of Shalmaneser III, Assyria had steadily lost ground until new independent kingdoms had been formed by combinations of native groups, among which the kingdom of Urartu developed noteworthy strength. The difficulties of the situation were increased by the other combinations of states in the interior of Syria and Palestine and along the Phœnician coast, formed to resist the tribute imposed upon these districts by Assyria. The Assyrian king was obliged once more to turn his attention to Syria and Palestine, with the result that the northern Hebrew kingdom became practically a province of Assyria, while Judæa's position was only a trifle less precarious, because its king had voluntarily submitted to become tributary to Assyria. The eighteen years of Tiglathpileser's reign (745–727 B.C.) were thus filled with events of great importance. By his more systematic efforts actually to govern distant provinces reconquered by him, as by his policy above outlined[76] to remove causes of fomentation among conquered peoples, he gave a more permanent character to the results of his many campaigns in Syria, Palestine, and in lands to the north and northeast. Less permanent were the efforts to control the east and southeast, and it was from this quarter—Media and Elam—that his successors had much to endure.

Of his son who ruled as Shalmaneser V for only five years (727–722 B.C.), we know little beyond his success in putting an end completely to the northern Hebrew kingdom which, relying perhaps upon help from Egypt, had refused the payment of tribute to Assyria. Before the capital, Samaria, actually fell, Shalmaneser died, succeeded by an usurper who on seizing the throne adopted as his name Sargon—associated as will be recalled with a most glorious dynasty of past ages.[77]

XVIII

Like Tiglathpileser IV, Sargon probably rose from the ranks, but he could hardly have attained his position without some violence which, perhaps, he deemed it wiser to pass over in silence in his annals. In many respects the campaigns of Sargon are repetitions of the conditions prevailing in the days of Tiglathpileser. In Babylonia we find the "sea land" organizing an attempt to place a native once more on the throne, Mardukpaliddin, who starts out as a local chief by ingratiating himself with Tiglathpileser IV, but as he grows in power

---

[76] Above, p. 175. See also p. 135.
[77] Above, p. 133.

takes advantage of the change of dynasty to make himself master of all Babylonia in the very same year that Sargon begins his rule. A first and immediate attempt to suppress Mardukpaliddin failed, and for the next years Sargon was so much occupied with campaigns against the Hittite state of which Carchemish was the capital, against the petty kingdoms of northern Syria and in the regions to the northeast that it was not until the year 710 B.C. that he succeeded in putting Mardukpaliddin out of the way, and in himself again assuming as king of Assyria the direct rule over the south as well. Sargon sets up the claim of being the deliverer of Babylonia and inaugurates a policy marked by great consideration for the ancient rights of the populace. The policy, however, was of little avail. Babylonia continued to chafe under the humiliation of a northern rule imposed upon her. The large centres were hotbeds of intrigue and opposition to Assyria. Uprisings beginning usually in the extreme south and fomented by Elam, which had hopes of again conquering her old enemy, followed in frequent succession until finally in the days of Sennacherib, the son of Sargon, the patience of Assyria was exhausted, and in 689 B.C. Sennacherib marched against Babylon and destroyed the ancient city entirely.

The reigns of Sargon (721–705 B.C.) and of his son Sennacherib (705–681 B.C.) thus mark further steps leading inevitably to the dissolution of the Babylonian kingdom after an existence of about two millenniums. The other new factor was the approaching conflict between Assyria and Egypt. Foreshadowed in the days of Sargon, the direct encounter between the two mighty powers took place in 701 B.C., through the assistance given by Egypt to an uprising of Syria, the Phœnician coast and Palestine against the Assyrian yoke. The Egyptians were defeated, the uprising broken up, but owing to disturbed conditions in Babylonia, Sennacherib was unable to follow up the ad-

12

vantage gained by him and hastened back to put things in order nearer home.

It is surprising that Assyria was able to bear the strain of these campaigns, organized on a larger scale than before, for the entire century intervening between Tiglathpileser IV and the destruction of Nineveh in 606 B.C. The stretch of her dominions passed beyond the borders of the Mediterranean. Under the greatest possible difficulties a fleet was added to the equipment, and Cyprus incorporated as a part of the Assyrian power.

Sennacherib fell a victim in 680 B.C., to the blow of an assassin, who was his own son or according to the Biblical account,[78] there were two sons involved. His son Esarhaddon, appointed by Sennacherib as the heir to the throne, succeeded in quelling the uprising and in establishing himself firmly. Reverting to the policy of his grandfather, Sargon, he decided to make an endeavor to reconcile the Babylonians by rebuilding the city of Babylon. Despite this, the "sea land" continued to be a centre of opposition and Esarhaddon passed through the same experiences as his predecessors.

Esarhaddon took the bold step of crossing over into Egypt. The victorious standard of Assyria was planted on the Nile, and in 670 B.C. the ancient capital Memphis fell into the hands of the Assyrian king. The ruling dynasty was overthrown, the government of the country reorganized under Assyrian control, though as a concession to tradition a native was recognized or set up by him as king of the twenty-two provinces or nomes into which Egypt was divided. In addition to Egypt, portions of northern and southern Arabia which had hitherto stood in a very loose connection with Assyria were brought under a firmer control, though it could hardly be said that the enormous tracts of central Arabia, so difficult of access and in which hordes of Bedouin tribes roamed at will, were ever really subject to Assyria.

[78] II Kings 19, 36–37.

PLATE XXVI

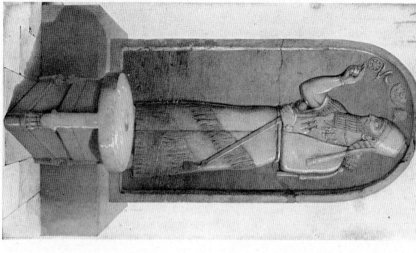

FIG. 1, KING ASHURNASIRPAL III OF ASSYRIA
(883–859 B.C.)

FIG. 2, KING ESARHADDON OF ASSYRIA
(680–669 B.C.) WITH TWO ROYAL

XIX

With the advent of Ashurbanapal in 668 B.C., we reach the climax in the glory of the Sargonide dynasty, as upon his death, in 626 B.C., the rapid decline sets in. Legend soon gathered around his name and as Sardanapalos among the Greeks he sums up as it were the spirit of Assyria's greatness. His efforts, to be sure, are largely taken up with maintaining the integrity of the vast empire claimed by Assyria. His campaigns in one direction or the other are therefore on the whole attempts to quell disturbances and to strengthen the hands of those governors of provinces who were merely the tools of Assyria. Now it is Egypt to which his armies turn, now Syria and Palestine which are forced to pledge themselves anew to do homage to the mighty power, and again it is the various groups of northern Syria, in and beyond the Taurus range, and the mountain hordes to the northwest which have to be kept in check. In two directions Ashurbanapal branches out even beyond the ambitious scope of Esarhaddon. Lydia comes within his grasp on the one side, while in a series of campaigns he deals a severe blow against Elam, the old enemy on the east, and with the capture and death of Teumman, the Elamite king, puts an end for the time being to the independence of this district.

The opposition to Ashurbanapal began once more in the south, and it was the king's own brother, Shamash-shumukin, whom he had appointed as governor of Babylonia, who organized an uprising on all sides against the Assyrian yoke. Ashurbanapal wreaked vengeance on those who had assisted his treacherous brother and, after quieting Babylonia, proceeded to inflict punishment on Elam and Arabia for their share in the great uprising. The agitation in the north, too, gradually subsided, but the greatest danger to Assyria, the pressure of hordes pouring into Asia Minor towards the south, was one that even Ashurbanapal was unable to resist. Already in the days of Esarhaddon new groups like the Cimmerians, Mannai and Ashguzeans make their appearance in the royal annals, representing a wave of Aryan migration across the Caucasus range and that appears to be one of a series of *Völkerwanderungen* in this general region. Esarhaddon and Ashurbanapal were able to keep the advance in check, but only by tremendous efforts involving the dispatching of Assyrian armies of large size into the mountain ranges to the north and northeast. Twenty years after Ashurbanapal's death, Nineveh fell, through a combination between the Babylonians and the wild hordes of the northeast—at that time grouped under the general designation of Manda.

The rapidity with which Assyria declined after 626 B.C., when Ashurbanapal passed away, will always remain a puzzling phenomenon. A gradual decline through exhausted vitality was to be expected, but that within twenty years the achievements of centuries should have crumbled like a house of cards is a sad reflection not only upon the transitoriness of mere worldly power, but upon the weakness of the foundations upon which the structure was reared.

A country divided against itself cannot endure. Babylonia fell under Assyrian sway because the south was pitted against the north and preferred to have recourse to intrigue and to combinations with the enemy to the east—Elam—or with Bedouin hordes from the west and southwest rather than to unite with the north. Only strong rulers, as they arose from time to time, were able to keep the north and south of the Euphrates Valley firmly knit together. Similarly Babylonia and Assyria, although the latter was the offshoot of the former and both had practically everything in common, never held together, while even within Assyria as she expanded factions arose which threatened her unity at

frequent intervals. Assyria and Babylonia both succumbed to this inherent weakness, but Assyria fell first
because of the exhaustion of her vitality through
incessant warfare.

XX

We must not, however, take leave of her without
considering briefly the other side of the picture—her
achievements in other fields than conquest. It is a
relief to find that her rulers, even those whose greed
for power and for the extension of Assyria's borders
was strongest, were zealous also in the promotion of
works of peace, more particularly the embellishment of
the capital in which they resided, though their concern
was extended also to other places. Wars were undertaken in the name of the gods, and with their help,
and when victory crowned the Assyrian arms, to the
gods belonged the glory. The kings, thus feeling at all
times close to their gods, took every occasion to show
their homage. Attached, therefore, to the annals detailing their military expeditions are accounts of the
enlargement of the temples, of repairs to sacred edifices,
which were so frequently required in the case of brick
structures that building and rebuilding became synonymous terms. Next to the temples, the royal palaces,
built in close proximity to the chief temples in each
centre, engaged the attention of rulers; and they are
equally proud of their efforts at improving conditions
of life for the people by providing new canals to provide good water supply and transportation facilities,
laying out parks and gardens, regulating commercial
dealings, affording protection to all classes of the community. With the extension of political power, commercial intercourse with distant lands also expanded,
and the priestly organization kept pace with the development of the military strength.

Ashurbanapal, though perhaps not the greatest of
Assyrian rulers, becomes the typical *grand monarque,*

who, in addition to his campaigns organized on so large a scale, is the promoter of art and patron of learning. Nineveh, which from the time of Tiglathpileser IV on is selected as the capital, reaches the height of its splendor under the Sargonic dynasty. Its temples and palaces are worthy of the pre-eminent position acquired by Assyria as the mistress of the nearer Orient. Ashurbanapal embellishes his new palace with sculptured slabs representing scenes from his campaigns, engaging for this purpose the services of the best artists, and, following the initiative of Sennacherib, brought together in his palace copies of the most important literary productions of the past which his scribes copied from the originals in the temples of the south.[79] He thus made Nineveh a cultural as well as a military and political centre, for he succeeded in really gathering together a collection of tablets that merits the term royal, embracing as it did, every branch of the literary activity of Babylonia during the long period of her existence, together with the additions to native literature made by Assyria.

XXI

The death of Ashurbanapal was the signal for the final uprising of Babylonia, and in 625 B.C., Nebopolassar, of humble birth and who came from the "sea land" in the extreme south which had always been the centre of political fermentation, became the independent king of Babylonia, after having previously served as governor under Assyrian supremacy. He not only maintained himself against endeavors on the part of Assyria to overthrow him but he was able on his death, in 604 B.C., to pass over the succession to his son, Nebuchadnezzar. He founded a dynasty which lasted till close to the downfall of Babylon. Nebopolassar's reign was largely devoted to the strengthening of the

[79] Above, p. 21.

kingdom and to rebuilding and improving the capital. He also took a part in the movement which led to the fall of Nineveh, though more as a fomenter of the opposition to Assyria than as a direct participant in the final attack. Nebuchadnezzar, however, was an active warrior as well as a promoter of prosperity in his own domain. A renewed spirit of aggressiveness had entered Egypt with the accession of Necho II, who had the ambition once more to make the nearer East, especially Palestine and Syria, subservient to the Pharaohs. His success threatened the existence of Babylonia, and accordingly Nebuchadnezzar was sent by his father to an encounter with the Egyptian army at Carchemish, the old Hittite centre, which ended in a decisive victory for the Babylonians and checked the further advance of Egypt.

During the next twenty years he made himself master of Syria and Palestine, crushing the little Hebrew kingdom, which had maintained a semblance of independence despite the weight of the Assyrian yoke. Egypt came to the rescue of Judæa and of the other principalities of this district, but it was of no avail. The fall of Jerusalem, in 586 B.C., marks another turning point in the affairs of the nearer east, for it meant the renewed ascendency of Babylonia and the decline of Egyptian influence. It was no easy task, however, for Nebuchadnezzar to bring the coast towns on the shores of the Mediterranean, notably Tyre, to subjection, and so it is not until 562 B.C. that we find him ready to invade Egypt. He seems to have proceeded into the heart of the country triumphantly, but nevertheless fails actually to incorporate Egypt as a part of his own empire. But even without this he had succeeded in giving to Babylonia an extension and a power almost equal to that of Assyria in her most glorious days.

Nebuchadnezzar II followed the example of the Assyrian monarchs in adding to the glory of his reign by extensive building operations. The city of Babylon was the primary object of his concern, and the boast recorded in the Book of Daniel,[80] "Is not this the great Babylon that I have built?" correctly associates the name of Nebuchadnezzar with the new Babylon that arose out of the ashes of the destroyed one.[81] Nebuchadnezzar did not, however, confine his interest to the capital city. The temples at Borsippa, Sippar, Larsa, Uruk, Ur and Dilbat were restored and beautified by him during the course of his reign. When Nebuchadnezzar died, in 561 B.C., he left to his son, Amêl-Marduk ("man of the god Marduk"), a legacy which only a strong monarch could maintain intact. The son did not possess this quality and after a reign of only a year fell a victim to a conspiracy against his life, fomented by his brother-in-law Neriglissar. This act marked the beginning of the decline of the neo-Babylonian empire, though before the end came we find a usurper, Nabonnedos, who maintained himself for a period of sixteen years, from 555 to 539 B.C. Internal dissensions hastened the end, so that when Cyrus the Mede marched against Babylon he was hailed by the priestly party, who were dissatisfied with Nabonnedos' policy, as a deliverer come to restore the glory and dignity of the god Marduk. So quietly was the transfer of the control of the Euphrates Valley made to the old enemy to the east, that probably the people hardly felt that an epoch in the world's history had come to an end.

Cyrus himself adopted a conciliatory policy towards the conquered land. His desire was to leave conditions undisturbed, and accordingly we find him and his successors maintaining the cult of the Babylonian gods in Babylon, Borsippa and in the other centres. Even the introduction of Zoroastrianism (or Zarathustrianism) as the official religion of Persia in the days of Darius I towards the end of the sixth century did not materially change conditions in Babylonia, except possibly in giv-

[80] Chap. 4, 27.

[81] See above p. 55, for the excavation of this new city of Babylon.

ing a new impetus to the movement to look upon Marduk as the god who embodied the attributes of all the other gods—a kind of Babylonian counterpart to Ahura-Mazda. On the other hand, the presence of a religion of so spiritualized a character as Zoroastrianism acted as a disintegrating factor in leading to the decline of faith in the gods of Babylonia. Both the religion and the culture of the Euphrates Valley had fulfilled their purpose. The time was ripe for the appearance of new forces in the world—first Persia and then, two centuries after Cyrus, Greece. Alexander's entrance into Babylonia in 331 B.C., where by a curious freak of historical chance he dies in the very palace which Nebuchadnezzar had erected for himself, marks another epoch in the world's history. Even after Alexander, the religious and social life of Babylonia goes on unchanged to outward appearances, but the contact with Greek civilization destroyed what little vitality had survived the impetus of the new force represented by Persia and Zoroastrianism. Up to within a few decades of the Christian era, the Babylonian language and script continued in use, but Greek ideas and Greek usages had made their way not only into the government of the country but also into the life of the people.

If, in a final summing up, the question be asked, What was the legacy which Babylonia and Assyria left to the world after an existence of more than three millenniums, the answer would be, that through the spread of dominion the culture of the Euphrates Valley made its way throughout the greater part of the ancient world, leaving its impress in military organization, in the government of people, in commercial usages, in the spread of certain popular rites such as the various forms of divination, in medical practises and in observation of the movements of heavenly bodies—albeit that medicine continued to be dependent upon the belief in demons as the source of physical ills, and astronomy remained in the service of astrology

—and lastly in a certain attitude towards life which it is difficult to define in words, but of which it may be said that, while it lays an undue emphasis on might, is yet not without an appreciation of the deeper yearnings of humanity for the ultimate triumph of what is right.

The most unfortunate blot on the escutcheon of Assyria more especially is the craving for power, the ambition to extend her rule beyond the natural boundaries, and which affected Babylonia as well though not to the same degree. Alexander, Cæsar and Napoleon are the natural successors of the Babylonian rulers who first laid claim to being the "king of the four regions." War for conquest made both Assyria and Babylonia cruel and remorseless, as it proved to be the undoing of Rome.

CHAPTER IV

THE GODS OF BABYLONIA AND ASSYRIA

I

THE hybrid character of the Babylonian-Assyrian civilization, the result, as we have seen, of the commingling of a non-Semitic or Sumerian element with the Semitic or Akkadian contingent, is reflected in the religion which in the formation of the pantheon, in the doctrines and in the cult is the outcome of the combination of these same two factors. To be sure, the mixture of the two factors is so complete that it is no longer possible to specify the features contributed by each, except along very general lines. This is particularly the case in the conceptions formed of the gods, for both those of Sumerian origin and those that may with more or less probability be regarded as Semitic in character take on the color demanded by the unfolding of social and political life. We know, for example, that a prominent deity in the earliest period, known as Enlil, and who indeed remained for a long time the head of the pantheon, was brought to the Euphrates Valley by the Sumerians. All indications point to his having been conceived by the Sumerians as a grim power who manifests himself in the storm and whose voice is heard in the thunder. As such his seat was placed on the top of the mountains, whence the storms sweep down. Such a deity belongs to a people whose rugged character would be formed by the mountainous region in which they dwelled. The Sumerians became agriculturists as the Akkadians had been, and they also engaged in the more peaceful pursuits incident to growing commercial activity. Corresponding to this transformation, Enlil became also an agricultural deity,

187

who was appealed to as the power able to bring about the fertility of the fields and the success of the crops. Now, agricultural deities are either conceived as personifications of the power residing in the sun as the chief factor involved in vegetation, or as the personification of the earth pictured as the female element in whose womb the seed ripens and in time brings forth fruit. Enlil, therefore, while not losing the fierce traits belonging to him as a mountain god whose element is the storm, absorbs the attributes of a solar deity, while his consort, Ninlil,[1] becomes the mother goddess who nurtures the seed and spreads blessings among mankind. Attempts have been made by various scholars to distinguish in the case of religious doctrines between Sumerian and Akkadian nuances, but without much success.

Naturally, if we were in a position to trace the development of religious thought and practice in Babylonia and Assyria, we could differentiate more sharply between the Sumerian and the Akkadian elements. The material, however, at our disposal, though ample for obtaining a knowledge of details regarding the pantheon, the beliefs and the chief cults, is quite insufficient for tracing the history of the religion itself, except in general outlines. We can distinctly see the Sumerian conquerors imposing the names of their deities on the country, just as they imposed their language and script. As the superior cultural element, Sumerian beliefs predominate in the earliest periods, and the cult is similarly in its chief aspects to be regarded as Sumerian, while the earliest religious literature, including the form given to the popular myths, is entirely in Sumerian. And yet we must not be misled by these external features to set aside entirely the participation of the Akkadians in the unfolding of religious belief and practice. There are traces of

---

[1] Nin designating "lady," as En is "lord."

PLATE XXVII

TERRA-COTTA VOTIVE IMAGES OF THE GOD ENLIL AND OF HIS CONSORT NINLIL (NIPPUR)

Semitic influences in the oldest votive inscriptions of Sumerian rulers. Semitic words make their way into the Sumerian language.

Corresponding to these early Semitic influences, we find the Sumerians representing their gods generally with beards, after the fashion of the Semites, while they portray themselves as clean-shaven—a further indication that the Sumerians identified the deities whose worship they brought with them, with such as already formed the object of a cult marked by crude images of the deities to whom appeals were directed. Similarly, the characteristic Sumerian plain or flounced skirt, falling from the waist, gives way to a kind of plaid draped around the body from the left shoulder down, with or without a slit in the front, which appears to have been the Akkadian form of dress.[2] We are therefore justified in concluding that the Sumerians, thus assimilating even in external traits their gods with those which they already found in the country, also incorporated religious practices of the Akkadians into their cult; they would naturally do this in order to ensure the good-will and favor of the indigenous gods whom they identified with their own.

In this way we can account for the striking fact that in the long course of the Babylonian-Assyrian religion, running parallel to the history that extends over several millenniums, there is no sudden break, but, on the contrary, a continuous line of development. The gods worshipped in the latest period of Babylonian history are practically the same as those found in the

---

[2] See on this whole subject Eduard Meyer's important monograph, *Sumerier und Semiten in Babylonien* (Berlin, 1906), whose general conclusions seem to me to be definitely established, though in matters of detail there is room for differences of opinion. So, *e.g.*, the two kinds of plaids found on early monuments are not so distinct as to justify us in regarding one variety as Sumerian and the other as Akkadian. Both represent, as I believe, the "Semitic" fashion of the country, as against the plain or flounced skirt.

earlier stages. The relationship of these deities to one another changes with the vicissitudes of political transformations that the country undergoes. These vicissitudes also carry in their wake the absorption on the part of certain deities of attributes belonging to others. Semitic designations replace in some cases, though by no means in all, the Sumerian forms, but the chief personages of the Babylonian pantheon in the latest period can all be traced back to the old Babylonian epoch. The change of political control from the Sumerians to the Akkadians, of such fundamental significance in the history of Babylonia, leaves the religion practically unchanged, except for the rise of the local god of Babylon, Marduk, to the head of the pantheon by virtue of the pre-eminent position acquired by Babylon as the political centre of the government, while the subsequent rise of Assyria to supremacy similarly carries with it no momentous changes in the pantheon or in the cult, beyond the rise of the god Ashur, originally a solar deity and the local patron of the city of Ashur, the early capital of Assyria, to the headship of the pantheon as finally constituted in the north.

II

Bearing in mind this general aspect presented by the religion of Babylonia and Assyria, we may proceed to a consideration of the chief deities which we encounter in the pantheon. These deities are all, at least originally, personifications of nature—an indication that among the Sumerians as among the Akkadians the basis of worship was an animistic conception of nature, as we find it among all peoples at a certain stage of culture, and which involves as a primary supposition the identification of all forms and manifestations of life in nature with that of which we are conscious in ourselves. Life is power, according to this view, and *vice versa* where there is a manifestation of power, there must be life behind it. Moon and sun are two most obvious manifestations, active and powerful, moving from place to place, both spreading light, and the sun in addition to light also warmth. Behind the manifestation, therefore, of these two powers there was life, and the same conclusion was drawn with respect to trees and fields, renewing their life with uninterrupted regularity yearly after a period of steady decay and apparent death. Storms and rains to the accompaniment of thunder and lightning were by a similar logic ascribed to the activity of powers having the essential quality of life, and lastly there was life in the running waters and the bubbling springs and even in rocks and stones, which by their peculiar and often fantastic formations suggested a petrification of objects that once possessed activity. As for the animal world around man, the activity put forth by the largest and the smallest species and one in so many respects of the same character as his own—running, feeding, struggling, attacking, growing, languishing—forced on him the conclusion that the life within them was identical with that which conditioned his being. The gods worshipped by a people in this stage of culture are thus merely personifications of powers of nature —the sun, the moon, the power manifesting itself in the storm, in trees and fields, in the waters and in stones, while the form given by fancy to these powers may either be human or animal, or under certain conditions a combination of the two.

Naturally, the material at our disposal for the study of the religion of Babylonia and Assyria being of a literary character belongs to an age that has long left behind it the purely animistic conceptions and has advanced to more abstract views of the relationship of man to the powers around him. The growth of village communities living under agricultural conditions leads to the association of a particular deity as the special patron and protector of the community, though we must not fall into the error of supposing that such a specific association excludes the worship of other deities. The importance of the sun for an agricultural community, since upon his favor the blessings of the fields depend, leads in many instances to the choice of the sun-god as the special deity of a place, though a cognate association of ideas, with the earth pictured as the gracious and fruit-bearing female element, might result elsewhere in making the great mother goddess the patron of some centre. Again, the presence of a large body of water flowing past some agricultural settlement would bring about a close affiliation with the life-spirit of the watery element, personified like the sun and like the earth as a divine power. To a people in the nomadic stage the moon as the measurer of time and as the guide for wanderings by night is of more significance than the sun, and it may happen that, by force of tradition, in some centres the moon-god will be chosen as the patron saint. Be this as it may, we find in the earliest period to which our material leads us back, sun-gods, the earth-goddess, water deities and moon-gods closely bound up with the various centres of Sumerian and Akkadian settlements in the Euphrates Valley. The lists of deities drawn up by the priests show us a bewildering array of local deities, and in connection with each deity we must perforce assume a local cult. Many of these local gods or goddesses play a minor part in the history of Babylonia so far as known to us, and still more of them no part at all, so that they are little more than names for us. In many cases we cannot even tell whether the deities concealed behind the strange-sounding Sumerian appellations are personifications of the sun or of the earth-goddess, of the moon or of the watery element. Only in the case of those local cults which, because of the political role played by the respective centres, come within the historical horizon are we in a position to specify the attributes assigned to them. When, in addition to votive inscriptions in their honor, we have hymns and prayers addressed to them, the details of the conceptions formed of them are clearly revealed. In this way we obtain a stately array of the main figures of the old Babylonian pantheon—Enlil, Ninib, Ningirsu, Nergal, Anu, Ea, Shamash, Sin, Adad, Marduk, Nabu and their consorts, and of the chief goddess, Nanâ or Ishtar.

III

In the preceding chapter we pointed out that the oldest historical and literary documents reveal a varying number of little states or principalities in the Euphrates Valley, grouped around some centre, with now one of these centres, now another, exercising a measure of control over a larger section. This political picture is complemented on the religious side by the corresponding growth of the local deity to a position commensurate in proportion to the political control acquired by the centre in question; and as the local deity extends his sway, he is endowed with attributes that are quite independent of the power of nature which he originally personified. The tendency also becomes pronounced for the deity associated with a powerful centre not only to be given the attributes of other local deities but actually to absorb minor deities, so that the names of the latter become designations of the more powerful one. The conquest of a district carried with it the conquest of its gods, and in case the latter are not entirely absorbed, they are placed in a dependent position, as children, servants or officials of the triumphant god. In this way, through the close interrelations between the states of the Euphrates Valley—usually hostile in character and constantly shifting—there arises a pantheon which involves a selection out of the large number of once existing local deities, prompted by the rise to prominence of a limited number of centres. Naturally, in the development of

13

religious doctrines and in the unfolding of religious organization other factors besides the political one enter into consideration, so that the parallel between the shifting political panorama and the relationship of the gods of the various centres to one another is not complete. The latter relationship, when once it becomes definite, is not changed by every turn in political affairs but only through transformations of a large character; and even then gods whose position in the pantheon is fixed by tradition are not seriously affected by the vicissitudes of the centres to which they originally belonged; they survive the decline and even the complete eclipse of these centres. The religious life of a people is always more enduring than its political fortunes. The organization of a pantheon ensures for those gods fortunate enough to find a place therein a permanency, both theoretical and practical, which is often in contrast to the political history of the centres in which their worship arose. The god Enlil, to whom we had occasion to refer several times, is an illustration in point. Through circumstances which we are no longer able to follow, the city of Nippur became the seat of the cult of Enlil. Nippur became so thoroughly identified with Enlil that the name of the city was written by a series of signs designating it as the "place of Enlil." A storm-god, partaking of the aggressive character of his worshippers, Enlil is naturally pictured as a mighty warrior who leads his subjects to victory. He is present in the midst of the fray. To him as the god of war the victories are ascribed and paeans are sung in his honor in his temple at Nippur, which in view of his original seat is appropriately known as E-kur, "the mountain house."

An invocation that occurs frequently in a series of lamentation songs,[3] bewailing catastrophes that have

---

[3] See Langdon, *Sumerian and Babylonian Psalms*, pp. 90, 106, *seq.*, 114, 126, etc.

swept over the land, portrays the strength ascribed to him:

> "Lord of lands,
> Lord of the true word,
> Enlil, father of Sumer,
> Shepherd of the dark-headed people,[4]
> Seeing through his own power,
> Strong guide of (his) people,
> Causing multitudes to dwell together."

The original personification of Enlil as the mighty, onrushing storm whose voice is heard in the roar of the thunder leads to an elaborate symbolism of the "word" of the deity, which becomes a synonym of his power. In many variations this "word" of the storm-god is celebrated.[5]

> "The word which rages in the heavens above,
> The word which causes the earth below to quake,
> The word which strikes terror among the Anunnaki.[6]
> Beyond the seer, beyond the diviner,
> An onrushing storm which none can oppose,
> Raging in the heavens above, causing the earth below to quake,
> Tearing mother from daughter like a burû-reed.
> It overwhelms the marshes in full verdure,
> It overflows the harvest in season,
> A flood tearing away the dams,
> It uproots the huge *mesu*-trees,
> Reducing all things to submission."

Such is Enlil who, as the chief god of Nippur, becomes the head of the pantheon with the Sumerian conquest of the country and who retains this position long after Nippur has ceased to be the political centre. The cult of Enlil, in fact, lends to his patron city a significance far outreaching its political prestige even

[4] *I.e.*, the Sumerians.

[5] *E.g.*, Reisner, *Sumerisch-Babylonische Hymnen*, No. vii, rev. 13–25.

[6] A collective name for a minor group of deities. Even the gods fear the word of Enlil.

in the heyday of its glory. As a religious centre, Nippur becomes a sacred city, not unlike that of centres of pilgrimage in our own days like Jerusalem, Benares, Mecca and Rome. The sanctity of Nippur survived the downfall of both Babylonia and Assyria, and the sacred quarter of the city in which the temple stood was converted into a burial place acquiring sanctification by its time-honored associations to which even Jews and Christians manifested their attachment down to the seventh century of our era.[7]

The position of the god as the head of the pantheon entailed as a natural consequence the grouping of the other chief deities and of many minor deities about him. Smaller temples and shrines were erected for these deities, forming as it were the court of Enlil, around the chief sanctuary. In the extracts from religious compositions above given, he is regarded also as the power which brings forth vegetation. The storm god has become a solar deity. The control of the watery element is likewise assigned to him so that he becomes a water deity as well. The tendency grew to associate with Enlil as many gods as possible, with the implication that the latter derived their powers from this association. The gods stand in dread of him, precisely as do his subjects. He is the god of all lands, controlling gods and men alike.

IV

There are good reasons for believing that a deity whose name is provisionally read as Ninib, but the real pronunciation of which was probably Enmasht,[8] was

---

[7] See Montgomery, *Aramaic Incantation Texts from Nippur* (Philadelphia, 1913).

[8] See Clay, *Amurru*, p. 197. The names of the gods (as to a large extent proper names in general) being written in ideographic form, we cannot in all cases be sure of the exact pronunciation, particularly when the names are Akkadian and merely written in their Sumerian form.

an earlier patron deity of Nippur who was forced to yield his position to the all-conquering Enlil. If, as has been made probable,[9] this deity was of Amoritic origin, whose cult was brought to Babylonia by Semites coming from the northwest, we would have a further proof for the thesis which assumes that the Semitic settlers preceded the Sumerians in the Euphrates Valley. The secondary position of Ninib after the advent of Enlil is indicated by the title "son of Enlil" or "offspring of E-kur,"[10] almost invariably attached to his name in invocations. This relationship of father and son is merely the formula to find a place for two deities associated with the same centre, or to indicate a control of one centre by the other, just as the designation of one deity as the servant of another or as holding some official rank in the service of a god is the manner in which Babylonian priests expressed, in the case of two gods representing originally the same natural power, the supremacy of the one over the other. Ninib in contrast to Enlil is a solar deity, who protects the fields, causes the verdure to grow and brings prosperity and the blessings of rich crops to the population. It is from Ninib that Enlil takes over the milder attributes of an agricultural deity, a *Baal* or "lord" of the fields, but in return Ninib, adopted by the Sumerians, becomes like his father, a war-god, armed for the fray and whose presence is felt in the thick of battle. Indeed, so prominently is this trait emphasized, especially in the votive and historical inscriptions of both Babylonian and Assyrian rulers, that it overshadows

---

[9] Clay, *ib.*, p. 121. If the god Enmasht is of Semitic origin, then we must assume that the Sumerian element En, meaning "lord," was attached to the name by the Sumerians to whom also the method of writing the name as Nin-ib must be due. The problem is an exceedingly complicated one and cannot be discussed here. "Amorite," it should be added, is a general designation for northwestern Syria.

[10] The name of Enlil's temple is often used for the god himself.

the original solar and beneficent character of Ninib.
One of these hymns, shading off into an incantation
for the exorcising of a demon of disease, begins:[11]

"O, Ninib, mighty god, warrior, ruler of the Anunnaki, controller
    of the Igigi,[12]
Judge of all things, who shuts off the door of darkness, who dis-
    sipates the obscurity,[13]
Who renders decisions for mankind in their settlements,
Resplendent lord, bestowing power on the land through his decision,
Who seizes the demon Ti'u [14] and drives him back to his place.
Merciful one, granting life, bringing the dead to life,
Who controls right and justice, destroying evil(?),
Whose active weapon destroys all enemies."

The solar character of Ninib is clearly revealed in
the power ascribed to him of dissipating darkness, as
well as in epithets emphasizing his brilliancy. In the
course of the hymn he is expressly described as a
"burning fire," with a direct allusion to the glow of
the sun's rays. The sun-gods, moreover, are always
associated in the religious literature of Babylonia and
Assyria with justice and the punishment of the evil-
doers. His enemies are the evil-doers, the law breakers
who are brought to justice and punished in accord with
the righteous decrees that are traced back to him. It
is Ninib, the sun-god, who is celebrated as the one who
renders decisions, who dispenses justice to all mankind,
who overthrows evil and scatters the enemies who are
identified with evil-doers. Even as a warrior, Ninib
does not cast off his role as a judge. His weapon is
raised in order to smite evil. The cause of his subjects
is a just one, and therefore he accords them his powerful aid. His temple in Nippur, known as E-shu-me-du,
occupies a rank only second to E-kur itself; and as a

---

[11] See Jensen, *Kosmologie der Babylonier*, pp. 470–472.

  [12] A collective name, like Anunnaki, for a group of minor deities.

  [13] *Sc.* "of the night."

   [14] A demon of disease, the cause of troubles having their seat in
the head.

trace of the former's independent position occupied by Ninib, the New Year's day continued, even after Enlil had become the head of the pantheon, to be celebrated as the festival of Ninib when gifts were offered to him and his consort Gula, and ceremonies enacted in his temple, symbolical of his marriage at the beginning of a new year. His festival was also the occasion when the fates of individuals for the coming year were decided by him. The beneficent character of Ninib crops out also in assigning to him and his consort the power of healing, to which references are likewise made in the quoted hymn. Ninib saves his subjects from the clutches of the demons of disease. It is in this sense that he is spoken of as bringing those near death back to life. The other more aggressive aspect leads to making Ninib the deity who presides over the chase of wild animals—a favorite sport of the Assyrian kings. The chase is a species of warfare and it seemed natural, therefore, to dedicate the spoils of the chase to Ninib and to pour out libations to him over the dead bodies of lions and wild bulls [15] laid low by royal hunters.

V

The pre-eminence enjoyed at one time by Ninib over other solar deities associated with other centres is shown by the identification of such deities with him. The names borne by other solar deities become epithets of Ninib. Prominent among these is Ningirsu, the chief deity of a centre, Lagash, in southern Babylonia, where, it will be recalled,[16] extensive excavations have been carried on. The name signifies "lord of Girsu" —Girsu being the name of a section or quarter of Lagash, presumably the one in which the temple of the god stood. For a long period Lagash played an important role in the early political history of Babylonia;

---

[15] See Plate LV in Chapter VII.
[16] See above, p. 39, *seq.*

its rulers extended their sway over a considerable portion of southern Babylonia, but eventually they were reduced to a secondary position, and it must have been at this time that Ningirsu was practically identified with Ninib, becoming, as it were, merely a manifestation of the great solar deity of Nippur. Ningirsu's consort, Bau, similarly becomes synonymous with Gula, the consort of Ninib. Precisely like Ninib, Ningirsu is commonly designated as a warrior, the son of Enlil, armed with powerful weapons that create havoc among the enemies of his subjects. On monuments found at Lagash he is thus represented, notably on a remarkable stele,[17] graphically illustrating a severe conflict between Lagash and Umma—which ended in the triumph of Eannatum (c. 2920 B.C.).[18] The victory, however, is due to the intervention of Ningirsu, who is portrayed in majestic size, holding the standard of Lagash in one hand, while in the other he has a huge net in which the enemy is held captive. The temple of Ningirsu at Lagash, known as E-ninnu ("house of fifty"), was filled with votive offerings of all kinds dedicated by rulers or high officials to Ningirsu. Like Ninib, Ningirsu also manifests a beneficent aspect as the god of vegetation.

The fate of Ningirsu in being absorbed by Ninib also overtakes another solar deity, Zamama, the patron of Kish, which was a centre that at one time exercised a wide sway.[19] Like Ningirsu, Zamama becomes little more than a designation of Ninib, and as a war-god is likewise addressed as the "son of Enlil"; and the same applies to the solar deity of Dilbat, Urash, whose name becomes an epithet of Ninib. The force of the tradition acquired by Nippur seems to have maintained the cult of Ninib even after Shamash of Sippar becomes the sun-god *par excellence*. Ninib's cult is transferred

---

[17] See Plate XLVII.
[18] See above, p. 128.
[19] Above, p. 126, *seq.*

to Assyria. A temple to him is erected by Ashurnasir-pal III (883–859 B.C.) in Calah, for a time the capital of Assyria.[20] A statue of the god of colossal dimensions is placed in the sacred niche, and provision made for the maintenance of the cult and for the celebration of the time-honored festival of Ninib and Gula. The kings of Assyria are fond of invoking Ninib among the powers which grant victory to the Assyrian armies, and we have seen the role which Ninib plays in Assyria as the god of the chase. Despite this, however, some of his prestige is lost in the course of time through the pre-eminence acquired by the sun-god of Sippar, whose Sumerian name is Babbar but who is more commonly known by the Akkadian designation Shamash, the common term in all the Semitic languages for the sun.

VI

The great antiquity of Sippar is vouched for by the results of excavations conducted on the site,[21] but it is still an open question whether another seat of Shamash worship at Larsa is not even older. We must, at all events, assume some relationship between the two centres, for in both places the names given to the patron deity and to his temple, E-Babbar ("resplendent house"), are identical. It is a direct consequence of the Semitic control of Babylonia which becomes pronounced in the days of Sargon and Narâm-sin [22] that Shamash acquires his pre-eminent position as the sun-god *par excellence,* for Sippar is in close proximity to Agade and shared with the latter the prestige of being the capital of the kingdom that rose to supremacy under Sargon. Shamash is represented on monuments and on numerous seal-cylinders [23] as a majestic figure

---

[20] So in the days of his successor Shelmaneser III.

[21] Above, p. 37, *seq.*

[22] Above, p. 135, *seq.*

[23] See Plate LXXV, Fig. 3, and Plate LXXVII, Fig. 1, at the close of Chapter VII.

seated on a throne, or stepping over a mountain, or passing through gates to symbolize the rise of the great
orb of light, or sailing in a boat across the heavens.
Frequently also rays are depicted as issuing from his
shoulders. As the god of light, he is the general object
of adoration, and the specific association with Larsa or
Sippar does not stand in the way of his becoming a
deity whose worship extends throughout Babylonia and
passes northward into Assyria. In all large centres
temples or shrines to Shamash were erected. Babylonian and Assyrian rulers from the oldest to the
latest period include Shamash in the invocations to the
chief gods of the pantheon at the beginning of votive
or historical inscriptions. So, to give an example of
the early period, Lugalzaggizi, the king of Uruk (c.
2750 B.C.), designates himself in the introduction to
one of his inscriptions [24] as

"The great *patesi* [25] of Enlil, endowed with understanding by
Ea,[26] whose name was called [27] by Babbar (*i.e.*, Shamash), the chief
minister of Sin,[28] the lieutenant of Babbar, the provider for Innina,
the child of Nisaba,[29] nourished with the milk of Ninkharsag,[30]
the servant of Mes,[31] the priest of Uruk."

At the other end of Babylonian history we find the last
king of Babylon, Nabonnedos (555–539 B.C.), particularly devoted to the service of Shamash, enlarging and
restoring his temples in Sippar, Larsa and Babylon,

---

[24] Hilprecht, *Old Babylonian Inscriptions*, I, 2, No. 87, Col. I,
15–30.

[25] A sacerdotal office which, however, also included secular
functions.

[26] Written En-ki. See below, p. 210, *seq.*

[27] *I.e.*, called to his high station.

[28] The moon-god, written En-zu. See below, p. 222.

[29] A goddess presiding over vegetation.

[30] "The lady of the mountain," a title of the consort of Enlil.

[31] An otherwise unknown deity.

and invoking his aid almost to the exclusion of other gods in the political crisis which ended in the advent of Cyrus and in the fall of the neo-Babylonian empire.[32]

The hymns in honor of Shamash, of which we have a large number, belong to the finest specimens of Babylonian and Assyrian literature, celebrating the god as the benefactor of mankind who sheds his light and his warmth in all directions, whose rays ripen the produce of the fields, who is the source of prosperity and of all manner of blessings, who spreads justice, who rewards the virtuous and punishes the wicked and who is also the judge who protects his people, and as a mighty warrior accomplishes the overthrow of the enemy on the field of battle.

A hymn which was evidently composed as a greeting to Shamash as he appears on the horizon begins as follows:[33]

"O lord, illuminator of the darkness, opening the face (of heaven?),
Merciful god, raising the humble, protecting the weak;
For thy light the great gods wait,
All the Anunnaki look for thy appearance,
All tongues [34] dost thou direct as a single being.[35]
With raised heads they look expectantly towards the sunlight;
Thou art the light for the remotest bounds of heaven,
The banner for the wide earth art thou;
All mankind look upon thee with joy."

Briefly but effectively the expectant moments just before sunrise are described, the gods joining with mankind in waiting anxiously for the appearance of the great orb; and when the tension is released and the light spreads to all sides, all creation is represented

---

[32] See above, p. 184.
[33] Rawlinson IV,[2] Pl. 19, Nr. 2.
[34] *I.e.*, all peoples.
[35] The sun guides all humanity as one directs a single individual.

as breaking out into joy. No less impressive is the description and praise of the sun at sunset: [36]

"O, Shamash, on thy entrance into the heavens,
  May the resplendent bolts of heaven greet thee,
  May the gates of heaven bless thee,
  May Meshara,[37] thy beloved messenger, direct thee!
  Over E-Babbar, the seat of thy rule, let thy supremacy shine,
  May Â, thy beloved consort, step joyfully before thee,
  May thy heart be appeased,[38]
  May the table of thy divinity be spread,[39]
  O, Shamash, powerful warrior, be thou glorified!
  O lord of E-Babbar, pass on, thy course be rightly directed!
  Take thy way, on a firm path [40] move along!
  O Shamash, judge of the world, giver of all decisions art thou."

We find in all ancient religions a certain fear associated with moments of transition, whether it be the transition of one season of the year to another, or the transition of one phase of the moon to the succeeding one, or the transition of the child from the womb into the light. In accord with this the appearance of the new moon and the time of full moon are fraught with special significance, and similarly in the case of the sun, the moment of sunrise and that of sunset. Hence the hope expressed in the hymn that the sun may safely enter into the midst of the heavens and be properly directed to pursue the correct path, so as to be certain to make its appearance in the morning at the expected time. If the sun should by any chance lose its way, disaster would follow. Emphasis is laid on the guidance afforded by Shamash. It is he who directs mankind into the right path, just as the sun pursues the right road in moving across the heavens. The right

---

[36] Abel-Winckler, *Keilschriftexte zum Gebrauch bei Vorlesungen* (Berlin, 1890), pp. 59–60.

[37] "Righteousness"—personified as an attendant of Shamash.

[38] *I.e.*, may Shamash show himself gracious and not be angry.

[39] May rich offerings be placed before Shamash.

[40] The "firm path" along which the sun moves is the ecliptic.

path for mankind is justice, and it is through Shamash as the supreme judge that the cause of the righteous is protected and hidden enemies brought to light.

In the case of a religion unfolding and developing hand in hand with advancing culture, and following more or less closely the political vicissitudes of the country, we must be prepared for the theoretical elaboration of the doctrinal aspects of the current beliefs, by the side of a steady enlargement in the organization of the cult and the priesthood in connection with the chief deities of the pantheon. The result of such a process continued for many centuries is to lead to attempts at a systematization of the currents and counter-currents of popular beliefs. It is part of the system devised by priestly activity to find a place in the pantheon for deities that personify the same power of nature. The god Ninib, we have seen, absorbed the roles of the other local sun-gods in the earlier Babylonian period, but was obliged to yield his prerogatives to a still greater solar deity, Shamash. Such, however, was the force of tradition that Ninib could not be entirely set aside in favor of Shamash. A place had therefore to be found for Ninib in the pantheon, and this was done by differentiating between the phases of the sun according to the seasons of the year. The sun in a sub-tropical climate like the Euphrates Valley with only two seasons, a rainy one beginning in the fall and lasting till the spring, and a dry one during the summer months, presents two aspects, as a beneficent and revivifying force in the spring, driving away the rains and the storms and bringing new life in the fields after the apparent extinction of all vitality during the winter months, and as a raging and destructive one during the torrid months when its fierce rays scorch the earth, and the intense heat brings suffering, sickness and often death. Shamash was the sun as a whole, while Ninib became in the theological system of the priests the sun of the springtime, and by a natural association also the morning sun. The sun as a destructive and hostile force was symbolized by another solar deity, Nergal, who, originally the local deity of an important centre in southern Babylonia, Cuthah, became the sun of the midsummer season and the sun of the noon-time. The cult of Nergal takes us back again to the old Babylonian period when Cuthah [41] was the political focus of one of the principalities in the Euphrates Valley, enjoying an independent existence and exercising sway over a considerable territory, even though the details of the history of the kingdom of Cuthah still escape us. Nergal was too prominent a solar deity to be absorbed by Ninib. His temple at Cuthah, known as E-shidlam, acquired great prominence at an early period. We find him represented by a shrine or sanctuary at Nippur within the sacred area in which E-kur stood, and when Babylon became the political and religious capital of the country, the cult of Nergal was transferred to this centre and continued in force to the end of the Babylonian monarchy. Like Ninib and Shamash, Nergal was pictured as a warrior but one of an invariably grim countenance, a god of battle, whose destructive power was directed against all mankind. True, he also leads his subjects to victory, but more commonly he deals out pestilence and death. He strikes unawares and he strikes apparently without discrimination. He is not a just judge like Shamash, but a god, filled with rage, stalking about in the heat of the day on the lookout for victims. Nergal is thus primarily the god of death. When pestilence sweeps over the land, it is ascribed to Nergal's activity. Because of this forbidding aspect, it was all the more important to raise one's appeal to him in the hope of averting his wrath. The hymns to Nergal, of which we have quite a number,[42]

---

[41] See above, p. 124, and below p. 455.

[42] See Böllenrücher, *Gebete und Hymnen an Nergal* (Leipzig, 1904).

all emphasize the severity and irresistible power of the god. He is pictured as a lion, which animal becomes his symbol. His solar character crops out in epithets that describe his brilliancy. Like Ninib, he is the son of Enlil who carries out the commands of his father, and as a god of death his presence is naturally felt also in the midst of battle. One of the hymns to him begins as follows: [43]

"Lord, strong, supreme, first-born of Nunammir,[44]
Ruler of the Anunnaki, lord of battle,
Offspring of Kutushar,[45] the great queen,
Nergal, mighty one among the gods, beloved of Ninmenna,[46]
Thou shinest on the brilliant heaven, high is thy station;
Great art thou in the realm of the dead, without a rival art thou;
By the side of Ea,[47] thy counsel is supreme in the assembly of the gods,
With Sin,[48] thou overseest all in heaven.
Enlil, thy father, entrusted to thee, the dark-headed, all living things,
The animals of the field and all swarming creation into thy hand."

The solar character of Nergal is unmistakably revealed in these lines, which also indicate the endeavor to connect the god with other leading figures of the pantheon. As the god of pestilence and death, his special realm, however, is the lower world where the dead are huddled together and which was regarded as a dark, gloomy prison with Nergal and a goddess, Allatu, as the merciless overseers to prevent the escape of any of the prisoners back to the upper world.

There is still another solar deity, originally a local patron of an ancient centre, and who retains his identity in the systematized pantheon by being advanced to the

---

[43] King, *Babylonian Magic and Sorcery*, Nr. 27.

[44] A title of Enlil, conveying the force of "hero of rulership."

[45] A goddess.

[46] "Lady of the crown"—a title of Kutushar, one of the names of the consort of Nergal.

[47] The god of humanity.

[48] The moon-god.

general control of the heavens or the upper regions.
This is Anu who is so closely associated originally with
Uruk in southern Babylonia as to leave no doubt of
his being at the start merely the patron deity of that
place. The theoretical aspect of the Babylonian religion to which attention has been directed [49] is illustrated by the position accorded to Anu. He becomes
the god of heaven, just as Enlil is placed in control
of the earth and the atmosphere above it, and a third
deity, Ea, originally the god of the Persian Gulf, becomes the power in control of the watery element in
general.

This threefold division of the universe—heaven,
earth and water—with the assignment of one deity to
each division is clearly the work of the priestly schools
attached to the Babylonian temples. It has an academic flavor. It is only through a phase of speculation
which has all the earmarks of the school that the notion
arises of the heavens as a distinct section of the universe with some god in general control, just as further
speculation of this character leads to the predication of
the other divisions of the universe—the earth with the
atmosphere above it and the watery expanse; and since
even the advanced speculation unfolded in the schools
adopts the language and metaphors of the animistic
view of all nature, the threefold division of the universe leads to assigning to each one a god in control,
Anu for the heavens, Enlil for the earth with the surrounding atmosphere, and Ea for the waters. As the
god of heaven, Anu becomes the "king of the gods"
and their "father." The triad Anu, Enlil and Ea are
invoked at the beginning of votive and historical inscriptions in a manner which shows that the original
and specific character of these deities has been entirely
lost sight of. Enlil was chosen as the second figure of
the triad because he was the most prominent of the
gods whose power was manifested on the earth and in

[49] Above, p. 205.

the atmosphere above it, while the choice of Ea as the third member was a similar logical process because he was in control of the greatest body of water known to the Babylonians. As the god of the Persian Gulf, Ea was naturally selected as the personification of the watery element in general.

The conception of Anu as the king and father of all the gods furthermore reflects the period when the seat of the gods was projected on the heavens. Such a view is closely entwined with astrological notions, and rests upon the theory which identifies planets and stars with the gods of the pantheon and quite independent of their original character places the seats of all the gods, the one who presides over the divisions of the drawn up by Babylonian and, later, by Assyrian priests are to a large extent compiled in the interest of the astrological system devised in the schools, and which necessitated designations for a large and ever increasing number of stars. It is therefore in an astrological sense that Anu is viewed as the king and father of the gods, the one who presides over the division of the universe in which each one of the gods has his assigned station, and since sun and moon are also suspended in the heavens, Anu as the god of heaven is supreme also over the two great orbs of light. In the actual cult of Babylonia, Anu plays a relatively minor part. We do not find hymns and prayers addressed to him, and even in his original seat of worship, it is a goddess, Nanâ, the personification of the female element in nature, who appears to have been within the period embraced by historical documents the chief object of worship.

In an enumeration of the pantheon, however, in the old Babylonian period Anu is rarely omitted, and, instead of Nanâ, a consort, Antum, is assigned to him— a name representing merely a feminine form of the god Anu. All the gods and goddesses being children of Anu and Antum, the name of Anu is often added both

14

in votive inscriptions and in the religious literature in connection with the name of a deity. So for example, Gudea frequently adds to the name Bau, the consort of Ningirsu, that she is the "daughter of Anu" or "the chief daughter" [50], and even Enlil is designated as the son of Anu.[51] Occasionally instead of the triad, we find only Anu and Enlil enumerated as summing up the manifestation of divine power among mankind.

Ordinarily, however, the third member of the triad is included. As a matter of fact the god Ea is one of the most important as well as one of the most interesting figures in the Babylonian-Assyrian pantheon. He begins his career as the local deity of Eridu, so that he becomes the personification of the watery element in general because the Persian Gulf on or near which Eridu was situated [52] was the largest body of water known to the Babylonians, the "father" of all waters. The oldest settlements of the Euphrates Valley are those nearest to the Persian Gulf. The part that water plays in the life of mankind and in the development of human culture is quite sufficient to account for the unique position acquired by Ea in the pantheon as the protector of humanity, the friend and guide of man in his career, subject to such constant vicissitudes. He is the teacher also who instructs man in the various arts.[53] It is Ea who endows the rulers with intelligence as it is he who presides over the fine arts, instructing men in architecture, in working precious metals and stones and in all the expressions of man's intellectual activity. Thus Ea may briefly be defined as the god of civilization. The friend of mankind, it is to him that one turns in the first instance when other gods

---

[50] *E.g.*, Statue B, Col. 8, 58.

[51] By Lugalzaggisi in the inscription above (p. 202) referred to, Col. 3, 16.

[52] Owing to the steady accumulation of the soil, Abu-Shahrein, the site of Eridu, is now some sixty miles from the head of the Gulf.

[53] Cory, *Ancient Fragments*, (2d ed.) p. 22, *seq.*

PLATE XXVIII

FIG. 1, THE GOD MARDUK IN CONFLICT WITH THE MONSTER TIAMAT

FIG. 2, PROCESSION OF GODS

seem hostile. When the gods in counsel decide to bring on a destructive rain-storm, it is Ea who reveals the purpose to a favorite of his who by constructing a ship for himself and his family escapes destruction; and similarly in another myth it is Ea who tries to secure immortality for mankind, though he alas! fails to do so.

The healing qualities of springs, which man must have ascertained at an early period by experience, was no doubt a factor in making Ea a chief figure in the incantation rites for the purpose of driving out the demon supposed to be the cause of disease and bodily suffering. An elaborate exorcising ritual was developed by the priests of Eridu which continued to be down through the period of the Assyrian empire the model and prototype for all other methods of healing disease. The sick man was sprinkled with holy water, and various other rites, symbolizing the hoped for relief from the clutches of the demons or supposed to act directly on the demons, were performed in the name of Ea.

VII

Ea stands in a particularly close relation to the god who with the rise of the city of Babylon as the political centre becomes the head of the pantheon—Marduk. The latter is invariably designated as the son of Ea, and since Marduk's sanctuary at Babylon bears the same name, E-sagila ("the lofty house"), as that of Ea at Eridu, we are perhaps justified in concluding that the settlement of Babylon itself is an offshoot of Eridu. Marduk is originally a solar deity like Anu, Ninib, Shamash and Nergal. As such he may very well have been worshipped at Eridu by the side of Ea until his cult was transferred to Babylon. But however we are to explain the association of Ea with Marduk, the relationship of father and son points to a dependence of the latter upon the former, and a dependence of so decided a character that, although Marduk comes to be the lord over gods and mankind, he never ceases to acknowledge Ea's priority, even though in the religious literature the honor of Marduk is protected by representing Ea as rejoicing in the supreme position attained by his well-beloved son. So in the incantation texts, when the appeal is made to Marduk to release the sufferer from the grasp of the demons, Marduk, the dutiful son, goes to his father, Ea, and asks what can be done for the sufferer. Ea invariably replies,

> "My son, what dost thou not know that I could tell thee?
> What I know, thou also knowest." [54]

In this manner, the way is paved for the application of the Eridu ritual, but through Marduk Ea's authorship is acknowledged, and at the same time Marduk's equality with his father is indicated. Marduk owes his position in the pantheon to the union of the Euphratean states definitely brought about by Hammurapi (c. 2120 B.C.), as a consequence of which Babylon becomes the political capital of the kingdom, setting aside for all times the prerogatives formerly enjoyed by Nippur, Uruk, Eridu, Lagash, Kish, Sippar, Ur or any of the other centres of the Euphrates Valley. Even Enlil must yield some of his prestige to Marduk. Naturally, Enlil retains his position as the second member of the triad, but Enlil transfers of his own accord the headship of the pantheon to Marduk. He is represented as doing this at the close of a tale in which Marduk's triumph over a monster, Tiamat, symbolizing the primeval chaos, is described in detail.[55] All the gods assemble to celebrate Marduk's great deed. They bestow fifty glorious names upon him, the names symbolizing the attributes of Marduk, on whom, as the head of the pantheon, the qualities of

---

[54] This conversation occurs again and again in the incantation rituals, *e.g.*, *Cun. Texts*, xvi, Pl. 20, 128–138; 45, 119–148; xvii, Pl. 12, 20–31; 19, 31; 21, 118–142; 26, 48–63, etc.

[55] See below, p. 442.

all the gods and goddesses grouped around him as the courtiers gather around the royal throne are thus heaped. Enlil steps forward and bestows his name as "lord" upon Marduk. The bestowal of the name, according to the prevalent view in antiquity, carries with it the power and position of the one bearing it. The god Ea follows Enlil's example, and thus without a conflict the rule passes to Marduk.

The ritual of Nippur is carried over to a large extent to Babylon, with additions so as to adapt it to the cult of Marduk. Instead of the "word" of Enlil, that of Marduk is celebrated. The "lord of lands" is no longer Enlil but Marduk who becomes the *bêlu* or Baal *par excellence* to such a degree that Bêl becomes a common designation of a god, passing beyond the confines of Babylonia to other countries. "There is no god like Marduk" is the burden of the many hymns in honor of the god that have fortunately been preserved for us. So we read in a text found at Sippar,[56]

"Mighty lord of gods, strong Marduk,
Counsellor, beloved of Ea, of all pervading command,
Before his mighty command the great Igigi [57] bow;
(In thy?) holy chamber the Anunnaki bow before thee;
Lord of all below, merciful one, producer of fertility,
Guardian of sacrifices for the gods, founder of cities,
Guide of the sources, opener of fountains,
Lord of lands, king of heaven and earth, granting prosperity,
God without whom in the depth the fate of mankind is not determined.
Thou lookest on the habitations of the wicked and destroyest their power.
What god in heaven or earth is like to thee?
Supreme art thou over all gods;
Among the gods, thy counsel prevails;
Thou art superior to Ea, the father who produced thee."

---

[56] Scheil, *Une Saison de Fouilles à Sippar* (Cairo, 1902) pp. 97–98.

[57] A collective name, like Anunnaki, for a series of minor deities.

The hymn may well have been originally a composition in honor of Ea, composed for his cult at Eridu and then recast so as to adapt it to Marduk, with the express purpose of emphasizing the transfer of Ea's attributes to the head of the pantheon, who, although the son of Ea, becomes, as the hymn declares, superior to his father.

It is interesting to compare this hymn with one [58] in which in a similar manner descriptions belonging to Enlil as the storm-god and whose "word" is heard in the roar of the thunder are transferred to Marduk.

> "Who can escape thy gaze?
> Thy word is a great net stretching over heaven and earth;
> It encloses the sea, and the sea is stirred up,
> It encloses the marsh, and the marsh groans,
> It encloses the billows of the Euphrates.
> The word of Marduk troubles the river bed(?).
> Lord, thou art supreme, who is like unto thee?
> Marduk, among all the great gods thou art supreme."

The net is a metaphor for the storm which sweeps along in fury. The description fits a storm-god but is hardly appropriate for a solar deity, such as Marduk is. In the descriptions of Enlil's "word" of which a specimen has been given above,[59] the same picture of a great, all encompassing net is introduced. There is no reason to question that the hymn in question also represents such a modification of an old composition in honor of Enlil, intentionally made to emphasize that Marduk has usurped the place of the older head of the pantheon.

In a large proportion of the hymns to Marduk that have been preserved, these two aspects of the god—his functions derived from Ea and those transferred from Enlil—are prominently dwelled upon and indeed to such an extent as to overshadow his original role as a solar deity. Anu is also associated with Enlil and

[58] Rawlinson IV² Pl. 26, No. 4.
[59] P. 195.

Ea, in according to Marduk supremacy over the gods so that all three figures of the triad combine in doing homage to him. A particularly impressive hymn to Marduk [60] begins as follows:

"I pay homage to thy name, O Marduk, the strong one of the gods, the ruler of heaven and earth,
Glorious being, who alone is supreme,
Thou possessest the power of Anu, the power of Enlil, the power of Ea—rulership and majesty,
Thou art in control of all wisdom, perfect in strength,
Circumspect counsellor, lofty ruler, powerful and mighty,
Whose rule Anu praised as a preparation for the conflict.[61]
In heaven thou art supreme, on earth thou rulest, wise counsellor (of the gods),
Founder of all settlements, who holds the ends of the starry heavens in his grasp."

The hymn ends in a direct appeal to the god for divine grace and long life.

"I implore thee, mighty, powerful lord, may thy enangered heart be appeased, thy stirred up liver be quieted,[62]
Have mercy, let me live in fear of thee, ruler of the gods, supreme Marduk,
The splendor of Sarpanit, thy great consort, wife of En-bilulu,[63] daughter-in-law of Ea.
I will glorify, the son of Mummu [64] will I humbly glorify forever."

The humble petitioner who has felt the anger of his god is no doubt, as in most of the hymns, the king himself. Some misfortune has come over the land or

---

[60] Craig, *Assyrian-Babylonian Religious Texts*, I Pl., 29–31.

[61] An allusion to Marduk's conflict which Tiamat to which he is encouraged by Anu who declares that Marduk alone can overthrow the monster. See below p. 433 *seq.*

[62] Heart and liver are in this way very frequently combined, the heart as the seat of the intellect, and the liver as the seat of the emotions.

[63] A title of Marduk.

[64] A personification of the watery deep and here used as a designation of Ea. The son of Mummu is, therefore, Marduk. See p. 428.

over the royal house, and in a penitent spirit the king
seeks out the divine throne for forgiveness. This
attitude of the king, setting the example for the people,
is further illustrated by the prayers to Marduk which
we find in considerable number attached to royal inscriptions, particularly those of the neo-Babylonian
dynasty.

In eloquent and impassioned terms the great
Nebuchadnezzar, the son of Nebopolassar, addresses his
god upon ascending the throne of his father.[65]

"O, eternal ruler, lord of the universe, grant that the name of
the king whom thou lovest, whose name thou hast proclaimed,
flourish as may be pleasing to thee. Lead him in the right path. I
am the prince who is subservient to thee, the creature of thy hand.
Thou hast created me and thou hast entrusted the rule of mankind
to me. According to thy mercy, O lord, which thou bestowest upon
all, may thy supreme rulership be merciful. The fear of thy
divinity implant in my heart. Grant me what may seem good to
thee, for thou art the one who has granted me life."

Such prayers,[66] beautiful and simple in diction and
filled with a deep religious fervor, show us the religion
of Babylonia at its best. The spirit of humility and
reverence does not fall short of the attitude towards
Yahweh in the Psalms, and the conception of Marduk
rises to a height of spiritual aspiration which comes to
us as a surprise in a religion that remained steeped in
polytheism and that was associated with practices and
rites of a much lower order of thought.

Marduk, as the supreme god, naturally assumes the
rôle of creator of the universe, and the creation marking the beginning of the calculation of time, Marduk's
festival is coincident with the new year. This festival
which, as we have seen,[67] was celebrated at Nippur in
honor of Ninib and Gula, and at Lagash was sacred to

---

[65] Rawlinson I, Pl. 53, Col. I, 55–II, 1.

[66] For further specimens see Jastrow, *Religion Babyloniens und Assyriens*, I, pp. 400–420. and below pp. 465–469.

[67] Above, p. 199.

Ningirsu and Bau, becomes in Babylon the season dedicated to Marduk. In its developed form the New Year's festival of Babylon extended over eleven days with special rites for each day. The transition *motif* was also carried over from ancient days, as shown in the current conception which represents Marduk sitting in a sacred chamber, surrounded by the other members of the pantheon and determining the fate of individuals for the coming year. This point of view lent a sombre aspect to the New Year's festival. The statue of the god in E-sagila was carried in solemn procession to the special shrine which contained the "chamber of fates" as it was called, and at the close of the conclave of the gods was brought back to its resting place, accompanied as accorded with his dignity by the images of the other great gods.

The process involved in the absorption of the roles and attributes of other gods which we have noted in the case of Enlil, Ninib and Shamash appears to have gone to even greater lengths in the case of Marduk, who is addressed in terms which give one the impression as though he were the one and only deity. The monotheistic strain in the prayers and hymns addressed to Marduk is sometimes so pronounced that if one substitutes Yahweh or God for Marduk, they might form part of a Jewish or Christian service of to-day. A god on whom the other gods bestow fifty names [68] is well advanced on the way to become the one and only power, as the source of all the phenomena of nature.

Still, the limitations of the monotheistic tendency in Babylonia must be recognized. Not only do the other gods of the pantheon continue to receive recognition in their temples and sanctuaries scattered throughout the land, but neither Babylonians nor Assyrians ever passed beyond the point of regarding gods as personifications of powers of nature. Marduk, too, remains on this basis.

---

[68] See above, p. 212 and below, p. 443.

Just as Marduk is invariably associated with Ea as
his father, so another deity, Nabu, whose name we have
already encountered is closely attached to Marduk as
his son. Like all the other gods of Babylonia, Nabu
starts on his career as a local patron. He belongs to
the city of Borsippa, lying in such close proximity to
Babylon on the west bank of the Euphrates as to become, with the extension of Babylon, almost a suburb
of the latter. It is this close relationship between the
two cities that finds an expression in making Nabu the
son of Marduk. There are reasons, however, for believing that Borsippa rose to importance earlier than
Babylon, and that for some time Nabu was a serious
rival to Marduk. The original character of the deity
of Borsippa is still in doubt, but indications point to
his being originally a water-god—perhaps the water-
spirit in the Euphrates—and as such he would naturally become also a god of vegetation, since the fertility
of the land is dependent upon the overflow of the rivers
during the rainy season. The association of water with
knowledge and culture which, we have seen,[69] dominates
the views held in regard to Ea would account for the
chief trait of Nabu as revealed in inscriptions and in
the religious literature, to wit, his rôle as the god of
writing more particularly and then in general as the
god who gives understanding and wisdom. His symbol
is the stylus of the scribe. He is the secretary of the
gods who, at the time of the New Year's assembly of
the pantheon when the fates of individuals are determined for the coming year, records the decisions of the
gods. It is he who inspires the priests to collect the
hymns, incantations, omens and other parts of the
ritual as a guide for further ages. Secular wisdom is
also due to him. Writing is his invention communi-
cated to mankind, and Ashurbanapal in the subscripts
to the tablets of his royal library rarely fails to acknowledge the aid of Nabu and of his consort, Tashmit,

[69] Above, p. 210.

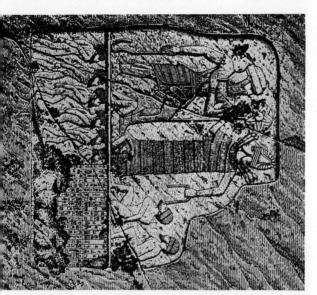

PLATE XXIX

as the ones who inspired the ruler with the idea of collecting the literary productions of the past. The close association with Marduk leads naturally to a similarity in the terms in which they are addressed, but the distinctive character of Nabu as the god of writing on whose tablets one can read the future is rarely omitted even in the prayers of late Babylonian rulers like Nebuchadnezzar, where Nabu is generally invoked only in connection with his father. A prayer of this ruler on the completion of the tower attached to Nabu's temple at Borsippa reads as follows: [70]

"Oh Nabu, legitimate son,[71] sublime messenger, triumphant, beloved of Marduk, graciously look in joy on my handiwork. Long life, numerous progeny, a firmly established throne, enduring rule, conquest of the enemy's land grant me as a gift! On thy unchangeable tablet which marks the bounds of heaven and earth, proclaim length of days for me, inscribe offspring (for me)! Before Marduk, the king of heaven and earth, the father who produced thee, make my deeds pleasing, intercede on my behalf and proclaim that Nebuchadnezzar is indeed a king who beautifies."

The tablet of Nabu is the starry expanse on which the future is written for him who can read the signs in the heavens. Nabu, however, is merely the recorder of the decision which rests with Marduk.

This close association of Nabu with Marduk finds many other expressions both in the cult and in the religious literature. Babylon and Borsippa were combined so as to form practically a single conception in the minds of priests and populace. The one could hardly be thought of without the other. In Babylon, shrines and sanctuaries to the leading members of the pantheon were grouped around the central temple, E-sagila, as was done in earlier days at Nippur,[72] where E-kur, the temple of Enlil, grew to be the designation of the sacred quarter of the city.

---

[70] Rawlinson I, Pl. 51, No. 1, Col. II, 16–31.

[71] Sc. of Marduk.

[72] Above, p. 196.

In the official correspondence it became customary to introduce in the greeting with which the letters began the names of Marduk and Nabu, and similarly in historical inscriptions the two names were constantly entwined. Indeed it would appear that at times attempts were made to play off the one god against the other. It is probably not accidental that three of the rulers of the neo-Babylonian empire [73] bear names compounded with Nabu, and it looks as though the founder of this dynasty wished to place the son on an equality with the father. Cyrus, who overthrew this empire, claims to have come to Babylon to reinstate Marduk in his full dignity. In Assyria, where Marduk was regarded as in a manner the rival of Ashur, the head of the Assyrian pantheon, we find the kings disposed to pay their homage to the son rather than to the father as the chief figure of the Babylonian pantheon. An official of one of these kings, Adad-nirari IV (810–782 B.C.), erects a statue to Nabu and inscribes on it: [74]

"O offspring, rely on Nabu. Put your trust in no other god."

Ashurbanapal, the greatest of the Assyrian kings (668–626 B.C.), is among those who pay homage to Nabu in a manner which betrays the tendency to make him more than a mere appendage to Marduk.

It is interesting to note that the cult of Nabu (as that of Marduk) survives the fall of the Babylonian empire and even the substitution of Greek governors for the Persian rule. We have a prayer of the Seleucid ruler, Antiochus Soter (281–261 B.C.), addressed to Nabu on the occasion of that ruler's restoration of Nabu's temple, E-zida, at Borsippa. The prayer, though modelled upon those of the rulers of the neo-Babylonian dynasty, is nevertheless of sufficient interest to warrant an extract here. [75]

---

[73] See above, p. 182, seq.

[74] Rawlinson I, Pl. 35, No. 2, line 12.

[75] Rawlinson V, Pl. 66, Col. I, 16–II, 29.

"O Nabu, sublime son, mighty lord of the great gods, whom to praise seems meet, first-born son of Marduk, offspring of Erua,[76] the queen, creator, look in joy! At thy supreme unchangeable command which has brought about my victory over the enemy, grant a just kingdom, an auspicious rule, years of prosperity, plentiful progeny to the kingdom of Antiochus and of Seleucus, his son.

. . . .

By thy supreme stylus which fixes the bounds of heaven and earth, through thy glorious utterance may my salvation be proclaimed. May my hands conquer the lands from sunrise to sunset,[77] compel their tribute in order to complete E-sagila and E-zida. O Nabu, royal son, upon thy entering into thy legitimate temple,[78] proclaim favor for Antiochus, the king of (all) lands, for the king Seleucus, his son, and for the queen Stratonike."

Even in this late composition Nabu is still the scribe who writes down the decrees of the gods. The king is careful also to drag in Marduk and his temple, and as an interesting new touch he includes in his prayer his son, associated presumably with the father in the government, and his queen.

VIII

We have still to consider one of the most notable figures of the Babylonian-Assyrian pantheon, one whose cult assumed great prominence in the earliest days to which we can trace back the history of the country with which we are concerned, and who retained his position despite all political and social vicissitudes, throughout all changes in religious thought down to the disappearance of the Babylonian-Assyrian civilization—the moon-god, Sin. There were chiefly two centres of Sin worship in Babylonia, one at Ur in the extreme south, and the other at Harran in the north.

---

[76] A title of Sarpanit, the consort of Marduk.

[77] *I.e.*, from east to west.

[78] With an allusion to the name of Nabu's temple, E-zida, "the legitimate house."

The former of these two is the older and by far the more important. By the side of Sin, the moon-god also bears a name, Nannar, which designates him as a "luminary." In Sumerian the name is written with two signs, En-zu, which describes him as the "lord of knowledge" and of which Sin—divided into Si-in— may be a derivative by an inversion of the two syllables, which is not uncommon.[79] These two qualities, as a light-giving power and as a god of wisdom, are the two traits of Sin most prominently dwelt upon in votive and historical inscriptions and in religious texts. In the art,[80] the moon-god is represented as an old man with a flowing beard, with the moon's crescent as his symbol. On the so-called Boundary Stones,[81] the crescent alone is used for the moon, as the circle with numerous rays stands for the sun. The horns suggested by the moon's crescent were probably a factor in representing him also figuratively as a bull, and a frequent epithet given to him is "the young bullock of Enlil," which illustrates also the endeavor to associate him with the old Babylonian pantheon grouped around the god of Nippur. The crescent also suggests a bark, and in very old invocations he is pictured as sailing across the heavens in a bark. One of these reads in part as follows:[82]

"In the resplendent bark of heaven, O self-appointed ruler,
Father Nannar, lord of Ur,
Father Nannar, lord of E-gishshirgal,[83]
Father Nannar, lord of Namrasit,[84]
Lord Nannar, first-born son of Enlil,
As thou sailest along, as thou sailest along,

---

[79] So we have Zu-ab, "house of knowledge," becoming *apsu.*

[80] See Plate LXXVII, Fig. 2.

[81] See p. 416, *seq.*

[82] Cun. Texts, XV, Pl. 17, and Reisner, *Sumerisch-Babylonische Hymnen,* No. 38.

[83] Name of Sin's temple in Ur.

[84] "Rising in light," an epithet of the moon-god.

PLATE XXX

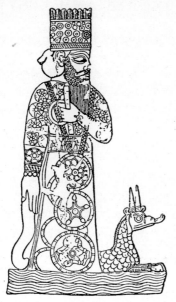

FIG. I, MARDUK, THE CHIEF DEITY OF BABYLON

FIG. 2, ADAD, THE GOD OF STORMS

In the presence of thy father, in the presence of Enlil, **thou art**
    ruler;
Father Nannar, thou art ruler, thou art leader,
In the bark riding through the heavens,—thou art ruler.''

In this manner the litany proceeds, the lines of
which are evidently intended to be chanted by a leader
and chorus alternatively, or by two choruses of priests.
Though Sin or Nannar is constantly addressed as
father in his capacity as the chief luminary in the
starry heavens, the endeavor is clearly made to bring
him into association with Enlil whose first-born son
he is therefore declared to be, and in the course of the
process of the incorporation of the Sin cult into that
centring around Enlil, the ''word'' which we have
seen is the specific quality of the chief god of Nippur
in his role of a storm deity is likewise transferred to
Nannar, as it was transferred to Marduk, to Shamash,
to Ea and in fact to all the chief figures of the pantheon,
quite independently of their original character.

IX

A totally different god is Adad, the storm-god, who
is represented as brandishing the thunderbolt and
hurling the lightning. Adad is a counterpart of Enlil,
but, unlike the latter, who, as we have seen, takes on
other traits, Adad or Ramman (''the thunderer''), as
he was also called, retains his forbidding character of
a god who when he manifests himself does so because
his wrath has been aroused. Gods as well as men stand
in terror of Adad as is well brought out in one of the
hymns to him.[85]

''When the lord is enraged, the heavens tremble before him,
  When Adad is enangered, the earth quakes before him,
  Great mountains are cast down before him.
  At his anger, at his wrath,
  At his roar, at his thunder,

---

[85] Rawlinson IV² Pl. 28, No. 2.

The gods of heaven retire into the heavens,
The gods of earth recede into the earth,
The sun passes into the foundation of heaven,
The moon disappears into the zenith of heaven.''

He is the destroyer who sweeps across ''the heavens, the land and the waters'' as we read in another invocation to him. When the gods decide to bring on a deluge, it is Adad who is the chief executive of the divine decree.

But just because of his power and his violence, the attempt is made to gain his favor. When the storm ceases, the rainbow appears in the sky and the sun comes out from the clouds, it is a sign that Adad has been reconciled. Applying the association to human conditions, sickness, loss of life, destruction of crops, as a result of storms lead king and subjects to appeal to Adad's mercy, if happily they can arouse it. It is hoped that the god may feel flattered by being addressed as merciful and forgiving. So in a series of invocations to Adad we actually read:[86]

''Merciful one among the (great) gods,
I have directed my thoughts to thee, I implore thee humbly (?)
Be merciful, O lord, hear my prayer,
Destroy my enemies, drive away my opponents,
May the poison, poison, poison of the sorcerers not touch me,
Have mercy and proclaim grace for me.''

While Adad is also brought into association with the Nippur pantheon and with that grouped around Marduk, he is to a larger extent than the other members of the pantheon an independent figure. This may be due to the fact that so far as our material enables us to judge, he is not brought into connection with any important political centre. In this respect he marks a decided exception. He impresses one as an intruder whose cult may have been brought to the Euphrates Valley from the north, for in Assyria we find one of

---

[86] King, *ib.*, No. 21, lines 61–66.

the oldest temples dedicated to Anu and Adad—Anu as the old solar deity, afterwards replaced in Assyria by Ashur,[87] and Adad the storm-god.

There is still another phase of the cult of Adad to be briefly considered. He is a god of oracles and in this capacity is invariably associated with the sun-god, Shamash. In addition to divining the future through reading the signs in the heavens at night—in the moon, planets, stars, and constellations—the phenomena observed in the sun and those seen in storms, hurricanes, clouds, rain, thunder, lightning and earthquakes were gathered into an elaborate system, supplemental to astrology proper.[88] The deities presiding over these phases of divination are naturally Shamash and Adad, who therefore become, as the "lords of divination," oracle gods, frequently designated as such in the inscriptions of Babylonian and Assyrian rulers.

It is as a further reflex of astrology and supplemental forms of divination that by the side of the combination of Shamash and Adad into a duality, we have a triad, Sin, Shamash and Adad, very frequently appearing in invocations attached to votive and historical inscriptions as well as in religious texts, by the side of the greater triad Anu, Enlil and Ea.[89] As the latter symbolize the three chief divisions of the universe—heaven, earth and water—so the second triad sum up the chief manifestations of nature, the sun which conditions vegetation, the moon standing for the entire starry heaven, and the storm with all its accompanying phenomena, rain, floods, thunder, lightning, earthquakes and all other abnormal occurrences, more or less directly connected with the activity of the storm-god.

There are, however, two elements of nature not

[87] See below, p. 229.
[88] See, for details, Jastrow, *Religion Babyloniens und Assyriens*, II, p. 577–612 and 705–748, and also below p. 262, *seq.*
[89] See above, p. 208.

represented in this triad, the earth itself and fire. As to fire, this element appears to have been in part associated with the sun and with lightning, and in part to have been looked upon as an independent force. Both views come to the surface, but of the two the latter may be regarded as the more popular belief, while the derivation of fire from the sun and from lightning assumes a point of view of a more speculative character. Among all peoples of antiquity we find fire looked upon as a separate element, in the possession of the gods to be sure, but not identified with any particular one, not even with the sun-god.

The fire-god appears under various designations, Gibil—also written in the reversed form, Bil-ge—Girru, Gisbbar, Ishum and Nusku—the latter designation being the common one in Assyria. We do not find in connection with any of these names a special place selected as the centre of the cult, and this is quite what we should expect in the case of a god who does not represent a personification of a specific power of nature like the sun, moon, the water or the earth, for fire is to be found everywhere, on the earth and in the heaven and even within the bowels of the earth. The fire-god is a free lance as it were who, however, performs service for both gods and mankind. He is appropriately termed therefore the "messenger of the gods." Of the actual cult of the fire-god we learn little. His chief function is in connection with incantation rites to drive off the evil demons. As a sacred element, the fire is regarded like water as a purifying element. Hence by the side of a water ritual, associated as we have seen primarily with the god Ea, we have a fire ritual which consists of such ceremonies as burning images, made of various materials, of the sorcerer or sorceress by whose direct intervention some victim has been bewitched, or consigning to the fire such objects as onions, dates, palm blossoms, seeds or bits of wool to the accompaniment of magic formulas emphasizing the hope that as these materials are consumed, so the demons as the cause of the disease and suffering may be consumed or forced by the heat to abandon their victim.[90] All this falls within the category of sympathetic magic, involving a symbolical action to bring about the reality. Thus we have two series of incantation rituals which, because of the prominence given to fire in the rites, are known as "Maklû" and "Shurpû" —both terms having the force of "burning" or consumption through fire. Hymns to Nusku, illustrating the current conceptions in regard to him, are interspersed in these rituals. One of these reads as follows:[91]

"Nusku, great god, prince of the great gods,
  Guardian of the offerings of all Igigi,
  Founder of cities, renewer of sanctuaries,
  Resplendent deity, whose command is supreme,
  Messenger of Anu, carrying out the decrees of Enlil,
  Obedient to Enlil, prince, leader of the strong Igigi,
  Mighty in battle, whose attack is powerful,
  Nusku, consumer, conqueror of enemies,
  Without thee no sacrificial meal is given in the temple,
  Without thee the great gods do not inhale any sweet smelling
      offering,
  Without thee Shamash, the judge, does not make a decision."[92]

But the fire is also the indispensable aid to man in his advance along the path of civilization. The bricks for the construction of houses, temples and walls are burnt in the fire, the metals are tempered through the sacred element, and so in almost all the operations of man the fire is his faithful ally. Nusku is therefore hailed as the founder of cities, through whom sanctu-

---

[90] See specimens in Jastrow, *Religion Babyloniens und Assyriens*, I, p. 305, *seq.*, and 328, *seq.*

[91] Tallqvist, *Die Assyrische Beschwörungsserie Maqlû*, II, 1–11.

[92] Referring to offerings in connection with securing an oracle from the sun-god.

aries are built and renewed. The fire associated with
Shamash becomes like the latter the judge to whom
the appeal for a just decision is made. So in the
formulæ accompanying the symbolical burning of a
bronze image of the sorcerer or sorceress, Nusku is
apostrophized as [93]

> "Mighty fire-god, awe-inspiring glow,[94]
> Guiding gods and princes,
> Judging the cruel one and the wicked woman,[95]
> Step forward to my cause like Shamash, the warrior,
> Judge my cause, proclaim my decision,
> Burn the sorcerer and the sorceress,
> Destroy my enemies, censure my opponents,
> May thy raging glow come upon them!"

X

We have several times had occasion to point out
the dependence of Assyria upon Babylonia, extending
to all aspects of Assyrian civilization, though we must
not lose sight of some additions made to Babylonian
culture by the northern empire, or of the modifications
introduced by Assyria in what she took over from the
south. In the case of the pantheon we have only one
striking figure, embodying the spirit of Assyria and
who represents an entirely original contribution—the
god Ashur. We now know that the city bearing the
name Ashur on the site of which successful and most
thorough excavations have been carried on for the
past fifteen years,[96] represents the oldest capital of the
northern kingdom, and that in fact from Ashur as a
centre Assyria begins to extend her dominion about 2000
B.C., though the settlements in the north by migrations
from the south as well as through incursions from the
northwest are to be carried back to a much earlier

[93] Maqlû II, 114–121.
[94] Literally "day."
[95] I.e., the sorcerer and sorceress.
[96] See above, p. 55, seq.

PLATE XXXI

FIG. 1, ASHUR (?), THE CHIEF DEITY OF ASSYRIA

FIGS. 2 AND 3, WINGED DISCS AS
SYMBOLS OF THE GOD ASHUR

period. The name of the god being dependent upon that of the city, Ashur is thus the god of the city of Ashur. The original solar character follows from the common symbol of the god, a reproduction of the solar disc, frequently with the rays of the sun clearly indicated.[97] He is addressed also in hymns and invocations in terms which betray the original conception, though this trait is naturally overshadowed by the supreme position accorded in Assyria to Ashur, who, taking the place assigned to Marduk in the south, becomes like the latter the creator of everything, the ruler of gods as well as of all mankind. At the dedication of an image of Ashur made at the instance of King Sennacherib (705–681 B.C.), the king addresses his god as follows:[98]

"To Ashur, the king of the totality of the gods, his own creation, father of the gods,
Whose power is unfolded in the deep, king of heaven and earth,
Lord of all gods, controller of the Igigi and Anunnaki,[99]
Creator of the heaven of Anu and of the world below, creator of mankind,
Dwelling in the resplendent heavens, Enlil [100] of the gods, determiner of fates,
Dwelling in E-sharra in Ashur—for his lord, Sennacherib, King of Assyria, has made an image of Ashur."

The god who dwells in the heavens is a solar deity like Anu himself was, as we have seen. Naturally, Ashur takes on the traits also of Marduk. The role of creator is transferred by virtue of national pride from Marduk to Ashur. As the universal creator, Ashur controls the deep as well as the heavens. He is Anu,

---

[97] See Plate XXXIII, Figs. 2 and 3, and Plate XXXII, above the tree of life.

[98] Craig, *Assyrian and Babylonian Religious Texts*, I, Pl. 83.

[99] The group designation for the minor order of heavenly and earthly deities.

[100] In the sense of "supreme lord."

Enlil, and Ea thrown into one. The process towards concentrating all divine attributes in one being is carried to even further lengths in Assyria than in Babylonia, for Marduk is always associated with Ea as the father and with Nabu as the son. Ashur stands entirely alone in his majesty. Representing the spirit of Assyria which was so intensely martial as to make her at one time the greatest military power of the ancient world, Ashur naturally becomes primarily a warrior. The artists of Assyria yield to this influence and spoil the beautiful symbol of the god by placing a warrior with bow and arrow within the solar disc. Without this addition, the disc might indeed have become a symbol of a spiritualized power, as the swastika and the cross became. For the rulers, more particularly, Ashur is merely the warrior whose standard is carried into the midst of the battle field so as to ensure the presence and aid of the god. "By the might of Ashur" is the standing phrase in the votive and historical inscriptions of Assyrian kings. It is Ashur who mows down the enemies, who burns and pillages cities, who captures the women and children, and who spreads the misery and desolation incident to bloody warfare.

As Ashur reflects the genius and spirit of Assyria, so the god follows the varying fortunes of the country. With the transfer of the capital to Calah and thence to Nineveh, the centre of Ashur's cult shifts to the political stronghold. Wherever the kings reside, there is Ashur's seat; and when the king himself leads the military exploits, Ashur follows. Ashur is not *bound* to a definite centre like his two older rivals. He and Assyria become synonymous terms in a sense which never applied to Marduk. He becomes the *lord* or Bêl, *par excellence,* who has nothing to fear from any possible rival. A centralizing tendency arises more pronounced than previous endeavors in this direction, and without disturbing the time-honored traditions that grew up around Nippur, Sippar, Uruk, Cuthah,

Eridu and other sites. Nineveh as the capital of Assyria rises to a supremacy equal to the rank acquired by Ashur himself—unsurpassed in majesty, without a rival in power and glory.

XI

We have thus passed in review the chief figures of the Babylonian-Assyrian pantheon and in the course of this review have endeavored to show the close association between the conceptions formed of the gods and the course of political development in the south and the north. We have seen how as a consequence of this association solar gods, moon gods, storm gods and water gods lose their original character by having attributes given to them which are intended to symbolize the supremacy they assumed because of the political prestige acquired by the centres in which they were worshipped. Attempts are made in earlier and later periods to specify the relationship of the great gods to one another and also to the minor local deities. A pantheon arises with Enlil as the head which is subsequently replaced by another with Marduk taking the rank of Enlil, while in Assyria, Ashur eclipses both Enlil and Marduk. Gradually, a selection out of the large number of local deities is made. The pantheon takes on a more definite shape. The hundreds of minor gods fade into the background, becoming merely designations or attributes of the more important gods, or are placed in lists drawn up by the priests in the relation of members of the household,—relatives, servants, officials—of a great god. Through a process reflecting the speculations in the temple schools, a triad is evolved, consisting of Anu, Enlil and Ea, dividing among themselves the three parts of the universe—heaven, earth and water. A second triad is placed by the side of this one, summing up the chief manifestations of divine power in the universe, Sin (the moon), Shamash (the sun) and Adad (the storm, including water). In the case of each triad, a fourth figure is often added, Nin-lil, originally the consort of Enlil, or Nin-makh ("the great lady") to the first, and Bêlit ("the lady") or Ishtar to the second—both, however, symbolizing the female element which, fructified by the male, is the indispensable complement to the production of life, vegetation, fertility and all blessings that go with the never ending process of vitality, growth, decay and regeneration in nature. This leads us to a consideration, before leaving the pantheon, of one notable female figure, the great mother-goddess, frequently identified with the earth viewed as a fruitful mother but who should rather be regarded in a still wider sense as the mother of all that manifests life, embracing therefore the life in man and the animal world as well as in the fields and mountains in nature in general.

This natural association of a female element as a complement to the male one leads to assigning to every deity a consort who, however, has no independent existence. So Enlil has at his side Nin-lil, Ninib has Gula ("the great one"), Ningirsu has Bau, Shamash has Â, Sin has Nin-gul, Nergal has Laz, Anu a female counterpart Antum, to Ea a consort Shala ("the woman") is given, to Marduk, Sarpanit or Nin-makh ("the great lady"), to Nabu, Tashmit ("obedience"), while Ashur's consort appears as Nin-lil or Bêlit and at times as Ishtar. All these figures with the single exception of Ishtar are merely shadowy reflections of their male masters, playing no part in the cult outside of receiving homage in association with their male partners. Ishtar, however, although assimilated in the Assyrian pantheon to the consort of Ashur, is an independent figure, who has her own temples and her distinct cult. She appears under a variety of names —Nanâ, Innina, Irnini, Ninni, Ninâ—all of which contain an element having the force of "lady," as is also the case with Nin-makh and Nin-lil, likewise used

as epithets of the great mother-goddess. Corresponding to the Sumerian element, we have in Akkadian Bêlit "lady" or "mistress" as one of the gen-
eric designations of Ishtar. All this confirms the view
that Ishtar is merely the symbol of the female element
in the production of life, and that the specific name is
of secondary significance. The circumstance that Nin-
lil, the consort of Enlil, is also (though in texts of a
later period) identified with the mother-goddess would
seem to show that the female associate of the head of
the pantheon was always an Ishtar, though in a certain
sense, as we have seen, the consorts of all the gods
were Ishtars.

The oldest cult of the mother goddess, so far as
our material goes, appears indeed to have been in Uruk
where she is known as Nanâ, but we may be quite sure
that the cult was never limited to one place. The
special place which Nanâ has in the old Babylonian
pantheon is probably due to the peculiar development
taken by the chief deity of that centre, Anu, who as
we have seen became an abstraction—the god of heaven,
presiding over the upper realm of the universe. Her
temple at Uruk known as E-anna "the heavenly
house" and revealing the association of the goddess
with Anu as a solar deity became one of the most
famous in the Euphrates Valley. It is in connection
with the cult of Nanâ that we learn of a phase of the
worship of the mother-goddess which degenerates into
the obscene rites that call forth the amazement of
Herodotus.[101] As the mother-goddess, Nanâ or Ishtar
is not only the source of the fertility displayed by the
earth and the kind, gracious mother of mankind, but
also the goddess of love—the Aphrodite of Babylonia.
The mysterious process of conception and the growth
of the embryo in the mother's womb gave rise at an
early period to rites in connection with the cult of the

[101] Book I, § 199.

mother-goddess that symbolized the fructification through the combination with the male element.

There is, however, another side to Ishtar which comes particularly to the fore in Assyria, though it is also indigenous to Babylonia. She is not only the loving mother but, as the protector of her offspring, a war-like figure armed for the fray and whose presence is felt in the midst of the battle. She appears to her favorites in dreams and encourages them to give battle. It is she who places in the hands of the rulers the weapons with which they march to victory. To Ashur-banapal she thus appears armed with bow and arrow and reassures him: "Whithersoever thou goest, I go with thee." [102] As far back as the days of Hammurapi, Ishtar is thus viewed as the one who encourages her followers for contest and battle.

Both phases of the goddess, as the gracious mother and as the grim Amazon, are dwelt upon in one of the finest specimens of the religious literature of Babylonia in which a penitent sufferer, bowed down with sickness and misfortune, implores Ishtar to grant relief.[103] The hymn is addressed to the goddess of Uruk but she has become the general mother-goddess and is instead of Nanâ addressed as Ishtar. Ishtar is here identified with the planet Venus and assigned to a place therefore in the heavens. As such she is called "the daughter of Sin," the moon-god. She is thus the daughter of Anu, of Enlil and of Sin at one and the same time, a further indication that such epithets merely symbolize a relationship to various gods, according to the traits assigned to her. The composition, too long to quote entirely, begins:

---

[102] Cylinder B (ed. Geo. Smith, *History of Assurbanapal*, p. 125), Col. 5, 61–62. Ishtar is frequently represented as goddess of war on seal cylinders. See Ward, *Seal Cylinders of Western Asia* (Washington, 1910), Chapter XXV.

[103] King, *Seven Tablets of Creation*, I, p. 222–237.

"I pray to thee, mistress of mistresses, goddess of goddesses,
Ishtar, queen of all habitations, guide of mankind,
Irnini [104] praised be thou, greatest among the Igigi [105]
Powerful art thou, ruler art thou, exalted is thy name,
Thou art the light of heaven and earth, mighty daughter of Sin,
Thou directest the weapons, arrangest the battle array,
Thou givest commands, decked with the crown of rulership,
O lady, resplendent is thy greatness, supreme over all gods.

. . . .

Where is thy name not? Where is thy command not?
Where are images of thee not made? Where are thy shrines not
    erected?
Where art thou not great?—where not supreme?
Anu, Enlil and Ea have raised thee to mighty rulership among
    the gods,
Have raised thee aloft and exalted thy station among all the Igigi.
At the mention of thy name, heaven and earth quake,
The gods tremble, the Anunnaki quake.
To thy awe-inspiring name mankind gives heed,
Great and exalted art thou!
All dark-headed ones,[106] living beings, mankind pay homage to
    thy power.

. . . .

I moan like a dove night and day,
I am depressed and weep bitterly,
With woe and pain my liver is in anguish.
What have I done, O my god and my goddess—I?
As though I did not reverence my god and my goddess, am I treated.

. . . .

I experience, O my mistress, dark days, sad months, years of mis-
    fortune.''

As the planet Venus, the movements of Ishtar in
the heavens form a basis for divining what the future
has in store.[107] The prominent part taken by the observation of Venus-Ishtar in Babylonian-Assyrian

---

[104] An epithet of Ishtar. See above, p. 232.

[105] Here used as a general designation of all the gods.

[106] Here used for mankind in general.

[107] See for details, Jastrow, *Religion Babyloniens und Assyriens*,
II, pp. 612–638.

astrology is reflected in many of the hymns to her. The influence of the priestly speculations in thus combining the popular animistic conceptions of the gods and goddesses with points of view derived from the projection of the gods on to the starry heavens is one of the features of the religion of Babylonia and Assyria.

Ishtar under one name or the other becomes a favorite subject for myths symbolizing the change of seasons, her period of glory when the earth is in full bloom being the summer followed by the rainy and winter months when nature decays, and which was pictured as due to the imprisonment of the goddess in the nether world. She takes her place in popular tales, half legendary and half mythical, and we have a number of compositions [108] further illustrating how the popular myths and tales were embodied into the cult.

---

[108] See pp. 453–461.

CHAPTER V

THE CULTS AND THE TEMPLES OF BABYLONIA AND ASSYRIA

I

In the course of discussion of the views held of the gods and goddesses, the general features of the religion have been revealed, as well as the relation of religious beliefs to the course taken by the political fortunes of Babylonia and Assyria. A close interdependence between the position of the gods and the changing political conditions in the Euphrates Valley, needs to be kept in mind as the most important factor, leading to a divorce in the conception of the gods from the animistic starting-point as the personification of some specific power or manifestation of nature. We have seen how in the case of such figures as Enlil, Marduk and Ashur this process resulted in a tendency towards the unification of all such manifestations in a single deity. A spiritual impulse is thus given to the view of divine government of the universe, the significance of which is not diminished by the limitation pointed out and which prevented the rise of a genuine monotheism in Babylonia and Assyria. As a reflex of the higher point of view such members of the pantheon as Shamash, the sun-god, Sin, the moon-god, Ea, the water-god, Nabu, originally the god of Borsippa, Nusku, the fire-god, and Ishtar, the mother-goddess rise far beyond the original animistic level, and become in a measure symbols of the beneficent influence exerted by the powers of nature on man. Ethical traits such as mercy, justice, love, forbearance are superimposed on the original attributes of strength and violence, at times to such an extent as to obscure the older aspects. As a result of this tendency towards giving the personifications of powers of nature an ethical import, we find increasing prominence given to the thought

237

that the gods send sickness, suffering, misfortune, drought, pestilence and national catastrophes of a larger character, defeat in battle and invasions of the country, as a consequence of misdeeds, primarily on the part of the rulers who stand nearer to the gods than the ordinary individual. To be sure, the misdeeds grouped together under the general designation of sins, may be either of a genuinely ethical character or purely ceremonial neglect or even ritualistic errors. While this decided limitation in the ethics of Babylonia and Assyria which clings to the religion down to the latest period must be given due consideration, nevertheless it marks a decided step forward to recognize that the displeasure or anger of the gods as shown by the punishments sent by them is not aroused without some good cause,—good naturally from the limited point of view here emphasized. All misfortunes are looked upon as punishments from angry deities, and the punishment itself is the natural and necessary consequence of sin. The obvious corollary is that the gods are on the whole and ordinarily favorably disposed towards mankind. Some are more merciful by nature than others, some like the god Ea are in a special sense the protectors of man, revealing to him even the secret counsels of the gods, some like Ishtar bewail catastrophes sent against mankind by angered deities, but all are open to appeals and, it might even be said, prone to mercy and inclined to be forgiving.

A second factor of fundamental importance for our estimate of the religion of Babylonia and Assyria is the recognition of the part taken by the endeavors on the part of the priests to systematize the current religious beliefs, with the result of building up a theological system of no small proportions. The most prominent outcome of this endeavor was the theory of a threefold division of the universe with the assignment of a deity in control of each. The setting up of this triad which may be traced back to the old Babylonian period marks a further step in the dissociation of the gods from their original limitations. Anu, Enlil and Ea become symbols of divine government of the universe, and similarly, though not to the same extent, the second triad, Shamash, Sin and Adad, sum up the chief manifestations of divine power in so far as it affects mankind—the sun, the moon and atmospheric phenomena, while the addition of a further figure in the case of both triads, Ninlil [1] for the first, and Ishtar for the second, symbolizes the female element which combines with the male to bring about the renewal of nature and the reproduction of animal and human life. While the theoretical constructions perfected in the temple schools no doubt exercised a decided influence on popular beliefs, yet it is natural to find that the masses clung to the traditional animistic conceptions of the local deities. To the people, the head of the pantheon, whether Enlil, Marduk or Ashur, remained the local divine patron; and so in the other centres, Shamash, Ea, Sin, Nabu, Nergal as the case may be, remained on the level of personifications of powers of nature, attached as protecting spirits to the locality in question. The larger and higher point of view comes to the fore in the hymns and prayers which are distinctly the product of the priests of the temple schools, but the very circumstance that they are in most cases attached as introductions to pure incantation formulas, the popular basis of which is just as evident as is the more scholastic character of the hymns, shows that the consequences of the expansion in the conceptions of the gods were not drawn when it came to the actual cult.

II

From this point of view it is therefore significant to find the large place taken in the practice of the religion by incantation rituals and divination prac-

[1] Or Nin-kharsag—another designation of the consort of Enlil. See above, p. 202.

tices. It is inconceivable that the hymns and the incantations should be the product of the same order of thought, and as we proceed in our study of the religion of Babylonia and Assyria the evidence increases for the thesis that the incantation texts, growing by accumulation from age to age, represent the older products which are retained by the side of compositions expressive of more advanced thought. The power appealed to to furnish relief must be addressed, and naturally the priests will endeavor to embody in this address the conceptions of the god or goddess that have been developed as a result of their speculations and attempts at systematization. The technical term *shiptu* for "incantation" is therefore attached to the hymns as a further indication that they form an ingredient part of this subdivision of the religious literature.

Taking up the incantations proper, we find the basic idea to be the theory that sickness and all forms of bodily suffering are due to the activity of demons that have either of their own accord entered the body of the victim, or that have been induced to do so through the power exercised by a special class of sorcerers or sorceresses who are able to bewitch one with the aid of the demons. This theory of ailments of the flesh is of course the one commonly held among people in a primitive stage of culture, and which is carried over to the higher phases. That aches and fevers should be ascribed to the activity of demoniac forces within one is a natural corollary to the animistic conception controlling the religion of Babylonia and Assyria, and which ascribes life to everything that manifests power. A cramp, a throbbing of the head, a shooting pain, a burning fever naturally give the impression that something—to speak indefinitely—is inside of you producing the symptoms; and modern science curiously enough with its germ theory to account for so many diseases comes to the aid of the

PLATE XXXII

FIG. I

FIG. 2

FIG. I, TYPES OF DEMONS
FIG. 2, HUMAN-HEADED LION

primitive notion of demoniac possession. To secure relief, it was therefore necessary to get rid of the demon —to exorcise the mischievous being. It was also natural to conclude that the demons, ordinarily invisible, lurking in the corners, gliding through doors, hiding in out of the way places to pounce upon their victims unawares, should be under the control of the gods as whose messengers they thus acted. The presence of a demon in the body was therefore a form of punishment sent by a deity, angered because of some sin committed. But besides the gods, certain individuals were supposed to have the power over the demons to superinduce them to lay hold of their victims. Giants and dwarfs, the crippled and deformed, persons with a strange expression in their eyes, inasmuch as they represented deviations from the normal, were regarded as imbued with such power, and curiously enough women were more commonly singled out than men, perhaps because of the mysterious function of the female in harboring the new life in her womb. As a survival from this point of view, we find the witch far down into the Middle Ages a commoner figure than the sorcerer, and in fact surviving the belief in the latter.

In whatever way the demon may have found his way into the victim, the appeal had to be made to a god or goddess to drive him out; nor was the theory that the demon represented the punishment sent by an angered deity affected by the power ascribed to certain individuals to bewitch individuals, for it was also in this case because the deity was offended that the sorcerer or sorceress could exercise his or her power. With the good will and favor of the gods assured, one was secure from demons and sorcerers alike.

The existence of several elaborate incantation series in Ashurbanapal's library, prescribing a large number of formulas to be recited in connection with symbolical rites to get rid of the demons, furnishes the proof for the practical significance attached to incantations in

16

both Babylonia and Assyria. These series, Babylonian in origin, revert to Sumerian prototypes and represent compilations stretching over a long period, with additions intended to adapt them to conditions prevailing in Assyria. The scribes of Ashurbanapal were not indulging in a purely academic exercise in copying the archives of Babylonian temples; their purpose, as was also the aim of the king, was to make Nineveh the central religious authority as well as the political mistress by having in their control the accumulated experience of the past, in dealing with the religious needs and problems of their own age.

A feature which these incantation series [2] have in common is the recognition of a large number of demons, with special functions assigned in many cases to the one class or the other. So, for example, there is a demon Labartu, represented as a horrible monster with swine sucking at her breasts,[3] who threatens the life of the mother at childbirth; a group known as *Ashakku* who cause varieties of wasting diseases, another demon Ti'u, whose special function was to cause diseases, manifesting themselves by headaches accompanied by fever, and so on through a long list. It will be apparent that there is no differentiation between the demon and the disease. The one is the synonym of the other, and accordingly in medical texts the demons are introduced as the designations of the diseases themselves. The names given to the demons in many cases convey the "strength" or "size" ascribed to them, such as Utukku, Alu, Shedu, Gallu, or they embody a descriptive epithet like *Akhkhazu*, "seizer" (also the name of a form of

---

[2] Large portions of five series have now been published, having the names: (1) *Utukki limnûti* (the evil utukki), (2) *Ashakki marsûti* (disease ashakki), (3) *Labartu-series*, (4) *Shurpû* (burning), (5) *Maklû* ("consuming"). See copious specimens in Jastrow, *Religion Babyloniens und Assyriens*, I, pp. 273–392.

[3] See the illustration at the bottom of the bronze plaque, Plate LXVI, Fig. 1 and p. 411.

jaundice); *Rabisu,* the one lying-in-wait; *Labasu,* "overthrower"; *Lilu* and the feminine *Lilitu,* "night-spirit"; *Etimmu,* ghost or shade, suggesting an identification of some demons with the dead who return to plague the living, *Namtar,* "pestilence," and more the like. The descriptions given of them, cruel, horrible of aspect, blood-thirsty, flying through space, generally invisible though sometimes assuming human or animal shape or a mixture of the two, further illustrate the conceptions popularly held. A group of seven frequently occurring in the texts and depicted on monuments [4] is described as follows: [5]

"Seven, they are they seven,
In the deep they are seven,
Settling in heaven they are seven.
In a section of the deep they were nurtured;
Neither male nor female are they,
Destructive whirlwinds are they,
They have no wife, they produce no offspring.
Mercy and pity they know not,
Prayer and petition they hear not,
Horses raised in the mountains [6] are they.
Hostile to Ea [7] are they,
Throne bearers of the gods are they,
To hem the way they set themselves up in the streets.
Evil are they, evil are they,
Seven are they, they are seven, twice seven are they."

Their universality as well as their function in seizing hold of their victims, taking up their seat in any part of the human body, is emphasized in another description.

More specific is the description of the demon Ti'u, the demon of head troubles and of fevers. [8]

---

[4] See Plate LXVI, Fig.1, and Plate LXVII, Fig. 2.

[5] Cuneiform Texts, XVI, Pl. 15, 28–57.

[6] *I.e.,* wild horses.

[7] The god of humanity. See above, p. 210, *seq.*

[8] Cun. Texts, xvii, Pl. 19, 1–30.

"The head disease roams in the wilderness, raging like the wind,
Flaming like lightning, tearing along above and below,
Crushing him who fears not his god like a reed,
Cutting his sinews like a khinu-reed,
Maiming the limbs of him who has not a protecting goddess,
Glittering like a star of heaven, flowing like water,
Besetting a man like a whirlwind, driving him like a storm;
Killing that man,
Piercing another as in a cramp,[9]
So that he is slashed like one whose heart has been torn out,
Burning like one thrown into the fire,[10]
Like a wild ass whose eyes are clouded,[11]
Attacking his life, in league with death,
So is Ti'u, who is like a heavy storm whose course no one can follow,
Whose final goal no one knows."

Elsewhere the invisibility of the demons is dwelled upon. Of the Ashakku it is said [12] that, sweeping along like a storm, driving through the streets and highways

"He stands at the side of a man, without anyone seeing him,
He sits at the side of a man, without anyone seeing him,
He enters a house, without anyone seeing his form,
He leaves a house, without anyone observing him.".

III

The methods of obtaining release from the demons are as various as the demons themselves, though they all rest on two *motifs*—the power supposed to reside in certain formulas urging the demons to leave their victim, and the performance of certain rites based on sympathetic or symbolical magic, either mimicking the hoped-for release or applying certain remedies; but always with the idea that they will drive the demon

---

[9] He writhes in pain like one seized by a cramp, literally "cutting of the inside."

[10] A description of a burning fever.

[11] In the medical texts the blinding headache is described in this way as clouding a man's vision.

[12] Cun. Texts, xvii, Pl. 3, 21–28.

away, rather than that they will have any direct beneficial effect on the patient.

The magic formulas invariably involve the invocation addressed to some divine agent or to a group of deities. The names of the gods have a certain power, the name being, according to a widely prevalent view, part of the essence of the being. Besides, words as such are also imbued with power—a thought naturally suggested by the command of a superior which is obeyed by the one dependent upon a chief, and reinforced by the mystery of writing as the reflex of the spoken word.

A few specimens of the formulas will not be out of place. A brief and comprehensive one that is frequently found is

"By the name of heaven be ye forsworn, by the name of earth be ye forsworn,"

Or the exorciser appeals to all the gods as

"By the name of the gods, I adjure you"

or certain gods are specifically named as at the close of a rather elaborate command to the demons to leave the body [13]

"Away, away, far away, far away,
Be ashamed, be ashamed! Fly, fly away!
Turn about, go away, far away,
May your evil like the smoke mount to heaven! [14]
Out of my body away,
Out of my body far away,
Out of my body in shame,
Out of my body fly away,
Out of my body turn away,
Out of my body go away.
To my body do not return,
To my body do not approach,

---

[13] Maklû series (ed. Tallqvist, Tablet V, 166–184).

[14] The line assumes, as an accompanying rite, the burning of images of the demons.

To my body draw not nigh,
My body do not afflict.
By Shamash, the powerful, be ye forsworn,
By Ea, the lord of the universe, be ye forsworn,
By Marduk, the chief diviner of the great gods, be ye forsworn,
By the fire-god, who consumes you, be ye forsworn,
From my body be ye restrained!''

The magic formulas with the invocation to the gods constitute, however, only half of the exorcising ritual, the other and in many respects more important half being marked by ceremonies, accompanying the formulas, which as suggested either represent dramatically and symbolically the destruction or driving out of the demons, or fall within the category of medicinal charms that are supposed to have a direct effect on the demons. We have already had occasion in discussing the views held of Ea, the water-god,[15] and of Nusku (with various other designations),[16] the fire-god, to point out that water and fire constitute the two chief elements in the symbolical rites for exorcising the demons. The Ea-ritual involved washing or sprinkling the body of the victim with water that is to be taken from the Euphrates or Tigris as the sacred streams, or from some bubbling source coming directly out of the earth. So we read:[17]

"With pure, clear water,
With bright, shining water,
Seven times and again seven times,
Sprinkle, purify, cleanse!
May the evil Rabisyu depart!
May he step to one side!
May the good Shedu, the good Lamassu, remain in my body!
By heaven, be ye forsworn,
By earth, be ye forsworn.''

[15] Above, p. 211.
[16] Above, p. 226, *seq.*
[17] Haupt, *Akkadische und Sumerische Keilschrifttexte* (Leipzig, 1892), p. 90, col III, 1–13.

An image is frequently made of the demon or of the sorcerer or sorceress, placed on a little boat and sent over the waters to the accompaniment of formulas, voicing the hope that as the image passes along the evil spirit may depart. The little boat is made to capsize and the image is drowned, or it is directly thrown into the water and thus again the hoped for release is dramatically reproduced. The variations in the rites are naturally endless. It is merely a further modification of the Ea ritual if we find elsewhere directions to surround the bed on which the sick man lies with some kind of porridge made of water and barley, to symbolize the isolation of the individual, and with this isolation to secure his release from the torturing demons.

As the Ea ritual revolves around the use of water, in all kinds of variations, so the Nusku ritual is primarily concerned with the use of fire as a means of exorcising the demons, or of destroying the sorcerer and sorceress. The most direct method was to make an image of the demon and burn it, in the hope that the imitation might bring about the reality.[18]

"I raise the torch, their images I burn,
The images of the Utukku, Shedu, Rabisu, Etimmu,
Of Labartu, Labasu, Akhkhazu,
Of Lilu, Lilit and maid of Lilu,
And all evil that seizes men.
Tremble, melt and dissolve,
Your smoke rise to heaven,
Your limbs may the sun-god destroy.
Your strength may Marduk, the chief exorcisor, the son of Ea, restrain!"

Or for the sorcerer and sorceress:[19]

"On this day step forward to my judgment,
Suppress the uproar, overpower evil,
As these images flutter, melt and disappear
So may the sorcerer and sorceress flutter, melt and disappear!"

---

[18] Maklû, Tablet I, 135–143.
[19] Maklû, Tablet II, 132–135.

The images were made of various materials such as pitch, clay, dough and bronze. A variation of this fire ritual consisted in taking substances such as onions, dates, palm cones, bits of wool, and seeds, and throwing them into the fire to the accompaniment again of magic formulas. A single specimen of such an incantation will suffice.[20]

"As the onion is peeled and thrown into the fire,
Consumed in the flaming fire,
In a garden will never again be planted,
In furrow and ditch will never be imbedded,
Its root will never again stick in the ground,
Its stalk never grow, never see the light of the sun,
Will never come on the table of a god or king,
So may the curse, ban, pain and torture,
Sickness, aches, misdeed, sin, wrong, transgression,
The sickness in my body, in my flesh, in my muscles,
Be peeled as this onion,
This day be burned in the flaming fire.
May the ban be removed, may I see the light!"

Similar formulas are prescribed for the other substances.

In addition, however, to burning the images of demons or sorcerers or throwing them into the water, a large variety of other symbolical actions are introduced in the incantation series, all falling within the category of sympathetic magic. The image is bound, hands and feet, so as not to be able to move, its eyes are pierced or filled with spittle, its tongue pulled out or tied, its mouth covered, or poison dripped into it or stuffed with dust, its body slit open [21] and the like; and thus mutilated, it is thrown into water or fire or on a dust heap. From such rites it is not a long step to the endeavor to transfer the demon from the victim to some substitute—a lamb, a pig or a bird, which appears then to

[20] Shurpû-series (ed. Zimmern), Tablet V–VI, 60–72.
[21] See e.g., Maklû-series, Tablet III, 89–103 and Tablet VII, 97–107.

have been offered up as a vicarious sacrifice for the life of the victim.[22]

"The lamb as a substitute for a man,
 The lamb he gives for his life.
 The head of the lamb he gives for the head of the man,
 The neck of the lamb he gives for the neck of the man,
 The breast of the lamb he gives for the breast of the man."

The underlying thought is that the demon passes out into the animal which is offered to the gods, to appease their anger against the human sufferer. We are justified in drawing this conclusion from the caution expressly given [23] not to eat the animal which is declared to be taboo:

"Take a white lamb of Tammuz,[24]
Place it near the sick man,
Tear out its insides.
Place in the hand of the man,
And pronounce the incantation of Eridu.
That lamb whose insides thou hast torn out,
Cover it up as forbidden food for that man,
Consign it to the flame or throw it into the street.
That man shut up in a room and pronounce the incantation of
    Eridu."

The animal has become unclean through the demon that has been transferred to it; therefore it is not to be eaten, and while it is offered to the gods as a means of diverting their anger from the man on whom it has been visited, it is not a sacrifice in the ordinary sense. The demon may be also transferred to a bird which is caught for the purpose, slaughtered and cut up, after which the blood together with its skin and some portions of the body is burned in the fire [25] to the accompaniment of an incantation.

---

[22] Cun. Texts, xvii, Pl. 37, Tablet 2Z, 15–22.
[23] Cun. Texts, xvii, Pl. 10, 73–11, 87.
[24] *I.e.*, born in the month of Tammuz—the spring season.
[25] See Cun. Texts, Part xxiii, Pl. 49, 3–6.

IV

We have still to consider an aspect of the incantation rites which brings them into close relationship to medical remedies. The incantation, in so far as its aim is to cure the patient, is a precursor of medical treatment, and so long as the theory of disease which regarded all sickness as due to the presence of a demon in the body prevailed, medicine could never cut itself loose from the principle underlying the various methods resorted to, for releasing the victim from the clutch of the demons. Incantations, magic rites, symbolical ceremonies had precisely the same object in view as medicine proper—to drive or coax the demon out of the body, or, *vice versa,* medical treatment was supposed to act on the demon, while the cure of the patient was merely an incidental though obvious consequence that followed upon the exorcism of the demon. Such we find to be actually the theory on which medicine rested among the Babylonians and Assyrians down to the latest days; it formed an integral part of the incantation division of the religious literature, and while prescriptions of a purely medical character are to be traced back to quite an early period, they are invariably accompanied by certain magic rites of precisely the same character as are found in incantations proper. But the question may be asked, did not the Babylonians and Assyrians recognize that there were substances and certain remedies which effected a cure? Certainly, but it is just because medicine arises as an empirical science, based wholly on experience, that it could flourish though attached to so primitive a notion as the exorcism of demons. If a certain treatment was good for a patient, it was so because it was bad for the demon. If certain herbs and certain concoctions acted favorably on a sick man, it was because the demons did not like the smell or taste of the herbs, or because the ingredients of which the concoction was made were unpleasant to the demons and caused them to leave their victim, rather than be subjected to the annoyance of unpleasant ordeals. In the case of stomach troubles, for example, which naturally belonged to the most common of diseases, the remedies resulted in vomiting or in loosening the bowels, and it was supposed that in this way the demon was forced out of the body through one end or the other. Experience taught the people that for cramps and certain pains manipulation of the parts of the body involved furnished relief, but in such cases it was again perfectly natural to conclude that the demons did not enjoy such manipulation, and preferred to quit their victim rather than to submit to it again. The theory could thus be made to fit any conditions. If we now look at the prescriptions in the medical texts of Babylonia and Assyria, of which we have a considerable number,[26] we are struck by the large proportion of bitter, pungent, ill-smelling substances which were frequently ordered to be given, including a large number of downright nasty substances, such as putrid food, fat, crushed bones, earth, dirt, urine and excrements of human beings and of certain animals. The purpose of these was evidently to disgust the demons through the evil smell, and to induce them to fly to more agreeable surroundings; and if we also find pleasant ingredients like milk, honey, cream, sweet-smelling herbs and pleasant oils and unguents, we are justified in concluding that the aim of these was to gently coax the demons to leave their victims, just as the gods are bribed and their anger appeased by sweet-smelling incense added to the sacrifices.

An incantation in connection with the use of butter and milk, frequently prescribed in medical texts, reads:[27]

---

[26] See a paper by the writer on ''The Medicine of the Babylonians and Assyrians'' in the Proceedings of the Royal Society of Medicine (London) for March, 1914 (pp. 109–176), for further details.

[27] Cun. Texts, xvii, Pl. 23, 170–191.

"Butter brought from a clean stall,
Milk brought from a clean fold,
Over the shining butter brought from a clean stall recite an incantation:
May the man, the son of his god,[28] be cleansed,
May that man like butter be clean!
Like that milk cleansed,
Like refined silver shine,
Like burnished copper glitter!
To Shamash, the leader of the gods, commit him,"
Into the gracious hands of Shamash, the leader of the gods, be his
salvation [20] committed."

In connection with a medical prescription consisting of eight ingredients, an incantation is added in which by a play upon the name of each of the substances the hope is expressed that the power of the sorceress may be broken: [30]

"Like the mint may her charm be crushed,[31]
Like the sapru-herb may her charm destroy her,[32]
Like a thorn weed may her charm pierce her,[33]
Like the sammu-weed may her charm make her blind,
Like cassia may her charm bind her,
Like khaltappan-herb may her charm terrify her,
Like kitmu-herb may her charm cover her,
Like araru-herb may her charm curse her,
Like mukhurtu-herb may her charm cut her lips."

Oil as one of the most common of remedies is also introduced into the incantation texts, and by a natural association with water is attached to the Eridu-ritual.

---

[28] *I.e.*, his protecting deity.

[29] From out of the clutches of the demon. The word used conveys the idea also of a complete cure.

[30] Maklû-Series, Tablet V, 30–38.

[31] Ninu (mint) with a play on *enû*, "humble."

[32] Ṣapru—the name of a medicinal herb—with a play on *ṣapâru*, "destroy."

[33] Sikhlu (a thorny weed), with a play on *sakhâlu*, "to pierce"; and, similarly, in the case of the other substances.

The priest in rubbing the victim with oil pronounces formulas that imply the appeal to Ea, the god of Eridu.[34]

"Pure oil, shining oil, brilliant oil.
Oil which makes the gods shine,[35]
Oil which mollifies the muscles of man.
The oil of Ea's incantation, with the oil of Marduk's incantation
I pour over thee; with the healing oil,
Granted by Ea for easing (pain) I rub thee;
Oil of life I give thee;
Through the incantation of Ea, the lord of Eridu,
I will drive the sickness with which thou art afflicted out of thee."

Not infrequently purely medical prescriptions are inserted into the incantation texts,[36] and as a further indication of the close bond between incantations and medical treatment, we have large groups of texts [37] in which such prescriptions alternate with purely magic formulas, accompanied by directions of a ritualistic character, just as in the medical texts proper such directions are introduced as an essential adjunct.[38]

Lastly, we have amulets of various kinds prescribed as a protection against the demon, and which have also the power of driving the demons away after they have taken up their seat in some part of the body. The most common of such amulets are stones, supposed to have magic power, which are strung together into a chain and attached to the hands, feet, eyes, as the case may be, or placed around the head or hung about the neck. The directions are specific to use white, black or red strands of wool. A large variety of stones are thus introduced, and from other sources we know of the good

---

[34] Maklû-Series, Tablet VII, 31–38 and Weissbach in *Beiträge zur Assyriologie*, IV, p. 160.

[35] An allusion to the anointing of the statues of the gods.

[36] *E.g.*, Rawlinson IV,[2] Pl. 16, No. 2; 26, No. 7.

[37] *E.g.*, Cun. Texts, xxiii, Pl. 1–22.

[38] Many examples in Cun. Texts, xxiii, Pl. 23–50.

luck associated with some stones, and of the bad luck with others.[39] Threads also, spun from virgin kids and knotted, were looked upon as protections against the demons and, like the stone charms, were attached to the head, neck, hands or limbs of the patient, and even tied about the bed. The ramifications of the incantation *motif* are thus almost endless. It was no easy task to fit one's self to become an exorciser, and so for the guidance of priests, as for the education of those being trained for temple service, elaborate handbooks were compiled in which all the details were set forth with almost painful accuracy.[40] Everything depended upon the correct application, upon the proper arrangement of the various ingredients for the symbolical rites to accompany the incantations, and upon the recitation of the proper formulas in the proper way. The slightest error might prove fatal, and in case of failure to heal the sick, the explanation was ready at hand that some error had been committed, or that a wrong method had been applied to drive the demons off.

V

The constant fear of the demons in which the people passed their lives lent a somewhat sombre aspect to the religion of Babylonia and Assyria which crops out also in the methods devised for determining what the gods had in mind, and thus to be at least prepared for what the future had in store. Incantations which were resorted to when the evil had come and had manifested itself through disease and suffering correspond to curative medicine, into which, as we have seen, it shades

---

[39] See Jastrow, *Religion Babyloniens und Assyriens*, I, p. 464, *seq.* For stones in incantation and medical texts see Jastrow, *ib.*, I, p. 338, and Cun. Texts, xxiii, Pl. 34, 29–31, and Pl. 42, 17–19.

[40] The texts published by Zimmern in Part II of his *Beiträge zur Kenntniss der Babylonischen Religion* (Leipzig, 1901), pp. 81–219, represent portions of such handbooks.

over. Divination, as the endeavor to forestall coming evil, has its counterpart in a measure in preventive medicine. Sickness and suffering were so common that the individual needs could not be overlooked. In the case of a general pestilence, to be sure, the anger of the gods manifested itself against the country as a whole, and in such cases the guilt attached itself primarily to the rulers upon whose good standing with the gods the general and public welfare depended, but when the demons· confined their tortures to certain individuals, the latter would naturally repair to the temples or have the priests come to them, bring sacrifices and with the aid of the priests endeavor to rid themselves of the demons. Incantation rites thus played a considerable part in the religious life of the masses.

It was somewhat different when it came to divining the future. Foreknowledge of this kind was important before proceeding to war and at other crises affecting the general weal; and even when the signs were not deliberately sought out but obtruded themselves on one, as in the case of phenomena in the heavens or of extraordinary occurrences, the common belief was that the portent bore on public affairs rather than on the fate of the individual, always excepting the rulers and the members of the royal family whose welfare was so closely bound up with the general condition of the people and the country. This applies more particularly to such cases where the sign revealing the intention of the gods had to be sought out, for divination methods are of two kinds, the one involving the interpretation of a sign which is looked for as an indication of the divine purpose, the other the explanation of a sign not of your seeking but which is obtruded on your notice. The chief example of the former method in Babylonia and Assyria is the system of divination for reading the future in the liver of a sacrificial sheep. Before an impending battle, before laying the foundation of a temple or palace, before

entering upon a treaty with some rival power and in
the face of any crisis affecting the country, including
even the outcome of sickness of the king or of a member of his family, the priests were directed to kill a
sheep, which must be without blemish, to take out the
liver and note carefully the shape of the lobes, the gall
bladder and gall duct, the two appendices of the liver,
and above all the markings on the liver of a freshly
slaughtered sheep, due to the traces on the surface of
the subsidiary ducts carrying the gall into the main
duct and thence into the gall bladder, there to be purified and discharged into the duodenum. Abnormal
peculiarities were particularly noted, such as the unusual shape or size of any part of the liver, and on the
general principle underlying all forms of divination
that the unusual sign points to some unusual happen-
ing, the conclusion was drawn by an association of
ideas suggested by the sign or by a record of what happened in the past on an occasion when the sign in
question was observed, whether the prognostication
was favorable or unfavorable. Thus an enlarged gall
bladder or an unusually large finger-shaped appendix
attached to the upper lobe of the liver portended increase, prosperity, success, added strength. But the enlargement may be limited to one side, and in such a case
the association of the right side as the favorable one,
and of the left as the unfavorable one, would lead to a
further differentiation, a sign being interpreted as
favorable to you, or as favorable to the enemy and therefore unfavorable to you, according to the side on which
the sign appeared. It will easily be seen how by further
ramifications, the field of observation could be extended
almost indefinitely, and the possible interpretations correspondingly increased. Handbooks were prepared in
which all possible and many impossible signs—
theoretically assumed—were entered, together with the
interpretations, such collections to serve as guides to
the priests in determining the meaning of signs noted

in the case of a called for inspection on any occasion.
The liver was chosen as the organ of divination, because
of the widespread belief among people in a primitive
and in a more advanced stage of culture which regarded
the liver as the seat of life,[41] superinduced, no doubt,
by the vast amount of blood—always associated with
life—to be found in the livers of both men and
animals.[42] The liver is the bloody organ *par excellence,*
so that the Chinese speak of the liver as the "mother
of blood." Life was synonymous among the ancients
with what we would call soul, and hence the liver was
regarded as the seat of all manifestations of soul
activity—thought and all emotions alike. It is only
gradually as a reflex of increasing anatomical knowledge that the differentiation takes place which popularly assigns thought to the brain, the higher emotions
to the heart, and only the lower ones such as jealousy
and anger to the liver.[43] The liver was originally regarded as the one and only organ of life. Corresponding to this stage, the liver of the sacrificial animal,
accepted by the deity to whom it was offered, would
thus be regarded as a reflex of the mind of the god.
Childish and naïve as all this may seem to us, yet hepatoscopy is redeemed in a measure by the theory on
which it rests; and it acquires a certain importance
from a general cultural point of view because of its

[41] See an article by the writer, "The Liver as the Seat of the
Soul," in *Studies in the History of Religions,* presented to C. H.
Toy (New York, 1912), pp. 143–168.

[42] One-sixth of the blood in the human body is to be found in the
liver; in the case of some animals the proportion is even larger.

[43] The Babylonians and Assyrians advanced to the stage which
saw in the heart the seat of the intellect, and the liver as merely the
seat of the emotions, though of all emotions (see above, p. 215), but
there are no indications that they ever recognized the function of
the brain. Our term phrenology, derived from the Greek word for
"midriff," is a survival of the period which placed the seat of
thought below the diaphragm, and not in the head.

17

spread among other nations—the Hittites, Greeks and
Romans—as a direct result of the extension of the
sphere of Babylonian-Assyrian influence in the ancient
world.

The same is even more the case in a second system
of divination, elaborated by the Babylonian priests and
which centred around the observation of the phenomena in the heavens. We have already had occasion[44]
to touch upon the wide sway of astrology in the conceptions formed of the gods, whose seats under this
sway were transferred to the heavens, quite independent of the powers of nature which they originally
symbolized. In contradistinction to hepatoscopy, where
the sign is sought out as a means of securing an answer
to the question as to the favorable or unfavorable disposition of the gods at a given moment, astrology represents a method of divination in which the sign is forced
upon one's attention and calls for an interpretation.
The sun, moon, planets and stars are there and the constantly changing appearance of the heavens was
brought into connection with the ceaseless vicissitudes
in the fortunes of man here below. Once the step was
taken of identifying planets and stars with gods, as
sun and moon were gods, the further corollary followed that the movements in the heavens represented
the activity of the gods, preparing the events that took
place on earth. Everything being dependent upon the
gods and everything in nature and in the life of mankind being due to the gods, the theory arose in the
schools of speculative thought of a correspondence between conditions to be observed in the heavens and
phenomena on earth. Astrology, or the interpretation
of the signs in the heavens, thus takes its rise as an outcome of speculation of a comparatively advanced character in contrast to liver divination, which rests upon
an essentially popular belief of the liver as the seat of
life. The second method of divination thus stands on

[44] See above, p. 209.

a far higher plane; it involves a careful observation of the movements of the sun and moon, far above the reach of the average mind, and to an even larger extent is this the case in endeavors to follow the slower and less conspicuous movements of the planets. The simplest form of astrology thus involves some astronomical knowledge, and it is not surprising to find that the endeavor to read the coming events in the heavens led from a pseudo-science to a real one, which in the later periods reached an astonishing degree of perfection. So strong, however, was the hold which astrology acquired that even after the point had been reached of recognizing the laws presiding over the phenomena in the heavens, priests continued to conclude from conditions in the heavens what was to occur on earth; and the priests of Babylonia were succeeded by the astronomers of Greece and the star-gazers of Rome, who applied and amplified the system of interpretation, evolved in the course of millenniums in the Euphrates Valley. Until the threshold of modern science astrology was cultivated as a discipline of genuine value throughout Europe, by the side of and in connection with astronomy.

The supposed correspondence between phenomena and movements in the heavens and occurrences here on earth was, however, not the only factor involved in Babylonian-Assyrian astrology. The two chief gods in the heavens were the sun and the moon, the former recognized by experience as the regulator of the seasons, the latter a means of calculating time. The movements of the sun and moon represent a constant transition, in the case of the sun from night to morning, in the case of the moon the regular succession of its four chief phases. This transition *motif* in the heavens had its parallel in the life of man, in the transition of the new life issuing out of the womb of the mother, the transition from childhood to adolescence marked by striking physical phenomena at the age of puberty, the transition from life to death. The dependence of man upon the sun and moon being a fact too obvious to be overlooked, the transition periods in connection with these two bodies were carefully noted as furnishing an indication whether one could look forward to a favorable or unfavorable turn in the affairs of mankind. Note was accordingly taken of the phenomena attending sunrise, whether the sun rose in a clear sky or enveloped in clouds; and in addition, any striking conditions under which the sun appeared at any time, with a halo around it, or through atmospheric disturbances appearing paler or brighter than usual, and above all an eclipse of the sun or an obscuration under circumstances which seemed to suggest an eclipse. Association of ideas and the record of events that followed in the past upon the observation of certain striking phenomena in the sun, formed again the two chief principles involved in the interpretation. The unusual because abnormal pointed to some occurrence out of the ordinary—an eclipse or obscuration of the sun by a natural association portending some disaster —bad crops, defeat in war, sickness in the royal family, destructive storms, inundations, pestilence, a plague of locusts or what not.

For the moon the scope of observation was still wider. Of the phases of the moon, the appearance of the new moon, the time of full-moon and the disappearance of the moon for a few days at the end of each lunar month represented the chief periods of transition. All three were marked with great significance. The disappearance of the moon naturally aroused uneasiness. Popular myths arose, representing the cause of the disappearance as due to the capture of the moon by hostile powers; and great was the rejoicing when the new moon appeared. The time of the disappearance as of the reappearance could only be approximately determined, and according as the disappearance took place on the 27th or 28th day, it presaged a different event. Similarly, in the absence of any exact astronomical calculation, the new moon might appear to be delayed, which was always looked upon as a bad omen. The length of the lunar months varying somewhat in the calendar as fixed by the priests, the day on which the moon appeared to be full might be the 14th or 15th day, while through defective calculations it might appear not to be full till the 16th day, or as early as the 13th day. A too early or a belated appearance of the new moon or full moon was generally regarded as an evil omen, though under other attendant circumstances, the unfavorable sign might be converted into a favorable one.

Thirdly, we have the further extension of the scope of astrological divination by the identification of the great gods of the pantheon with the planets, Jupiter with Marduk, Mercury with Nabu, Mars with Nergal, Saturn with Ninib, and Venus with Ishtar. The conditions under which the planets appeared, whether bright or pale, their relative position to one another, to certain stars and to the moon, and such phenomena as the phases of Ishtar, were noted and interpretations recorded. The ecliptic as the road along which the sun and the planets appeared to move was recognized, and a three-fold division set up corresponding to the three-fold division of the universe. Adopting the terminology for the latter, the northern section of the ecliptic was assigned to Ea, the middle to Anu, and the southern to Enlil; and according to the position of any planet at any time, a further means of securing differentiating interpretations was obtained. Various other devices, all of a more or less artificial character, were resorted to in order to build up a system of interpretation, as for example the parcelling out of the four directions, South, North, East and West among the four countries, Babylonia, Assyria, Elam and Amurru, and according as a phenomenon was observed on one side or the other of the moon or sun or of one of the planets, the interpretation was applied to the corresponding country.

Without entering into further details, suffice it to say that for obvious reasons astrology was a form of divination that bore almost exclusively on the public welfare—the outcome of a military expedition, the crops, general prosperity or national catastrophes, the effects of storms, inundations, the invasion of the enemy, the sickness or death of the ruler, rebellion, change of the dynasty, and the like. The individual had a very minor share. Only the faint beginnings of an attempt to read in the stars the fate of the individual can be detected in Babylonian-Assyrian astrology. That phase of the pseudo-science was taken up by the Greeks, who appear to have cultivated astronomy long before they came into contact with Babylonian-Assyrian astrology, and who, as we know,[45] took over the astrological system perfected in the Euphrates Valley and grafted it on to their own astronomy.

Lastly, the observation of atmospheric phenomena such as winds, storms, earthquakes, thunder and lightning and the movements and shapes of clouds was added as a supplement to astrology proper, as a fertile field for determining what the gods, who controlled these phenomena likewise, intended to bring to pass on earth. The factor of fancy entered into this subdivision of divination even more largely, and according to the direction of the wind, the number of thunder claps, the character of the lightning, the fanciful figures of the clouds, and the conditions under which these and various other phenomena appeared, the interpretations, usually bearing on matters of public weal, varied.

[45] See, for the proof, Jastrow, *Religion Babyloniens und Assyriens*, II, pp. 703, *seq.*, and 744, *seq.*, and the monograph of Bezold and Ball, *Reflexe Astrologischer Keilinschriften bei Griechischen Schriftstellern* (Heidelberg, 1911).

VI

A third system of divination that flourished in Babylonia and Assyria and, like the two others, made its influence widely felt in antiquity was the interpretation of abnormalities of all kinds in the case of infants and the young of animals, observed at the time of birth. The new life issuing so mysteriously out of the mother marked a transition to which all the greater importance was attached because of the profound impression made by the mystery of life in general. This system falls, as does astrology, in the class of omens which are forced on one's attention—not deliberately sought out, as in the case of hepatoscopy. The observation of birth-signs shares, however, with hepatoscopy its bearing on the fate of the individual as well as on the public welfare, and indeed to a greater extent than is the case in divination through the liver of the sacrificial animal, resorted to, as we have seen, chiefly for public and official purposes. The house in which an infant with anomalous features is born or the stall in which an animal deviating in one way or the other from normal conditions makes its appearance were supposed to be directly affected by the unusual phenomenon, but in many cases an alternative interpretation is offered, bearing on public affairs, while in the event of an extraordinary deviation such as the birth of an unusually large litter, or so rare an occurrence as triplets or four or even five infants born to a woman, or the birth of some monstrous creature, the sign was an ominous one for the whole country primarily, if not exclusively. The range of anomalies recorded in the compilations of the diviners and in official reports is exceedingly large and, as more texts come to light, reaches proportions almost too large to be controlled. In general the deviation from the normal was regarded as an evil omen, though there are not infrequent exceptions. The distinction between the right as the favorable side and the left as the unfavorable one, is introduced as a basis for varying interpretations. Thus, if a lamb is born with the right ear lacking, it signifies that "the rule of the king will come to an end," "confusion in the land," "loss of cattle" and the like, whereas the lack of the left ear prognosticates corresponding misfortunes to the enemy and his country, and is therefore favorable to Babylonia and Assyria. Again, two ears appearing on the right side and none on the left is an unfavorable sign, whereas two ears on the left and none on the right is unfavorable for the enemy and therefore favorable for you. In the enumeration of anomalies we must again take into account the factor of fancy and the desire to make the collections complete so as to be prepared for all emergencies. Many of the entries are therefore purely "academic."[46]

The factor of fancy manifests itself in these hand-books of the Babylonian-Assyrian diviners in a form which is especially interesting, because of the explanation it affords for the widespread belief in antiquity in hybrid creatures such as satyrs, mermaids, fauns, harpies, sphinxes, winged serpents and the many fabulous monsters of mythology and folk-lore. We have long lists of the young of animals having the features or parts of the body of another animal. Instead, however, of being recorded as a mere resemblance, an ewe giving birth to a lamb having a head which suggests that of a lion, or of a dog, an ass, of a fox or a gazelle, or ears or eyes which suggest those of another animal, it is stated that the ewe has given birth to a lion, dog, ass, fox gazelle, as the case may be. In the same way, since it often happens that the face of an infant suggests a bird, a dog, a pig, a lamb, or what not, the fancied resemblance leads to the statement that a woman has given birth to the animal in question, which thus becomes an omen, the interpretation of which varies according to the

---

[46] See, for details, Jastrow, *Babylonian-Assyrian Birth-omens and their Cultural Significance* (Giessen, 1914).

PLATE XXXIII

THE TREE OF LIFE WITH ASSYRIAN KING AND WITH WINGED CREATURE AS GUARDIAN AND FERTILIZER OF THE TREE—SYMMETRICALLY REPEATED

ideas associated with the particular animal. A lion
suggests power and enlargement, and therefore a lamb
or an infant with a lion-like face points to increase and
prosperity in the land and to the growing strength of
the ruler, and is also a favorable sign for the stall or
house in which such a creature is born. Favorable ideas,
though of a different order, are associated with the
lamb, pig, ox and ass, whereas with the dog as an unclean animal in the ancient as well as in the modern
Orient, the association of ideas was unfavorable, and
similarly with the serpent, wild cow and certain other
animals, the interpretation refers to some misfortune,
either of a public or private character, and occasionally
of both. This feature of a fancied resemblance between one animal and another and between an infant
and some animal was the starting-point which led,
through the further play of the imagination, to the
belief in hybrid creatures and all kinds of monstrosities. The case of an infant being born with feet
united so as to suggest the tail of a fish is actually
recorded in our lists of birth-signs, and from such an
anomaly to the belief in mermaids and tritons, half
human and half fish, is only a small step, rendered still
more credible by the representation in art which converts the resemblance to a fish tail into a real tail.
Since we have the direct proof [47] of the spread of the
Babylonian-Assyrian system of divination from birth-
omens, as of the two other systems above discussed, to
Asia Minor, Greece and Rome, there is every reason to
believe that we are justified in tracing back to this
system the belief in fabulous beings of all kinds, though
it may of course be admitted that there are also other
factors involved. We find this belief in Babylonia and
Assyria, where we encounter in the ancient art hippocentaurs as well as bulls and eagles with human faces,
and in the Assyrian art the winged monsters with

---

[47] Given in the author's monograph on *Babylonian-Assyrian
Birth-omens*, pp. 50–64. See also Plate XXXII, Fig. 2; Plate
XXXIII; Plate LII and Plate LXXIV for hybrid figures.

human faces and the bodies of bulls or winged human figures with eagle faces. The process once begun would naturally lead to all kinds of ramifications and combinations.

VII

The three systems of divination which we have analyzed all entered directly into the religious life of the people and illustrate some of the religious practises which were maintained, like the incantation rituals, throughout all periods. The longing to pierce the unknown future, to pull aside the veil which separates us from a knowledge of coming events, is so strong in man as to have all the force of an innate quality—an instinct of which he himself only gradually becomes fully conscious. It plays an unusually prominent part in the religion of Babylonia and Assyria, indeed so prominent as to justify us in asserting that by the side of the ever present fear of the demons, the significance attached to omens was the most conspicuous outward manifestation of the religious spirit of the people taken as a whole. This conclusion is strengthened by the knowledge that we now have of other forms of divination, such as pouring a few drops of oil into a basin of water, and according to the action of the oil in forming rings and bubbles that sink and rise and the directions in which they spread, conclusions were drawn of a more or less specific character, and suggested by a more or less artificial association of ideas with the action of the oil—bearing either on public affairs or on private matters, according to the questions asked of the diviners, to which they were expected to give an answer.[48]

Within the other category of involuntary divination where the sign is obtruded on your notice, falls the importance attached to dreams, the interpretation of

[48] For details see Jastrow, *Religion Babyloniens und Assyriens,* II, pp. 749–775.

which formed in fact one of the most important functions of the Babylonian-Assyrian priests acting as
diviners. References to dreams are frequent both in
the older and later inscriptions of Babylonian and
Assyrian rulers.[49] A majestic figure reaching from
earth to heaven appears to Gudea in a dream; it turns
out to be the god Ningirsu. A female figure also rises
up with a tablet and a stylus who is the goddess Nisaba.
The sun mounting up from the earth is explained to be
the god of vegetation, Ningishzida. Various utensils
and building material and an ass to carry burdens
which the ruler sees in his dream leave no doubt as
to the interpretation of the vision. It is the order to
Gudea to build a temple according to the plan drawn
on a tablet by a second male figure appearing to him,
and who turns out to be the god Nin-dub. The interpretation is given to the ruler in this instance by the
goddess Ninâ as whose son he designates himself.
Ordinarily, however, it is to a priest to whom rulers
and people go to learn the meaning of dreams, in the
belief that dreams are omens or signs sent by the gods
as a means of indicating what is about to happen; and
even in Gudea's case we may safely assume that the
interpretation ascribed to the goddess directly was
furnished to him through the mediation of the priests.
At the other end of Babylonian history, we find Nebuchadnezzar and a goddess appearing to Nabonnedos,
the last king of Babylonia, in dreams to explain certain
strange signs that had lately been reported. In the
inscriptions of Ashurbanapal, the great king of Assyria, there are several references to dreams. The
goddess Ishtar rises before him and encourages the
king to give battle. A diviner has a dream in which
he sees certain ominous words written on the moon.
The priests made compilations of all kinds of phenomena that might appear to people in dreams with the

[49] See examples in Jastrow, *Religion Babyloniens und Assyriens*,
II, p. 955–958.

interpretations added, and no doubt the endeavor was made also in these handbooks to be prepared for all emergencies. If one dreams of carrying dates on one's head, it meant distress, if vegetables that things will go well, if salt that he will suffer some injury, if a mountain that he will have no rival. If one dreams that one is flying away, it is a prognostication that good fortune will take wings; if he descends into the earth and sees dead persons, it is an indication of approaching death. Eating figs and drinking wine in a dream are good omens; dust, clay and pitch are bad signs, and so on *ad infinitum*.

The movements and actions of animals formed another fertile field of divination. Among the animals, snakes and serpents, dogs, cows, sheep, goats, gazelles, falcons, mice, horses, pigs, foxes, eagles, chickens, swallows, fishes and various insects occur in lists of such omens preserved for us. Seeing a snake on getting up in the morning on New Year's Day was interpreted as an indication of approaching death; if the snake falls on a man, it means severe sickness or serious misfortune; if it falls behind a man, the omen was a good one; if it falls on the right side, that he will be seized by a demon of sickness, whereas on the left side the omen was partly favorable, partly unfavorable. The interpretations vary again according to the month and the day of the month on which the incident occurs, so that once more the field is enlarged to almost limitless proportions.

A white dog entering a palace means siege of a city; a yellow dog, that the palace will escape disaster; a dog of mixed colors, that the enemy will plunder the palace. Dogs barking at the gates prognosticate a pestilence, mad dogs the destruction of the city, howling dogs the overthrow of the city. A falcon flying into a man's house means that his wife will die; if the falcon carries off something from a man's house, that the man will die of a lingering disease; if a bird builds its nest and lays its young in a man's house, at the entrance or in the court, the omen is unfavorable.

These examples will suffice to illustrate the general character of the collections as well as the nature of the interpretations, based in part upon the same association of ideas which we encountered in the case of the other systems of divination, and in part no doubt on the record of what happened in the past when the sign in question was observed. In addition we must always allow a large leeway for fancy and the purely arbitrary factor, as well as the "academic" character of very many of the omens registered which probably never occurred, and are entered merely through the desire of the priests to be prepared for all possibilities —and impossibilities.

VIII

To complete the general survey of the religion of Babylonia and Assyria, it remains for us to summarize the organization of the temples and to add some indications of the festal occasions on which special rites were observed in honor of the gods, and the manner in which on such occasions they were approached.

We have already indicated, in connection with the discussion of the chief figures in the pantheon, the tendency to group around the cult of the patron deity of an important centre the worship of other gods, and we have seen that this tendency goes hand in hand with the political expansion of such a centre, but that the centre is apt to retain a considerable portion at least of its religious prestige even after the political decline has set in. The force of tradition, playing so effective a part in religion everywhere, would help to maintain rituals and practices once established, even if the conditions giving rise to such rituals and practices no longer prevailed. Confining ourselves to the larger centres and to those best known to us, like Nippur, Lagash, Uruk, Ur, Kish, Eridu, Sippar, Babylon and

Borsippa in the south, and Ashur, Calah and Nineveh in the north, we note the gradual extension of the area within which the main temple stood to become a more or less extensive sacred quarter. So in Nippur E-kur, the name of Enlil's sanctuary, becomes such a designation to include the temples and shrines erected to the numerous deities grouped around Enlil and brought into a relationship of subserviency to their master, as his sons, daughters, servants, body-guard, ministers and officials. Similarly in Babylon, E-sagila, as the name of Marduk's temple, grows to be a spacious quarter with numerous sanctuaries, large and small, to Nabu, Ninmakh (or Ishtar), Shamash, Ea, Nergal, Ninib—to name only the most important. The general arrangement of these temples, as we shall have occasion to see in more detail in the chapter on the architecture and art,[50] was in all cases the same, following an ancient prototype which provided an outer and an inner court of almost parallel dimensions, with a corridor leading from the inner court to the innermost smaller chamber, reserved for the priests and the rulers and in which, enclosed in a niche, the image of the deity in whose honor the temple was erected stood. Grouped around the three divisions was a series of rooms, varying in number according to the size and importance of the edifice, for the accommodation of the priests and for the administration of the temple, while in the case of the largest centres, special buildings were erected as store-houses for the temple possessions, stables for the animals, and dwellings for the numerous attendants and officials incident to the growing complications of the larger temple organizations. A feature of the main temple in every centre that was never lacking was a stage-tower, consisting of from two to seven stories, and placed either behind or at the side of the temple proper.[51]

---

[50] Chap VII. See also Plate XXXVIII.

[51] See p. 374 *seq.* on the special significance of these towers.

Corresponding to the growth of the temples, we find the organization of the cult extending its scope; and with this extension, the steadily increasing power and authority of the priests. In the small beginnings of the Euphratean cities, the priestly and secular functions no doubt rested in one and the same person. The ruler of a city or district, as we have seen,[52] was regarded as the representative of the deity. As such he stood in a special relation to the deity, acting as a mediator between the latter and the people, while upon his good standing with the god, the general welfare of the people depended. On the very ancient monument of Ur-Ninâ[53] we find the ruler himself offering the libation to the god, though behind him stands an attendant who is probably a priest to assist in carrying out the rite. As early, however, as the days of Gudea (c. 2450 B.C.) the ruler himself is led into the presence of the deity through the mediation of a priest. Gudea is so depicted on seal cylinders and other monuments, and presumably therefore the marked differentiation between priest and ruler thus illustrated was at the time an established custom of long standing. The mediatorship may, indeed, be set down as the chief prerogative of the priest in Babylonia and Assyria. With this as a starting-point, his other functions as sacrificer, as exorciser, as inspector of the liver for the purpose of ascertaining the disposition of the deity, as astrologer and as diviner in general, interpreting birth-signs, dreams, and furnishing the answer as to the meaning of all kinds of occurrences that deviated from the normal or that in any way aroused attention, may be derived. The people could proceed as far as the inner court of the temples, where an altar stood, but beyond that the priests alone could venture, and the rulers only if accompanied by a priest who as the privileged servitor of the deity had access to the divine presence.

[52] Above, p. 127 and Plate XLVI.
[53] See above, p. 255 and below p. 468.

Intercession is thus a distinguishing function of the priest, as a corollary to his role as mediator.

The growth of the temple organizations along the lines above set forth naturally resulted in a differentiation of priestly functions. Besides a number of general names for priest, such as *shangû, ênu,* "votary" and *ummânu* (expert), with gradations of rank as indicated by the title *shangû makhkhû,* "high priest," we find over thirty classes of priests recorded in the material at our disposal. The "exorciser" (*mashmashu* or *âshipu*) is separated from the "diviner" (*bârû,* literally "inspector"), and these two from the "singer" (*zammeru*), "anointer" [54] (*pashishu*), and "musician" (*kalû, lallaru, nâru,* etc.) and from the "snake charmers" (*mushlakhkhu*), who formed a class by themselves and perhaps had other functions than the name suggests. Each of these had numerous subdivisions such as "libationist" (*ramku, nisakku*), "anointer" (*pashishu*),[54] "dream interpreter" and "oracle" (*sha'ilu*) and others such as *urigallu,* and the *abkallu, abarakku,* whose exact functions still escape us.[55] Women also took a large part as priestesses of one kind or another in the temple service [56]—as singers, "howlers" (chanting the lamentations), musicians, exorcisers and furnishing oracles. We find also several classes of holy women leading a secluded life in special homes which would correspond to our cloisters and nunneries, and who were regarded as constituting in a measure the harem of the god to whose service they were dedicated. Some of these were "sacred prostitutes," and it is in connection with this class of priestesses that rites were practised in the temples which, while probably regarded as purely symbolical to promote fertility among mankind and in

[54] Perhaps, however, the one who merely prepares the ointment.

[55] See the full list with discussion in Frank, *Studies zur Babylonischen Religion* (Strassburg, 1911), I, pp. 1–37.

[56] See Frank, *ib.,* pp. 47–50.

the animal world, were unmistakably obscene, or at least degenerated into obscene rites.

In addition to the purely religious duties in connection with the temple service, the priests were also the scribes, the judges and the teachers of the people— all three functions following naturally from the religious point of view involved in writing, in legal decisions and in knowledge in general. The tradition once established, the priests continued to act as the official scribes in the case of the thousands upon thousands of legal and commercial documents that have come down to us from all periods, though, to be sure, in later days we occasionally come across a scribe who does not appear to have been a temple official.

The gods are the law givers, as all decisions are originally divine oracles furnished by their representatives, the priests. We have an interesting trace of this point of view among the Hebrews in the phrase "to go before God," used in the oldest legal code of the Pentateuch.[57] The word for law in Hebrew, *tôrâ,* has its equivalent in the Babylonian *têrtu* which means "oracle," that is, a divine decision. Hammurapi places as the headpiece of the monument containing the laws of the country,[58] an effigy of himself in an attitude of adoration before Shamash, "the judge," as the ultimate source of the laws. Down to the latest days of the Babylonian and Assyrian kingdoms, the temples were also the law courts, and in the large centres, no doubt, special quarters were provided for the numerous offices and officials required to carry out this part of the temple service, which grew to large proportions with the spread of commercial activity and increasing business complications incident thereto. Respect for law thus deriving its sanction from the religion marks rulers and people alike; and even those kings who ap-

[57] Exodus 21, 6. The rendering "judge" in the English version embodies the later interpretation.

[58] Plate XXXIV.

18

peared to be most ambitious to extend their power and authority, whose cruelty to enemies and conquered nations knew no bounds, who openly boast of the ravages they committed in fierce warfare, bow before the majesty of the law and emphasize the care with which they protected the rights of their subjects.

The temples themselves had their own business affairs which in the case of the larger centres assumed the proportions of extensive commercial establishments. As the organization of the priesthood became more complicated, there was much work which had to be done for the temples. The needs of the priests and of the temple service had to be attended to. Contracts were given out for garments to be made, for temple property to be tilled and improved, for necessary repairs and for new edifices to be erected. A feature of the temple organization in both Babylonia and Assyria which throws a less favorable light on the religion was the gradual increase in their land holdings, and the accumulation of large resources with the help of which the priests themselves became important factors in the commercial activity of the country. We find the temples in the large centres engaged in renting out lands and houses, in all manner of barter and exchange, in lending large and small sums on interest, and in entering directly on the customary commercial enterprises. At certain periods, the temples in fact assume somewhat the aspect of national banks, without, however, ever becoming financial monopolies. In the later days of the Babylonian monarchy we find priestly factions arising, who help to bring about the internal dissensions which made Babylon fall such an easy prey before the army of Cyrus.[59] The religion of Babylonia and Assyria, however, survives the political downfall of both the north and the south, and well on through the period of Greek domination following upon Persian control, we find the temples in the old centres still the

---

[50] See above, p. 184.

object of veneration and worship, to which the new rulers come to share with the people in the homage to the ancient gods. From the earliest to the latest period the priests continued to act as the teachers of the people. With the art of writing in the hands of the priests, the secrets of the gods could be unlocked by them only. The mysterious art naturally formed the basis of an education which the priests alone could impart. On the tablets all the extant knowledge was recorded, and to the tablets the wisdom and experience of the past was committed. Only through the handbooks was it possible to acquire the details of the various rituals and to carry out the requirements without danger of missteps. To provide for the uninterrupted continuance of religious tradition and its expression in the cult, the priests of the coming generation had to be trained by the present one. In all the larger temples and no doubt in the smaller ones as well, schools were established by the priests to hand down to their successors the wisdom of the ages as recorded in the compilations and collections which each large temple made in response to practical needs, though only in so far as these needs dictated. For the benefit of the pupils, lists of the signs used in the script were prepared with their values as syllables and as words. Grammatical paradigms both for the Sumerian and the Akkadian texts were drawn up, exercises in the use of the phrases and terms occurring in the hymns, incantations, omens, and in legal and historical texts were worked out in almost bewildering profusion, and texts edited with commentaries to explain difficult or obscure passages. Much of the Babylonian literature has thus come down to us in the form of school editions; and this applies also to mathematical tablets, chronological and geographical lists and medical prescriptions for which long lists of trees, plants, herbs and stones served as supplements, just as lists of all kinds of animals, of vessels of all kinds were prepared as aids for instruction in the omen literature. There followed instruction in the temple service in all its ramifications, and for this purpose the scribes of each temple had committed to writing all the necessary details and had preserved from one generation to the other the incantation rituals, the hymns and prayers, the omen collections and also as supplements, closely bound up with the cult and the current beliefs, the myths and fables and miscellaneous productions of the past. The larger the centre, the larger naturally the official and school archives. The sciences that were evolved out of the cult, such as astronomy and mathematics in connection with astrology, medicine and botany as an outcome of the incantation rituals were likewise in the hands of the priests and remained so till a very late period. The temple schools thus continued to be the intellectual centres of the country, and no doubt these schools furnished the incentive to the cultivation of the fine arts as well. The priest as scribe and as judge leads to the priest as teacher. In this threefold capacity he dominated the entire civilization unfolded in the course of millenniums.

IX

The occasions on which the people repaired to the temples have been touched on at various points in the course of our survey of the chief aspects presented by the religion. In general it was when sickness or some other kind of misfortune ensued, that the people sought the mediating help of the priests. On such occasions the elaborate incantation rituals were drawn upon, the appropriate formulas selected and the ceremonial details punctiliously carried out. Reports were sent to the rulers, announcing the appearance of the new moon and officially recording the exact time of full moon. All strange occurrences in the heavens and on earth were interpreted, and the priests were kept busy answering the questions put to them by the rulers at critical periods, or by the people when strange happenings took place in houses, streets or stalls, or when any unusual experience occurred. Owing to the large aspect taken on by the official character of the religion, the times when the rulers proceeded to the temples were particularly numerous. The official cult played a far larger part in the religion than the satisfaction of the religious needs of the ordinary individual, but at the important festival celebrations, occurring at the transition periods of the year, the people joined the rulers in thronging the courts of the temples, witnessing the offering of the sacrifices which they provided for such occasions and perhaps taking a direct, albeit a minor, part in the ceremonies incident thereto. The sacrifices embraced animals and land produce, as well as precious woods and special votive gifts. Lists embodied in Gudea's inscriptions,[60] which may be regarded as typical, enumerate oxen, sheep and goats, doves and various other domesticated birds, chickens, ducks and geese(?), various kinds of fish, dates, figs, cucumbers, butter, oil, cakes. In what way the animals to be offered were selected we do not as yet know, but it is eminently likely that with the perfected organization of the priesthood, regular tariffs were set up, prescribing what was to be brought on each occasion and in what amounts—very much as in the various Pentateuchal codes and in Phœnician sacrificial tarifs. The New Year's festival, celebrated at the commencement of the spring season and marking the transition from the winter—the period of nature's silence —to the reawakening to new life was the most solemn occasion of the year. Its celebration may be traced back to the old Babylonian period. In Lagash it was pictured as the marriage day of the solar deity Ningirsu with his consort Bau, the mother-goddess, the union, accordingly, of the male and female element,

[60] Statue E, cols. 5–6 and G, cols. 4–5 and elsewhere (Thureau-Dangin, *Sumerisch-Akkadische Königsinschriften*, pp. 80–84).

issuing in the new life pulsating throughout the earth in the joyous springtime. The sacrifices offered at the festival were designated as the wedding presents for the divine pair. No doubt in other centres of sun cults —and we have seen that most of the patron deities in the large centres were solar gods—similar rites were observed, so that the celebration in Babylon centring around Marduk and his consort Sarpanit, of which we know many details, represents a combination and elaboration of ancient traditions. The gods were carried about in solemn procession, bringing their homage in common with that of mankind to the great solar deity who had become the head of the pantheon. Nabu came from Borsippa to pay a visit to his father enthroned in E-sagila.[61] The festival lasted for ten days, during which interval the gods were supposed to assemble in the "sacred chamber of fates," there to decide the fates of the individuals for the coming year, with Nabu acting as the secretary and recording the divine and unalterable decisions. A sombre character was thus given to the festival, the ritual for which included penitential hymns, embodying appeals for forgiveness of sins and for divine mercy. The Babylonian-Assyrian *akitu*, as the New Year's festival was called, became the prototype for the New Year's season of the Hebrews, which likewise embraces a period of ten days and closes with a solemn fast, the main burden of which is the confession of sins and the appeal for forgiveness so that one may be "inscribed for life for the coming year," as the phrase in the Jewish ritual runs. The seventh month, as the beginning of the second half of the year which was divided into twelve lunar months,[62] also acquired a sacred significance; it marked the season of the final harvest, preceding the beginning of the rainy season. The transition *motif* thus also

---

[61] See above, p. 217.

[62] Regulated to accord with the solar year through intercalating a month at certain intervals.

dominates the fall festival which, like the one in the spring, appears to have extended over a considerable part of the month. Indications point to its having been marked by the rejoicings incident to a harvest festival, though the approach of the wintry season of the year must have tempered the joy. There are indications that the Babylonians, from a certain time on, recognized two "New Year's" seasons,[63] one in the spring which remained the official one, and one in the fall which appears to have been suggested by the agricultural and climatic conditions of the Euphrates Valley.

The period of the summer solstice was also marked by a festival, though we are still in the dark as to the character of the ceremonial prescribed for it; it is eminently likely moreover that we will come across some rites marking also the winter solstice. Besides these occasions, marking the transition from one season to the other, the two transition periods in the phases of the moon, the new moon and the full moon, were festive occasions, the former characterized by rejoicings at the reappearance of the silvery orb, the latter of a more solemn aspect as marking the transition to the waning of the moon.

X

Lastly, a few words as to the belief of the Babylonians and Assyrians regarding the fate of man after death has set in. In common with all peoples of antiquity, Babylonians and Assyrians believed in the continuation of conscious existence in some form in the grave. As an heritage of the limited mental horizon of primitive culture, they could not conceive of life once begun coming to an absolute standstill. The analogy between sleep and death, and the constant renewal of

[63] See Jastrow, *Religion Babyloniens und Assyriens*, II, p. 462, and now with further details, Weidner, *Alter und Bedeutung der Babylonischen Astronomie und Astrallehre* (Leipzig, 1914), p. 31, seq.

life in nature after its apparent extinction reinforced the popular conception that the dead, though condemned to inactivity, yet retained consciousness. The fate of the dead was, however, a sad and gloomy one. Earth burial being the prevailing method of disposing of the dead among both Sumerians and Akkadians, the dead were pictured as huddled together in a great cave under the ground to which the name *Aralû* was given. In poetic compositions [64] this dwelling place is at times spoken of as a city and again as a palace, but the conception loses none of its gloomy aspects by such terms. In Aralû the dead lie, like prisoners, bound hand and foot, unable to move, doomed to perpetual inactivity, subject to pangs of hunger and thirst unless their needs are provided for by surviving relatives through food and drink placed on the graves. The method of burial remained at all times exceedingly simple. In earlier days it appears to have been customary to bury the dead naked in the ground, in later days to cover them with reed mats, or to enclose them in large earthen jars or barrels and to place them in subterranean vaults of a simple construction. No doubt, in the case of the rulers and of the high officials more elaborate methods of burial were introduced, but in striking contrast to conditions in Egypt, we find little care bestowed on the preservation of the body. Libations and sacrifices were offered to the dead, pots and jars with food were placed near them in the vaults, and in later periods models of objects needed by them, as well as ornaments, trinkets, and perhaps toys for the children. There was a special pantheon for the dead presided over originally by a cruel goddess, Ereshkigal or Allatu, to whom afterwards Nergal, the grim god of mid-summer, associated with sickness and death, is assigned as a consort. The pair act as prison keepers,

[64] See p. 454, and for further details Chapter IV on "Hebrew and Babylonian Views of Life after Death," in Jastrow, *Hebrew and Babylonian Traditions* (New York, 1914).

assisted by a host of demons, headed by Namtar, the demon of pestilence, in keeping the dead confined within the gloomy hollow, portrayed as dark and dusty.

The faint beginnings of a timid reaction against this primitive conception are to be seen in tales of favorites of the gods to whom a happier future is accorded. So the hero who escapes from the deluge is removed to a land at the confluence of streams, and there enjoys a genuine immortality like that of the gods.[65] Another hero, Gilgamesh,[66] described as two thirds god and one third man, may in one version have also been accorded this boon, but in the composite story of his achievements which became current as the national epic of Babylonia, he is pictured as fearing death like the rest of mankind. His companion, Eabani, who is associated with him in some of his deeds of prowess is obliged to submit to the "law of the earth" as it is called, and from the tomb sends Gilgamesh a message describing the state of the dead in the nether world. The last word on the subject is therefore a note of despair, an injunction to enjoy life as long as it lasts, for after death all joys cease.[67]

That under the circumstances the ethics of the Babylonians and Assyrians were nevertheless of a relatively high order, as seen in the laws, the regulations of the courts, in the methods of business, in the family relationships, and even in the attitude of the kings towards their subjects speaks well for the whole-

[65] See p. 452.

[66] See Chapter XXIII of the author's *Religion of Babylonia and Assyria* (Boston, 1898).

[67] See pp. 461–463.

[68] Further details in Chapter V, "Hebrew and Babylonian Ethics," in the author's *Hebrew and Babylonian Traditions* (New York, 1914), and Chapter VI, "Ethics and Life after Death," in the author's *Aspects of Religious Belief and Practice in Babylonia and Assyria* (New York, 1911). See also "Maxims of Conduct," pp. 464–465.

some influence exerted by the religion.[68] No doubt the
constant fear of the demons acted as an impelling motive in inducing the people to maintain favorable relations with the gods, paying tribute to them by sacrifices and gifts, seeking out their shrines to obtain
directions through the priests for proper conduct, taking the necessary steps to ascertain the meaning of
signs sent by the gods, imploring their forgiveness
when divine anger had manifested itself in one way or
another, but apart from all purely material motives
there must have been a serious realization of the obligations resting upon ruler and people alike to regulate
their lives according to fixed standards which, with
due recognition of their limitations, must yet have been
of a high order. The gods, as we have seen, were
pictured as on the whole kindly disposed toward mankind, acting from motives of justice tempered with
mercy. Such conceptions must have reacted favorably
on the disposition of the masses to carry out in their
own lives the example set by the divine rulers from
whom they believed all blessings to flow. The hope of
obtaining these blessings, which were in the main of
a purely materialistic order—long life, plenty of offspring, ease, comfort and joy—were no doubt the main-
spring of conduct, as they still dominate the general
ethics of the masses at the present time; but such is
the complicated and contradictory nature of man that
ideals may spring up from a materialistic foundation.
This was the case in the civilization of Babylonia and
Assyria. When Hammurapi, the great and rather
ruthless conqueror, declares as his highest ambition to
be remembered as a "father to his people,"[69] we can
no longer doubt the sway exercised by religious conceptions and by ethical aims, quite independent of the
material rewards to be expected by following the
standards of right and justice.

---

[69] In the Introduction to his famous code.

CHAPTER VI

LAW AND COMMERCE

I

WE are fortunate in possessing the code of laws according to which Babylonia was governed in the second millennium before this era. This code, the oldest compilation of laws in the world, inscribed on an obelisk of black diorite standing about eight feet high, was found in 1901 in the course of excavations conducted under the leadership of M. J. de Morgan on the site of the ancient city of Susa. The monument, dating from the reign of Hammurapi (c. 2123–2081 B.C.), was originally set up in the temple of Marduk at Babylon, known as E-sagila ("the lofty house") whence it was carried as a trophy of war by an Elamitic conqueror in the twelfth century B.C. A striking feature of this code, written in Babylonian, is its comprehensive character, covering as it does almost all phases of public and social life in Babylonia. No less significant is the circumstance that the code reverts to an older Sumerian original of which some fragments have been found,[1] so that Hammurapi's share in this great compilation appears to have been limited to preparing a translation of the older and later laws of the country into the Semitic speech and to publish the Code officially as the laws of the country for all times.[2]

---

[1] See Clay, *Orientalistische Litteratuzeitung*, 1914, Sp. 1–3.

[2] Clay copies of the Semitic text were prepared, of which the University of Pennsylvania possesses a large fragment, published by Dr. Arno Poebel, *Historical and Grammatical Texts* (Phila. 1914) No. 93. The first publication of the Code with phototype reproductions, transliteration and translation into French, we owe to Vincent Scheil (Délégation en Perse, Mémoires, Vol. IV., Paris, 1902, pp. 11–162); an English translation with the original text and transliteration, as well as a complete glossary was published by the late Prof. R. F. Harper, *The Code of Hammurabi* (University

There are indications in the code itself of its being a mixture of older with later elements. It opens, in fact, with two statutes which show the ordeal as a test of guilt still in force; it assumes in certain instances the *lex talionis* as the basis of punishment, but by the side of such primitive views and procedures, it contains many statutes revealing an advanced stage of society with highly developed ethical principles and elaborate means of establishing the guilt of the one accused of a crime or misdemeanor, with correspondingly nice distinctions in the endeavor to bring about a coördination between guilt and punishment, and accompanied also by efforts to curb parental and marital authority.

The reason for the retention of old laws by the side of later ones lies in the view common to antiquity of law as a divine decree—an oracular decision of a deity. The Hebrew word for law, *tôrâh,* has its equivalent in the Babylonian *têrtu* which means an " oracle." The decision in a dispute between parties was rendered by the deity and originally no doubt before the image of the god. It was, therefore, binding for all times. But while it could not be abrogated, modifications were introduced which practically changed its tenor, and since these modifications take on the form of regulations superimposed on the original law, the old was formally retained by the side of the new. Thus in the oldest code of the Hebrews—the so-called Book of the Covenant (Ex. 21–23, 19)—slavery, while formally recognized,

---

of Chicago Press, 1904) ; another English translation in convenient form we owe to C. H. W. Johns, *The Oldest Code of Laws in the World* (Edinburgh, 1903) ; the best German translation is that of Prof. Arthur Ungnad in a publication in conjunction with Prof. J. Kohler, *Hammurabi's Gesetz* (5 parts, Leipzig, 1904–1911), containing in addition to the translation comments on the legal aspects by Prof. Kohler, and a selection of business and legal documents of the Hammurapi period, illustrating the application of the code in actual practice. The spelling of the name with " p " appears to be a more correct form and is now generally adopted by scholars.

PLATE XXXIV

THE CODE OF HAMMURAPI, KING OF BABYLONIA (C. 2123—2081 B.C.)

is changed practically into an indenture by the stipulation that when one buys a slave, he must be set free at the end of six years. So in the code of Hammurapi the *lex talionis* is not infrequently modified into a fine regarded as a *quid pro quo,* in place of the original literal interpretation. We are not in a position to indicate the age of the oldest portions in the laws of Hammurapi, but from an important document of the reign of a far earlier ruler, Urukagina (c. 2700 B.C.), we learn of legal reforms instituted by him,[3] which presuppose the formulation of the laws for the regulation of temple fees, of marriage and divorce, of restitution, of wrongful acquisition of property, and the like. We are, therefore, safe in assuming that as early at least as 3000 B.C., and probably considerably earlier, the endeavor was made to provide for the orderly conduct of public and private affairs of the country by legal procedures.

The code of Hammurapi is thus not only an index of the state of law in the second millennium, but is also a witness to the high antiquity to which the formulation of laws in the Euphrates Valley reverts. Taking Hammurapi's code as it stands, it is both interesting and important to detect the systematic manner in which the statutes are put together.[4] After a series of introductory regulations on evidence and judicial decisions, the entire domain of law under the two aspects of things and persons is divided into six groups, Personal Property, Real Estate, Trade and Business Relations being treated under the former aspect, and the Family, Injuries and Labor under the second aspect.

Under Personal Property, we have theft of objects, further subdivided according as the theft is from a

---

[3] Thureau-Dangin, *Sumerisch-Akkadische Königsinschriften*, pp. 44–56. See above p. 130.

[4] I follow Professor D. G. Lyon's admirable analysis in the Journal of the American Oriental Society, vol. xxv, pp. 250, *seq.*

temple or palace or from an individual, kidnapping a minor, fugitive slaves, aggravated forms of theft, as burglary, highway robbery, robbery with murder, and theft from a burning house. Under Real Estate there are first treated the laws regarding the holdings of state officials with their duties, rights and restrictions, and covering such subdivisions as the loss of one's holdings through various causes, the relation of the holder to claimants, inalienable holdings of animals or realty. There follows the division of private realty with subdivisions like hired fields and payment of rent, unreclaimed land, subletting, payment of debt on one's field, mortgages, damages to fields and crops, laws in regard to orchards or date groves, leasing of productive groves, lease of houses, etc.[5] Under Trade and Business, the regulations for suits against or by merchants and peddlers, wine-selling, debts, suits for debts, storage and deposits.

This closes the first of the two larger divisions dealing with things. Among the most interesting features of the code are the statutes in the second division, treating of the family in all of its many aspects, including the definition of marriage, adultery, the suspect wife, remarriage, desertion, divorce, rights of wives, relation of wives to concubines, slave wives, deserted wife, mutual responsibility of wife and husband, killing of husband, incest, breach of promise, dowries, rights of children, status of widows, daughters who became votaries, adopted children and disinheritance. A second of the larger subdivisions takes up the important subject of injuries, specifying the punishment or fine in case the injury is done to males,—further distinctions being made as throughout the code between

---

[5] There is a break in the text at this point, due to an intentional erasure on the part of the Elamitic conqueror who carried off the code, and who had intended to write a commemorative inscription of his own deeds on this part of the stone. For some reason this was not done.

PLATE XXXV

THE FIRST EIGHT COLUMNS OF THE CODE OF HAMMURAPI

injuries to freemen and to slaves,—and to females, more specifically in the case of a woman with child who is maltreated. The third subdivision may be grouped under laborers and labor, and comprises injuries done by doctors, surgeons and veterinarians whose profession comes under the category of skilled labor, building and shipping accidents due likewise to laborers included under the head of skilful, while the other general category of unskilled labor covers such miscellaneous subjects as damages to or by oxen, farm hands, wages of shepherds and accidents caused by them, hire of laborers of various kinds and finally slaves.

This carefully considered arrangement was on the whole consistently carried out, though it resulted in a certain confusion because of the necessity of treating the same subject (as, for instance, slaves and injuries) under various subdivisions instead of massing them together, and because of the addition of later elements in the form of modifications and special illustrations to the older subdivisions.

II

Coming now to the code itself, it may be useful to give some illustrations of its provisions as a further means of grasping the spirit in which legislation in Babylonia was conceived. I have already referred to the survival in the code of the ancient ordeal as a punishment and as a test. After announcing in the first paragraph that the false accuser shall be put to death, it provides that if the accusation is sorcery, the one so charged shall be immersed in a stream. If, as the phrase runs, " the river (spoken of as the river god) holds him in his grasp," *i.e.*, if he sinks and is drowned, his guilt is established and the accuser obtains possession of the sorcerer's property; if, however, the river deity acquits him, *i.e.*, if he does not drown, the one accused obtains possession of the property of his accuser.

Now nothing could conceivably be more primitive, and from the point of view of modern justice more absurd. The stipulations, however, well illustrate the ancient point of view that all decisions in cases of doubt rest with the gods. The contestants bring their suit before the deity, who through a sign or an oracle renders a verdict,[6] and as a survival of such beginnings of legal procedure, the custom continues to prevail till the latest days in Babylonia to have the court of justice within the temple or the temple precinct, and to have priests as the representatives of the deity to act as the judges, though, as we shall see, not exclusively. The circumstance that the accuser shall receive the property of the accused in case the latter's guilt is established, and that the former shall forfeit his own property in case of a false accusation, also shows a point of view totally different from the principles upon which our ideas of justice rest. A fine or compensation for a false accusation seems reasonable, but that the accuser should receive a reward for an accusation which turns out to be correct reveals social conditions that antedate the existence of rational equity. There is an advance to a higher stage in the third paragraph which provides that he who bears false witness or who cannot prove his testimony in a criminal case involving life or death, shall himself incur the death penalty. Here the principle underlying the *lex talionis* comes into play. Since the testimony, if established, would lead to the death of the accused as a punishment, the false witness—and he who cannot prove his testimony falls within that category— should receive the punishment which is involved in the testimony itself. The application of the same principle leads to the further statute, that if the case is a civil suit involving as the phrase runs " grain or money," or as we say merchandise or currency, the penalty im-

---

[6] In the Book of the Covenant—the oldest of the Pentateuchal codes—the phrase to have a lawsuit still runs "to bring before god" (Ex. 21, 6).

posed in case the testimony is correct falls on him who has borne false testimony, or who cannot prove that to which he testifies.

A fifth paragraph which concludes the section of the code devoted to what we may call general legal procedure tells us that the judge who renders a decision duly attested and sealed and then changes the decision shall himself be called to account in court, fined to the amount of twelve times the sum involved and expelled by a popular assembly from his "judgment seat," that is, deprived forever of his judicial functions.

Since a deity cannot make a false decision, it follows that a judge who does so does not represent a deity. Such a person is a fraud—practically an inconceivable contingency, and therefore the code merely provides for the conceivable case that a judge changes his decision. Since a deity cannot in the nature of the case do so—an oracle being both the first and the last resort—the judge who is guilty of this misdemeanor logically forfeits his claim to act as the representative of a deity. It is from this point of view that the statute with its severe punishment must be considered. The appeal, which in modern law is considered in many instances the privilege of the accused or of the loser in a suit, is thus precluded by the very nature of a decision as conceived by the Babylonian spirit. The law as an "oracle," is infallible; hence the judge, too, must be infallible.

III

Passing to the next group of statutes dealing with the general subject of theft of property, we again note as a curious principle a distinction according as the object stolen is sacred or profane. Under sacred property is included whatever belongs to a temple or to a palace, for the palace is also sacrosanct as the dwelling of the king, who is originally also a priest and who continues to be regarded as the representative of the

19

deity even after the differentiation of his religious from
his secular functions. The palace is always adjacent to
the temple, and indeed the two edifices are viewed under
the same aspect, the temple being the dwelling of the
deity and the palace the temple of the deity's representative on earth. Taking temple or royal property,
therefore, is sacrilege and he who is guilty of the act
is put to death, as is also the one who receives such
stolen property. Such is the original law as it stands
without qualification (§§ 6–7). A later paragraph
(§ 8) makes an exception in the case where the object
is an ox, sheep, ass or pig—that is a domesticated animal—or a boat. A fine of thirty-fold the value is imposed, whereas if the stolen animal or property is from
a plebeian, the fine is only ten-fold, but if the thief
have not the wherewithal to pay, that is if he does not
or cannot pay the fine, he is put to death. Evidently
there is here a concession to the milder spirit of a more
advanced period which revolted against the forfeiture
of life independently of what was stolen. The old rigid
law is retained in theory, but the practice is modified
apparently on the principle that it is not sacrilege, but
merely a particularly grievous offence to take from a
temple or palace something that is not directly connected with the cult, the specification of a domestic
animal or a boat being introduced as an illustration of
the conditions under which the milder punishment of
a heavy fine is substituted for capital punishment.

A principle which, dating apparently from an early
stage and quite consistently carried out, is the aggrava-
tion of a crime through the proof of intentional fraud.
For this reason the receiver of stolen property, if aware
of the theft, suffers the severest punishment, and from
this point of view the one who aids a slave to escape,
whether from the palace or the city gate, or harbors a
fugitive slave, is put to death (§§ 15, 16, 19)—a cruel
law indeed from the modern point of view, but intelligible on the basis of the Babylonian principle that con-

nivance in depriving a man of his legal property is more
reprehensible than direct theft. The severity of the
code is, however, one of its less favorable features which
points to the retention in it of enactments reflecting a
crude state of civilization, for the progress of law is
towards mildness and indulgence, whereas the further
back we go the greater the severity of punishment,
approaching often to merciless cruelty. The number
of instances in which death is prescribed as a
punishment may serve as a test for this aspect of the
code. That man-stealing[7] and brigandage (§§ 14 and
22) should have been regarded as capital crimes is
natural, but that a purchase made without witnesses
or a formal contract should involve a death punishment
(§ 7), on the assumption that a claim made under such
circumstances points to fraud has a meaning only from
the Babylonian point of view, that fraud is established by the mere absence of a formal contract. The
punishment no doubt rests on a provision that every
purchase must be confirmed by a contract, but to extend
the law beyond the establishment of the validity of a
transaction indicates extreme crudity in its interpretation. The primitive law of retaliation accounts for a
large number of the instances in which death is set
down as the punishment, as, for example, that in case
of the collapse of a defective building, the architect is
to be put to death if the owner is killed by the accident,
and the architect's son if the son of the owner loses his
life (§§ 229–230), or that if through a blow inflicted
by some one on a man's daughter, the latter dies, the
daughter of the one who inflicted the injury should be
put to death (§ 210). It is significant that these provisions occur within a group of statutes (§§ 195–225)
all dealing with the application of the primitive *lex
talionis,* just as we find traces of this law in the Penta-

---

[7] The specific case instanced (§ 14) is the case of a man stealing
a minor, but no doubt the application is general.

teuchal codes.[8] The one who destroys the eye of another shall lose his eye; if he breaks a man's bone, his
bone shall be broken, and if he knocks out a man's tooth,
one of his teeth shall be knocked out. It is likewise the
extension of the same principle which provides that a
physician who performs an unsuccessful operation resulting in the loss of a patient's eye or in the patient's
death should have his hands cut off, or that in case a
veterinary operates on an ox or ass and the animal dies,
one fourth of its value should be restored to the owner.
The very extension of the principle while leading to
crudities also paves the way for a juster valuation of
damages. It is still a most absurd application of the
principle which leads to the enactment that if a nurse
to whom a child has been entrusted and who substitutes
another child in place of the one so entrusted which
has died on her hands, the woman is to have her breasts
cut off so as to deprive her of the possibility of the
repetition of the crime (§ 194), but on the other hand
a more advanced stage is represented by the provisions
for suitable compensation in the case of bodily injuries.
So immediately following the direct enunciation of the
lex talionis in regard to destroying a man's eye or
breaking his bone (§§ 196–197), we find the provision
converting the underlying principle into a basis for
adequate compensation. The fine for destroying the
eye of a plebeian is one mina [9] of silver, whereas in case
the injured party is a slave, only half of that sum is
imposed.

---

[8] Hurt for hurt, eye for eye, tooth for tooth, etc., with additions
and variations in the three principal codes, viz., Ex. 21, 24 (code
of Covenant); Deut. 19, 21 (Deuteronomic code); Lev. 24, 20 (Holi-
ness code).

[9] A mina (or mana) is 60 shekels. The actual silver value of a
shekel is less than 50 cents in modern coinage, but is a standard
coin in antiquity. Its purchasing value, fluctuating according to
commercial activity, was much higher—perhaps at times as much
as five dollars in our days.

IV

This distinction of classes in fixing of fines and punishments is characteristic of the code throughout, and follows as a natural corollary from the principle of the *lex talionis* which thus reveals its hold even after the stage of literal interpretation had been passed. With class distinctions recognized in all walks of life, it was a logical conclusion to connect with the aim of bringing about a just proportion between punishment and crime—which is the basic principle of the *lex talionis*—a differentiation according to the rank of the injured party. A free plebeian being of higher grade than the slave, and the nobleman above both, the illegality was regarded as of a higher or a lower severity corresponding to the difference in ranks. In other words, while according to modern ideas a crime is viewed independently of the one by whom or on whom it is committed, ancient law as long as it remained under the influence of the *lex talionis* could not dissociate the act either from the actor or from the one who suffered through it. So if a man injures another, the fine varies according as one strikes a person of superior rank, in which case public whipping—sixty strokes with a leather thong—is prescribed (§ 202), whereas if one strikes a man of one's own rank, a fine of one mina of silver is imposed, though in the case of any plebeian striking a plebeian, the fine is only ten shekels of silver, that is one-sixth of a mina (§ 204). A slave, on the other hand, is more severely treated, his ear being cut off in case he strikes a man's son (§ 205), as an adequate punishment for the assault; and we may conjecture that in this case the abandonment of the more literal application of the *lex talionis,* which would have suggested that the slave's hand be cut off, was due to loss in the value of the slave as property through such a punishment. A further advance in the direction of more humanitarian justice is indicated in the provisions for the case that a bodily injury is inflicted without intent. According to the original spirit of the *lex talionis* this element does not enter, but Hammurapi's code stipulates that if a man can swear, " I did not strike with intent " in a quarrel with another, he is let off with the payment of the doctor's bill; and in case the victim dies of the blow, a fine of half a mina is imposed if the one who has inflicted the fatal injury belongs to the general class of inhabitants, whereas a plebeian pays only one-third of a mina. A miscarriage as a result of an unintentional injury to a man's daughter entails a fine of ten shekels, for the daughter of a plebeian only five shekels, and for the daughter of a slave only two shekels. If the woman dies, in case she is the daughter of a plebeian, the fine is one-half of a mina of silver, for a female slave one-third of a mina of silver, whereas—curiously enough—the old law of *lex talionis* is retained in case the victim is the daughter of a free citizen, the code providing (§ 210) for such a contingency the death of the daughter of the man who has struck the blow which ended fatally. The *lex talionis* as the basis of adjustment between a crime or an injury and the punishment or fine leads by a natural evolution also to an equitable compensation for benefits conferred as well. Under this aspect, the physician's fee in case of a cure through an operation or otherwise is regulated with regard to the value of the cure. A successful operation which saves a man's eye is valued at ten shekels in the case of an ordinary citizen. A plebeian pays only five shekels, and the owner of a slave two shekels to the physician who has saved a slave's eye. For setting a broken bone or for an ordinary physical trouble, the fee is five shekels if the patient is a free citizen, three shekels for the plebeian who is throughout the code a somewhat privileged personage, obliged to pay less, whether a fine or a fee, and for the slave two shekels paid for as usual by the master. The Code in the same way endeavors to regulate the cost of building a house, the hire of boats and even of animals. That such regulations are all viewed under the general aspect of the *lex talionis* in its double extension to all kinds of injuries on the one hand, and to benefits on the other, is shown by the juxtaposition of the building and hiring stipulations with losses incident to such agreements, whether through neglect or through unforseen causes. In fact the principle of compensation involved in the primitive *lex talionis*—its underlying justification as it were—becomes the starting point for the further development of justice in the regulation of dealings of man with his fellow. Responsibility for damage or loss of cargo on a boat hired to carry goods to any place rests on the boatman, if carelessness on his part can be proved. The cargo must be replaced as well as the boat; and in case the boatman succeeds in refloating the original boat, a compensation to the extent of one-half of the value of the boat is to be given the owner, to make good the diminished value of the boat by reason of the accident (§§ 237–238). In the case of a collision between two boats resulting in the sinking of one, it is assumed that the ship moving up stream is responsible as the one which could more easily get out of the way. The owner of the boat lost in going down stream must make a sworn declaration of his loss, which as well as the boat or its value must be made good by the owner of the other boat (§ 240).

The hire of oxen, of field-laborers and of herdsmen is similarly regulated by law (§§ 242–243; 257–258), and the same distinction made between accidents due to neglect and such as could not have been prevented Thus the one who hires an ox or an ass cannot be held responsible if the animal is killed by a lion. The owner in that case must bear the loss (§ 244), but if the death of the hired animal is caused by neglect or abuse, its value must be restored; and the further attempt is made to regulate the extent of loss through an injury to the animal. The loss of an eye involves a fine of one-half of the value of the ox, the breaking of a horn, or the cutting of the tail or injury to its flesh through the yoke, one-fourth of its value, but if the injury is such as to ruin the usefulness of the animal, as, for example, if its foot is crushed or it is hamstrung, then an ox of equal value is to be restored to the owner (§§ 246–248). If an ox gores a man as it goes through the street, this is regarded as an unavoidable accident and entails no penalty (§ 250), but if the ox has been known to be vicious, and the owner has been warned and its horns have not been tied up, a penalty of half a mina of silver is imposed if the ox fatally gores a man of the ordinary class, and if it be a slave one-third of a mina (§§ 251–252).

V

The two large fields of activity in ancient Babylonia were agriculture and commerce. In the endeavor to regulate on an equitable basis the obligations resting upon those who own and those who rent fields for purposes of cultivation, as in the complications arising from contracts and agreements entered upon by merchants and money lenders, the code is equally explicit. A few extracts from the sections dealing with these phases of activity will suffice to illustrate the principles underlying the regulations. In renting fields for cultivation, the stipulation was in general (a) a return through a percentage of the yield, according to the size of the property, calculated on an average crop and applying to both fields and date-tree orchards, or (b) through a division of the yield in terms agreed upon, with further special provisions in the case of virgin fields. The general term of rent was for one year, except in the case of virgin soil where the term was usually for three years.[10] The code provides that in case the failure of the crop can be traced to the neglect of the tenant, the latter is responsible for the share

---

[10] See further below pp. 327 and 349.

according to the contract, on the basis of the yield in adjacent fields; and if in addition it is shown that he has not even cultivated the field, he must till and harrow it before returning it to the owner (§§ 42–43). Similarly in the case of a virgin field, rented out for three years, if the tenant neglects to carry out his obligation to till it properly, he must return the field in the fourth year hoed and harrowed, and hand over to the owner a return on the basis of ten Gur for every ten Gan [11] (§ 44). If, on the other hand, the failure is due to causes beyond his control—an inundation or lack of sufficient rain— the tenant is not obliged to make any return for that year, and a new contract is made for the ensuing year (§ 48). If, however, an inundation occurs, ruining the produce of the field after the tenant has already paid the share of the crop due to the owner—who presumably therefore is entitled to the first yield—the tenant must bear the loss (§ 45).

Pasturing sheep in a field without an agreement and without consent of the owner entails as a fine a return of twenty Gur of grain for each ten Gan, or double the amount of the ordinary rate of return for letting out a field for cultivation; and under aggravated circumstances when the owner of the flock deliberately turns his flock into another's field, sixty Gur for each ten Gan, the assumption in the former case being that the sheep strayed into another's field (§§ 57–58). In the case of money obtained as a loan with a field as security, the interest may be paid in the yield or directly according to the usual rate of interest. If the latter is stipulated and the debtor cannot pay cash, then he must pay from the crop at the market rate of its value; nor can the obligation in either case be avoided if the crop is a failure. The contract is valid even though it is stipu-

---

[11] A Gur is about 120 litres and a Gan about 6½ Ka. or 25 acres. The amount is, therefore, based no doubt on the average yield, 1200 litres for 250 acres, i.e., about twenty per cent. of the total crop.

lated that the interest is to be paid in the crop of that year. [The basic principle is throughout that agreements must be made in good faith on both sides, and that exemption from obligations can only be claimed if circumstances beyond control arise, and then only if the agreement is of such a character as to justify the assumption that the agreement was not to be kept in such a contingency.]

This principle is well illustrated in a series of laws to regulate the relationship between a wholesale merchant and his retail agent who acts as a salesman or negotiator. When the transaction is directly in cash which the agent is to use in mercantile enterprises, the latter is to hand in a detailed account, and interest is to be charged according to the length of time for which the money is used (§ 100).[12] In other words it is not an ordinary loan for a stipulated time, for which no special provision need be made, but an agreement with some one acting as the representative of the merchant. The responsibility rests upon the agent, who takes all risks except that of being robbed. If he swears an oath to this effect, he is free of obligation (§ 103), but failure of the enterprise through any other cause entails a fine of double the amount received (§ 101). This seems hard and it is strange that the law should not have been content with the return of the capital plus the interest. One suspects that such a provision is a survival of the period when transactions of this kind involved great risks on the part of the merchant who was thus to be protected against fraud by the agent, who could easily pretend not to have been successful. In accord with this we find a fine of threefold the original sum imposed as a fine in case the agent is convicted of fraudulent intent (§106). On the other hand, the agent is protected against any improper advantage being taken by the merchant by a written account of what he takes on

---

[12] There is a large gap just before this paragraph so that the enumeration of paragraphs from this point on is merely approximate.

commission—grain, wool, oil or anything else—and by
taking a receipt duly sealed in the presence of witnesses
for the money which he returns to the merchant (§ 104),
though it is also stipulated that failure to take such a
receipt does not oblige the agent to pay it again if he
can prove that it has been paid (§ 105)—a stipulation
which impresses one as a later judicial decision rather
than as a logical inference. If fraudulent intent is
proved against the merchant, the latter must refund
as the fine six times the amount paid by the agent
(§ 107). In case the money is given to an agent as a
favor, by which presumably is meant that the agent
does not take it as his risk, in case of failure to carry
out the enterprise, only the principal need be returned
(§ 102). This stipulation again impresses one as of
later origin to obviate the earlier and entirely too
severe law which placed all the risks on the agent. In
this way the agent could choose the conditions on which
he might act for another, or at all events the opportunity would be afforded of avoiding the consequences
of the earlier law, provided an express stipulation was
made that the agent received the commission "as a
favor"—which must be regarded in this instance as a
technical term to designate a commission without in-
curring all the risks in case of failure of the enterprise.

VI

It is interesting to note also the endeavor of the
Code to protect the debtor against undue pressure and
maltreatment when seized for debt, evidently with a
view of counteracting abuses that had crept into
practice, and which had given creditors a merciless
hold upon those who had been unsuccessful in their
enterprises. The general point of view of the Code is
still that a man who contracts a debt which he finds
himself unable to pay is a criminal, even though free
from criminal intent. He is treated as such in later
law codes (down almost to our own days), when debtors

could be thrown into prison. No one has the right to incur an obligation which he is not certain of being able to carry out. At all events if he takes a risk, he must endure the bitterest consequences. Apparently in Hammurapi's days a member of the debtor's household could be seized as a hostage by the creditor and kept as a prisoner in the latter's house till a settlement was made, or he might seize the debtor's slave or his son, holding him as a hostage; and if the one so seized dies while a prisoner through natural causes, there is no charge to be brought against the creditor (§ 115). This was going pretty far, and evidently to prevent the possibilities of foul play, it is provided in what is clearly a later statute, modifying the earlier one, that if it can be shown that the one seized for a man's debt died through blows or other inhuman treatment (as, for example, starvation), then the old *lex talionis* comes into play, and if the debtor's son is the victim, then the son of the creditor is put to death, and if it is a slave, then one-third mina of silver is imposed as a fine, and the debt is forfeited (§ 116). An unwarranted seizure for a hostage entails the same fine as in the case of a slave being seized and allowed to die through abuse— one-third of a mina of silver (§ 114), but the debt is not forfeited, which shows that even in Hammurapi's code the advantage was always on the side of the stronger, except when fraudulent intent or deliberate injury can be proved. From this point of view it is as much as could be expected that if a creditor, holding a debt of grain or money against a man, reimburses himself out of the debtor's granary without the latter's consent, the creditor shall be called to account, return what he has taken, and because of his greed forfeit the total amount of his debt (§ 113). The aim of the statute is clearly to protect the debtor against a wilful and cruel creditor, who even though he is entitled to what he has taken, commits a crime because not acting by order of the court. The statute implies that the proper procedure is to bring the case before a judge, and to secure an execution to seize the debtor's granary for the amount. It marks a considerable advance thus to insist upon legal procedure, even when there is no question of what is due to the creditor. In another direction, the Code evidently aims to modify the hard condition of the debtor, who under the primitive view that wife and children are part of a man's chattels, could sell them for debt and, indeed, was in certain cases probably forced to do so. To curb the ancient practice without abolishing the underlying principle, the Code provides that if a man is held for debt and sells his wife, son or daughter or hands them over to the control (sc. of the creditor), he can do so for only three years. In the fourth year their freedom must be given them (§ 117). The provision, evidently made in the interest of the debtor's family, practically changes the legalized sale into an indenture, precisely as the old Hebrew law, desirous of abolishing slavery in so far as it affected members of the group, converts the sale into an indenture of six years.[13] On the other hand, male or female slaves sold for debt may be further disposed of by the merchant into whose possession they pass. An exception, however, in the further interest of more humanitarian conditions, provides that a maid who has borne children to her master, if sold for debt, is to be ransomed by her master when he is able to do so.

Deposits with any one of gold or silver or anything else must be made in the presence of witnesses and the exact terms stipulated. Accordingly, a claim for a deposit without witnesses and written agreements is invalid. If these conditions are fulfilled, and the one with whom the deposit has been made disputes the claim, a fine of double the amount is imposed on the fraudulent trustee (§§ 122–124). The trustee is responsible for what he receives on deposit, and in case

---

[13] Above p. 288.

through his neglect, it is stolen or otherwise removed, he must restore the full loss to the original owner, but may reimburse himself if he succeeds in regaining the lost property (§ 125). A supplemental provision covers the case of a false claim on the part of one who has made a deposit, entailing a fine of double the amount of the claim, which must be set forth in detail before a decision is rendered as to its being false or not (§ 126).

VII

Almost one-fourth of the Code is taken up with the regulation of family relationships, including such subjects as adultery, false accusations, divorce, rights of wives, slave wives, desertion, widows, adoption, rights of daughters, and disinheritance. Taken together, these family laws, as we may collectively call them, throw more light on social conditions prevailing in ancient Babylonia than any other portion of the Code; and since in addition they furnish further illustrations of legal procedure and of the underlying principles of justice, it is worth while in concluding our analysis of the code to take up some features of these laws.

A wife is still viewed as an acquisition, and therefore no marriage is valid without a contract (§ 128). Divorce can be granted in case of a childless marriage, but the marriage gift, as well as the dowry which the woman has received from her father's house, must be returned to her; and if there was no marriage gift the husband must in that case give his wife a mina of silver[14]—an amount which is reduced to one-third in case the husband belongs to the plebeian class (§§ 138–140). Two other causes for divorce are (a) improper conduct on the part of the woman or (b) incompatibility between husband and wife. If the improper conduct goes no further than that the woman

---

[14] An older (?) law (Rawlinson, V., Pl. 25, col. iv, 8–12) fixes the amount at one-half of a mina.

is in the habit of going out and, as the Code puts it,
" commits indiscretions," neglects her house and husband, then the husband has the choice of dismissing
her without giving her anything, or he may reduce her
to the rank of a maid and take another wife in her
place (§ 141). If, however, the woman goes further
than this and lays herself open to suspicion, she is
thrown into the river, by which is presumably meant
that she must submit to an ordeal (§ 143). Incompatibility is expressed by a euphemistic phrase to indicate
her unwillingness to have sexual intercourse with her
husband. If it can be shown that she is otherwise without reproach, or that her husband has neglected his
duties towards her, then the woman receives her dowry
and returns to her father's house (§ 142). This is as
far as the Babylonian law goes, but the advance over
former conditions may be seen from an older Sumerian
law which stipulates that a woman who refuses to have
intercourse with her husband is to be thrown into the
river,[15] without further investigation as to the cause
or whether the woman is otherwise without reproach.

The authority of the husband was at one time absolute, as was the authority of either parent over the
children. The father or mother could disinherit the
son by the formula, " thou art not my son,"[16] which de-
prives the son of all rights and privileges; " he is ex-
cluded from house and wall "—as the phrase runs,
while the son who disowns the authority of his father
or mother by the formula, "thou art not my father,"
or, "thou art not my mother," is branded as a slave
and sold if he rebels against his father, and branded
and driven from home and town if he rebels against his
mother.[17]

The Code endeavors to curb this absolute authority
without denying the principle—on the conventional

[15] Rawlinson, V., Pl. 25, Col. iv, 1–7.
[16] Ib., Col. ii, 34–39.
[17] Ib., Col. ii, 22–33.

supposition that a once existing law cannot be annulled, because it represents a divine decision. In the case of the son, it provides that the father must bring his intention to disinherit his son to the notice of the court. A decision of the judges is needed and the judges are instructed to inquire into the merits of the case. If they find that the son has not been guilty of a crime sufficient to justify the disinheritance, the father is restrained from carrying out his intention (§ 168); and the law goes even further in providing that the first offence must be condoned. Only in case of a second offence, can the disinheritance be regarded as legal (§ 169). The older and severer law, however, remains in force in the case of an illegitimate child or one of low estate who, if he says to his foster father, "thou art not my father," or to his foster mother, " thou art not my mother," i.e., if he rebels against their authority, has his tongue cut out. In case the son discovers the identity of his father, and rejects his foster parents in order to return to his father's house, his eye is plucked out (§§ 192–193), the principle involved being that such a child if once adopted belongs absolutely to the foster parents and cannot be reclaimed (§ 187). A trace of the older status of absolute authority of the pater-familias is to be seen also in the provision that a legally adopted child cannot be reclaimed after it has been reared, but then follows immediately the later modification that if the child after being taken, longs (?) for his father and mother, it must be returned to his father's house (§§ 185–186). The purpose of the modification is to protect the child against forcible adoption. Similarly, the adopted child must be given the same status as the other children, and if that is not done he may return to his father's house even after he has been reared. According to the Babylonian laws an artisan may adopt a child who is apprenticed to him, and after the former has taught the apprentice his trade, no claim can be put in, but if he fails to teach the child a trade, he may return to his father's house, that is, the contract of adoption is annulled (§§ 188–190).

The Code recognizes the legitimacy of the children of a handmaid or concubine, provided the father during his lifetime recognizes them as his own by pronouncing the formula "my children" in regard to them, that is, by a formal adoption. In that case they share in the paternal estate equally with the children of the main wife. If the formal adoption has not taken place, then the children of the handmaid have no share in the estate, but on the other hand protection is given to them by the grant of their freedom after the death of the father; and it is specifically provided that the children of the main wife have no claim on the service of their half-brothers or sisters. A man's heirs are his children—not his wife. His widow receives her dowry and the marriage gift on the death of her husband and is allowed to remain in her husband's house as long as she lives, but she is not allowed to sell it, for it belongs to her children (§ 171). If no marriage gift has been made, then the widow receives in addition to her dowry, an amount equivalent to the share of a son. The widow is further protected from maltreatment by her children, who may not force her to leave the husband's house without good cause. If, however, she leaves of her free will, then she forfeits the right to the marriage gift, but can dispose as she pleases of the dowry and is allowed to marry whom she pleases (§ 172). On her death, the dowry shall be divided between the children of the first and second marriage, or if there is no issue from the second marriage, then the dowry goes to the children of her first marriage (§§ 173–174). In no case, therefore, does the husband receive the dowry. A widow whose children are still minors cannot marry without the consent of the court. To obtain that consent an inventory of the estate must be made, and the woman and her second husband must agree by a written contract to administer the estate for the benefit of the

20

children whom they are obliged to rear. They may not dispose of the estate, and he who makes such a transaction forfeits his claim (§ 177). The children inherit the dowry of the mother. If the mother dies, and the husband takes a second wife and has children by her also, upon the death of the father the children of the first wife receive the dowry of their mother, and after this is deducted the paternal estate is divided between the children of both wives (§ 167). Under ordinary circumstances it would appear that the estate was equally divided, but the father had the right to favor one son if he so chose. In that case the special property —field, orchard or house—is given outright to the son so favored, and the balance of the property divided (§ 165). The question must have arisen whether a son who had not reached the age of majority on the death of the father should receive the same share as the others. The Code provides that if all the other sons having reached the age of majority are married, that is, have established households of their own, they shall set aside from the estate an amount equivalent to a marriage gift [18] for the minor brother so as to enable him to take a wife (§ 166).

---

[18] A passage like this proves that the marriage gift or settlement, as we would say, is made by the bridegroom, but is deposited with the bride's father for her benefit. The dowry on the other hand is given by the bride's father to the prospective son-in-law. Of the two customs, the marriage gift on the part of the husband appears to be the older,—a survival of the custom of marriage by purchase, dating from a time when the husband owned his wife and children as part of his chattels. The dowry, on the other hand, while originating likewise from the days when a child was obliged to do service for the father and representing the pay for such services on the change of the daughter's status to become the property of another, nevertheless represents a higher stage of society, recognizing the obligation not to send the daughter away empty-handed—as though she were merely a piece of property, thus disposed of.

VIII

These instances will suffice to illustrate the great care that was taken to prevent, as Hammurapi says in the introduction to the Code, " the strong from oppress-pleased. Even prior to the promulgation of the Code, throughout is to protect those who need to be secured against an advantage that may be taken of them— wives, widows and minor children. The attempt was also made to make the position of daughters more secure than it must have been in an earlier period when the father had the right to dispose of his daughters as he pleased. Even prior to the promulgation of the code, the period had been passed when fathers could sell their daughters to their husbands. The dignity of marriage and of family life had been recognized to the extent that the father gives the daughter a dowry on her marriage, and that a portion of the estate is settled upon her, though the latter does not appear to have been obligatory. It is expressly provided, how-ever, that if the father fails to give his daughter a dowry, she is entitled to a share in the estate on the father's death equivalent to that of a son, with the re-striction, however, that after her death it reverts to her brothers.

From an early period, the custom of devoting daughters to the service of a deity continued in force down to the end of the Babylonian-Assyrian monarch-ies. In the earliest form of this custom, such votaries were sacred harlots. We know of several classes of such votaries at the temple of Nanâ in Uruk,[19] and it is more than likely that they formed part of the organization in every religious centre. In how far prostitution prac-tices were carried on as part of the temple rites we do not know, but the circumstance that in Babylonia and Assyria, the lay prostitute had a certain standing may

[19] Shurpu Series (ed. Zimmern), Tablet V–VI, 145–147.

be taken as an indication that prostitution retained, from its connection with the ritual, a measure of sanctity which it is difficult for us from the modern point of view to appreciate. But besides acting as sacred prostitutes, female votaries performed other services including certain distinctly priestly functions.[20] Such votaries and priestesses never entered into wedlock. The Code, accordingly, makes special provisions for them and places, as we have seen, the lay prostitute in the same category. Strange to say, however, the latter is placed on a par legally with a bride, whereas the sacred prostitutes, of which the Code recognizes two classes—the *kadishtu* ("pure" or "holy woman")[21] and *zermashitu* ("disregarding or neglecting the seed")[22]—receive, in case no dowry is given to them, only one-third of a son's portion after the father's death (§ 181), presumably because these votaries were provided for by the temple organization to which they belonged, whereas the lay prostitute was under necessity of making her living by her trade. The *kadishtu* and *zermashitu* could not dispose of their inheritance, which reverted on their death to the male heirs, whereas a votary attached to the Marduk cult at Babylon could dispose of her portion, and will it to

---

[20] See the list of the various classes of priestesses occurring in legal and other documents given by Frank, *Studien zur Babylonischen Religion,* pp. 47–50, and which can be still further extended. Kings set the example by devoting one of their daughters to the service of a deity. See the illustration in the author's *Bildermappe zur Religion Babyloniens und Assyriens,* Nr. 26 and Dhorme's article "La fille de Nabonide," in the *Revue d'Assyriologie,* xi, pp. 105–117.

[21] Sumerian Nu-Gig = *kadishtu,* (Brünnow, *Classified List* No. 2017). The same term *kedēshâ* is used in the Deuteronomic Code (Deut. 23, 18) as well as the masculine *kādēsh* for such female and male votaries, which were forbidden by the Hebrew legislation.

[22] Nu-Par = *zermashitu* (Meissner, *Seltene Assyrische Ideogramme,* No. 1147.).

whomsoever she pleased (§ 182). A general name for a woman attached to a temple was " *entu* " or " woman of a deity." Such votaries lived in a separate portion of the temple known as "dormitory" and equivalent to our nunnery, but there were also votaries who were not so confined. The Code is severe on a votary who opens a wine-shop, which was the brothel in Babylonia and Assyria, for the penalty is death by burning, and this law is applied also to a votary or nun who even enters a wine-shop, the assumption being that she does so for purposes of prostitution with men who congregate there (§ 110). In passing it may be noted that the Code assumes that the proprietors of these wine-shops or brothels are women; they appear to have been women of the lowest class—quite different from the lay prostitutes. They naturally had a most unsavory reputation. Outlaws gathered in the dens kept by these women, and the Code provides that if a woman harbors such outlaws sought for by the courts, she suffers death as a punishment (§ 109).

The Code still recognizes, as a survival of an earlier day when the leading idea connected with marriage was to provide for offspring, the right of a wife to give her husband a concubine whose children would be recognized as though they were her own. We are familiar with this custom from the incident in the cycle of Abraham stories where the childless Sarah transfers her maid Hagar to her husband (Gen. 16, 3), and Bilhah, the maid of Rachel, is given to Jacob so that "she may bear on my knee and I acquire offspring through her " to indicate that Bilhah's children will be regarded as hers (Gen. 30, 3). Such a concubine, however, did not have the rank of a wife (§ 145). With this as a starting point, the Code endeavors to protect both the wife and the concubine, the former by providing that in case she does bear children, the husband may not take a concubine (§ 144), the latter by stipulating that the mistress, that is, the legitimate wife, may not sell the concubine who has born her husband children, but she may place a slave mark upon her and reckon her with the slaves (§ 146). In case, however, the concubine has not born any children, then the mistress may sell the concubine (§ 147) who, it is assumed throughout, is as in the case of the Biblical parallels the property of the wife—a special handmaid.

It was not obligatory for a father to give a daughter who becomes a concubine a dowry. If he does so, then she has no further share in the property of her father upon his death (§ 183), whereas if he does not do so, then the brothers after the death of the father must give their sister a dowry proportionate to the amount of the paternal estate (§ 184); and it is furthermore provided that they shall provide a husband for their sister. In both cases it is assumed that the concubine may be given by her father to a husband. In the former case he does so, in the latter he does not. It would seem therefore that the term concubine is applied in the Code in a double sense, (a) as the handmaid of a wife brought to the husband for the purpose of bearing children and (b) as an additional wife, not having the status of the man's wife, but at the same time not a handmaid of either the husband or of the wife. Bearing in mind the Biblical parallels, the older practice appears to have been that in the case of a childless marriage, the wife brings to her husband her own handmaid, whereas with more advanced social conditions the husband could choose any woman as his concubine and place her in his household as a legitimate wife, though subservient in status to the chief wife. The concubine thus becomes the partner or rival of the first wife— parallel to the case of the two wives of Elkanah, Hannah and Peninnah in the story of Samuel (I Sam. 1, 6) where Peninnah is spoken of as the "rival" or partner of Hannah in the possession of the husband.

IX

The old severity towards those who endangered the sanctity of the marriage tie or of family relations was maintained in full rigor. The woman caught in the act of adultery is thrown into the water together with the culprit, though an additional clause gives the husband or the king the right to spare the woman's life if either feels so inclined (§ 129)—a provision intended no doubt to cover cases where extenuating circumstances existed. If a betrothed woman is forced to the act which takes place in her father's house, the culprit is put to death but the woman goes free (§ 130), and if the woman accused by her husband of adultery can swear an oath that she is innocent, she may return to her husband's house (§ 131). If, however, another than her husband accuse her, then she must submit to the ordeal by throwing herself into the water (§ 132). The assumption in all these cases of course is that she has not been detected in the act. The punishment for the one who brings an accusation of adultery but cannot prove it is to be branded on the forehead (§ 127), and this applies to such a charge brought against a votary as well as against a wife.

Starting from the principle that a man must provide for his wife, the Code adds a number of decisions to distinguish between desertion and enforced absence. If a man is captured but there is provision made by him for his wife she must remain faithful to him. If she fails to do so, she is to be thrown into the water; but if the husband fails to provide for her, she is free from blame if, as the phrase in the Code reads, "she enters the house of another " (§§ 133–134); and if she bears children to her second husband, and then the first one returns, she is to be taken back by her first husband, while the children from the second one are placed in charge of the father (§ 135). Such cases arose frequently in consequence of the numerous wars in which

the petty states and afterwards the united states of the
Euphrates Valley were engaged, as a consequence of
which wives might be in doubt whether their captured
husbands would ever return. Making provision for
the wife was, however, taken as an indication of the
husband's intent to return, and therefore, the woman
was bound to him until she heard that he had perished.
The same would apply of course to a husband absent
from home on business, and it is interesting to compare
with the Code the discussions and decisions on the complications arising from such circumstances in the
Talmudical treatise setting forth the Jewish practice,[23]
with the same endeavor to distinguish between enforced
absence and actual desertion. On the latter subject,
the Babylonian Code is brief and explicit. The woman
can marry another, and if the first husband returns,
she is not to go back to him (§ 136).

Lastly, as a further illustration of the aim of the
Code to maintain proper standards in family relations,
we may instance the series of punishments for incest
which will also show the grades of such conduct recognized. The man who violates his own daughter is driven
out of the city, that is, loses his right of citizenship
(§ 154). If a father violates the son's betrothed after
the son has known her, he shall be bound and thrown
into the water; but if the son has not yet known her,
then the man is let off with a fine of half a mina of
silver; he also restores to the girl whatever she may
have brought from her father's house, and the girl may
marry whom she pleases (§ 155). The point of view
is that found generally in primitive society which looks
lightly upon sexual intercourse with a woman before
marriage or before she has known the man to whom
she is promised, but is exceedingly severe upon the
same act with a married woman. As a consequence even
the illicit intercourse between a father and his virgin

---

[23] Treatise Kethubîn, fol. 110b.

daughter does not entail the severest punishment,
whereas if a son has intercourse with his mother after
his father's death, both are to be burned (§ 157). If,
however, the intercourse be with one of his father's
wives who is not his mother, he is merely expelled from
the family, because the grade of incest is less than in the
case of his own mother (§ 158). The distinction, however, appears to belong to a later age. Breach of
promise is treated from two points of view. A marriage representing primarily an agreement between
the father of the bride and the prospective husband, a
refusal to marry may emanate from the latter, and a
refusal to give in marriage from the former. If the
prospective husband rejects his bride merely because
he prefers another woman, that is to say without adequate cause and he has already fixed a marriage gift
for the girl, and in accordance with prevailing custom
has given the father-in-law the present which takes
the place of the older purchase-money for a wife, then
the father-in-law retains the settlement. If the father
of the bride refuses to give his daughter in marriage
after the gift has been turned over, then double the
amount is to be returned to the bridegroom. If the
father-in-law, after the marriage settlement has been
given, refuses to abide by the agreement because he
listens to the defamation of his son-in-law, to some idle
gossip from a " friend," the same fine of double the
amount of what had been given is imposed on the
father-in-law. The " friend " who slandered the bridegroom is not permitted to marry the girl (§§ 159–161).
The three cases are set down as typical and form the
basis for deciding other cases that may arise.

X

The Code closes (§§ 278–282) with a series of enactments regulating dealings in slaves. As a protection
to the purchaser it is stipulated that if within a month

a purchased slave is taken with a *bennu* sickness [23a] which incapacitates him, he is to be returned to the seller and the purchase money given back, the assumption being that the slave was not what he or she was represented to be. In accord with this, the seller is responsible in case of a prior claim on the slave, in which case the sale is likewise invalid. Similarly, a sale of a slave is invalid if made in a foreign land and the owner of the slave recognizes his former property when the slave is brought into the district in which the former owner dwells. Such a slave is granted his freedom if he belongs to the district in which the original owner dwells, but if slaves sold under such circumstances be not natives, they are to be bought back by the former owner. The law is of interest as pointing to an endeavor to protect slaves against being bandied about without regard to their feelings of pride. The court decides that a slave who is not sold directly through his master gains his freedom if he is brought back to the district to which he originally belonged. In this way a restriction was placed on traffic in slaves. The law in thus assuming that a slave is purchased to be put into service and is not to be regarded as mere merchandise marks a decided step in advance to protect the dignity of human life. To be sure, the underlying principle that slaves *are* chattels is maintained, and the right is accorded to the owner to dispose of him, but if he is sold to a foreigner and in the course of time is resold and brought back to his native place, his dignity is protected by his being granted his freedom. In this case, the Code proceeds on the principle found in modern law *emptor caveat*. The purchaser takes the risk and should assure himself of the circumstances of the slave's provenance before closing the bargain. On the other hand, to prevent an abuse of the privilege, the old law providing that a slave who rebels against the

---

[23a] Perhaps epilepsy. See below p. 343 *seq.*

authority of his master is to have his ear cut off is added (§ 282), to cover the case also of a slave who has run away and who is not under any conditions to have the privilege of securing his freedom through a fortuitous chain of circumstances, or by a fictitious sale in a foreign district. The Code of Hammurapi is particularly severe on any one who aids a slave to escape or who harbors a runaway (§§ 15–19), death as a penalty being imposed precisely as in the case of man stealing (§ 14) ; and if a slave escapes from the person who has captured him, the latter must swear an oath to that effect (§ 20), so as to free himself from the suspicion of having connived at the escape. On the other hand, a reward of two shekels is to be given to the one who returns a runaway slave (§ 17).

XI

We may now pass on to some illustrations of the manner in which existing laws were applied in the regulation of commercial transactions, which cover an exceedingly wide scope from actual sales of houses, land, orchards, goods, cattle and slaves to loans of money or chattels, rent of houses or fields, deposits, transfer of property, covering also legal transactions such as contracts of all kinds, including marriage deeds, division of estates, partnerships, hiring of laborers, commercial agencies and testaments.[24] Incidental to such transactions and contracts, we have numerous cases of lawsuits brought before a tribunal which, after an examination of the facts, renders its decision on the basis of the prevailing statutes. In this way, a constant succession of new cases is brought before the judges, and each new decision carries with it some supplement to the recognized code. Law in Babylonia

[24] See the admirably arranged bibliography for this section of Babylonian-Assyrian literature in Johns, *The Relations Between the Laws of Babylonia and the Laws of the Hebrew Peoples* (London, 1914), pp. 76–89.

and Assyria is thus a progressive process, and as we
pass from older to later periods, we can follow in detail
the modifications in both legal procedure and practice
incident to the growing complications of commercial
expansion and the various forms of social activity. The
many thousands of legal and business documents found
in the course of excavations and that have been published up to the present time thus unfold a picture of
the inner life of the communities in both the south and
north, which complements the data to be derived from
the annals and votive inscriptions of the rulers and
from the official correspondence in the form of letters,
orders and reports of all kinds.

A striking feature thus revealed for a very early
period, the time of the Ur dynasty (c. 2450–2330 B.C.)
and for several centuries before this age, is the great
business activity displayed by the temple organizations
in the larger centres. As an example we may instance
the extensive temple archive discovered at Telloh, the
site of the ancient centre Shirpurla or Lagash,[25] the
most extensive of the kind that has as yet come to light.
The temples in this early period owned extensive lands
which were either farmed out with stipulations of adequate returns of the yield, or were directly cultivated
through a large body of officials connected with the
temple organization. The temple accounts were most
accurately maintained, records being kept of all transactions, of purchases or sales, of the income from temple
property, of the wages assigned to the many workmen
engaged, and the numerous other details involved in the
management of temple property. Receipts were given,
and records made of offerings and gifts for the temple
and of taxes or contributions that were levied. Such
receipts of which there are hundreds upon hundreds
give us lists of animals—cattle, sheep, goats, asses,

[25] For a list of the chief publications of tablets from Telloh, see
Myhrman, *Sumerian Administrative Documents dated in the reigns
of the Kings of the Second Dynasty of Ur*, pp. 13–15.

birds and fishes—that were brought to the temple, as were all kinds of produce from the fields—fruits, vegetables, grain, flour, oil, perfumes and the like. The rulers in these early periods still exercised priestly functions, or at all events were so closely associated with the temples that the management of their affairs formed an integral part of the activities of temple officials. We find hundreds of accounts dealing with the royal exchequer, gifts and allowances apportioned to the members of the royal household, records of expenses incurred in connection with the royal estates, special lists of royal offerings to the gods, payments to palace officials and to the numerous body of workmen coming directly under the authority of the palace, and more the like. The functionaries of the temple and palace include commercial agents, overseers of workmen, gardeners, grain measurers, shepherds, fishermen, butchers, superintendents of temple and palace granaries, storehouses and stables, beside various classes of priests, diviners, doorkeepers, guardians, scribes and judges, including at a very early period female votaries and active priestesses attached to temple service in various capacities.

Completing the picture of the extensive activities of temple and palace, we have hundreds of lists of produce of the field brought to the temple by the officials, wool from sheep, garments, oil, bread, salt, spices, silver, bronze, beverages, lists of workmen, of barges, inventories of slaves, salary accounts, memoranda of provisions for voyages of temple and palace officials, of food for the cattle and the flocks, and more the like.

What applies to Telloh holds good for the other large centres like Nippur which likewise yielded an extensive temple archive [26] as a result of extended excavations

---

[26] Above, p. 46. Many temple documents from the older and later Babylonian periods are included in the series of publications of the Museum of the University of Pennsylvania by Myhrman (Ur dynasty), Poebel and Ranke (1st Babylonian Dynasty) and Clay (Cassite and later periods). See above p. 50, note 66.

conducted on that site, and for later periods we have
the thousands upon thousands of business and legal
documents found at Abû Habba, which was the site
of the ancient city of Sippar. Quite recently thousands of such documents have been found by marauding Arabs at Drehem, not far from Nippur, dating
from the Ur dynasty, and there is no doubt that similar collections still lie beneath the soil at such sites
as Eridu, Uruk, Ur, Umma, Kish and other places in
the south that rose to importance in the Euphrates
Valley.[27]

The temples were, however, not merely the most
extensive business establishments of the country; they
were also the centres of justice to which all classes of
the population repaired. In the temples sat the tribunals, composed in the earlier periods of priests who
heard complaints and rendered decisions. Within the
temple precincts were the offices of the notaries where
contracts were drawn up and duly registered in the
presence of witnesses. The temples in both the larger
and smaller centres included record rooms in which
copies of agreements, settlements of estates, and judicial
decisions were stored. At every turn, we thus find
the temples entering closely into the life of the people. Commercial methods take their cue from the
activities of the temple organizations; private business is largely an offshoot of the extensive operations carried on by the temple and palace officials.
Correspondingly, legal formulæ, legal procedure, and
legal decisions, in so far as they deal with business
and commercial aspects of life in Babylonia and
Assyria, reflect the points of view acquired in the
course of the business and commercial activities of
the temples.

---

[27] From Uruk and Umma have come several thousand tablets,
dug up there by Arabs and sold through dealers.

XII

Taking up by way of illustration some legal con-
firmations of transactions, found among the documents
of the oldest period, we will be in a position to see for
ourselves both the authority exercised by the courts,
and the methods of procedure followed in the regulation of the commercial affairs of the population. In the
days of the Sumerian Ur dynasty (c. 2450–2330 B.C.),
the official before whom parties went to obtain a legal
confirmation of transactions was known as the *mashkim*
who corresponds in a measure to our notary public,
though he also exercised to some extent the functions
of a magistrate. The purchase of a cow is confirmed
by the *mashkim* in the following terms:[28]

"A cow at the price of 6½ shekels [29] of silver from Lugal-
erin to Lu-absa, son of Shipra, is confirmed. Ur-Ish-Bau, son of
Ur-dun (and) Kalamma, the *nipush*,[30] have sworn. Ur-nigin-gar,
mashkim."

Simple as the procedure is, we may here see the elements needed for the most formal kind of an agreement,
the two parties involved, the specification of the facts,
the witnesses to the transaction and the official record.
The date alone which does not appear to have been a
necessity at this time is lacking, though it was usually
added. So in another document of the same general
tenor:[31]

"Judicial settlement: 7½ shekels of bright (?) metal . . . the
price of which before Ud-sar-gi-makh (sold by) Bashumu, the

---

[28] F. Pelagaud, "Textes Juridiques de la 2de Dynastie d'Our,"
Nr. IV (Babyloniaca III, p. 102 and Pl. II).

[29] A shekel was equivalent to about fifty cents, but in equivalents of ancient coin it must always be borne in mind that money had
a much larger value in ancient times. See above note 9.

[30] A profession of some kind.

[31] Thureau-Dangin, *Recueil des Tablettes Chaldéennes* (Paris,
1903). No. 292.

merchant to Ur-Ish-Bau, the *pashishu* priest,[32] is confirmed, Lu-shimashu being the *mashkim*. Ur-lamma patesi, year when Bur-Sin became king.''

The attest is dated in the accession year of King Bur-Sin of the Ur dynasty corresponding to c. 2374 B.C. Such formal attests by which transactions between individuals were made binding were deposited in the temple archives, which thus in very early days must have had a division corresponding to the office of the recorder of deeds in our days. The official character of these attests, embodying also decisions in disputed cases, follows also from the circumstance that two entirely different transactions were combined on one tablet. An instance of this kind dealing with purchases of slaves by different parties reads as follows:[33]

''Judicial settlement: 6½ shekels of silver, the price of (the woman), Nin-mu-nanga-mu, Lugal-azag-zu has received from Daga. Daga has confirmed this on oath in the presence of Ur-Bau and Dadaga as witnesses, Albamu, the *sukkallu*,[34] being the *mashkim*.''

''Two shekels of silver, the price of Shab-gu-bi, the slave of Lu-kani, which Lu-kani has received from Ama-shim, Dadaga claims from Ama-shim. Ba-ni-nibi, Lu-ab-sa and Ganab-ka (?) are witnesses to this, Lugal-Dungi being the *mashkim*.''

The only point of contact between the two transactions is the probable identity of the witness Dadaga in the first attest with the claimant in the second case, but it is not likely that this circumstance has anything to do with the combination of the two transactions. The second case introduces as a new feature of judicial

---

[32] A class of the priesthood, whose function, to judge from the name, was to act as ''anointer,''—perhaps they were also the ones to prepare the oinments. See above p. 272.

[33] Thureau-Dangin, *Recueil*, etc., No. 294.

[34] Designation of some high functionary, acting as the representative of the ruler, somewhat like a viceroy. A god associated with a superior deity is often spoken of as the *sukkallu* of the higher one.

procedure the method of placing an injunction on a commercial transaction. Ama-shim owes Dadaga some money which apparently is due. To secure this, or at least a part of the debt, Dadaga lays claim to the sum which Ama-shim, who is evidently in hard straits, has received through the sale of a slave. Dadaga goes to the *mashkim* with his witnesses who testify to the debt, and obtains an order from the court for the money.

We have among documents of this order an interesting one from which it appears that at a very early date slaves with a family could not be transferred without their consent from one master to another. A judicial decision in such a case reads: [35]

"Judicial settlement (in the case of) Tili, a slave, Nitidam, his wife, with son and daughter were sold for ½ mina of silver by Ana-khane . . . to Aba-bil-gimshu.

"The declaration of Nitidam, the wife of the slave, to be restored is confirmed (sc. through witnesses). The male and female slave with son and daughter are confirmed for Ana-khane, Ur-Lamma, son of Kalla, being the *mashkim* and Lu. . . . and Lu-Urash-gal, Lu-Dingirra and Ur-Ka-silim being the judges."

Marriage agreements were likewise confirmed before the notary in the presence of judges whose decree thus takes the place of a modern license. A document of this order reads: [36]

" Judicial settlement: Ninmar, son of Lu-Nannar, appeared and said, 'In the name of the king,[37] Lu-Dingirra, son of Guzani, is to marry Damgula, my daughter.' Arad, son of Ur-lamma, and Ur-shid, son of Lu-Nannar, take an oath to this.[38] Lu-dingirra has been married to Damgula." [39]

---

[35] Thureau-Dangin, *Recueil*, etc., No. 290.

[36] Scheil, in Recueil des Travaux relatifs à la Philologie et l'Archéologie Egyptienne et Assyrienne, xxii, p. 153–154.

[37] *I.e.*, an oath invoking the king's name.

[38] Confirmed the declaration of the father. One of the witnesses, be it noted, is the brother of the bride.

[39] Such is the court's confirmation.

21

"Ninmar for a second time appeared and said: 'Nin-azag-zu, daughter of Guzani, is to marry my son, Sib-kini.' It is attested that the name of the goddess Ninmar and the name of the king were invoked in an oath.[40] Sib-kini, the shepherd, has been married to Nin-azag-zu, Til-e-makh-ta being the *mashkim*, Lu . . . and Ur-ka-silim judges. In the year following the destruction of Simanu."[41]

Here again a single document records two distinct transactions which presumably were settled in short succession of one another. Similarly, settlements of divorce were made before the notary.[42]

"Judicial settlement: Lu-Babbar, son of Nig-Bau, rejects Gin-Enlil (his wife). Gin-Enlil appeared and said: 'In the name of the king give me 10 shekels of silver in lieu of a judicial settlement.' He has paid her 10 shekels of silver. Duggi-ul and Uku-il, farmer, have sworn to this, Ur . . . being the *mashkim*. In the *patesiate* of Ur-Lamma.[43] The year of the destruction of Kharshi and Khumurti."[44]

According to the older Sumerian law, a man on divorcing his wife must pay her one-half of a mina, which would be thirty shekels.[45] Apparently, Gin-Enlil has agreed under oath to be satisfied with less than that amount, and this being confirmed, the notary

---

[40] *I.e.*, witnesses confirmed the declaration of Ninmar by swearing to it.

[41] *I.e.*, the fourth year of Gimil-Sin of the Ur dynasty, corresponding to c. 2361 B.C.

[42] Thureau-Dangin, *Recueil*, etc., No. 289.

[43] *Patesi* of Lagash.

[44] 58th year of Dungi, the second member of the Ur dynasty, corresponding to c. 2374 B.C.

[45] Rawlinson, V., Pl. 25, Col. IV, 8–12. In the days of Hammurapi, the divorce settlement had advanced to one mana in ordinary cases, and one-third mana if the husband was of the plebeian class (Code §§ 139–140). See above, p. 302.

formally records that the amount has been paid, and the record deposited in the archives of Lagash, where the settlement took place.

XIII

Agreements could be made, however, between parties in the presence of witnesses without the intermediary of a *mashkim*, and it is a reasonable conjecture that in time these formal attests became restricted to cases where a dispute had arisen obliging the parties interested to appear before the court in order to have the terms officially recorded, or a decision rendered and deposited in the archives of the temple. The legal formulæ for all kinds of transactions and contracts became fixed as early at least as 3000 B.C. A few specimens taken from the time of the Ur dynasty (c. 2450–2330 B.C.) will suffice to illustrate the general method followed. In the case of simple receipts for a loan made or for produce delivered, names of witnesses are commonly not added, but it is safe to assume also that the court would not ordinarily recognize such receipts as testimony unless they bore the seal of the party who had received the loan or produce. The case was, of course, different when it came to documents dealing with temple affairs, as most of the business tablets are, which have come down to us from the earliest period. Here the mere deposit of a receipt in the official archives would be a sufficient attest to the transaction. The formula for receipts reads as follows:[46]

"One-half mina of silver at an interest of one shekel for five shekels[47] from Ur-Dun-pa-e, Gir-ni-ni-shag has received. Month

---

[46] Myhrman, *Sumerian Administrative Documents dated in the reigns of the kings of the second dynasty of Ur* (Phila., 1910), No. 22.

[47] *I.e.,* at the rate of twenty per cent. per year.

Gan-gan-e [48] in the year when the lord of the goddess of Uruk was appointed." [49]

A receipt for produce from the same Ur-Dun-pa-e reads: [50]

"Three Gur of *kharshu* grain [51] at an interest of 90 Ka [52] for each Gur, from Ur-Dun-pa-e, Ishme-ilu has received. Month Engardu-a,[53] 19th day, in the year when Simuru was destroyed." [54]

In the same way a receipt for dates reads: [55]

"Two Gur of dates at the (usual) interest for each Gur,[56] from Lugal-iskim-zi, Kalam-de(?)-e has received. Month She-kin-kud,[57] first day." [58]

Purchases are recorded in the presence of witnesses, the object being named first, followed by the price, the purchaser and seller, thirdly the witnesses and lastly the date. Thus the sale of a slave is recorded as follows: [59]

"One male slave . . . -lum by name, for 11 shekels of silver, to Ur-E-Lugal-ani, Ur-Nusku, the commission broker [60] has bought.

---

[48] Ninth month.

[49] Perhaps "high priest." The date has not been identified.

[50] Myhrman, No. 23.

[51] We find a large number of such specifications of grains mentioned in these business documents the exact nature of which still escapes us; they seem to designate qualities or special varieties.

[52] A Gur equals 360 Ka, *i.e.*, therefore, at a rate of 25 per cent. interest.

[53] Eighth month.

[54] 35th year of Dungi, corresponding to c. 2397 B.C.

[55] Myhrman, No. 31.

[56] That is, 25 per cent.

[57] First month.

[58] Year broken off.

[59] Myhrman, No. 15.

[60] *Damkar*—a general term for a commission merchant, and also for trader without specification.

In the presence of Gudea, the MU of the archive,[61] Shu (?)-dug-ga-zi-da, the *kalu* priest.[62]

. . . .

as witnesses. Month Azag-Shim,[63] 9th day,[64] in the year when Bur-Sin destroyed Urbillum."[65]

An agreement to refund a sum advanced in connection with some business transaction reads as follows:[66]

"One mana and ten shekels of silver, which as the balance of a transaction Lu-Babbar has received from Ur-Lukh. He swears an oath in the name of the king to pay back on the seventh day of the month of Shu-Kul.[67] In case he does not pay back (sc. at the time agreed upon), the amount will be doubled. Sworn to in the name of the king before Lugal-azag-su, Lugal-itu-da, A-Khush-a, Ur-Mami, in the month of Sig,[68] the document (?) was drawn up, in the year when Gimil-Sin, king of Ur, built the great ship of Enlil and Ninlil."[69]

We also have at this early period formal agreements to become surety for repayment of loans. A document of this nature is worded as follows:[70]

"In case the obligation of Ur-Enlil for 10 Gur of grain is not redeemed, that amount of grain Ur-Damu will bring in. In the name of the king he swore, Ur-shu-makh, Adda-kalla, Kalamma-ne-mu, Ut-shag-ga being witnesses. The year when Simuru was destroyed."[71]

---

[61] Literally "house of tablets," *i.e.*, the official archives. The MU is some official connected with the archives.

[62] The names of the other witnesses are broken off.

[63] Unidentified month, perhaps the 7th month.

[64] Indicated by $10 - 1 = 9$, like the Roman IX.

[65] Second year of Bur-Sin, corresponding to c. 2372 B.C.

[66] Myhrman, No. 13.

[67] Fourth month.

[68] Third month.

[69] Eighth year of Gimil-Sin, corresponding to c. 2357 B.C.

[70] Myhrman, No. 7. A detailed study of surety in Babylonia and Assyria with numerous illustrations from legal documents of all periods will be found in Koschaker, *Babylonisch-Assyrisches Buergschaftsrecht* (Leipzig, 1911).

[71] 35th year of Dungi, corresponding to c. 2397 B.C.

These specimens of legal forms perfected at an early period, will suffice to illustrate the general character of such documents. Supplementing them by the many hundreds of business documents dating from the Ur dynasty, and which for the larger part are accounts of transactions and not formal contracts or agreements, we obtain a remarkable picture of the extent of business activity in the third millennium before this era in the Euphrates Valley, both such as was carried on in the temples, and such as represent private business affairs.[72]

The usual rate of interest at this period was twenty per cent. for loans of money, and thirty per cent. in the case of produce. Slaves varied in price from two to twelve shekels, and no doubt in some cases the price went beyond the latter amount. Laborers were commonly paid in produce, though occasionally in currency. Wages were calculated at so many Ka[73] of grain per month of thirty days, varying from forty to ninety Ka. In addition we find the laborers receiving wool, dates, oil and drink in part compensation; and we also find commission agents of all kinds who engaged workmen, or who had them at their command to be hired out for any purpose.

From the period immediately following that of the Ur dynasty, we have specimens of business documents which supplement the picture and furnish further illustrations of the manner in which purchases were made and agreements drawn up. Thus a document recording the purchase of a house shows the manner in which the property was described, beginning with the

---

[72] Legrain, *Les Temps des Rois d'Ur* (Paris, 1912). Legrain gives (pp. 49–92) a survey of 389 texts of the Ur period published by him, and which may serve as an index of the scope covered by business documents of this character.

[73] A Ka is about 4/10 of a litre.

size of the lot and passing on to the terms of the transaction. It reads as follows: [74]

"7½ Gin improved property, adjoining the house of Ali-Akhati, with the long side facing the street, the house of Adad-rabi son of Ur-Innanna, from Adad-rabi, son of Ur-Innanna, Apil-Sin, son of Bulalum, has bought. As its price in full 2½ shekels and 15 She of silver he weighed out. For all times, Adad-rabi shall not make any claim on the house. In the name of the king he has sworn an oath, before Sin-gamil, son of Gubbani-dug, Elali, son of Nabi-ilishu, Ur-Ningishzida, son of Nurum (and) Azag-Nannar (as) the scribe. Month of Gan-Gan-e,[75] in the year when King Sin-ikisham made a statue of gold and silver." [76]

The names of purchaser and seller as well as some of the names of the witnesses are Semitic—an indication that we are approaching the period of growing Semitic influence as a reaction against the Sumerian predominance in the Ur dynasty.

A contract for the rent of a house, the ordinary period being one year, has the following form: [77]

"The house of Damu-ribâm, from Damu-ribâm, Sin-idinnam, the commercial agent,[78] has rented as a dwelling and possession [79] at a yearly rental of ⅓ of a shekel of silver. In the presence of Sin-magir, son of Zibû'a, (and) Ina-ekur-rabi,[80] the scribe. First day of the month Shu-Kul,[81] in the year when King Samsu-iluna, in accordance with the oracle of Enlil, etc." [82]

---

[74] Chiera, *Legal and Administrative Documents from Nippur, Chiefly from the Dynasties of Isin and Larsa,* (Philadelphia, 1914), No. 22.

[75] Ninth month. 180 She are one shekel.

[76] Sin-ikisham ruled for six months only, c. 2195 B.C.

[77] Chiera, No. 90.

[78] Or merhcant (*damkar*). See above p. 324, note 60.

[79] That is, to do with it what he pleases, including therefore subletting for any purpose.

[80] Semitic name signifying "Reared in Ekur," the temple of Enlil in Nippur.

[81] Fourth month.

[82] Abbreviated dating for the 28th year of Samsu-iluna, corresponding to c. 2052 B.C.

Despite the fact that this deed is dated in the reign of Hammurapi's successor, and that the parties involved as the witnesses and the scribe bear Semitic names, it is nevertheless written in Sumerian, showing that in old Sumerian centres like Nippur (whence this tablet comes), Sumerian continued in use as the official language of the court, just as Sumerian remained for a long time after the complete Semitic control of the country the language of the cult, though both in court proceedings and in the cult, Akkadian in time supplanted the non-Semitic tongue, with a retention, however, of Sumerian legal phrases that had become too incrustated to be entirely removed.

Purchases and leases of fields for cultivation were drawn up in much the same manner. A document dated in the reign of a ruler of the Larsa dynasty reads: [83]

"1 Gan and 10 Sar [84] of a clover field, being part of a new (?) field adjoining (that of) Nannar-me-du, son of Uru-ma-kal, being the field of Sin-eribam, son of Gir-ni-ni-shag, from Sin-eribam, the son of Gir-ni-ni-shag, Warad-Sin, the son of Khundurum has bought. As its full price of 2⅓ shekels of silver he has weighed out. For all future time, neither Sin-eribam nor any heirs of Gir-ni-ni-shag, as many as there may be, shall have any claim against the field. In the name of the king they [85] have sworn in the presence of Lugal-melam, son of Alia, Ur-pa-bil-sag-ga, son of Khambia, Erib-Sin, son of Lugal ibila, Azag-Innina, son of Lul-Nin-shubur, Nûr-Shamash, son of Sin-ishmeanni, Aba-Enlil-dim, the scribe, month of Bil-Bil-Gar, [86] in the year when Warad-Sin, the king, built the great wall of Ur." [87]

Attached to the document is a reproduction of the seal of Sin-eribam, son of Gir-ni-ni-shag, rolled over the edge of the tablet twice as the attest of the seller.

More complicated in their nature are business docu-

---

[83] Chiera, No. 27.

[84] A Gan is about 25 acres and 10 Sar about 350 square metres.

[85] *I.e.*, Sin-eribam and the heirs of his father from whom the field descended to Sin-eribam.

[86] *I.e.*, fifth month.

[87] C. 2140 B. C.

ments dealing with such subjects as divisions of property. A case of this kind between two brothers leads to a formal agreement[88] in which first the share given to the one brother is set forth, then in detail what the other one receives, both swearing to the decision in the name of the king to annul any further claims on the part of either.

To equalize the division the younger brother also receives a certain amount of currency, from which one may conclude that a detailed inventory of the estate was made as the basis for the division.

Priests, it would also appear, retained their private property despite their being attached to the service of a specific temple; they inherited their share of the paternal estate, and we have plenty of evidence to show that they conducted business affairs as individuals as well as in their official capacity. The priestly office held by the father was also transferred to his heirs and formed part of the estate. In view of this, it is not surprising to find that priestly offices could be leased at a valuation, calculated according to the income through fees and gifts.[89]

Of special interest is a document of the time of the Isin (or Nisin) dynasty which illustrates the privileges enjoyed by a class of slaves who were attached to the palace service; they could own property in their own names and pass it on to their heirs. The document in question, drawn up in the days of Bur-Sin II (c. 2220 B.C.), is a deed of gift of a mother's property to the daughter, in return for which the daughter agrees to provide a specified amount of food for the mother every month. It reads as follows:[90]

"2/3 Sar improved property (and) Tuda-Ishtar, a female slave of Nin-me-dugga, the improved property and all its belongings, the property of Nin-me-dugga, her mother, which Nin-me-dugga to

---

[88] Chiera, No. 12.

[89] *E.g.*, Chiera, No. 15.

[90] Chiera, No. 1.

Nin-dingir-azag-mu, her daughter, has given. For all times, none of the children of Nin-me-dugga, as many as there may be, will have any claim. Nin-me-dugga has sworn in the name of the king. Fifteen (?) Ka of provision Nin-dingir-azag-mu to Nin-me-dugga, her mother, monthly shall give.''

Nin-me-dugga has rolled her seal over the document once, and no less than five times again over the envelope [91] in which the document was enclosed and which contains in addition, as a kind of docket, the indication of the contents of the document together with the date. The seal designates Nin-me-dugga as '' a palace slave,'' that is, belonging to the harem of the ruler but who, as we have seen, could herself own a slave as well as other property.

The business documents of the earliest period of Babylonian history thus complement the data derived from votive inscriptions and historical records proper by showing us the people in their daily life, how they lived, what their occupations were, the dealings they had with one another, the changing fortunes of life, the classes of the population, the position of the priests and the methods of the administration of justice.

XIV

An abundance of further details in all these and other aspects of social life is furnished by the many hundreds of business and legal documents that have been preserved from the period of the definite union of the Euphratean states under the rule of the Semitic kings of Babylon, the period of the so-called first

---

[91] In most cases where a document was placed in an envelope of clay, the outer case contained a duplicate of the text. The envelope served as a protection to the legal document. This fashion of having a duplicate of the document inclosed appears to have varied from time to time; it does not appear to have been obligatory at any time.

dynasty of Babylon, extending from c. 2225-1926 B.C. [92]
In contrast to the business documents of the Agade, Ur
and Isin dynasties which, as we have seen, are so largely
taken up with mere accounts and lists connected with
the temple organization in one centre or the other, those
of the first dynasty of Babylon are of a much more miscellaneous character and for the most part taken up
with transactions between laymen dealing with the
ordinary business affairs and with more or less elaborate lawsuits brought by contending persons. There is,
to be sure, every reason to believe that such documents
will also be found some day in abundance for earlier
periods, but for the present we must depend upon the
material dated in the reigns of the rulers of the first
dynasty and of subsequent periods for a more definite
picture of business activities among laymen and of the
manner in which justice was carried out in the courts
of the land. The business and legal documents of this
period, moreover, are written in Semitic or Akkadian
which makes the task of interpretation less precarious,
for despite recent progress in the interpretation of
Sumerian texts, there is much in such material that is
still obscure. When we reach Semitic texts, we are on
firm soil. It is also a great advantage to have as a guide
and control for the understanding of the business and
legal documents of this period the code of Hammurapi
of which we have for this reason given a rather full
analysis.[93] This great code became a standard for all
times, though as has been noted additions continued to
be made to it, and modifications were introduced to keep
pace with changing conditions and to embody new
decisions that were constantly being rendered, albeit
on the basis of the principles on which the code was
established.

[92] The definite determination of the chronology of this period
we owe to the researches of F. X. Kugler, *Sternkunde und Sterndienst in Babel* (Münster, 1910), ii, 1, pp. 234-311.

[93] Above pp. 283-315.

Before giving some examples of business and legal documents of the period of Hammurapi, as we may also call the age of the first dynasty of Babylon from its most prominent representative, it will be well to out-line the methods perfected in his days for the legal administration of the country.[94] In the first place, we note by the side of the older and original tribunals in the temples, entirely in the hands of the priests, a class of civic judges or magistrates before whom legal documents could be drawn up and to whom litigants came to have decisions rendered. Such magistrates acted in the name of the king, and it would appear that their functions were extended after the days of Hammurapi so that only specific cases requiring an oath in the presence of the gods were referred to the " judges of the temple," as the priestly officials in contra-dis-tinction to the lay judges were commonly designated. The institution of civil courts marks a decided decline in the authority of the priests, though as a court of last instance the temple continued to maintain itself to the closing days of the Babylonian empire. There are also traces of a kind of popular assembly with certain judicial functions,[95] and in addition, the governors of provinces and the chief magistrates of cities could be appealed to, to render justice. Furthermore, the promi-nence acquired by the city of Babylon as the capital of the country gave to the judges of Babylon a position not unlike that of a supreme court; and we have in-stances of cases, dealt with in Sippar and elsewhere,

---

[94] For details see Edouard Cuq, "Essai sur l'organisation judici-aire de la Chaldée à l'époque de la première dynastie Babylonienne (Revue d'Assyriologie VII, pp. 65–101).

[95] This assembly met at the "wall" of a city, and was accord-ingly known as the "wall of Sippar," "wall of Nippur," etc., according to the locality. Such an assembly may well have been a survival from primitive days when the "elders" constituted the tribunal before which litigants came—antedating, therefore, the formal organization of courts of justice in the temples.

being referred to the tribunal of Babylon. All this points to an elaborate system of administration, keeping pace with the union of the states of the Euphrates Valley under a central authority and to the growing complications of social life, necessitating the institution of lower and higher courts, and differentiating the functions of the many officials required to maintain law and order.

The large number of actual contracts of all kinds and legal cases embodied in the material at our disposal from the Hammurapi period also furnish us with an extensive legal terminology, as the result of many centuries of legal procedure. This procedure, furthermore, led to fixing a definite form for legal documents which all thus turn out to be arranged according to a definite sequence in the arrangement of the data. Inasmuch as the legal document involves, primarily, the disposition of some object—real or personal estate or a slave, child, wife or some member of the household—the person or object in question is first mentioned with such specifications as are needed to identify it, as, for example, the definite location of a house, field or orchard, and the description of the produce, article of merchandise, sum of money or individual in question. After this come the parties concerned, (*a*) seller and buyer, or (*b*) the parties to any kind of an agreement, or (*c*) the litigants, (*d*) slave owner and slave (or slaves), (*e*) father or mother and children, members of a household, and the like. The business transaction itself is then specified—loan, marriage agreement, sale or lease, gift, adoption, or claim is set forth as the third division, again with the necessary specifications, after which the formal decision reached is indicated, to which the parties involved agree in the case of the disposition of property by an oath to abide by the terms of the document and to renounce all further claims. The names of the witnesses and the date terminate the document.

The attachment of a seal or of seals [96] to legal documents was customary from the earliest period on, without, however, being obligatory. In the case of deeds of sale, it is the seller who attaches his seal, in the case of a lease the lessee, in the case of a loan the creditor, in the case of a work contract the contractor, in the case of an inheritance deed, the one who disposes of the property, and the guarantor in case of a bond,—in general, therefore, the one who gives up a claim, or who takes an obligation upon himself, while in cases where both parties take obligations upon themselves, both attach their seals. So, for example, in marriage contracts, the two contracting parties seal the document; the same in the case of partnership agreements, or in deeds involving exchange or division of property, while in cases of adoption, the father and the foster parents, though at times the foster parents only. The custom varies somewhat in different centres and at different times. So, for example, at Nippur the seal appears to have been made specifically for the document; it is more in the nature of a formal attest than the signature of the one party or of the two parties, as is shown by the fact that two names are combined on one seal, and the seal itself is in the form of a rectangular stamp made of a soft material and impressed on the clay like a die, and not a seal cylinder, made of some hard material and which is always that of an individual, rolled over the document. [97] In a general way it may be said, therefore, that the seal was a guarantee for the validity of the document on the part of the person or persons who yielded certain rights, or who took obligations on themselves, but in addition to this it also served as a protec-

[96] See for further details regarding the seal cylinders which were rolled over or impressed on the documents, at the close of Chapter VII. pp. 418–426.

[97] See on this subject of the "Nippur" seals Poebel's discussion in *Babylonian Legal and Business Documents from the first dynasty of Babylon* (Phila., 1909), pp. 51–55.

PLATE XXXVI

FIG. 1, LEGAL TABLET WITH SEAL

FIGS. 2 AND 3, SEAL IMPRESSIONS ON LEGAL AND COMMERCIAL TABLETS

FIG. 4, NAIL-MARKS ON LEGAL TABLETS AS SUBSTITUTE FOR SEAL

tion against alterations or additions to a document by
being rolled over the document wherever there was
room for it, and frequently even directly over words
of the document. This feature of the seal is particularly apparent in cases where the original document
was enclosed in a cover or envelope of clay, on which
often a brief docket of the nature of the document was
added with seals to prevent the cover from being de-
tached with fraudulent intent. In most cases, however,
the envelope contains a duplicate of the document, the
agreement of which with the inner one would furnish a
guarantee for the authenticity of the original in case
the question of genuineness were raised. The addition
of such a duplicate was not obligatory, though it became sufficiently common to lead to the decision that
the absence of a duplicate was no ground for question-
ing the validity of a legal document.[98]

In addition to these two purposes for which seals
were attached, the witnesses or even parties not named
as witnesses attached their seals as signatures which
might be appealed to in cases of dispute as proof for
the actual consummation of an agreement. In place
of a seal we find in documents down to the Cassite
period, the attachment of a bit of clothing imbedded in
the clay document while still in a soft condition, and
specifically referred to in the document as a substitute
for the seal. The technical term for such a guarantee
imbedded in the document (as in the case of the seal)
by the one who disposes of a right or claim, or by the
one who takes an obligation upon himself is *sissiktu*
(or *sisitu*) which appears to designate the fringe
attached to a garment.[99] Again, in place of the seal, the

---

[98] See Winckler, *Die Gesetze Hammurabis* (Leipzig, 1904), p. 86
(§ 2, 4–14).

[99] See on this term and the custom which it illustrates Ungnad
in Orient. Litteraturzeitung, vol. ix, sp. 163; xii, sp. 479; and
Clay, *Babylonian Expedition*, XIV, pp. 12–14. The Hebrew term

finger-nail marks of the contracting party or parties are scratched on the tablet in lieu of a seal.[100] This may have happened originally in the case of persons who had no seal, but in time became quite a common attest to a legal document, of which the cross or mark, still recognized in modern times as a signature to legal documents, is a direct successor. The most solemn feature in connection with legal documents was the oath which was by no means obligatory in all agreements; it was restricted chiefly to cases where individuals through sale, exchange, or dissolution of partnership, or through a testament or deed of gift renounced certain claims and, as already pointed out, it is always the person who gives up further claims who swears the oath, as it is he who attaches his seal by way of further confirmation.[101] We also find the oath where obligations are imposed on individuals, though limited, as it would appear, to marriage contracts, deeds of adoption, appointment of heirs and manumission of slaves—all being transactions involving family and household affairs. The oath is not taken in the case of loans, leases, labor contracts, commissions and the like. We have seen that in the earliest days the oath is taken in the name of the king, who in his capacity as the representative of the deity [102] has the quality of sanctity attached to him. In the days of Hammurapi, the gods

---

sisît for the fringe to be attached to garments according to the Priestly Code (Num. 15, 38) is probably a loan word from the Babylonian.

[100] Specifically stated as such in the document.

[101] See on the oath in Babylonian and Assyrian inscriptions a monograph by S. A. B. Mercer, *The Oath in Babylonian and Assyrian Literature* (Paris, 1912), with supplementary articles in the Journal of the American Oriental Society, vols. 33 and 34, and in the American Journal of Semitic Languages, vol. 29, No. 2.

[102] Above, p. 288. The rulers of Agade and of Ur have the determinative of deity attached to their names. The divine descent of kings thus reverts to a very early period in the history of man.

either take the place of the king or the name of the king is added to that of the gods, and frequently also the name of the city or temple in which the document is drawn up. The change points to the growing secularization of the royal office, leading to the substitution of the gods as a more solemn affirmation. The oath was taken by the " raising " of the hand,[103] and the place where it was taken was naturally in the temple. Before the civil courts, sitting outside of the temple, no oath could be taken, and when it became necessary in a suit brought before such a tribunal to introduce the oath, the case was transferred to the " temple " judges.

XV

We are now ready to take up some illustrations of legal procedure and of business methods in the time of the first dynasty of Babylon and of later periods, restricting ourselves mainly to such specimens as will also show the practical workings and application of the regulations in the contemporary code of Hammurapi which we have discussed. The scope of the published documents from this period [104] is exceedingly extensive, covering all kinds of loans, sales of houses, fields and orchards, mercantile transactions in produce, in live stock and goods, leases of houses, fields, commission brokerage, hire of boats, of animals and of workmen, partnership, surety and guarantees, gifts to members of one's family, inheritance and disinheritance, slave trade, marriage and divorce, adoption, and manumission being some of the subjects covered, besides

[103] From the stem *nashû*, "to raise," a noun *nîshu* was formed which acquired the technical force of "taking the oath." See Schorr, *Altbabylonische Rechtsurkunden*, p. xxxiii, note 1.

[104] See the bibliography in Schorr's *Altbabylonische Rechtsurkunden*, p. xlix–lvi. Schorr's work itself comprises translations of 318 documents with commentary, glossary and indices of proper names. It is a valuable compilation, despite many inconsistencies in the translations, and many omissions in the glossary and indices.

22

many instances of lawsuits which illuminate the legal procedure of the courts.

The formulæ for loans are much the same as those which we have already come across in Sumerian documents, with interest fluctuating from 5½ to 25 per cent. for loans of money, and from 20 per cent. to 33⅓ for loans of produce. (Loans without interest, naturally, were made at all periods as a kind of personal accommodation.) Women often appear both as creditors and debtors; and it is significant that we find a large number of instances of priestesses [105] engaged in money and in produce lending, and in other mercantile transactions. Fines are occasionally stipulated in case of failure to return the loan at the time agreed upon. [The temples in the large centres continue to act as financial institutions, lending money and produce and making investments in real estate, selling property, making labor contracts of all kinds and dealing in slaves.] The kings also engage in mercantile pursuits through their accredited agents; they appear to have utilized their large holdings more particularly for wool-growing, the extensive sheepfolds in various parts of the realm being directly under the supervision of the governors appointed by the king.[106] [The breaking of the tablet recording a loan was the formal termination of the transaction.] Receipts were also given, though not obligatory. [Debts could be transferred, and in case of the death of the debtor, the obligation rested upon the heirs.] Failure to pay gave the creditor the right to levy on the produce or other property of the debtor;

[105] Chiefly of the temple of Shamash at Sippar, though this is of course largely accidental, owing to the provenance of many of the documents.

[106] An old title of the Babylonian kings frequently introduced in votive and historical inscriptions is "shepherd," which thus turns out to be more than a mere *epithetum ornans,* and reflects the actual occupation of the rulers, who naturally became the largest land owners in their realm.

and if there was no property, the person of the debtor falls into the hands of the creditor, though he could substitute for his person, his wife, child or slave. To relieve such hardships, the law provided that someone could become surety for the debtor at the expiration of the term of the loan and agree to reimburse the creditor within a short period. Precautions were also taken against usurious rates of interest, though the creditor usually succeeded in driving a sharp bargain by being permitted to lend produce at the current price at the time of the loan—usually in the winter or spring, before the harvest—with a return of this amount at the harvest season when the price was considerably lower, and the creditor therefore received more produce back than he loaned.

A promissory note from the days of Darius may be taken as a sample of the general form employed.[107]

"One mina and five shekels of silver (due) Nabu-mukin-zêr, son of Idinnâ, son of Gakhul, from Nabu-tabni-usur, son of Aplâ, son of Gakhal. Monthly for each mina one shekel of silver shall increase against him—apart from his share of a record of a seed field on the Kish highway, held in partnership with his brothers, as a pledge for Nabu-mukin-zêr. The total amount of silver against him he shall pay. Witness: Nabu-etir, son of Nergal-ushallim, son of Sha-nashishu, Bel-iddin, son of Tabnea, son of Warad-Nergal, Nabu-napishti-usur, son of Shuma, the fisherman, Nabu-mukin-zêr, the scribe, son of Shamash-akh-iddin, son of Nashishu. Babylon, month of Simanu,[108] 23rd day, 4th year of Darius,[109] king of Babylon, king of the lands."

---

[107] Clay, *Legal and Commercial Documents dated in the Assyrian, Neo-Babylonian and Persian Periods* (Philadelphia, 1908), No. 105. In the documents of these late periods, the names of individuals are carried back to the third generation, the "grandfather," however, being in many cases the family name. The dating (since the Cassite period), is according to the years of the reigning king.

[108] Third month.

[109] Corresponding to c. 518 B.C.

The interest here, as in general throughout the later periods, is at the rate of twenty per cent. per year, though in Assyria it fluctuated from twenty per cent. to as high as a hundred per cent. Attached to the record of a loan is a reference to another document, previously drawn up, in which Nabu-tabni-usur has given Nabu-mukin-zêr his share of a sown field held in common with a brother as a guarantee—a collateral, as we would say, to obtain the loan.

Loans could of course be made for any specified time, but in an agricultural country it is in the fall and more especially in the spring that farmers and land owners needed money to pay their laborers and to provide seed and other necessities of the fields, which they could return at harvest time. A loan of this kind made in Sippar reads: [110]

"One shekel of silver for Mâr-irsitim, ⅓ shekel for Ilu-abi, the sons of Makhnubtim(?), at the usual rate of interest of the Shamash temple, received from Â-rishat, the priestess of Shamash, daughter of Shamshatum. At the time of the harvest they will repay the silver with the interest. In the presence of Akhuni, son of Lu-Gul . . . and of Sin-magir, the diviner, in the month of Gan-Gan-e [111] in the year when the throne of Innina was made." [112]

We see from this and from many other instances that the rate of interest in temple transactions was fixed —presumably twenty or twenty-five per cent.—and that a priestess could act as a money lender. In the same way we find another priestess lending produce at interest.[113]

"181 Gur of grain, on interest at the usual rate (sc. of the Shamash temple), from Nishi-inishu, the priestess of Shamash, daughter

---

[110] Ungnad in *Vorderasiatische Schriftdenkmäler der Kgl. Museen zu Berlin,* Heft viii, Nos. 117–118 (case tablet with seal on the outer tablet).

[111] Ninth month.

[112] Fourteenth year of Hammurapi, corresponding to c. 2109 B.C.

[113] *Vorderas. Schriftdenkmäler,* etc. Heft viii, Nos. 93–94 (case tablet).

of Khuzalum, Sin-imgurrani, son of Sin-rabi, has received. At the
harvest in the month of Shandutim [114] he shall measure out the grain
and its interest. In the presence of Warad-Sin, son of Mâr-irṣitim,
Etel-pi-Adad, son of Belanum, son of Mâr-ibik-irṣitim. Month of
Dul-azagga,[115] first day in the year when the throne of Nannar was
made.'' [116]

An interesting loan made by four persons through a
palace commissioner, payable on demand, reads as
follows: [117]

"One talent [118] of wool of the palace,[119] worth 10 shekels of
silver which Ilushu-ibni, overseer of the merchants, has received
from the palace through (?) Utul-Ishtar, the scribe, Taribum, son of
Ibi-Shamash, Ibku-Mamu(?), Beliatum, sons of Ilushu-bani, and
Kubburum have borrowed from Ilushu-ibni, the agent. On the
day that the palace demands it, the money shall be brought to the
palace. In the presence of Warad-ilishu, the scribe, month of
Kin-Innina,[120] 22d day, in the year when Ammi-ditana set up his
image as leader of the army.'' [121]

In the case of purchases, the greatest care was taken
in the formal deed to protect the purchaser against
fraud or even unintentional deception by the assurance
on oath of the seller that he renounces all claims for all
times as a consequence of the *bona fide* sale. Not infrequently the further assurance is included that the
seller guarantees through a third party against any
claims on the property or object sold. This precaution
was particularly required in the sale of land or houses
which, as forming part of a family estate, could not as a

---

[114] A designation of one of the months in the fall of the year.

[115] Seventh month.

[116] Third year of Hammurapi, c. 2120 B.C.

[117] Cun. Texts viii, Pl. 36ᵃ.

[118] That is, the weight of 3600 shekels (or 60 mina), equal to
about 30 kilograms.

[119] That is, royal property. See above p. 338.

[120] Sixth month.

[121] 26th year of Ammi-ditana, corresponding to the year c.
1988 B.C.

survival of earlier conditions of family joint-ownership be disposed of by the head of the family, to the detriment of his heirs, or of those otherwise entitled to a share of the estate. The heirs and possible claimants are accordingly at times brought into the proceedings when a sale of a house or field is consummated, to guarantee the purchaser against future trouble. The purchase was ordinarily a cash transaction, though there are instances of part cash payment and the rest on credit. Certain formalities were observed at the sale, noticeable among which is, in the case of deeds drawn in Sippar, Babylon and Dilbat, the handing over of a staff by the seller to the purchaser [122] as a symbol of the agreement. A still older custom that can be traced back to pre-Sargonic days [123] is the addition of a small *bonus* over and above the price agreed upon, equivalent to about five per cent. of the total value in the case of real estate and from one per cent. to five and a fourth per cent. in the case of slaves.[124] It may be, as has been suggested, that the custom which is encountered also in Græco-Egyptian documents is to be traced back to an earlier prohibition of disposing of land as belonging to the gods, leading to a fictitious sale by giving not the purchase price but a higher amount, so as to lend to the transaction the form of a gift made by the seller rather than an actual bargain.

The most interesting feature of these deeds of sale is the various specifications that they contain, setting forth both the rights and the restrictions imposed upon the purchaser, the exact details regarding the property or objects sold and the terms of the sale. A purchase

---

[122] *Bukânu.* See Schorr *l.c.*, p. 116 and note on p. 122 with the references there given.

[123] Genouillac, *Tablettes Sumériennes Archaiques* (Paris, 1909), p. xxxv, *seq.*

[124] So according to Cuq, "*Etudes sur les Contracts de l'époque de la première Dynastie babylonienne,*" in Nouvelle Revue Historique de droit Français et étranger, vol. xxxiv, p. 463.

of a house made by one brother from another is recorded as follows: [125]

"One-third of a Sar and six Gin of improved property,[126] adjoining the house of Ea-idinnam, poultry dealer (?), being the house of Amurru-malik, son of Erish-sumatum, from Amurru-malik, Apil-Amurru, his older brother, has bought. As the full value, he has weighed out nine shekels of silver. For all times, Amurru-malik and his heirs, as many as there may be, renounce any claim on that house. In the name of the king he has sworn."

There follow the names of four witnesses, of the scribe and the official seal-maker,[127] together with the date, the ninth day of the eighth month in the ninth year of Samsu-iluna.[128] The seal of the seller is attached to the document, rolled twice over the tablet in the space just before the date.

In the case of purchase of slaves, the seller assumes the responsibility for the good condition of the slave by agreeing to revoke the sale in case within a month the slave is seized with a sickness known as *bennu* [129] which would incapacitate him. This is in accord with § 278 of the Hammurapi code.[130] A document of this class reads as follows: [131]

"A female slave, Ina-e-ul-mash-banat by name, from the city Ursum, belonging to Damik-Marduk, son of Libit-Ishtar, Usria, son of Warad-za, has bought from Damik-Marduk, son of Libit-Ishtar, her master. As the full price he has weighed 5/6 mina and one shekel [132] of silver, besides 2/3 of a shekel as *bonus*. Three days are allowed for investigation, and one month for a revocation in case of *bennu* sickness, according to the laws of the king."

---

[125] Poebel, *l.c.*, No. 33.

[126] The distinction is thus made between land and ground with a house.

[127] Above p. 334.

[128] Corresponding to the year c. 2071 B.C.

[129] Perhaps "epilepsy."

[130] Above p. 314.

[131] *Vorderas. Schriftdenkmäler*, Heft vii, No. 50.

[132] That is, 51 shekels—a very high price for a slave.

The names of five witnesses and of the scribe are attached to the document which is dated 15th day of the 9th month of the 7th year of Ammi-ditana.[133]

The guarantee against the *bennu* sickness as an assurance that the slave was sold in good condition was extended in Assyria to one hundred days, an indication of the frequency with which the development of the sickness after more than a month must have occurred. Moreover, the seller in Assyria was also obliged to guarantee that the slave was tractable. As in other purchases and agreements, a heavy fine is imposed for any suit brought in future to reclaim the slave. An Assyrian document of this kind recording the sale of three slaves reads: [134]

"Seal of Sharrâni, owner of the persons herewith legally transferred. Im-sha-i (?), the slave, . . . Shar-Ashur, Urkît-â . . . total three persons, . . . Akhu-tali (?), the mayoress of the central quarter of the city [135] has acquired for four mina of silver.[136] The silver has been paid in full. These men have been bought and taken over. Revocation or law suit there shall not be. Whosoever presses a suit against the mayoress, shall pay a fine of 15 mina of silver. Against their being seized (with *bennu* sickness) a guarantee of 100 days, against rebelliousness for all times." [137]

The transaction is attested by nine witnesses,—an unusual number in Assyrian documents, and due in this case probably to the fact that three slaves are involved. The date is the 18th of the 12th month in the eponymate of Bel-imur-ani, the general-in-chief, corresponding to the year 685 B.C. in the reign of King Sennacherib.[138]

---

[133] Corresponding to c. 2007 B.C.

[134] Johns, *Assyrian Deeds and Documents*, No. 232. The text is defective at the beginning.

[135] A curious office to be held by a woman!

[136] A high price, being an average of 80 shekels per slave.

[137] That is, a guarantee that the three slaves were tractable.

[138] On the Assyrian method of dating documents see below p. 351.

The position of the slaves in Assyria was much the
same as in Babylonia. They could hold property in
their own right and could even have slaves of their
own. They could act as witnesses and had their seals
with which to attest transactions made by them. Slaves
could even marry daughters of freemen, and we have
also instances in Assyria of a slave with two wives.[139]
The law also protected the family of a slave so that the
members were not torn away from their surroundings.
In many cases slaves formed an integral part of landed
estates and were sold together with their families with
the property to which they were attached.

XVI

As a survival of early conditions when women were
purchased as wives, we have in the marriage agreements
of the Hammurapi periods the same general form as
in the case of other purchases, even though this point
of view is no longer present in the subsequent relations
of man and wife; and the form undergoes only slight
modifications during the later periods of Babylonian
history and in Assyria.

In the marriage contract,[140] there are two parties as
in the ordinary bill of purchase—the parents disposing
of the daughter, or in default of both, the father or
mother, or if both are dead, the brothers and sisters,
while on the other side we have the bridegroom acting
for himself, though occasionally his parents act for
him.[141] The original purchase money is replaced by
the " gift," [142] given by the bridegroom to the parents
or representatives of the bride, but which already in

---

[139] See Johns, *l.c.*, No. 229.

[140] For details of marriage in the Hammurapi period, see Cuq's
admirable article, *Le Mariage à Babylone d'après les Lois de
Hammurapi* (Revue Biblique, 1905, pp. 350–371).

[141] See Cun. Texts, viii, 7b.

[142] *Tirkhatu.*

the days of Hammurapi is kept in trust for her, to be passed down to her children and of which her husband can at most use the interest for his business enterprises. The gift or dowry of the parents to the daughter appears at all times to have been optional, and while at the husband's disposal, is to be returned to the wife in case of a divorce brought about through no fault of the wife. [As we have seen,[143] the wife as well as woman in general possesses all the rights of a person whose independent legal status is recognized. She can buy, lease and sell, make contracts and can dispose of property belonging to her. She can enter into business partnership with the husband and both are held equally responsible for obligations thus entered upon. Women act as witnesses, as scribes [144] and even as judges [145] and hold other official posts. It would appear, indeed, that the relatively high status of woman in ancient Babylonia results from her position in the cult as a priestess. The woman, as part of the temple organization, would naturally share in the growth of the organization. Hence the priestess like the priest enters into commercial life, and with this had to be given a legal status equal to that of a priest. The ordinary form of a marriage contract reads as follows: [146]

"Bashtum, daughter of Belizunu, the priestess of Shamash, daughter of Uzibitum, has been taken to wife by Rimum, the son of Shamkhatum. . . . shekels of silver [147] as the amount of her

---

[143] Above p. 305, *seq.*

[144] *E.g.*, Cun. Texts vi, Pl. 24b (Amat-Mamu, the female scribe of the document in question).

[145] Cun. Texts, viii, Pl. 28b (Ishtar-Ummu, daughter of Abbanibum, female scribe and judge in the temple of Shamash).

[146] Meissner, *Beiträge zum altbabylonischen Privatrecht* (Leipzig, 1893), No. 90.

[147] The number of shekels is broken off. The amount of the gift varies naturally according to the financial status of the parents; it is quite frequently very low, four to ten shekels.

'gift' she has already received. Her heart is satisfied. If Bashtum says to Rimum, her husband, 'thou art not my husband,' [148] she is bound and thrown into the river; [149] and if Rimum says to Bashtum, 'thou art not my wife,' he weighs out to her ten shekels as divorce money. In the name of Shamash, Marduk, Samsu-iluna and the city of Sippar they have sworn.''

Seven witnesses, among them a woman, bear attest to the document. The circumstance that the bride, apparently, must declare her satisfaction with the marriage gift or settlement for her benefit shows how far removed we are from the days of marriage by purchase. In another document, [150] likewise dating from the days of Samsuiluna (2080–2043 B.C.), there is instead of a mention of a gift on the part of the bridegroom, a clause in regard to the dowry of 19 shekels of silver brought by the bride as a dowry to her husband. It is stipulated that the husband forfeits the dowry if he divorces his wife, besides being obliged to pay a compensation of half a mina, whereas if the woman rejects her husband, she loses the dowry and must pay a fine of half a mina. '' By mutual consent they have sworn in the name of the king,'' the document adds.

We have seen [151] how the Code endeavors to protect the first and chief wife against being shoved into the background through more attractive rivals. In illustration, we have an interesting marriage agreement between a man and two sisters, with a stipulation regarding the status of the second in order to make clear her subsidiary position in the household. The docu-

[148] *I.e.*, refuses to cohabit with him or desires to leave him.

[149] An alternative punishment is ''to be thrown from a column,'' *e.g.*, *Vorderas, Schriftdenkmäler*, Heft viii, No. 4, 24–25 (case of a female slave married to a freeman), and in the text below.

[150] From Nippur and couched in Sumerian. See Poebel, *l.c.*, No. 40.

[151] Above, p. 309, *seq.*

ment from the days of Sin-muballiṭ (2144–2124 B.C.) reads: [152]

"Warad-Shamash has married Tarâm-Sagila and Iltani,[153] daughter of Sin-abushu. If Tarâm-Sagila or Iltani says to Warad-Shamash, 'thou art not my husband,' they shall cast her down from a column; and if Warad-Shamash says to Tarâm-Sagila or Iltani, his wife, 'thou art not my wife,' he loses house and furniture. Furthermore, Iltani shall wash the feet of Tarâm-Sagila (and) carry her chair to the temple of her god. Iltani is to help Tarâm-Sagila with her toilet and (otherwise) assist her and she is not to use her seal. She must grind 10 Ka of flour and bake for her." [154]

These curious stipulations are all evidently intended to indicate the inferior position which the second wife is to occupy by the side of her sister, to do personal and menial service, in fact, to be in the position of a handmaid who, as will be recalled,[155] might also be given by the wife to her husband as a concubine.

XVII

In illustration of the paragraphs in the Code of Hammurapi dealing with leasing of houses, shops, barns, fields and boats, and the hiring of workmen and of animals, we have a large number of legal documents that throw further light on business practices in ancient Babylonia, and which underwent merely minor modifications in the transfer to Assyria and in the later periods of the Babylonian history, down through the time of Persian and Greek supremacy. The rent of houses varies naturally according to size and location,

---

[152] Cun. Texts ii, Pl. 44. We have also another special marriage contract between the same Warad-Shamash and one of the sisters (Iltani). See Meissner, *ib.*, No. 89.

[153] More literally they have entered into a relationship of "wife and husband," with Warad-Shamash.

[154] The names of ten witnesses are attached.

[155] Above, p. 309.

from two-thirds of a shekel to six shekels annually in the documents of the Hammurapi period, which appears to be very low from a modern point of view. We must remember, however, that the private houses were at all times very simple affairs, of one story, built of clay, with a varying number of rooms around a central court. The period of the lease was usually one year, occasionally six months, while in later times the period is two years. Repairs during occupancy had to be made by the occupant, who is also held responsible for damages. The same applies to ships. The rent was due at the end of the lease, though in most cases a portion was paid at the beginning of the term, amounting to as much as fifty per cent. of the entire rent. The general form of a house lease was as follows:[156]

"The house of Ribatum, the priestess of Shamash, Ninshubur-nasir, son of Nûr-alishu, has rented from Ribatum, the priestess of Shamash, daughter of Ibgatim, for one year. As rent for one year, he is to weigh out three shekels of silver. As part payment of the rent, 1½ shekels have been received. On the first day of the month Warakh-shamna[157] he moved in. Three festival gifts for Shamash, one piece of meat and 10 Ka of wine he shall furnish. In the presence of Amel-Adad, son of Sin-eribam, and Adad-bani, son of Marim. Month of Warakh-shamna, first day, the year of the goddess Tashmit."[158]

"Regarding the outlay for the house which rests on the tenant, if the owner of the house says to the tenant, 'Get out!' he (i.e., the owner) forfeits the outlay, but if the tenant moves out of his own accord, he is responsible for the outlay.

"In the presence of Bur-Adad, son of Bur-Adad, Idinnam-lagamal, Akhushina, son of E-Sharra, month of Warakh-shamma, first day, the year of the goddess Tashmit."

[156] Ranke, *Babylonian Legal and Business Documents from the time of the first Dynasty of Babylon* (Philadelphia, 1906), No. 35 and 36—two copies of the tablet with slight variants.

[157] Eighth month. The duplicate has *tîru* which appears to be a variant name for the month.

[158] 41st year of Hammurapi, corresponding to 2083 B.C.

We find this same priestess leasing a shop to a certain Atidum for one year at a rental of 1⅙ shekels of silver to be paid on moving into the house on the 20th of the fifth month, in the third year of Samsu-iluna, corresponding to the year 2077 B.C. [159]

As a curious custom we find cases of a builder being paid for the construction of a house by occupying it for a term of years; so in one instance [160] eight years in return "for his outlay," which implies that the builder pays the cost. The assumption is of course that the ground belongs to the one who engages the builder. Since the period of occupation is based on the cost of the house, we may conclude that on an average the yearly rent represents 12½ per cent. of the total cost, or about half the amount of the average interest on money loaned. From the other end of Babylonian history in the days of Seleucid rulers (312–65 B.C.) we have a lease with stipulations about repairs. It reads as follows: [161]

"A large house of Nanâ-iddin, son of Tanittum, son of Akhutu, which is in the district of the great park [162] in Uruk, which is at the side of the large house of Mushezibitum, daughter of Ishtar-akh-iddin, and alongside the centre of the field, at a yearly rental for the house of four shekels of silver is at the disposal of Anu-uballit, son of Kidin-Anu. Half of the silver at the beginning of the year, the balance of the silver in the middle of the year he shall pay. The bareness (of the walls) he shall repair, the cracks of the walls he shall close up. The amount for the work, bricks, reeds and beams, as much as he may need, shall be placed to his credit. During the year three *shugurrû* [163] he shall give. From the tenth day of the month of Tammuz of the eighth year of King Seleucus [164] that large house is at the disposal of Anu-uballit, son of Kidin-Anu."

---

[159] Ranke *l.c.*, No. 51 (case tablet).

[160] Meissner, *Beiträge zum altbabylonischen Privatrecht*, No. 66.

[161] Clay, *Legal Documents from Erech, dated in the Seleucid Era* (New York, 1913), No. 1.

[162] A public park (?).

[163] Perhaps festival gifts.

[164] That is, Seleucus I. whose eighth year corresponds to 304 B.C.

The document, witnessed and sealed, bears the date
of the fifth day of Tammuz (fourth month), eighth
year of King Seleucus, five days therefore before the
actual commencement of the lease. The stipulation
that the tenant is to be credited for the expense involved
in attending to necessary repairs is probably a special
agreement, due possibly to the neglected condition of
the house at the time that the lease was signed. It
will be observed, however, that the old form whereby the
tenant must undertake the repairs is observed—merely
that he is to be reimbursed by the deduction of the cost
from the rent. The annual rental being only four
shekels, one wonders how much was left for the owner
after the cost of repairs had been deducted.

The changes in legal procedure wrought through
the lapse of ages are all of a minor character. Since
the days of the Cassite rulers (c. 1760–1185 B.C.), the
reigns of kings were reckoned by years instead of by
the cumbersome method of a date for each year according to some event by which it was designated, and
which necessitated recourse to lists of dates prepared
by the scribes or votaries. The name of the place where
the document was drawn up is added. The tendency
also developed to reduce the number of witnesses
(though a uniform practice was never introduced),
and the word for "witness" was placed before the
names instead of the phrase "in the presence of."
In Assyrian legal documents the chief departure from
Babylonian models is marked by the reference at the
beginning of the document, to the seal or finger-mark
of the party who disposes of something or on whom an
obligation rests, while for the dating of the years an
independent method was followed, each year being
named after an official who acted as the eponym [165] for
that year, the ruling king leading off as the eponym
for the first year of his reign, followed by the highest

[165] The Assyrian term is *limu*.

officials and then by those of lower grade. The method was almost as cumbersome as the older system of Babylonia, and it is only by reference to lists of eponyms for each reign that we can determine the year of a ruler corresponding to the eponym named.[166]

Ships were commonly rented for transport of grain, and the return was generally reckoned in an amount of grain, and not in currency. The same was the case in fields which were rented naturally for cultivation, the stipulation being that the rent was to be paid in a percentage of the yield at the time of harvest. A contract of this nature is couched in the following terms: [167]

"A field of 9 (?) Gan—a meadow without an exit (?)[168] from Melulatum, priestess of Shamash, daughter of Ibkusha, proprietress of the field, (?) Bel-ludari, son of Liwirashum, as a field for cultivation on a return (of the produce) has rented. At the time of harvest the field to its full extent he shall garner and for each Gan 100 Ka of grain,[169] according to the standard of Shamash, at the wall of Sippar),[170] he shall measure out."

The names of four witnesses and of the scribe are attached to the document, which is dated on the 25th day of the 6th month in the year "when Ammiditana [restored] the power of Marduk," that is, the fourth year of the king's reign, corresponding to the year 2010 B.C. [171]

---

[166] See lists of such eponyms, in Schrader, *Keilinschriftliche Bibliothek,* I, pp. 204–215, some having merely the names of the eponyms, others the name with brief reference to some important event in that year. These lists, however, are very incomplete, covering only the 9th and 8th centuries.

[167] Cun. Texts, xxxiii, Pl. 33.

[168] The reference is perhaps to the lack of an irrigating canal leading into the field.

[169] About 40 litres.

[170] A term for the tribunal of Sippar, which had its seat at the wall of the city. See above, p. 332, note 95.

[171] The seals of Bel-ludari and of three of the witnesses are rolled over the tablet.

Workmen and slaves were hired for short and long periods, from a few days [172] up to two years, the wages being either in produce or more commonly in currency. Five shekels a year seems to have been an average price for a workman, though the amount is at times as low as two shekels. The stipulation is frequently added that the laborer is to receive his clothes during his term of service.[173] Presumably his board is taken for granted, since as a laborer he belongs to the household. As a specimen of such a contract we may select one which is interesting because it makes provision for three holydays each month.[174]

"Warad-Tashmetum has been hired for two months for team (?) work [175] by Sin-ikisham, the keeper of the archive (?) in the temple, from Idin-Lagamal, his brother. As his wages, he is to receive for two months 1⅙ shekels. In the month he is to have three days for himself. If he stops his work or goes away, he loses his hire. Before Ilushu-bani, son of Amurra-put-Adad, and Ina-palishu, son of Warad-Ishtar. Month of Airu,[176] first day, in the year in which king Ammi-saduka (erected) a golden throne."[177]

Similarly, animals were hired, and their value appears to have been rated higher than that of human beings. We have a case [178] of an ox hired for draughting for one month at the rate of one shekel, of which one-half, it is stipulated, is to be paid in advance. Flocks of considerable size were hired for a longer period with a return in currency, and also in a share of the offspring and the wool.

The hire passes over by an agreement of this kind

---

[172] Ten days in one instance for harvesting. (Meissner, *l.c.*, No. 57).

[173] We have, however, a case in which it is expressly stipulated that he is to provide his own clothes (Cun. Texts, vi, Pl. 40a).

[174] *Vorderas. Schriftdenkmäler*, Heft vii, No. 83.

[175] *shi-bi-ir sa-ma-di*, cf. Cun. Texts, xxxiii, Pl. 32, obv. 5.

[176] Second month.

[177] Eighth year, corresponding to c. 1969 B.C.

[178] *Vorderas. Schriftdenkmäler*, Heft vii, No. 92.

23

into a quasi partnership pact, since in return for a payment for the lease of the flock, the lessee shares with the owner the profit and increase during the period. The partnership agreement was usually quite simple in form, as the following document from the neo-Babylonian period shows:[179]

"One mina of silver Itti-Marduk-balatu, son of Nabu-akhe-iddin, son of Egibis [180] and Marduk-shapik-zêr, son of Nabu-shum-iddin, son of Nadin-sheim have invested in common. Whatever transactions they engage in they share as partners. Witness: Nabu-zêr-ikisha, son of Belshunu, son of Epesh-ili, Bel-udakhkhid, son of Shapik-zêr, son of the surveyor, and the scribe Marduk-shum-iddin, son of Aplâ, son of Bel-etir. Babylon, month Warakhshamna, third day, fifth year of Nabonnedos, king of Babylon."

Partnerships could also take the form of an investment in common of a sum of money and of merchandise which would then be managed for the partners by a third person as agent.[181] In that case the agreement is more explicit, as for example, in the following document, likewise from the reign of Nabonnedos.[182]

"Five mina of silver and 130 jars of incense belonging to Itti-Marduk-balatu, son of Nabu-akhe-iddin, son of Egibi, and Marduk-shapik-zêr, son of Nabu-shum-iddin, son of Nadin-sheim,[183] due from Kurbat-nabu-sabit (?), agent of Nabu-akhe-iddin and Nabu-dîn-epush, agent of Marduk-shapik-zêr, for current business. Whatever in the city or outside they acquire with it, is to be shared by Itti-Marduk-balatu and Marduk-shapik-zêr. Kurbat-nabu-sabit

[179] Strassmaier, *Nabonidus Inschriften* (Leipzig, 1889), No. 199.

[180] In the neo-Babylonian and later periods, the line of descent is carried further than the mention of the father. The third member is not necessarily the grandfather, but corresponds rather to our family name. See above, p. 339. Warakhshamena is the 8th month.

[181] In Strassmaier, nabonidus inschriften, No. 652, the agent is a woman.

[182] Strassmaier, *l.c.*, No. 572 (11th year of king = 544 B.C.).

[183] The same two partners as above.

(?) and Nabu-dîn-epush while engaged in this commission shall receive from it (*i.e.*, from the sum entrusted to them) food and clothing,[184] besides the use of the house at their disposal.''

During the continuance of partnership, debts contracted by one party entailed responsibility for the other. Partnerships were dissolved either naturally by the death of one partner or by mutual consent. The partners go before the tribunal to render an account, swear an oath that everything has been divided fairly and equally, and are then formally released from further obligations towards one another. It is interesting to compare two forms of such documents, one from the days of Hammurapi and one from the days of Nebuchadnezzar II. at the other end of Babylonian history, to see the substantial continuity of legal procedure, and at the same time note certain modifications in terms and phrases.

The former reads:[185]

"After Erib-Sin and Nûr-Shamash had formed a partnership, they went to the temple of Shamash and rendered an account. The currency, male and female slaves, everything outstanding, outside and within the city, they divided equally. After they had concluded this (settlement) of silver, male and female slaves, everything, outside and within the city, from straw to gold,[186] neither shall have a claim against the other. In the name of Shamash, Â, Marduk and Hammurapi they swore.''

The names of seventeen witnesses are attached to this document but no specific date.

The document of the later period reads:[186a]

---

[184] That is, their expenses shall be paid.

[185] Cun. Texts, ii, Pl. 28a.

[186] A phrase of frequent occurrence to indicate everything of value.

[186a] Strassmaier, *Nabuchodnosor Inschriften* (Leipzig, 1889), No. 116. Dated 8th of Shebat (11th month), 18th year of Nebuchadnezzar (586 B.C.).

"Business agreement (?) of Nabu-kin-apal and Nabu-bêl-shunu, his son, and of Shula, son of Zer-ukîn, son of Mushezib-bêl, the *shutapi* official, under which they carried on business from the eighth year of Nabopolassar, King of Babylonia,[187] to the eighteenth year of Nebuchadnezzar, King of Babylonia. They have rendered an account of their transactions before the judges. Fifty shekels of silver are still due from Nabu-bêl-shunu and Nabu-kin-apal, his father There will be no revocation or further claim among them. (The partnership) is dissolved, each one will go his own way. In the name of the people (?) and of the gods, each one has sworn. Their account with one another has been settled. The former documents in their names have been destroyed."

XVIII

Despite the advance marked by the Hammurapi period, it is full of survivals of an earlier age when the father exercised absolute control over his children. Thus a father could still sell his daughter to become a concubine and practically a slave in the household to which she was transferred, though she could not be again resold except for good reasons. We have such a case in a document from the 12th year of Hammurapi,[188] *i.e.*, c. 2111 B.C.

"Shamash-nûri, the daughter of Ibi-Sha-a-an, has been bought from Ibi-Sha-a-an, her father, by Bunene-abi and Belizunu.[189] For Bunene-abi, she is a wife, for Belizunu, a maid. At any time that Shamash-nûri says to Belizunu, her mistress, 'Thou art not my mistress,' she is branded [190] and sold for silver. The full price of five shekels has been weighed out. The staff (*bukânu*) has been handed over. The transaction is consummated. His heart (sc. of the seller) has been satisfied. For all times no claim

---

[187] *I.e.*, 617 B.C. The partnership lasted 31 years.
[188] Cuneiform Texts, viii, No. 22ᵇ.
[189] Man and wife.
[190] Literally "shorn," sc., of her hair, but which becomes the term for branding a person with some slave mark.

can be made by the one party against the other. In the name of Shamash, 'Â, Marduk and Hammurapi they have sworn."

A mother could sell her child. It appears not to have been uncommon for women to pass on their children to a nurse who is frequently a votary [191] for a term of years at a stipulated sum. In case the mother is unable to pay the amount, the child is sold to the nurse, who sometimes pays a certain sum in addition for the child which is hers to do with what she pleases. In a document, likewise from the reign of Hammurapi (–27th year, c. 2096 B.C.) we read as follows: [192]

" A certain Zukhuntum, wife of Ilu-kinum, has given her child to be nursed to the Iltani, the votary. The price of nursing for three years including food, oil and clothing,[193] she has not given to Iltani. 'Take the little one, let it be thy child,' Zukhuntum said to Iltani, the votary. Since she has so said, apart from the price of nursing for three years which she (i.e., Iltani) has not received, Iltani has handed over three shekels of silver to Zukhuntum. For all times neither party will have a claim against the other. In the name of Ib [194] and Hammurapi they have sworn."

The point of view in such documents is still that of the period when children were regarded as an asset of fixed monetary value because of the services that they could render after they had reached a certain age, just as the wife was an asset to her husband through her own services and through the children that she would bear. Hence the nurse who rears a child entrusted to her would feel compensated by the possession of the child in return for the pay which she would otherwise receive, though we have seen that the evaluation

---

[191] Nu-Gig-*Kadishtum.* See above, p. 308.

[192] *Vorderas. Schriftdenkmaeler,* Heft vii, Nos. 10–11 (case tablet with seals).

[193] Three standing terms for "support" also occurring in the Hammurapi Code, § 178.

[194] Perhaps to be read Urash.

of the child might also entail upon her to pay an extra sum over and above the compensation due her.

The adoption carried with it a full share in the estate; and this stipulation prevailed in Assyria as well, as is expressly set forth in a document dating from the middle of the 7th century B.C., which reads in part as follows: [195]

"Seal of Nabu-naid, the owner of his son, legally transferred. Ashur-ṣabatshu-iḳbi, a small child, son of Nabu-naid, has been adopted as their son by Sin-ki-Ishtar and (his wife) Râmtu. Should there be seven [196] children to Sin-ki-Ishtar and Râmtu, Ashur-ṣabatshu-iḳbi remains the oldest son.[197] Whenever at any time be it Nabu-naid, be it his brother, be it a governor, be it a relative should bring suit against Sin-ki-Ishtar, or his children, he will pay (a fine of) 1 mina silver and 1 mina of gold to the goddess Nin-lil,[198] 2 white horses he shall lay at the feet of the god Ashur, his eldest son he shall burn at the *khamru* [199] of Adad. Despite his suit he shall not obtain (sc. the child)."

The curious reference to an offering of horses as part of the fine is of frequent occurrence in Assyrian documents,[200] as is also the allusion to a free offering of children [201] which reminds one of the offering of children to Moloch in the pages of the Old Testament. Exactly how we are to understand this, whether literally or merely as a strong threat that was not actually carried out, is difficult to decide. Certainly on the face of

---

[195] Peiser in *Oriental Litteraturzeitung*, vi, Sp. 198.

[196] Here used as a large number, *i.e.*, ever so many.

[197] It follows from this that the couple was childless at the time that they adopted the child.

[198] An exceedingly heavy fine to be paid to the temple of Ninlil or Ishtar.

[199] The altar or some section of the temple.

[200] *E.g.*, Kohler-Ungnad, *Assyrische Rechtsurkunden* (Leipzig, 1913), No. 162, 164–178. Two to four horses are named as fines, besides a very large money fine for an unwarranted suit.

[201] *L.c.*, Nos. 158 (son or daughter to be offered in the fire to Belit-ṣêri), 163 (son offered to Sin; daughter to Belit-ṣêri).

it, the phrase suggests that at one time children were offered as sacrifices in the way indicated, though it is hard to believe that as late as the seventh century the practice still prevailed.

XIX

The manumission of slaves is also placed under the legal aspect of an adoption by the owner, though in time the adoption became a mere form—a kind of legal fiction, in order to give a definite status to the freedman or freedwoman, for a slave as such is never designated as the son or daughter of any one but merely by his or her name. The theory of manumission as an adoption is carried out to the extent that if such a freed slave rebels against the authority of his adopted father, he is punished as a son would be, not as a slave. The ceremony of manumission consists in removing the brand mark of the slave from the forehead, though both the branding and the cleansing from the brand may have come in the course of time to have been a formality—perhaps only symbolically carried out. In the case of a female slave, the manumission is often accompanied by the dedication of the woman to the service of some deity; she becomes a votary, in which case the temple as such adopts her, though the assumption is that her foster parents have presented her to the temple. The general form of such a document of manumission reads as follows: [202]

"A certain Zugagum by name [203] is (acknowledged as) the son of Sin-abushu [204] and of Ummi-tabat. Sin-abushu his father has cleansed his forehead.[205] As long as his father Sin-abushu lives, Zugagum, his son will support him. For all times, as regards Zugagum, son of Sin-abushu, Nutubtum, the priestess of Shamash

---

[202] Cun. Texts, iv, Pl. 42a.

[203] This form designates the individual as a slave.

[204] Signifying "the god Sin is his father."

[205] *I.e.*, has removed the slave brand.

and Nabi-Sin, her brother, the children of Sin-abushu, will not
have any claim on Zugagum, their brother. In the name of
Shamash, Marduk and the King Sumu-la-ilu, their father, Sin-
abushu has sworn. If Zugagum should say to his father, Sin-
abushu 'thou art not my father,' the punishment as in the case of
a son shall be imposed upon him.[206] According to the laws of
Sumu-la-ilu, they have destroyed the documents."[207]

The reference to the laws of Sum-la-ilu, the second
member of the first dynasty of Babylon (c. 2211–2176
B.C.), points to reforms instituted by that ruler who,
it is reasonable to conjecture, compiled a code as did
Hammurapi half a century later. That code must have
provided that the formal breaking of the clay documents represented the termination of the agreement
recorded therein. Accordingly, we find the ceremony
of the destruction of a document frequently referred
to either as an order of the court, or as a statement of
fact to indicate the termination of a contract, or a revocation or the cancelling of a debt or other obligation.
The manumission of a female slave by adoption and
who is then presented to the temple is recorded as
follows: [208]

"The female slave [209] Amat-Ishtar is the daughter of Kunutum.
Kunutum and Mukhadi have cleansed her. To Shamash and Â they
have presented her. [As long as Kunutum, her mother lives, she
(i.e., Amat-Ishtar) is to provide for her support. When her god

---

[206] According to the old Sumerian law (V. Rawlinson, Pl. 25,
col. ii, 23–28), such a rebellious son is branded as a slave and
sold for silver.

[207] I.e., the documents recording the former sale of the slave.

[208] Thureau-Dangin, Lettres et Contrats de l'époque de la
première Dynastie Babylonienne (Paris, 1910). Nos. 68–69 (case
tablet).

[209] Preceding the names of the slaves is an indication of the
number as "one head," "two heads" and the like, as we still say
one head of cattle, etc.

calls Kunutum to him,[210] no one is to have any claim on Amat-
Ishtar.] [211] Of the children of Shamash-idinnam,[212] male and female,
none will have any claim on Amat-Ishtar. In the name of Shamash, Marduk and Sin-muballit,[213] they have sworn.''

The inner document—without further specific date
—bears the names of nine witnesses, among them four
women, while the case or envelope has no less than thirteen witnesses, of whom eight are women. The remains
of seal impressions of four of the witnesses also appear
on the envelope—all, as the added titles show, connected
with the temple of Shamash at Sippar where the document was drawn up.

The children thus adopted took upon themselves the
obligation to provide for the support of their foster-
parents, but the phrase was probably introduced merely
to specify the duty devolving upon the adopted son or
daughter in case of necessity. The children as a survival of an earlier stage of society owed service to the
father or mother, and in lieu of their eventual share in
the property would be obliged to look after the parents
in case the latter became incapacitated. Sons were
obliged to care for their widowed mothers according
to the Hammurapi code, but it does not appear that the
parents were under ordinary circumstances actually
maintained by the children. On the other hand, to ensure themselves against want, it is frequently stipulated in the case of gifts made by a father or mother to
one of their children that in return, the support of the
parent devolves upon the child so favored. Such
phrases must, therefore, be taken as legal formulæ,

---

[210] *I.e.*, on the death of Kunutum. Mukhadi, who is mentioned
with Kunutum, may be the latter's daughter, who, as the heir agrees
to the manumission of the slave.

[211] These two sentences on the outside tablet only.

[212] The deceased husband of Kunutum.

[213] Sin-muballit, the immediate predecessor of Hammurapi, ruled
from c. 2144 to 2124 B.C.

introduced to provide for contingencies that might arise.

The laws of inheritance as set forth in the code of Hammurapi are illustrated by numerous documents from the period of the first dynasty. The practice varies, however, to some extent in different localities. So, *e.g.*, in Nippur and in Uruk and apparently, also, in Assyria, the oldest son received an additional share, though this appears to have been optional. In the same way the father could also make a special gift to any of his children, though the code takes precautions against his doing so to the serious detriment of the other children. Daughters inherit on equal terms with sons, and the mother, as we have seen, takes charge of the estate [214] (in case she survives her husband) until the children reach their majority. She is not, however, under ordinary circumstances the heir of her husband.

Naturally in a complicated form of society, many disputes arose in regard to estates, and some of the documents setting forth the settlement of property bequeathed by a father to his children are very elaborate. A final attest to a division is formally recorded in the following terms.[215]

"Nûr-Shamash, Ili-ma-akha, Palatum and Khumurum have divided all the possessions of their father. From straw to gold,[216] brother will not have any claim against brother. In the name of Shamash, Â, Marduk and Hammurapi, they have sworn. Before Ibik-Shamash, Ilu-nishtama, Sin-idinnam and Ibni-Shamash in the year of the Hammurapi canal."[217]

A more specific inventory is, however, the rule and generally the document is drawn up to settle the share

---

[214] Above, p. 305.

[215] Meissner, *Beitrage zum altbabylonischen Privatrecht,* No. 106.

[216] A phrase of frequent occurrence to indicate everything of value. See above, p. 355.

[217] *I.e.,* when Hammurapi dug a canal, called after him = the 9th year, corresponding to c. 2114 B.C.

of some one member of the family, as in the following instance: [218]

"Two Sar improved property at the side of the house of Sin-eribam, son of Warad-ilishu, its front facing the street, 2 Gar on the long side, 1 Gar on the front; *item,* one slave Warad-Erua, *item,* one slave Lumur-gamil-Shamash, who has escaped;[219] *item,* one female slave Taribum; *item,* one female slave Ashratum-ummi-is the share of Lipit-Ishtar, son of Bunini, which (at the division of the paternal estate) with Sinmagir, and Ibi-Sin, the sons of Buninî, with Sin-idinam and Rîsh-Shamash, the children of Ilushu-ibishu, [his brother],[220] he received. Also the share of Lamazi, the priestess of Shamash, reverts to the brothers between them.[221] They have divided everything from straw to gold, brother has no claim against brother. In the name of Shamash, Â, Marduk and Hammurapi [222] they have sworn."

Where in a deed of settlement, merely the share of one of the heirs is set forth, we must assume that similar documents setting forth the share of each of the others were drawn up, so that each heir would have documentary evidence in his possession, which would again become the basis for the division of his estate after his death.

We have, however, plenty of instances in which in one document the share of each of the heirs is detailed, as, *e.g.,* in one dated on the 17th of the 1st month in the 11th year of Samsu-iluna, corresponding to c. 2069 B.C., which reads as follows: [223]

---

[218] Thureau-Dangin, *l.c.,* No. 98–99 (case tablet).

[219] Counted in on the assumption that he will be caught and returned.

[220] So on the outer tablet. These are the nephews of Lipit-Ishtar whose father is dead, and who therefore receive the father's share.

[221] The priestess received her share during her lifetime, but it reverted to her brothers on her death. See above, p. 308.

[222] Dated in the 37th year corresponding to c. 2086 B.C.

[223] Poebel, *l.c.,* No. 32.

"Eleven (?)[224] Gin of improved property, adjoining the house of Lugal-Amaru, (with) one *zaggula* dish,[225] as a special possession because of his status as first-born, 1/3 Sar improved property, by the side of the house as a special possession,—the share of Apil-Amurru, the eldest son; one-third of a Sar, six Gin improved property by the side of the house of Apil-Amurru, his brother, the share of Lipit-Enlil, his brother; [one-third Sar six] [226] Gin improved property [at the side of the house] of Lipit-Enlil, his brother, the share of Lipit-Amurru, son of Apil-Shamash.

[One-third Sar, six] Gin improved property [by side of the house of] Ea-idinnam, the falconer (?),[227] son of Ea-tukulti, the share of Amurru-Malik. As heirs of Erisumatum they have divided the estate according to agreement. In the future, one will make no claim against the other. In the name of the King they have sworn."[228]

XX

To round out the picture of law, and of commerce and of social conditions in Babylonia and Assyria, we have for the older and later periods a large number of documents setting forth the judicial rulings in law-suits brought before the tribunals. These documents reveal the practical workings of legal procedure in civil cases, for up to the present at least we have not come across any records of criminal procedure, and the question has been raised whether such records were kept. The general form followed in cases brought before the courts was to begin with the statement of the case and of the claims made. The testimony on both sides was then set forth with the administering of the oath where called for, followed by the decision of the

---

[224] The number is not clear.

[225] Often mentioned in Nippur texts as a special possession of the first-born.

[226] Text defective. The restoration is made on the assumption that the share of the remaining brothers is equal.

[227] So Poebel's explanation.

[228] The document is written in Sumerian, which remained in use as the official language for a longer period than elsewhere in such strong Sumerian centres like Nippur.

court. There was commonly added an express prohibition against reopening the case, to which the party *appeal*
losing the suit consents by an oath. The names of the
judges and witnesses together with the date as usual
complete the record. The most important section in
such documents is the portion relating to the evidence,
which generally involves the production of legal documents and earlier court records bearing on the case.
In complicated affairs, such records often go back many
years and there are instances in which a large number
of documents are tested by the tribunal before reaching
a decision. With the advance from purely religious
tribunals to courts presided over by lay judges, as above
pointed out,[229] and the increased prominence given to
government officials, such as governors and city magistrates as against the former predominance of priests
in the judicial affairs of the country, we also find a
growth in the direction of finer distinctions and greater
scrupulousness in reaching a conclusion that should be
fair to the parties concerned. Efforts are also made by
the judges to bring about settlements by mutual concessions and by compromises so as to avoid bitter contests, which would entail delays and possibly hardships for both sides. On the whole, the picture thus
resulting is that of a country in which a high sense
of justice could be relied upon to protect those seeking
a vindication of their rights. Law and order prevailed
in the land, and while we learn occasionally of instances
of "graft" on the part of officials, as is natural in
a land in which government activities cover so large
a field, the general impression that one receives—and
this applies to Assyria as well as to Babylonia—is that
the citizens had a feeling of supreme confidence in
the courts as safeguards, under whose protection the
citizens could pursue their daily routine of barter and
exchange, and carry on their activities in the various

[229] See above, p. 332.

walks of life. It is a significant testimony to the spirit of justice and right thus emphasized by the courts in the south and in the north that Assyrian rulers who appear most ruthless in their campaigns of conquests, apparently concerned to promote their selfish ambitions, yet pride themselves in their annals, as did Hammurapi in his code, that they protected the rights of their subjects and sought to secure justice and to suppress violence and wrong. In a document [230] found in Ashurbanapal's library, setting forth certain special privileges accorded from olden days to the people of Sippar, Nippur and Babylon, some general sentiments as to the duty of kings are introduced which may be regarded as illustrating the prevailing point of view. We cannot do better than close our survey with an extract from this text:

"If the king does not hear the law, his people will perish, the power of the king will pass away.

If he does not heed the law of his land, Ea,[231] the king of destinies, will alter his destiny and cast him aside.

.   .   .   .

If he gives heed to the wicked, confusion will disturb the land.

If he follows the counsels of Ea, the great gods will aid him in righteous decrees and decisions."

---

[230] Cun. Texts, xv, Pl. 50.

[231] The god of humanity *par excellence*. See above, p. 210.

CHAPTER VII

THE ART OF BABYLONIA AND ASSYRIA

I

AT the outset of a discussion of the art of Babylonia and Assyria, it is natural to institute a comparison with that of the other great civilization of high antiquity—Egypt. Leaving aside the question not yet ripe for solution, whether the culture of the Nile is earlier than that of the Euphrates Valley or *vice versa,* though the indications at present are in favor of the former alternative, there are certain physical features which the two countries have in common, which help to explain the rise of a high order of culture in both. The warm climate during the greater portion of the year, suitable for a population as yet unable to protect itself against a more rigorous one, is divided in both the Euphrates Valley and in Upper Egypt into two seasons—a dry season beginning in the spring and extending till the late fall, followed by several months of rain and storms during which the Nile in Egypt, and the Euphrates and Tigris in Babylonia overstep their bounds and flood large areas. While this occurrence often brought about devastation prior to the construction of protective irrigation canals, through the perfection of a system to direct the overflow into the fields, it resulted in a fertility which rendered agriculture carried on with primitive methods, a comparatively easy task that was rewarded by rich returns.

The contrast between the two civilizations, on the other hand, which is particularly noticeable in the art, is due to the abundant presence of stone and wood in the one country, and the almost total absence of stone in the other. In place, therefore, of the massive stone structures of Egypt—temples with large stone columns,

elaborate rock tombs, mastabas and huge pyramids—
we have in the Euphrates Valley constructions limited
by the use of the clay of the native soil, which forms the
natural and practically exclusive building material.
Stones of various kinds from the hard diorite and basalt
to several varieties of limestone and alabaster were, to
be sure, imported at an early period from the mountainous district to the east and northeast as well as
from northern Arabia and probably also from Egypt
and Nubia, while wood was brought from the forests of
Lebanon and other districts; but the difficulties involved
in procuring such material had as a natural result its
rather limited use in architecture and proved a check
to the artistic instinct in the development of stone
sculpture. The hindrance was less felt in the case of
moulding and designing in copper and iron and in the
artistic employment of silver, gold and bronze and in
carvings on bone and shell in which a high degree of
skill was achieved at an early period. (See Pl. 74.)

The dependence of architecture upon the material
accessible for building purposes brings about a further
differentiation between Babylonian and Assyrian constructions, and this despite the fact that the art, as the
entire civilization of Assyria, is merely a northward
extension of the Euphratean culture. Limestone and
alabaster were abundant in Assyria, and the proximity
to the mountains made it possible to obtain harder
stones with comparatively little difficulty. The larger
employment of stone in the Assyrian temples and
palaces thus became a characteristic feature, whereas
the use of such material at all times remained exceptional in the large structures in the south.

Taking up first the older constructions in the south,
it is interesting to note at the outset the shape of the
bricks which during the period when the Sumerians
were in control were plano-convex and oblong, while
as we approach the time when the Semites assume the
supremacy, the older form yields to square bricks that

were also large and flat.[1] In time, a preference arose
for a smaller brick about twelve inches square, and
this remained in use with some variations. For the
important parts of the building, including the outer
layers, kiln-burnt bricks were used, but for the great
brick masses sun-dried bricks of crude variety appeared
to suffice.

At what time it became customary to paint colored
designs on the bricks we are unable to say, but from the
circumstance that painted pottery and vases of various designs were found in the lower layers at Telloh
and Nippur, it is a fair inference that the art reverts
to a very early period. At all events, we find it largely
employed in the bricks of Assyrian palaces of the ninth,
eighth and seventh centuries B.C., the colors either
being simply placed on a coating of plaster over the
bricks, or the designs were drawn on the bricks, placed
together and covered with a colored glaze or varnish,
which upon being burnt accentuated the brilliancy of
the hues. The chief colors employed were yellow, blue,
red and white.[2] It is in the constructions of the days of
Nebuchadnezzar II. that this art of glazed tiles reaches
its highest form of perfection. The procession street
leading to the temple of Marduk along which on festive
occasions the statues of the gods were carried in solemn
procession was lined with magnificently glazed tiles,
representing figures of lions marching along in majestic
dignity. The background is dark blue, the lion itself is
yellow, while running along the upper and lower edges
are small white rosettes with a touch of yellow in the
centre. Similarly, running along and around the outer

---

[1] At Nippur, e.g., the bricks of the Sargon period were found to
measure twenty inches square, but were only 3½ inches thick.

[2] An analysis of the colors showed that the yellow was anti-
moniate of lead, the blue glaze is copper with some lead to facilitate
the fusion of the lead, the white is oxide of tin, and the red a sub-
oxide of copper. Cf. Layard, *Discoveries in the Ruins of Nineveh
and Babylon* (New York ed. 1863), p. 166.

24

and inner walls of the great Ishtar gate, excavated by
the German expedition in Babylon and which formed
the approach to the temple of Marduk, there were
alternating rows of unicorns and dragons made in the
same manner as the lions, and showing the same traces
of the original, brilliant coloring. It is estimated that
there were at least fifteen rows of such glazed designs
rising to a height of about forty feet. From the Babylonians this elaborate and effective method of decorat-
ing exterior and interior walls passed to the Persians,
who carried it to an even greater degree of perfection.[3]
    Large numbers of painted and enamelled bricks
were found at Khorsabad and Nimrud by Botta and
Layard respectively, which exhibited the remains of
continuous patterns and of more or less elaborate designs, serving as decorations of the walls and arched
gateways of the royal palaces. One of these decorated
arches restored from numerous fragments portrays in
conventionalized form the familiar winged creatures
—a lower order of deities—standing before a large
palmette which has become one of the conventionalized
substitutes of the sacred tree.[4] Another elaborate design in one of the palaces of Nimrud, repeated like a
modern wall paper pattern, showed a crouching bull
with decorative borders above and below. This style
of decoration was extended to the gates and to the door-
ways leading from one division of the palace to the
other as well as to floors which were similarly often
found covered with elaborate geometrical and flowered
designs that bore traces of coloring.[5] We are therefore

---

[3] See the illustration in Perrot and Chipiez, *History of Art in
Persia* (London, 1892), facing p. 420.

[4] See Plate XVIII, Fig. 2 and Place, *Ninive et l'Assyrie* (Paris,
1867), Pl. 14–17.

[5] Traces of colored tiles—red, black and white—were found in
the case of the stage-tower at Khorsabad (see Botta et Flandin
Monument de Ninive, Pl. 155–156), but the conclusions drawn there-
from that each of the seven stages bore a different color and that
these colors stood in some relationship to the planets is not justified.

PLATE XXXVII

FIG. 1, DRAGON ON COLORED, GLAZED TILES (BABYLON)

FIG. 2, BULL ON COLORED, GLAZED TILES (BABYLON)

justified in concluding that it was customary in both
Babylonia and Assyria to cover the exteriors of temples
and gateways as well as of palaces with decorative designs, flowers, geometrical patterns and pictorial representations on glazed bricks and that this method of
decoration was extended to the interior halls and the
gates or doors, leading from one section of a temple
or palace to the other, and even to the exterior of the
staged towers, though the extent to which this was carried in the case of these towers is still in doubt. In the
case of interior decoration, less exposed to atmospheric
influences, direct painting on the stucco with which
the brick walls were covered frequently took the place
of glazed bricks. The effect of this manner of decoration and particularly of the colored glazed tiles must
have been striking in the extreme.

II

Outside of this feature, however, there was little in
the architecture of Babylonia and Assyria to arouse
one's admiration. The use of clay as the building material led in the direction of hugeness, but a hugeness
without beauty. The temples and palaces were large
brick masses surrounded by equally massive walls.
Some attempts at relieving the monotony were made
by gateways that had the appearance of towers, and
by turrets on the tops of the walls. The softness of the
soil made it necessary to exercise great care in order
to secure strong foundations for these immense struc-

Seven was not the customary number of the stages. Indeed there
was no fixed number, and four stages are more common than seven.
The ambition of the royal builders was solely directed to raising
the towers to as great a height as possible in imitation, as has been
suggested, of a mountain peak. It does not appear that any symbolism was associated with the number seven, even when this number
became a more common limit to the series of stages heaped on one
another.

tures, and it became customary at an early period to
erect a broad platform, often carried up to a considerable height, on which the temple or palace was reared.
Regarded as the dwelling of the god in whose honor
it was erected, the temple became literally the god's
house, and, as a consequence, the names of the temples
of Babylonia and Assyria invariably contain as one
of their elements the word "house." Thus Marduk's
temple at Babylon was known as E-sagila, "the lofty
house," which was also the designation of Ea's sanctuary at Eridu. Nabu's temple at Borsippa was called
E-zida, "the faithful house," Shamash's temple at
Sippar, E-barra, "the shining house,"—an appropriate
designation for the dwelling of the sun god; the temple
of the moon god Sin at Ur was called E-khul-khul,
"house of joys," and so on through the almost endless
list of temples in Babylonia and Assyria.

The prominent feature of the temple as the house
of the gods was an outer court immediately back of the
entrance, from which one entered into a long vestibule
leading into a second court with a large hall at one end,
at the back of which there was a recess or a small
chamber to receive the image of the god. Grouped
around the outer court were rooms for the priests and
for the temple administration. Similarly, corridors
led to rooms around the inner court and adjoining the
inner hall, all set aside for the various needs of the
temple service. The number of such rooms varied of
course with the size of the temples, just as the temples
themselves varied in size from comparatively small
dimensions—more in the nature of chapels—to large
areas with a perfect labyrinth of rooms around the
outer and inner court.[6] The temple of Ningirsu at
Lagash and known as E-ninnu, "the house of fifty,"
must have been an extensive structure, as described by

---

[6] See Koldewey, *Die Tempel von Babylon und Borsippa* (Leipzig, 1911).

FIG. I, RESTORATION OF THE TEMPLE OF THE GOD NINIB IN BABYLON

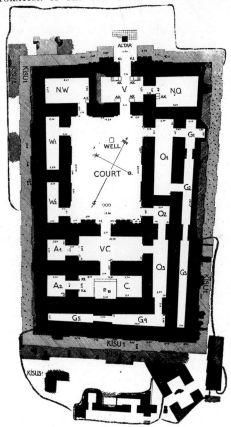

FIG. 2, PLAN OF THE TEMPLE OF THE GODDESS NINMAKH IN BABYLON

its builder Gudea, who tells us of the many rooms it contained for the accommodation of the priests, store rooms for grain, treasure rooms, stalls for the sacrificial animals, and various offices for the administration of the temple.   It will be recalled [7] that the temples became in the course of time commercial institutions, having large holdings of land, giving out contracts for work, hiring laborers, and engaging in the loan of money and other commercial enterprises.   For all these purposes, offices and store rooms had to be provided, and since the temple officials were also the judges and administrators of justice, further accommodations were needed for this phase of the temple activity.   An interesting variation of the Assyrian temples from the Babylonian models which in other respects were closely adhered to, consisted in the proportions of the outer and inner court.   While in the case of the Babylonian edifices the two courts were about the same shape, the inner court in the temples of Assyria was narrow and broader than the outer one, and led into a long and narrow hall, at the back of which was the "holy of holies," where the god had his seat.   The people assembled for worship in the large outer court where the altar stood on which the sacrifices were offered, while the inner court with the holy of holies in the rear was reserved for the priests and for the rulers who alone had access to it.   The impression conveyed by these sacred edifices is well described in an inscription of the Assyrian king Tiglathpileser I. who reigned about 1125 to 1100 B.C.[8]   He describes how, after laying the foundation of the restored temple of Anu and Adad in his capital city on the solid rock and enclosing the whole with burnt bricks, he built the temple of Anu and Adad of large stones.   He continues: "Its interior

---

[7] Above, p. 274 and 316 *seq.*

[8] Rawlinson I.   Pl. 15, 98–101.   Quoted also by Handcock, *Mesopotamian Archæology* (New York, 1912), p. 142.

I made brilliant like the vault of heaven, decorated its walls like the brilliancy of the rising stars and made it superb with shining brilliancy."

There were thus chiefly two features in the temple architecture of Babylonia and Assyria upon which the effect produced depended—the erection of the structure on an elevated platform, and the elaborate decoration by means of glazed tiling and through direct painting of the stucco-coated interior walls. The fondness for brilliant coloring so characteristic of Oriental art at all times may thus be traced back to the civilization of the Euphrates Valley, and in this respect, at least, the temples of Babylonia and Assyria must have surpassed the decoration of the sacred edifices of Egypt which, constructed of hard granite, lent themselves less to gaudy decoration. The use of various kinds of stone, chiefly a soft limestone and a harder alabaster, was an innovation introduced by Assyrian builders, but the stone was limited to the outer casings and to the sculptured figures that were placed at the entrances to temples and palaces and to the sculptured bas-reliefs with which the Assyrian kings from a certain period on were wont to cover the interior walls of the great palace halls—the throne rooms and reception halls. The great mass of the Assyrian temples continued to be built of kiln-dried and sun-dried bricks down to the latest period,—in slavish imitation of Babylonian prototypes. The main effect, therefore, of these structures was at all times that of huge square masses, usually with the corners orientated to the four directions, and merely interrupted by massive gateways and smaller entrances and the turreted tops of the enclosing walls to relieve the monotony.

III

This hugeness was further accentuated by the high towers that were attached to the temples in the case of the chief edifices of both Babylonia and Assyria and of many of the minor ones as well. The tower, as has already been pointed out, represents a mountain in miniature and is to be explained as an endeavor on the part of a people coming from a mountain home to reproduce in their new surroundings the belief which placed the seat of the gods on mountain tops. The tower as a sacred edifice thus rests on a totally different conception from the temple proper which is an outgrowth of the ordinary house; and since we find the tower as an adjunct to the temple in all the important Sumerian centres of the south, we may in connection with other evidence ascribe the tower to the influence of the non-Semitic element, and the temple as above described to be the sacred edifice expressive of Semitic ideas. The two together—and temple and tower are thus invariably combined—furnish, accordingly, another illustration of the composite character of the Euphratean culture.

The aim of the builders in harmony with the underlying *motif* of the towers was to make them as high as possible—an aim that is well expressed in the inscription of Tiglathpileser I., above referred to, who, speaking of two towers that he erected in connection with the double temple of Anu and Adad, states that he reared them "up to heaven." The simplest method of construction to convey the picture of a mountain was to place one stage above the other, each stage or story being somewhat smaller in proportions than the one immediately below it. The number of stages thus superimposed varied from four—which seemed in the earlier period to be the usual number [9]—to seven. It is of course possible that the number seven was associated with the moon, sun and five planets, but there is no satisfactory evidence that this was the case. Such symbolism could only have been introduced at a time

---

[9] Though towers of two and three stages also occur.

when the original purpose which inspired the building of these towers had been lost sight of. A tablet discovered by the late George Smith and recently published furnishes the height of the seven stories of such a stage tower in Babylon (*zikkurat,* "high place" as the Babylonians called it) as 300 feet. In this case each story was not only smaller in circumference, but the stages diminished in height as one proceeded to the top. Elsewhere, however, as at Khorsabad, the four lower stages were of equal height. Whether in all cases the outer casing of bricks were glazed and colored is a question that cannot be answered definitely, though the indications are that such elaborate decoration was exceptional and limited to the towers built in later periods by Assyrian rulers, who were fired with the ambition to outdo their Babyloniain predecessors in grandeur. It is probably safe to assume also that in the earlier periods, both in Babylonia and Assyria, the towers did not rise to more than 100 or 150 feet. Such a structure in comparison with the ordinary low one-storied houses —and even the temples and palaces, though higher, consisted of only one story—would seem huge indeed.

Up to the present the best preserved *zikkurat* found was that unearthed by Botta at Khorsabad, of which portions of four stages remain with abundant traces of coloring in the case of the exterior casings. Fortunately, we have two other means of forming more accurate views of the appearance presented by these towers when complete than would be possible by a conjectural reconstruction—in the first place by a representation of a tower on a Babylonian monument, and secondly through the preservation of a structure in the Euphrates district which, though dating from the Mohammedan period, is modelled on the pattern of a Babylonian zikkurat. The picture of a zikkurat occurs on a so-called Boundary stone,[10] recording the

[10] See Jastrow. *Bildermappe zur Babylonisch-Assyrischen Religion* No. 38.

PLATE XXXIX

FIG. I, STAGE TOWERS OF ANU-ADAD TEMPLE AT ASHUR

FIG. 2, MOHAMMEDAN TOWER AT SAMARRA ON THE TIGRIS (9TH CENTURY A.D.)

grant of a certain piece of property through a ruler of
the thirteenth century B.C.; it shows a structure of four
stages superimposed, with indications of a winding
ascent from one story to the other and crowned with
a chapel. The stages decrease in size as one proceeds
upward, and the same is the case with the very remarkable stone structure still standing at Samarra some
ninety miles above Bagdad. Here we have a stage
tower of seven stories on the top of which is a little
rotunda in which the *muezzin* takes his stand to call
the faithful to prayer. A glance at this Mohammedan
minaret is sufficient to show the direct and continuous
line of tradition leading from the *zikkurat* to the
towers of the Mohammedan mosques on the one hand,
and to the belfries, campaniles and steeples of Christian
churches on the other.[11] In Babylonian and Assyrian
architecture the tower is always separate from the temple proper—as though to symbolize the independent
origin of the two structures, the mountain-*motif* and
the house-*motif*. Generally the tower is back of the
temple, at times to one side, but, even when it is accorded
a position immediately adjacent to the temple, as in the
case of the two zikkurats attached to the temple of
Anu and Adad at Ashur, one standing to the right, the
other to the left of the double temple, the tower is yet a
distinct structure, the ascent being independent of the
temple. In the case of many mosques the Babylonian-
Assyrian tradition is followed through the virtual
independence of the minarets as adjuncts to the mosque,
though in others the minaret is directly attached and
eventually becomes a steeple placed on or at the side
of the mosque. Similarly in the church architecture of
Italy we find a tower built quite independently of the
church as in the case of St. Mark's in Venice and of the
cathedrals in Florence and Pisa, while in Norman archi-

---

[11] See on this subject Thiersch, *Pharos, Antike, Islam und Occi-
dent* (Leipzig, 1907).

tecture the belfry becomes attached to the church, and in Gothic architecture the tower becomes a steeple placed on the church, and with a complete departure from its Babylonian-Assyrian counterpart is looked upon as a symbol of the spirit of Christianity, calling upon its followers to direct their thoughts heavenward.

IV

There is another feature of Babylonian architecture which needs to be touched upon before we leave the subject. At Warka, Telloh, Nippur and Babylon remains of arches were found at a depth which left no doubt as to the great antiquity to which the construction of arches is to be traced back in the Euphrates Valley— at least to 3000 B.C. The span of these arches is not large and the construction is very irregular and crude, but nevertheless they illustrate the principle of the true arch; and it has been plausibly conjectured that the discovery was suggested by the arched form of the primitive reed huts—still in use by the natives in the villages. These early arches were used as tunnels through which drains passed to carry off the rain water and the refuse from the structures beneath which they were erected. The extent to which the arch may have been used in Babylonian temples and palaces as a part of the construction proper is a question still in dispute, but since we find it employed in connection with the gateways of Assyrian palaces in the eighth century, it is a reasonable conclusion that the Assyrians merely imitated in this regard as in so many others the example furnished by the architects of the south. This is all the more plausible because of the discovery at Bismya of a domed covering [12] for a structure that stood in close vicinity to the ancient temple at that place. We have at least one example of an arched gateway uncovered in the course of the excavations at Babylon by the German expedi-

---

[12] Banks, *Bismya*, p. 246.

PLATE XL

FIG. I, BABYLONIAN COFFINS OF THE OLDER PERIODS

FIG. 2, ASSYRIAN GRAVE VAULT

tion while illustrations on Assyrian monuments show
us temples with a series of domes—not unlike those
which constitute a feature of Mohammedan mosques
and chapels at the present time. The courts of the
temples, however, were uncovered and the public cult
took place in the open air. Nor are there any good
reasons for believing that either in the case of temples
or palaces or private houses flat roofs were ever introduced. The absence of stone and of wood to serve as
beams and rafters would prevent the architects from
introducing such a covering. The brick arch and the
dome were therefore the two resources which must have
been developed at a comparatively early period, and in
the construction of which the ingenuity of the builders
had an opportunity for wide play. The principle of
the arch was further applied in the construction of
vaults for the burial of the dead both in Babylonia and
Assyria. In the mound Mukayyar—covering the site
of ancient Ur—Taylor in 1854 discovered a number of
such arched vaults, averaging 5 feet in height and 3½
feet in breadth, and tapering from a length of 5 feet to
about 7 feet. About fifty years later, the German
explorers working at Kaleh-Shergat, the site of the city
of Ashur, came across vaults of precisely the same construction—an interesting and valuable index of the
continuity of architectural methods in both the south
and the north.[13] The depth at which these vaults were
found at Kaleh-Shergat showed conclusively that the
explorers were in the presence of tombs belonging to
the older Assyrian period. The span of the arch in
these Assyrian vaults was about five feet, the vaulted
portion above the perpendicular walls on which the
arch rested being a little over two feet high. The total
height of the tomb was therefore about five and a half

[13] See *Mitteilungen der Deutschen Orient Gesellschaft* No. 8,
facing p. 43; and for arches from Nippur and Uruk, Handcock,
Mesopotamian Archæology p. 170.

feet. The dead were placed in recesses along the walls or laid on the floor.

Digressing for a few moments to consider the methods of burial in Babylonia, we shall be led to the next subject to be considered—the pottery. The oldest form of burial appears to have been to place the dead in small clay coffins—not unlike a modern bath tub. Some of these were so small and so shallow as to suggest that the body was forced into these compartments by drawing up the knees and placing the body in a position that suggests the reproduction of the position of the child in the mother's womb. Instead of coffins proper, large jars were used and the body sealed as it were between two such jars, or again the bodies were placed on reed mats and covered with large earthen covers. In the later periods the tendency developed to increase the length of the coffins until in the neo-Babylonian and Persian periods we find long slipper-shaped receptacles with a narrow opening into which the body was forced. In the early periods, the coffins and jars were almost wholly without ornament, but on those of the later period, particularly on the slipper-shaped coffins, designs were worked out which, covered with a glaze, often gave a striking appearance to these coffins. By the side of vaults in which a number of bodies could be placed, we find square shaft tombs in each of which only one body was placed or a barrel-shaped tomb in which the dead was interred.[14] The general custom appears to have been to bury the dead naked, but in some Assyrian burial vaults at Kaleh-Shergat, Andræ believes to have found traces of clothing. The connecting link between these various methods of burial—and it would appear that the several customs were simultaneously employed and do not represent an evolutionary process—is the desire to imprison the dead securely

[14] See also Jastrow, *Bildermappe zur Babylonisch-Assyrischen Religion*, Nos. 113–115, and above, Pl. 14, Fig. 2.

PLATE XLI

FIG. I, SPECIMENS OF BABYLONIAN POTTERY (TELLOH)

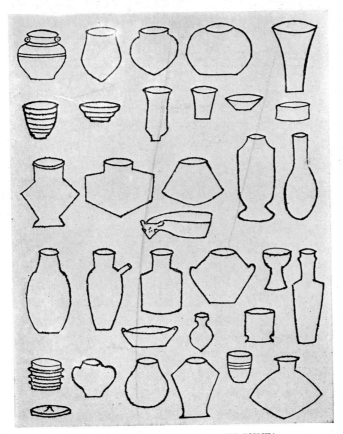

FIG. 2, SHAPES OF POTTERY FROM BISMYA

so as to prevent their troubling the living. The dis-
embodied spirit of the dead was a sort of menace to the
living, and with a view of symbolizing the hope for
security, the dead were forced into jars or coffins. Con-
comitant with this fear of the dead goes, however, the
reverence and pity for those who have left the world
of the living. Unable to provide for themselves, and
yet supposed to have the same craving for food and
drink and the same longing for activity as the living,
the surviving relatives placed jars with food, ornaments, utensils and weapons in the tombs.

V

It is through the contents of the graves that we
obtain an enlarged view of the various kinds of pottery
in use in Babylonia and Assyria, though naturally our
material is not limited to what was found in the graves.

A systematic study of this pottery—such as has been
made of Egyptian and Greek pottery—has not yet been
undertaken, and there is unfortunately much uncertainty as to the provenance of many of the specimens
at our disposal, while in only a limited number of cases
have we accurate data of the depth at which the material
available was found. The potter's wheel appears to
have been used at all periods, though many of the specimens show evidence of having been entirely hand-made.
The clay even in earlier times was burned to an almost
black color, though in the case of the cheap pottery for
every-day use this was probably not done, the clay being
merely sun-dried as in the case of the cheaper kind of
bricks. In the case of large urns and vases, straw was
mixed with the clay in order to give it more substance,
reminding us of the use of straw in the manufacture
of bricks in Egypt. The best collection of pottery
found up to the present time is that of Bismya, where
every conceivable shape and size occurs—from one inch

to almost three feet.[15]   The shapes likewise vary—
from a very simple and almost crude design with merely
a line or two at the top and bottom to elaborate decoration and very intricate shapes with graceful handles.
At Nippur and Telloh several specimens of unusually
large jars have been found, distinguished for their
regular rope pattern, while showing a still higher form
of art is a utensil—perhaps an incense burner—of
most intricate shape and beautifully enamelled with a
green color.   This specimen was found at Telloh.[16]

The clay furnished so profusely by the alluvial soil,
and which we have seen conditions the entire architecture of the Euphrates Valley, as it forms the writing
material, lent itself to all kinds of artistic purposes.
The earliest images of the gods as the earliest attempts
at ornamentation and at sculpture were in clay.   Some
of these attempts were naturally exceedingly crude.
These little images must have been manufactured in
large quantities and sold to pious worshippers, to be
kept in their homes as amulets to ward off the influence
of evil spirits, or deposited as offerings in the temples.
Clay moulds have been found into which the soft clay
was pressed to bring about conventional shapes.

Considerable skill was shown in the modelling of
the human face in these images, as may be concluded
from the figure of a goddess with uplifted hands.   There
is an expression of adoration and servility in the face
that is quite unmistakable and which is well supported
by the position of the hands, suggesting a petition to
some powerful being.   Even more carefully executed is
the picture of a goddess leading a worshipper into the
presence of the deity.   Strangely enough the portrayal
of animals is less successful, though of course it may
not be fair to judge from the few specimens at our dis-

---

[15] Banks, *Bismya*, pp. 175 and 261.

[16] De Sarzec et Heuzey, *Découvertes en Chaldée*, Pl. 44 bis
Fig. 6[a] and 6[b]; for large jars, Babylonian Expedition of the University of Pennsylvania I, 2 Pl. XXVI and Series D vol. 1, p. 406.

FIG. 1, VOTIVE STATUETTE OF CLAY

FIG. 3, THE GOD NINGIRSU AND HIS CONSORT BAU

PLATE XLII

FIG. 2, VOTIVE STATUETTE OF CLAY

PLATE XLIII

FIG. I, BABYLONIAN GODDESS

FIG. 2, VOTIVE TABLET OF UR-ENLIL FOUND AT NIPPUR

posal. Allowance, too, must be made for the individual
style of artists, and yet we are probably safe in saying
that except for the animals portrayed on glazed tiles,
there was something stiff and grotesque in the Babylonian artist's reproduction of animals—presenting a
contrast in this respect to Assyrian art, where the
portrayal of animals is superior to that of the human
face, which rarely rises above a conventional level.

VI

At a very early period the Babylonians conceived
the device to harden the clay by the admixture of substances which gave it almost the quality of a soft stone.
We have a variety of such artificial substances that
form a transition to sculpture in stone. A particularly
good specimen was found in Nippur, showing a sacrificial scene in two divisions. The upper portion represents a naked worshipper offering a libation before
Enlil, the chief deity of Nippur, repeated for the sake
of symmetry. In the lower portion are attendants
carrying some objects and driving two goats. Despite
the fact that the human figures are drawn in outline with
the aid of simple lines, there is dignity in the expression
on the face of the deity. The animal—apparently a
gazelle—drawing a plough (again repeated for the sake
of symmetry), is well reproduced in a second plaque
from Nippur, which shows the same naked worshipper
before Enlil (see Plate XLIII, Fig. 2).

In general, it may be said that in this early work
there is little expression in the human face. The eye
is lifeless, and, even when the face is in profile, the eye
is usually given in full. The crudeness of the art is to
be seen in the position of the feet, though occasionally
an artist succeeds in correctly representing a standing
position. So in the case of a bas-relief found at Nippur
which, though revealing all the characteristic traits of
the early art, is redeemed by the effective manner in
which a bearded priest is shown with his face half turned

towards a worshipper carrying a goat as an offering and being led into the presence of a goddess seated on a bird (Plate XLIV, Fig. 1). A limestone plaque with the figure of a Sumerian chief, standing at the entrance to the sanctuary of the god Ningirsu at Lagash, belongs to the same period, the dress of the worshipper being again of the same primitive character as in the Nippur bas-relief, with the exception that the single garb hanging from the waist reaches to the feet (Plate XLIV, Fig. 2). The elaborate pattern as well as the border of the garb which has a slit in front is due to the greater care in the artistic execution. Very striking is the arrangement of the hair falling down the neck and gathered together by a fillet around his head, while a long chin beard adorns the face. The eye is drawn in front view, and the positions of the feet also reveal the usual limitations of the early art. The long aquiline nose and long feathers as part of the head gear suggest a foreign conqueror who is here paying his respects to the patron deity of Lagash. The sacred poles with mace heads in front of the chief who grasps one of the poles with his right hand are religious symbols,—perhaps originally trees—placed near altars or in front of sanctuaries, not unlike the totem poles of the North American Indians.

A similar attempt to represent two different ethnical types may be recognized in a group of figures that are unfortunately only partially preserved. We have here apparently a procession of warriors, leading captives. The warriors wear their hair long, but the drawing is so conventionalized as to suggest wigs. The long aquiline noses remind one of the figure with the high feathers, as do the long almond-shaped eyes. The procession appears to have been arranged in two rows, and it is evident that the bald-headed and beardless figure in the second row is intended to represent a Sumerian. The folded arms are the gesture of adoration or devotion. It would appear then that we have here a portrayal of a scene in the early history of the Euphrates

PLATE XLIV

FIG. I, GODDESS SEATED ON BIRD

FIG. 2, SUMERIAN CHIEF

PLATE XLV

FIG. I, PROCESSION OF WARRIORS

FIG. 2, BAS-RELIEF, REPRESENTING A RELIGIOUS CEREMONY

Valley in which a foreign group succeeded in bringing the Sumerians into subjection. The two warriors facing one another would then represent the conquerors. Beyond, however, the indication of broadly distinctive types and a certain dignity and strength of posture these specimens of the earliest art do not go, so far as the human figure is concerned (Plate XLV, Fig. 1).

On the other hand, the art is rather remarkable in the skill with which a series of figures are grouped so as to convey a unity or a continuity of action. A good specimen is furnished by the fragment of what was, when complete, a limestone relief of an unusually large size. The fragment preserved is about four feet high. It is again divided into two sections, the upper one representing a procession of four figures being led into the presence of a deity, though it is possible that the third figure with uplifted hands represents a goddess, the consort of the god to whom homage is to be paid and who acts as an intercessor between the gods and the worshipper. In the lower portion the most significant feature is a seated figure—no doubt again a priest—playing on an eleven stringed instrument, the details of which even to the figure of a bull as a decorative portion of the frame are drawn with great precision. Despite the fragmentary condition of the scene portrayed, one obtains an impression of unity (Plate XLV, Fig. 2).

We can trace this artistic method in detail in a series of bas-reliefs, likewise on limestone plaques, portraying Ur-Ninâ, the king of Lagash (c. 2975 B.C.) and his family taking part in building the temple E-ninnu to Ningirsu in Lagash.[17] In the upper portion Ur-Ninâ is portrayed with the workman's basket on his head. He, as well as all the other personages, is beardless and without hair on his head. Naked to the waist,

---

[17] Two in the Louvre (*Découvertes*, Pl. 2 bis, fig. 1 and 2, and Pl. 2 ter, fig. 1) and two in the Museum at Constantinople—one of the latter in a very fragmentary condition.

25

the customary flounced skirt falls in three folds covering the lower part of his body. The dress of all the other figures is the same, only that in place of the flounced skirt, all except one are clothed in a simple form of skirt across which the artist has written the name of the personage portrayed. Behind the king stands an attendant priest with libation vase and cup; in front of him five members of his family with names attached, and it seems quite certain that the first of these is a woman and the king's daughter. In the lower portion the king is seated on the throne, pouring out a libation after the ceremonial rite of building. Behind him stands the attendant priest with the jar out of which a libation has been poured into the cup held by the king in his right hand, while before the king stand a priest (?) [18] and three other sons of the king. The pose of all the figures is entirely conventional, the crossing of the arms symbolizing devotion, and the same convention is observed in the manner in which the left arm is portrayed when the right one holds an object. No attempt is made to give any expression to the faces, all of which, therefore, look alike, but in keeping with the symbolism which pervades the art, the higher stature of Ur-Ninâ is intended to portray the supreme dignity of his royal office, just as by further contrast between the human and divine ruler, the god is represented in the early art as much larger than the king (Plate XLVI, Fig. 1).

VII

The progress of sculptural art is to be seen in the direction of an advancing complication in the design so as to tell as full and detailed a story as possible. The best specimen in this respect so far recovered is a large limestone stele, unfortunately found in a broken condi-

---

[18] The name of this personage is Dudu, but the title that follows is not clear. At all events he is not a member of the royal family, but some official.

PLATE XLVI

FIG. 1, UR-NINÂ, KING OF LAGASH (C. 3000 B. C.), AND HIS FAMILY

FIG. 2, THE GODDESS NINSUN

PLATE XLVII. FRAGMENTS OF THE "STELE OF VULTURES"

FIG. I, THE ARMY OF EANNATUM, RULER OF LAGASH (C. 2920 B.C.)

FIG. 2, THE GOD NINGIRSU, CAPTURING THE ENEMIES OF LAGASH IN HIS NET

tion, but of which enough is preserved to make clear the various episodes in a great struggle which it illustrates. The remarkable monument found at Telloh dates from the reign of Eannatum (c. 2920 B.C.) and portrays his successful engagement against the people of Umma with whom the rulers of Lagash had many a passage at arms.[19] Eannatum pictures the great god of Lagash, Ningirsu, as capturing the forces of the enemy in a large net. This symbolism is offset by a no less remarkable realism in portraying the course of the battle and its issue. One of the fragments, divided as usual into two compartments, shows the troops of Eannatum actually engaged in the conflict. The king is clad in a long skirt to which a cloak falling over the left shoulder is attached. The king's helmet differs also from the head gear of the soldiers by the ear-pieces with which it is provided. In his right hand he holds a weapon which has the shape of a boomerang. The march of the troops over the prostrate bodies of the enemy is portrayed with remarkable vividness and power. They form a solid phalanx, with their long lances held in the right hand, while with the left they protect themselves by rectangular shields that cover the entire body. To illustrate the various divisions of the soldiery participating in the battle, the "light" infantry is shown in the lower compartment, armed with lances and battle-axes but without shields. Again the king is portrayed at the head of his army, but this time riding in a chariot and brandishing a long lance to suggest another stage in the engagement, which probably extended over a considerable period of time. The entire obverse of the monument appears to have been taken up with the portrayal of the attack and the various stages in the engagement, while the reverse illustrated the result of the battle. Just as the king, to symbolize his preëminent rank, is drawn as of larger stature than his sol-

[19] See above, p. 128 seq.

diers, so the god Ningirsu is pictured as huge even in comparison with the king. The upper part of the head is wanting, but despite this, one is struck by the great dignity of the face, which is drawn with evident care. The eye is majestic, the mouth firm, while the long flowing beard adds to the impressiveness of the figure. In his right hand Ningirsu holds a powerful mace as his weapon, while in his left he clasps the heraldic standard of Lagash, the eagle holding two lions in his talons. This standard is frequently portrayed on seal cylinders and other works of art, and well illustrates again the symbolism that finds an expression in such various ways in the oldest art of the Euphrates Valley. The central idea of the design is strength—strength in a superlative degree. Before the god is the huge net with the prisoners to symbolize the capture of the enemy. To further indicate the impossibility of escape from the clutches of Eannatum, a prisoner who has thrust his head out of one of the meshes is being beaten back by the weapon in the hand of the god. The same combination of symbolism with extreme realism—so extreme as to be almost naïve—marks two other fragments of this monument continuing the tale of the victory and its results. One of these shows several rows of corpses, naked and with shaven heads, but evidently arranged in a certain order with great care. The burial of the soldiers of Eannatum who had fallen in battle is here depicted, by way of contrast to the scene preserved in part on the other fragment, showing vultures flying off with human heads, clearly intended to symbolize the punishment meted out to the slain forces of the enemy[20] (Plates XLVII and XLVIII).

---

[20] Because of this fragment the monument is commonly designated as the "Stèle des Vautours" ("Vulture Stele"). See for further details, Heuzey et Thureau-Dangin, *Restitution matérielle Stèle des Vautours* (Paris, 1911).

PLATE XLVIII. FRAGMENTS OF THE "STELE OF VULTURES"

FIG. 2

FIG. I

FIG. 3

FIG. 1, HEADS OF ENEMIES CARRIED OFF BY VULTURES

FIG. 2, BURIAL OF SOLDIERS OF EANNATUM

FIG. 3, THE CONFLICT BETWEEN LAGASH AND UMMA

VIII

It was evidently regarded as the highest aim of the older art of Babylonia to tell a story, and as the tendency towards elaboration increased, the result was an endeavor to give a continuous tale by means of successive scenes in which some details were symbolically indicated and others most realistically set forth. The lack, however, of a true artistic instinct comes out especially in the manner in which the accompanying inscription is allowed to interfere with the effect of the drawing or design, frequently running across figures, inserted wherever there was any room without regard to its effect upon the monument, as in the case of a sculptured votive offering from the days of Entemena, the nephew of Eannatum, interesting as furnishing a detailed drawing of the heraldic device of Lagash (Plate XLIX, Fig. 1) above referred to. The material is an artificial composite of clay and bitumen, having the appearance of black stone. The drawing is again divided into two compartments with an ornamental scroll-shaped design below. The eagle has a human face, an interesting testimony to the antiquity of the endeavor to reproduce in art the hybrid creatures which led in the course of further development to human headed bulls and lions in Babylonia and to the winged bulls with human faces in Assyria as well as to the sphinxes in Hittite art.[21] The combination of the human and animal form rests ultimately upon two features, the resemblance often so striking between the features of a child or a man and some animal, and, secondly, the occurrence of all kinds of anomalies in the young of animals and in the case of infants,[22] which suggested to the primitive mind the possibility of the actual production of "mixed"

[21] See Plate LIV, Fig. 1 and Meyer, *Kultur und Reich der Chetiter*, Figs. 9 and 61.

[22] See the elaboration of this thesis in the author's *Babylonian-Assyrian Birth Omens and their Cultural Significance* (Giessen, 1914) ; also above, Plate V, Fig. 1; Plate XXXII and Plate LIV, Fig. 1.

creatures. ` Symbolism seized hold of the belief and made of the combination the union of the powers and attributes suggested by the animal represented with human features. The crouching heifer in the second compartment is probably also to be taken as a symbol of power, just as on another monument we have the combination of the same two designs—the human headed eagle clutching lions and ibexes with crouching bulls.[23] In contrast to the eagle which gives a decidedly grotesque impression, relieved only by the force with which he clutches the lions, the natural force of the heifer full of life and vigor raises the work to a much higher degree of artistic execution. It is much to be regretted that a stele found at Telloh, illustrating in detail the course of a conflict with an enemy, should have been discovered in so fragmentary a state. In its complete form it must have told its story in a particularly effective manner. The two fragments that have been pieced together show us in the upper row the combatants marching to the encounter, in the middle the engagement itself and in a third presumably the victory, with a procession of captives and, perhaps, an offering to Ningirsu. It is a hand-to-hand encounter. The enemy is represented as naked, while the king's soldiers have helmets and short skirts. The scene is full of life and dramatic in the different pose given to each figure so far as preserved (see Plate XLIX, Fig. 2).

The highest point in this realistic portrayal of an actual conflict, which was obviously a favorite subject intrusted to the official artists of the rulers, is reached in a remarkable monument discovered in the course of the excavations at Susa and which formed part of the spoil taken from Babylonia by an Elamite conqueror in the twelfth century. The monument, a limestone slab, shows the king Narâm-Sin of Agade (c. 2550 B.C.) and his victorious army fighting in a moun-

---

[23] See below, Plate LXXI, Fig. 1.

PLATE XLIX

FIG. 1, HERALDIC DESIGN OF LAGASH

FIG. 2, CONFLICT WITH AN ENEMY

tainous district. The difficulties of the region are symbolized by the high steep cone which the king is about
to ascend. The manner in which the soldiers are distributed is also intended to convey the impression of
an army marching up the side of a mountain. A tree
is added to suggest a thickly wooded district. All this
is, to be sure, crude, but the main effort of the artist is
devoted to the delineation of the king as the central
figure, and in this he has been entirely successful. The
great stature as usual is supposed to accord with the
royal rank. He towers over the enemy as well as over
his own soldiers. His spear has sunk deep into the
neck of the enemy crouching before him, and he holds
a second spear in his hand ready to continue the attack.
The moulding of the right arm showing the strong
muscles and reproducing the strong grip of Narâm-Sin
on his weapon is admirable. The face is unfortunately
badly preserved, but the shape of the head, the carefully arranged beard, the tightly fitting helmet betray a
skill in keeping with the splendid poise of the body and
the well proportioned limbs. The horns attached to
the helmet are the symbol of divinity to which Narâm-
Sin laid claim. The numerous figures are so grouped
as to lead up to that of the king as representing the
climax. It was regarded sufficient to indicate by
the garb and by the pose the broad distinction between
the soldiers of the king and those of the enemy, but
within these limitations the stele of Narâm-Sin shows an
advance in the variations in the pose of individuals, in
contrast to the earlier conventional sameness.[24] This
marked tendency toward individual treatment is still
further accentuated in another monument of the days
of Narâm-Sin found near Diarbekr far up in the north-

---

[24] The original inscription accompanying the monument is almost
entirely missing, but on the cone, representing a mountain, Shutruk-
Nakhunte, the king of Elam who carried the monument to his capital
as a trophy in the twelfth century B.C., has written a record of this
act.

ern region of the Tigris, erected there by the triumphant king to commemorate his achievements in the extreme north.[25]   The material is again a soft stone on
which a large figure of the king has been sculptured in
a most effective manner. This is no longer a conventionalized face but an attempt to give a portrait of the
king. Despite the imperfect preservation of the monument, the face has an expression which is distinctly
individualistic. If we are justified in associating this
advance in sculpture with the age of Narâm-Sin, perhaps as a result of the intellectual stimulus incident to
the advance in the Semitic control of the Euphrates
Valley, then we may ascribe to the same period an
exquisite relief on black steatite which for grace and
attention to details belongs to the best that this high
antiquity has left to us.[26]   It represents the goddess
Ninsun seated on a throne. Her expression is singu-
larly attractive. There is a softness and beneficence in
her manner which add an element of great charm. The
dress, gracefully arranged in folds, covers the entire
body and a necklace adorns her throat. The neat
arrangement of the hair is in keeping with the exceedingly fine execution of the whole figure. The eye of
the goddess is correctly shown in profile—another proof
of the advance in art. The same quality of workmanship, though not so successfully carried out, is to be
seen in a fragmentary bas-relief picturing the divine
pair, Ningirsu the patron deity of Lagash and his
consort Bau.[27]   The latter is seated on the knees of the
god, who turns towards her with a look of extreme
tenderness. The expression on the face of the goddess
is less pronounced owing to defective preservation, but
one can still recognize the endeavor to give to her features a softness and femininity which are intended to
present a contrast to those of the male figure.

[25] See above, p. 136.

[26] Plate XLVI, Fig. 2.

[27] See illustration above, Plate XLII, Fig. 3.

FIG. 1, STELE OF NARÂM-SIN, KING OF AGADE

FIG. 2, BAS-RELIEF OF NARÂM-SIN, KING OF AGADE

PLATE L

IX

It may be accidental that in the sculptures in bas-relief of the later periods we do not encounter the same degree of perfection. In view of the many and large gaps in our material for tracing the development of Babylonian art, it is rather hazardous to draw conclusions, but it ought not to occasion surprise that after a period of strong art activity a reaction through some cause or the other should have set in. Comparing the stele of Narâm-Sin with the sculptured design at the head of the famous Code of Hammurapi [28] (c. 2123–2081 B.C.), one cannot help being struck by the stiffness and conventionality of the figures of both the god and the king on this diorite block, in contrast to the ease and grace of the earlier period. Hammurapi is standing in an attitude of adoration before Shamash, the sun-god, who as the god of justice is symbolized as the ultimate source of the laws compiled in the code. There is, to be sure, an attempt to reproduce the features and the general expression on the face of the king, as may be seen from a comparison with another bas-relief of Hammurapi which we are fortunate enough to possess. In so far the art of the second millennium continues the traditions of the past, and perhaps may even have improved upon them, but the figures are lifeless. The feet are reproduced in the usual conventional position. We also have a representation of the seated sun-god, dating from the middle of the tenth century, and showing that in the interval of more than a millennium, there had been no conspicuous change or improvement in the artistic representation of the gods and of the human figure in general. (See Pl. 10.)

Turning to sculpture in the round, it is natural in view of the greater difficulties involved to find the Sumerians and Babylonians so hampered by conven-

[28] See illustration above, Pl. 34; and for the other portrait of Hammurapi, Jastrow, *Bildermappe zur Babylonisch-Assyrischen Religion*, No. 5.

tionalism that there is very little progress to be noted in
a comparison of the oldest with later specimens. One
of the oldest is the statue of a king of Adab, found in
the course of excavations on that site and which is now
preserved in the Ottoman Museum at Constantinople.
The stone is hard marble, and the statue is noticeable
for its weight, which is about two hundred pounds. The
upper part of the figure is naked, and there is a total
absence of any attempt to show the muscles of the body.
The arms are attached to the stone, though less closely
than in some other specimens. The head is clean
shaven, the eye-sockets are hollow, with indications
however that they were once inlaid—probably with
ivory. This in itself shows the limitations of the art
which does not attempt to reproduce the individual
features, but contents itself with general and more or
less conventionalized traits. In comparing this with
another figure which may be somewhat earlier, it will
be noted that in the latter there is no attempt to reproduce the dress, that the arms are closely attached to the
body and that the feet are merely indicated and are
united to the pedestal. In these three respects, therefore, the sculpture in the round passes through a stage
of progressive development, and the statue of the king
of Adab shows us how the artists of Babylonia gradually overcame some of the difficulties which they encountered (see Plate XXII, Fig. 1; Plate XXIV, Fig. 1).

The treatment of the hair appears to have occa-
sioned special difficulties in this class of sculptures.
Ordinarily, the Sumerian artist contented himself in
the case of male figures with leaving the hair out entirely, which is natural since the Sumerians were beardless and may at a certain period have had the custom of
also shaving the hair of the head. Occasionally, however, the endeavor is made to show the hair, as in the
case of the statue of the Sumerian official above discussed, which, though cruder than that of the king of
Adab, is redeemed to a certain degree by this feature.

PLATE LI

FIG. I, DIORITE STATUE OF A WOMAN

FIG. 2, DOG, AS VOTIVE OFFERING

As a result of the growing prominence of the Semites, greater attention was paid to both hair and beard, since the Semites were bearded and wore their hair long. We have from Bismya, which yielded the statue of Lugal-daudu, a splendid specimen of the early portraiture of a Semite. The material is alabaster. While the strands of the beard are not indicated, nevertheless the general effect is pleasing and rather graceful. No doubt this is in part due to the good drawing of the head, the strong characteristic nose, the forehead and the vigor of the eye, although the eye-sockets are as usual hollow. The statue of an early Semitic ruler, Manishtusu, (c. 2600 B.C.), found in the course of the excavations at Susa, shows that the more careful representation of the beard was within the scope of the older Sumerian or Babylonian artists.[29] One can see also more of an attempt to reproduce personal features, such as the firm mouth and the broad nose. The portrayal of women, whose headdress at all times formed an important part of their toilet, acted as a further incentive to artists to perfect a method of representing the hair in a natural manner. We find this in the case of two heads that have come down to us from the earliest period, showing the hair carefully hanging in tresses that cover the ears and held back by a fillet. Nothing could be more charming and more graceful than the seated figure with her long hair falling in beautiful strands down her back, and the details of the closely fitting dress so carefully reproduced. Only in the arms closely attached to the body do we see the limitations of this early art. The most remarkable specimens of sculpture in the round that have come down to us from ancient Babylonia are the diorite statues from the days of Gudea. The king set up a large number of such statues of himself of which some are in sitting and

---

[29] Above, Plate XXIII, Fig. 2; for the head of a Semite (found at Bismya) Plate XXII, Fig. 2.

others in standing posture.[30]   Considering the hardness
of the material, which was imported by Gudea from a
great distance, it is surprising to see how gracefully the
garments fall over the body, and the degree of perfection reached in representing the muscles of the arms
and shoulders, and the lines of the neck and breast. The
clasped hands, no longer clinging to the body, are admirably executed. In the case of the feet of the standing statues, however, the artist betrays his inability
to detach them from the background, and which gives
to them a very awkward appearance. On the other
hand, in the case of the seated statues the artist has
overcome the difficulty and shows the feet free from
the pedestal and from the background. Ten such
statues were found, all decapitated, but through recent
finds, one statue can now be completed, and we have in
addition to this head fitting on the statue several other
heads of diorite which enable us to form a very satisfactory idea of the modelling of the human features
out of this hard stone. As was to be expected the expression is somewhat blank. The cheek bones and chin
are admirably modelled; the eyes are large and represented as wide open and with heavy eyebrows. Presumably, the hard substance prevented the artist from
making the eye-sockets hollow as in the case of statues
sculptured out of a softer stone, but there is a distinct
artistic gain in thus avoiding the temptation to insert
pupils of ivory or of some other substance. The turban
relieves the artist of the necessity of treating the hair,
but we are fortunate in having a statuette of a woman,
carved out of this hard substance and belonging to the
period of Gudea, from which we see how the artist overcame this difficulty to a certain extent. Here the arrangement of the hair is indicated by the curls held in
place by a fillet, while the hair falls in a thick mass in

---

[30] The standing ones measuring 1.10 to 1.58 metres; the sitting
ones 77 to 93 centimetres. See above, Plate XIII and *Découvertes
en Chaldée*, Pl. 7–20.

PLATE LII

FIGS. 1, 2, AND 3, HEADS OF LIONS

the back. The artist evidently could not go as far as in the case of the two figures above discussed, but on the whole the effect is pleasing. We may note in this figure also the skill of the artist in giving a feminine expression to the unusually regular features, and the rather elaborate dress which is admirably reproduced. The proportion of the head to the body is also correct, in contrast to the completed statue of Gudea where the head is out of proportion to the short and thick-set body, which gives the ruler almost the appearance of a dwarf.

X

Besides human figures, we have specimens of animals sculptured in the round, as well as some curious hybrid figures that are the forerunners of the huge winged creatures—the human faces with the body of an animal—which were placed at the entrances to large halls in Assyrian edifices.[31] An unusually good piece of work is a crouching dog carved out of steatite. The body is admirably drawn, the legs are in an easy position and true to nature, while the face is so carefully reproduced as to enable us to specify the breed of mastiff to which it belongs. It bears an inscription on its side, indicating that the object was a votive offering on the part of King Sumulailu, (c. 2211–2176 B.C.), to the goddess Nin-Isin, "lady of Isin."[32] Attached to the back is a cylindrical-shaped vase, but it is more than likely that this attachment which spoils the effect is of later date. At Telloh also a large number of heads of lions have been found serving as mace heads or as decorations on bowls, or supports for thrones (Plate LII). While some show greater perfection than others, they all testify to the skill displayed in representing the majesty and fierceness of the animal's features. It is only when we come to the mane that we encounter the influ-

---

[31] See Plate V, Fig. 1.
[32] See above, Plate LI, Fig. 2.

ence of conventionalism, though considerably less in some specimens than in others. In the combination, however, of the human with the animal, neither Babylonians nor Assyrians were ever able to overcome the impression of grotesqueness which is the natural result. We have nothing in Babylonian or Assyrian art that can be placed by the side of the remarkably harmonious combination of a human body with an animal head which we encounter in Egyptian art. In the case of the crouching bull with the human head, of which the Louvre has several specimens, the grotesqueness is heightened by the lack of proportion between the animal body and the human body. The head framed in by a mighty beard suggests that the symbolism is to be traced to Semitic influences. The features too are distinctly Semitic, while the strands of the beard ending in curls suggest the typical arrangement in the case of representations of Assyrian monarchs, merely somewhat simpler than the later more elaborate and more conventionalized style. The head, however, looks as though it had been stuck on the body as an after thought (see Plate LIII).

One of the two specimens of this hybrid figure is an interesting illustration of inlay work, of which the Babylonian artists were exceedingly fond. The inlaying was done with yellow shells inserted into the black steatite so as to give the effect of a streaked bull. The result is again a grotesqueness which reflects on the good taste of the artist. Because of the subject and manner of execution, mention may here be made of a steatite vase with strange mythical monsters, the effect of which is heightened by the incrusted little shells to represent the scaled backs of the winged serpents with scorpions' tails and talons resembling those of eagles. Like the human-headed bull, there is a latent symbolism, though perhaps of a different order. The serpent is no doubt to be regarded as the emblem of the god

PLATE LIII

FIG. 2

FIG. 1

FIGS. 1 AND 2, HUMAN-HEADED BULLS

Ningishzida to whom, as the accompanying inscription shows, the vase is dedicated by Gudea, the famous ruler of Lagash. The repetition of the symbol is for the sake of symmetry. Each of the serpents holds a hilted weapon, also encountered on other monuments. The other two serpents, more true to nature, entwined around a pole appear to serve merely decorative purposes, the mouths of the two serpents meeting at the edge of the vase, which evidently was a cult object, used in pouring out libations to the god to whom the vase is dedicated. The bodies of these serpents are likewise incrustated, and in contrast to the very grotesque mythical beings, the two entwined serpents are remarkably realistic. The whole object, unique in its design and original in its execution, ranks among the best specimens of Babylonian sculpture, and illustrates the wide range of that art. (See Pl. 71, Fig. 2.)

It may of course be an accident that we have not found nearly so many specimens of sculpture in the round as of bas-reliefs, but it is perhaps not unreasonable to conjecture that the difficulties involved may account for the fact. Custom, too, which is so large a factor in the development of art, may have led to the stele with a sculptured design as the type of the monument of an individual, having the advantage of more space for the accompanying inscriptions which was a chief motive with those who set up such monuments of themselves, or who had votive offerings prepared for themselves.

XI

It is time now to turn to Assyrian sculpture, which, while showing its dependence upon that of Babylonia, nevertheless strikes out in new directions and shows traits of a decidedly original character. In the choice of subjects Assyrian art reflects the ambitions of the rulers and the martial spirit of the people. Our material is not sufficient to enable us to follow the development of Assyrian sculpture through its various phases. We cannot carry it further back at present than the twelfth century, and the specimens up to the middle of the ninth century are so few that we must for the present begin the survey from the comparatively late period when Assyria was already approaching the zenith of her power. It seems, however, safe to assert that the general traits of Assyrian sculpture are already fixed several centuries before Ashurnasirpal III. (883–859 B.C.). The dependency upon Babylonian prototypes is seen in the portrayal of the human figure, which remains throughout the entire period stiff, lifeless and extremely conventionalized. On the other hand, there is considerable advance in showing soldiers and huntsmen in action, though here too conventionalism lays shackles on the freer development of the art, but the most striking contrast to the bas-relief sculptures of Babylonia is the breaking away from symbolism in the case of Assyrian art to become purely and completely realistic. The result is a decided advance in the direction of giving more life to the scenes depicted; they come closer to reality. The marching soldiers, being no longer chosen to symbolize the kind that marched to an attack, move with greater ease. The attack is effectively pictured in a continuous series of designs, each representing some striking moment in the battle, whether real or due to the fancy of the artist is of little moment. Even if the scene is based on a real occurrence, the execution is fanciful—a circumstance which affords a larger and freer scope to the artist's imagination, so essential to the development of a true art.

The palace walls of Ashurnasirpal were covered with bas-reliefs illustrative of incidents in the campaigns of the king, and picturing his activity in the chase, which was the favorite sport of the rulers. A few specimens of each will suffice to show the remark-

PLATE LIV

FIG. 1, HITTITE SPHINXES, SHOWING INFLUENCE OF ASSYRIAN ART

FIG. 2, ASSYRIAN ARMY, ATTACKING A FORT

able vigor displayed in portraying armies in action, as, for example, in attacking a city by means of a battering ram, reinforced by archers, who come into a hand-to-hand encounter with the enemy. The attention to details is also noticeable in the trappings of the horses and in the military equipment of rulers, of the high officers and of the common soldiers. The grouping of the figures is also carried out with taste and skill, though occasionally the scenes are too crowded, and the impression is blurred through the endeavor of the artist to show too much. A defect of the art at this period which is particularly noticeable in the hunting scenes is the stiffness and awkwardness in the drawing of the animals, so much inferior in this respect to the representation of the human figure. While the charioteer who drives the horses with the king at his side, discharging the arrows at the approaching lion, admirably displays the strain on the muscles of the arm and the tension in the face as he tries to control the dashing steeds, the horses themselves seem to be suspended in the air. The artist fails to convey the impression that the horses are speeding along, despite the posture of the forelegs, evidently intended to suggest a rapid dash. There is, indeed, a certain degree of force in the faces of the horses, but a comparison between a number of the bas-reliefs reveals that this expression is stereotyped and falls therefore under the ban of conventionalism. The limitations of the art are even more apparent when it comes to the portrayal of the lions in pursuit, or wounded by the arrows shot at them. The artist succeeds in his attempt to convey the impression of the pain and terror endured by the hunted animal, but the convulsions of the body are drawn in so awkward a manner as to border on the grotesque. We shall note as we proceed to later generations the progress made in this respect until at the highest point of its development, the Assyrian art is remarkably successful also in the naturalness and variety of the poses given to lions,

26

wild horses and other animals when pursued or wounded by the royal sportsmen (see Plate VIII).

The best specimens of the art in the early period are those in which the king is portrayed surrounded by his attendants or officers. These are marked by the most scrupulous attention to details, as, for example, in the scene where the king is portrayed with the bow in one hand and a bowl in the other containing a libation to be offered to the deity after the chase. The embroidery, borders and tassels of the royal garment are executed with the greatest possible care. Not a detail is overlooked, down to the embroidery on the edge of the short sleeves. Necklace, bracelets and ear-rings as well as sandals are similarly worked out in detail, while both in the case of the king and of the eunuch with the fly-flap standing before him, almost every strand of the abundant hair can be distinguished. The endeavor is also made to indicate the strong muscles of the arm, though owing to the substance—a rather hard limestone—this feature can hardly be termed an artistic success. The pose of the figures is easy and dignified, that of the king effectively conveying the impression also of royal majesty (see Plate LV).

The palace at Khorsabad [33] of Sargon, who ruled from 721–706 B.C., and the founder of the dynasty which gave to Assyria its most famous rulers, has yielded a large number of specimens of sculptured bas-reliefs which enable us to trace the beginnings of the art which manifests itself chiefly in the growing complexity of the designs. The artists of each succeeding age evidently vied with their predecessors in the endeavor to vary the monotony of the two main subjects chosen for illustration—war and sport—by the greatest possible diversity in the details. To accomplish this, the scale of representation was magnified, and each episode of

---

[33] See above Plate IV and V, and for further illustrations Botta et Flandin, *Monument de Ninive,* (Paris. 1849).

PLATE LV

FIG. 1, KING ASHURNASIRPAL III OF ASSYRIA (883–859 B. C.), HUNTING LIONS

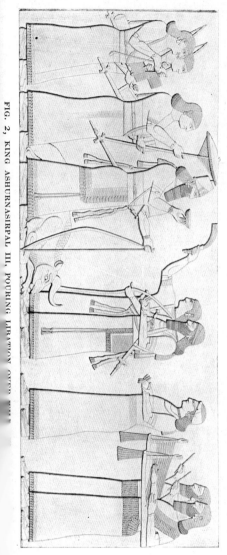

FIG. 2, KING ASHURNASIRPAL III, POURING LIBATION OVER DEAD

PLATE LVI

FIG. 2, TRANSPORTING WOOD ACROSS A STREAM (KHORSABAD)

FIG. 1, ATTENDANTS CARRYING THRONE (KHORSABAD)

the campaign or the chase selected correspondingly amplified by introducing as many figures as possible, and all in action.

There is, however, the same stiff conventionalism in the beardless figures carrying portions of the royal throne. Not only are the faces devoid of expression, but there is a total lack of any indication of muscular action. In contrast to these defects, great care is bestowed on the dress and on such details as the trappings of the horses and the carving of the ornaments of the throne (see Plate LVI, Fig. 1).

An attempt at introducing variety into what might otherwise be monotonous representations is to be seen in the portrayal of Assyrian workmen, transporting wood across a stream. The large variety of marine life is portrayed in a most vivid manner, and likewise the action of the sailors rowing the ships or loading or unloading large bars of wood which, it will be observed in some cases, are placed on a deck above the heads of the rowers, and in others are attached to the stern of the boat (see Plate LVI, Fig. 2).

The limits put upon the art through the extreme conventionalism is shown in the representation of attacks upon forts, such as the one here given, which despite its mutilated character is sufficiently well preserved to give the characteristics of the art of the period. Note the similarity of posture in the case of those appearing at the openings of the various parts of the fort, and the stiff and naïve method of representing the variour stories of the fort and the lack of perspective (Plate LIV, Fig. 2). Even more characteristic is the large figure of the Babylonian hero Gilgamesh represented in the act of strangling a lion, which evidently formed one of the achievements of the hero. The beard is drawn in the usual conventionalized style, but there is an expression of great power in the face, due, to be sure, more to the exaggeration of the features than to artistic delicacy. The expression on the lion's face is ludicrous, and the unequal proportion between the gigantic hero, and the diminutive lion is an indication also of the lack of humor on the part of the Assyrian artist, who did not recognize that it would have been more to the credit of the hero to strangle a really large lion than a little baby whelp (see Plate LVII).

XII

Of the same general character are the wall sculptures from the palace of Sennacherib, unearthed at Kouyunjik by Layard.[34] The later Assyrian artists were guided entirely by earlier models both in the selection of their subjects and in the execution. As we pass, however, from one reign to another we can note a certain advance in artistic execution and more particularly in the grouping of the figures. A good illustration of this advance is to be seen in the series of alabaster bas-reliefs, showing King Sennacherib sitting on his throne outside the city of Lachish in Palestine, and receiving the prisoners of war and tribute from the captive cities of the surrounding states. The wooded surroundings are indicated by trees which, although conventionalized in form, are executed with considerable attention to details. What one notices particularly is the manner in which the high officials of the captured towns, with a royal personage at the head, are represented, followed by common prisoners in various attitudes. Behind the prisoners are groups of captured women and children, some of them in wagons drawn by oxen, while interspersed throughout the long processions are the soldiers carrying the spoils of war. One receives the impression of a long triumphant procession passing by the royal throne, but without the usual exaggeration to which Assyrian artists were given and which spoils the effect in the case of many sculptures

---

[34] See above, p. 19, and for further illustrations Paterson, *Assyrian Sculptures, The Palace of Sinacherib* (The Hague, 1912).

PLATE LVII

GILGAMESH, THE HERO OF THE BABYLONIAN EPIC

PLATE LVIII

KING SENNACHERIB OF ASSYRIA (705–681 B. C.) AT LACHISH (PALESTINE)

by overcrowding. Here everything is drawn on a proper scale. There are just enough details to enable us to interpret the scene correctly, which thus answers the conditions suitable for the genuine illustration of an historical text. Less satisfactory is the endeavor to portray the actual attack on the city of Lachish, which evidently stood on an eminence. This portrayal involved problems of perspective which were beyond the range of the Assyrian artist, but despite this defect the grouping of the figures is again skilfully carried out. We receive the impression of a very large and successful army in the aim of the arrows of the soldiers, as well as in the damage done by the machines of war, hurling heavy catapults against the walls of the besieged town (see Plate LVIII).

Very effective, again, are a series of designs showing the loading and the transporting of one of the huge colossal human-headed bulls intended for the palace of the king. The mechanical devices for moving this heavy object are shown in so clear a manner as to make any further commentary useless. The bull is placed on a huge sled supported by rollers, which are moved as required so as to reduce the power necessary to pull the sled. The men carrying the extra poles and the extra ropes are shown, as well as the officers standing on the colossal figure and giving the necessary directions. Of particular interest is the representation of the manner in which the lever at one end is pulled down through the united strength of a large number of men, who attach themselves by means of ropes to the enormous crowbar (see Plate LIX).

Through these illustrations one also obtains an idea of the large number of workmen at the disposal of the rulers for the purpose of erecting their great buildings and for their building operations. Human life appears to have been an exceedingly cheap commodity in Assyrian days. There was never any lack of men to equip the enormous armies and, similarly, the king was never in lack of the many thousands required for the constant task of building temples and palaces and other huge edifices.

By far the most elaborate and on the whole the most artistic sculptural decorations of the royal palaces of Assyria date from the days of the *grand monarque,* Ashurbanapal (668–626 B.C.), in whose reign the artistic development of Assyria as well as her military glory reached its height. It is necessary to see for one's self at the British Museum, or in the series of photographs made from the originals, the extended group of the scenes of warfare and of the hunt sculptured on bas-reliefs that lined the walls of the large rooms of the palace of the king at Nineveh, in order to realize the general plan followed by the artists in thus illustrating the campaigns of the king and their royal master's sport (Plate LX). Such is the attention given to details that by means of these bas-reliefs we can follow, even without the accompanying descriptive texts and the elaborate annals that we possess of the king's reign, the course of his mad chase for power and glory. The criticism to be passed on many of the limestone or alabaster slabs is that the artist attempts, particularly in the battle scenes, to put too much in a limited space. The scenes are frequently too crowded for artistic effect. The horses in these scenes are particularly well executed; they dash along with fiery spirit and add to the impression of the fierceness of the fight (see Plate LXI).

The scenes here chosen are taken from the series illustrative of the campaign of Ashurbanapal against Teumman, King of Susa, Assyria's most powerful rival. We see the Assyrian monarch in his chariot in the midst of the fray, hotly intent upon capturing Teumman himself, who in one of the scenes is depicted as defended by his son. We see as the climax of the struggle the Elamite king decapitated, a part of the Susian army thrown into the river and the rest taken

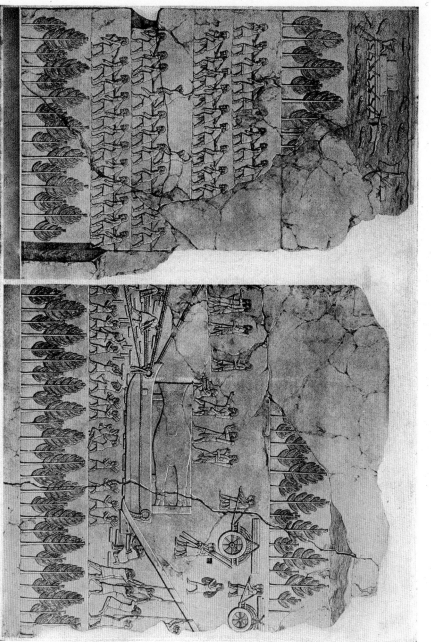

PLATE LIX

PLATE LX

FIG. I, DYING LIONESS

FIG. 2, ATTENDANTS CARRYING NETS FOR THE CHASE AND LEADING DOGS

prisoners. In a continuation of the campaign we observe the procession of prisoners and the head of **Teumman** carried off as a trophy of war in a chariot; and as the fitting close to the campaign, Ashurbanapal and his queen are seated in a garden, enjoying life, while as a ghastly, silent witness to the domestic scene the head of Teumman hangs in the arbor overarching the divans on which the king and queen are lying in an easy posture (Plate LXII).

XIII

A subdivision of the Babylonian-Assyrian art in which unusual skill was developed at an early period and which reached an even higher degree of perfection in Assyria was the work in metals—notably copper and bronze but also silver. Abundant evidence has been found that the Euphrates Valley had its stone age which no doubt overlapped as elsewhere into the age of metals. As early as the third millennium we find specimens of engraving on copper blades, and of copper and bronze statuettes and other votive objects that testify to the high antiquity of the metallurgical art. Despite its bad state of preservation, there is much to admire in the figure of a lion engraved on the tang of a copper blade, found at Telloh and which, measuring about 31½ inches in length, belonged to a lance which, as the partially effaced inscription shows, was dedicated by a "king of Kish" to some deity.[35] The head of the lion is well drawn and, but for the conventionalized shape of the mane, the general effect is pleasing. Another object of copper,[36] belonging perhaps to a still earlier period, shows a lion in a crouching position attached to a

---

[35] *Découvertes en Chaldée*, Pl. 5 ter, No. 1; see also *ib.*, Pl. 6 ter No. 2.

[36] Found at Bismya (see Banks, *Bismya*, p. 237). Banks speaks of the object as bronze, but it is probably copper, as Handcock, *Mesopotamian Archæology*, p. 251, suggests, with an accidental alloy.

spike. While the shape of the head betrays a certain crudeness, and the body is somewhat foreshortened, yet there is much life in the effect as a whole, due to the admirable manner in which the legs are portrayed, conveying the impression of an animal about to leap at some prey. Passing by some representations of animals moulded out of copper but so covered with oxidization as to be not clearly distinguishable, a fair idea of the traits of this art may be obtained from a series of votive statuettes, showing male and female figures carrying baskets on their heads, kneeling gods, female figures and animals in various poses. The basket bearers are of two types, one in which only the upper part of the body is shown, while the other portion, suggesting a skirt reaching to the feet, is taken up with a dedicatory inscription, the other in which the whole body is shown, the upper part and the legs being nude, while a short skirt hangs down from the waist, affording space for the inscription of the ruler who offers the statuette as a votive gift. The most striking feature of these figures is the graceful attitude of the hands in balancing the basket on the head; the least satisfactory is the blank expression on the face, and this despite the fact that the simple features are drawn in good proportion. In contrast to the awkward position of the feet on the sculptures in soft or hard stone, the pose is perfectly natural here. The figure stands firm and yet easy. There is also well expressed in the dignified attitude of the statues as a whole the devotion to a deity, symbolized, as in the case of the Ur-Ninâ plaques [37] by the workman's basket indicative of a direct participation in the erection of a sacred edifice. Belonging to a period not far removed from that of Gudea we have several specimens of votive objects, consisting of a cone to be fastened to some part of a temple or sanctuary and to which the figure of a kneeling god is attached—rather

[37] Above, Plate XLVI, Fig. 1.

PLATE LXI

FIG. I, ASSYRIAN ARMY AND CAPTIVES

FIG. 2, BATTLE SCENE. CONFLICT BETWEEN ASSYRIA AND ELAM

PLATE LXII

KING ASHURBANAPAL OF ASSYRIA (668–626 B. C.) WITH HIS QUEEN

awkwardly to be sure. The figures themselves, however, are exceedingly well executed. The body is well moulded, the features are clean cut, there is a vigorous expression in the eye, the nose is powerful and the mouth firm. The head is slightly out of proportion to the body, though not to such a degree as in the case of the statue of Gudea. We thus get the impression of a somewhat thick-set figure, which, however, is partly due to the fact that the Sumerians were a people of short build; they, therefore, pictured their gods in the same general style, though this did not hinder them from representing them as much taller than themselves, just as the kings were drawn as larger than the common folk (see Plate LXIII).

Much cruder are a series of votive statuettes, serving as amulets and stuck apparently into the walls as a protection against the encroachment of evil demons. They all have heads of females, but only the upper part of the body is clearly indicated. The clasped hands are poorly executed, the faces somewhat more carefully modelled, while the hair hanging about the neck has the appearance of a wig (Plate LXIV, Fig. 1). The grotesqueness is accentuated in some of the statuettes which are provided with a large flat ring shaped like a bird's tail, into which they were slipped to aid in bearing the burden of a tablet of stone attached to the heads (Plate LXIV, Fig. 2), and bearing a dedicatory inscription. In some cases, however, these tablets were bored with holes into which the heads of the statuettes were inserted. Such statuettes were found in groups, buried in hollows and walled in with bricks and bitumen. Perhaps the fact that they were to be kept out of view accounts for the little care bestowed on their execution. Rising again to a high degree of workmanship are heads and bodies of animals belonging likewise to a very early period. A crouching bull on the top of a nail provided with a point to be stuck into a wall is an admirable piece of work, the head being well modelled, the body in pro-

portion and the pose natural (Plate LXIII). Equally
good is a bronze bull standing on a flat support, though
the artistic effect is spoiled somewhat by the bits of
silver inlaid across the body to represent the variegated
coloring of the skin. The head with the gracefully
shaped horns is particularly well done. Still finer are
two animal heads hollowed out of copper, one a bull's
head found at Telloh, the other that of a Markhur goat
with elaborately crumpled horns. The eyes in the one
head are inlaid with mother of pearl, while the pupils
are of lapis lazuli; in the other case, the eyes are made of
shell, the pupils being colored dark brown(Plate LXV).

The extensive use to which copper was put in Babylonia is shown by the very large number and variety of
art objects and utensils found in the excavations at
various sites. Most of these utensils being made for
purely practical purposes, such as daggers, hatchets,
knives, fish hooks, spear-heads, and vases and dishes of
various kinds, have no artistic value, while others that
may have had were found in such a bad state of preservation as to render them uncertain witnesses. Moulds
of clay for metal casting appear to revert to a very early
age, and most of the smaller copper objects found were
prepared in this way. Earrings and jewelry of various
kinds were also made in the same way, as well as bronze
objects, which belong to a later period after the discovery of making bronze by adding an alloy of tin had
been made. The use of bronze becomes more common
as we pass down the ages until in the best Assyrian
period it gradually supplants copper.

Belonging probably to the later Babylonian period,
is a remarkable bronze plaque, detailing a ceremony
of exorcism of a demon of disease. The interesting
feature of this plaque from the artistic point of view
is the grouping of the figures in the second and third
rows. In the upper row we have a series of nine symbols of the chief gods of the pantheon, the crescent
standing for Sin, the moon god, the eight-rayed star

PLATE LXIII

VOTIVE OFFERINGS (COPPER) FROM TELLOH

PLATE LXIV

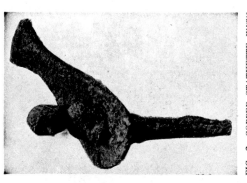

FIG. 2, COPPER STATUETTE WITH
FLAT RING ATTACHMENT

FIG. 1, VOTIVE STATUETTES (COPPER)

PLATE LXV

FIG. I, BRONZE BULL

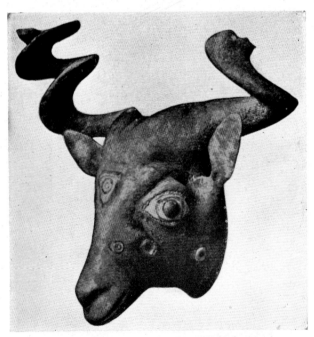

FIG. 2, GOAT WITH CRUMPLED HORNS (COPPER)

for the goddess Ishtar, the stylus to the left of the star for Nabu, the god of writing and wisdom, the adjoining spear for Marduk, the head of the pantheon, and so on through the list. In the second row is a group of seven demons, frequently referred to in the incantation formulas against the demons of disease, and who are regarded as responsible for the bodily ills to which human flesh is heir. The third row pictures the ceremonies for driving the demons of disease out of the victim who lies on a couch with uplifted hands. At either end of the couch stands an exorcising priest, dressed in a fish skin to symbolize that he is acting for Ea, the god of waters, and of whom the fish would be a natural symbol. The two deities chiefly invoked in incantation rituals [38] are Ea as the god of the watery element, and Nusku (or an equivalent) as the god of fire, water and fire being looked upon as the two chief purifying elements to purge the sufferer from disease which was conceived as a kind of impurity. These exorcising priests are performing some ceremony to symbolize the cleansing of the victim. At the left end is an altar with food which typifies the sacrifice offered by the sufferer as part of the ceremony. To the right of one of the priests the demons are pictured as being driven off. In the lowest compartment, the central figure is a representation of the demon Labartu, holding a serpent in each hand, and with pigs sucking at her breasts. She kneels on an ass, and is apparently being driven off in a boat by the demon to her left, who brandishes a weapon or whip in his uplifted hand. The various specimens of food to the right of Labartu may again represent offerings made to the demons to induce them to release their hold, or to the gods appealed to for their aid. The water below Labartu is represented by swimming fishes and the shore by two trees at the right end. The plaque thus tells the whole story of

---

[38] Above p. 246 *seq.*

the ceremony in a most realistic manner. The symbolism, it will be noted, dominates the scenes portrayed to such an extent that, if it were intelligible to us in all its minutest details, we would have a complete picture of the incantation rites and of the ideas underlying each incident in these rites (Plate LXVI).

The use of copper in Babylonia either pure or with an alloy which converted it into bronze was very extensive, indeed, as is shown by the large variety of objects, mirrors, daggers, spear heads, dishes, cauldrons, weights, etc., found in the mounds. Of the bronze objects found in Babylonia a bell, now in the Berlin Museum, merits to be singled out because of the unusually delicate design running around the cup, and which again represents demons portrayed as wild animals of hybrid character, in an upright posture and in a threatening attitude. Five of them have the heads of hyenas, but have human hands and apparently also human bodies; they are clothed in short skirts, and the grotesqueness is increased by the tails and clawed feet; the sixth has a human shape, while in the midst of these demons is again the exorcist, clothed in fish scales to symbolize him as the priest of the water god Ea with whose aid the demons are being driven away. The symbolism is extended to the handles of the bell which are in the form of serpents, and to the turtles and to another design the exact nature of which escapes us. Presumably these designs are emblems of the gods like those on the boundary stones,[39] added as further protection against the mischievous workings of the evil demons (Plate LXVII).

XIV

In Assyria we find bronze gradually supplanting the use of copper, though copper also continued in use to the latest period. Among the large variety of bronze

---

[39] See below p. 416 *seq.*

PLATE LXVI

FIGS. 1 AND 2, BRONZE PLAQUE (OBVERSE AND REVERSE) SHOWING EXORCISING
CEREMONY

PLATE LXVII

FIG. I, BABYLONIAN BRONZE BELL

FIG. 2, DEMONS ON BRONZE BELL

objects discovered in Assyrian mounds a series of
bronze weights in the shape of animals arrest our attention by the admirable drawing of the body and head
of the lions.[40] It is clear, of course, that such objects
were cast by means of moulds, and presumably in the
case of large and heavy objects, the moulds were of
stone or of bronze, while for smaller objects clay
moulds probably served as a more convenient and also
a simpler method. A high degree of art is reached in
repoussé work and engraving on bronze. Of the
former art we fortunately have some remarkable specimens in strips of bronze discovered at Balawat—the
site of an Assyrian town, Imgur-Bel—some fifteen
miles southeast of Nineveh and which were originally
attached to large wooden gates belonging probably to
the palace erected by Shalmaneser III. (858–824 B.C.),
at that place.[41] The doors themselves were over twenty
feet high, six feet wide and three inches thick. The
scenes represented on the bronze strips were intended
to illustrate the campaigns of the king. The method
followed was to beat out the designs on the reverse, and
then to finish it off with a graver on the right side.
There are indications of the hands of several artists in
the work, for some of the strips are superior in workmanship to those on others. The chief defect is in the
lack of perspective, which makes itself felt when large
numbers of personages are represented together and
who thus appear to be closely crowded; but considering the difficulties involved in the indication of details,
it is remarkable with what skill the camp life of the
Assyrian army and the same army in action is brought
before us, and this despite the fact that the animals,

[40] See *e.g.*, Mansell, *British Museum Photographs* No. 585 and
Layard, *Monuments of Nineveh*, 1st Series, Pl. 96.

[41] Birch & Pinches, *The Bronze Ornaments of the Palace Gates
of Balawat* (London, 1880); and Billerbeck and Delitzsch, *Die
Palasttore Salmanassars II von Balawat* (Beiträge zur Assyriologie,
vi, pp. 1–155 and 4 plates). See Plate LXVIII and LXIX.

more particularly the horses, are depicted in a very
conventional fashion. On the other hand the groups
of marching men—soldiers and prisoners—are frequently full of life and vigor, as are the scenes depict-
ing the attacks upon the walled cities of the enemy and
the camp scenes which are valuable also as illustrations
of details in the life of an Assyrian army. The finest
specimens, however, of the work of the engraver on
metal are a number of remarkable bronze bowls found at
Nimrud. The designs repeated like a pattern are series
of animals, gazelles, bulls, lions, ibexes, depicted with remarkable vividness, or griffins standing before a sacred
pole, the execution of which is particularly delicate
(Plate LXX). An interesting feature of these bowls
is the indication of foreign influence which raises
indeed the question whether they are native Assyrian
work. The griffins with the double crown of Upper
and Lower Egypt on their heads are distinctly Egyptian, but on the other hand the forms of the poles agree
with designs found in Babylonian-Assyrian seal cylinders. Some of the platters also contain inscriptions
in Phœnician characters, a circumstance that may be
due to the spread of Aramaic in Babylonia and Assyria
during the eighth and seventh centuries for which there
is other evidence.[42] The animals above referred to are
precisely the ones which we find on older Babylonian
works of art, and when, in addition, we encounter so
genuinely Babylonian a design as the conflict between
bulls and lions on the bronze bowls, there can scarcely be
any doubt that we are in the presence of native work,
which in the later centuries of Babylonian-Assyrian
history was particularly subject to foreign influences.
  The wide use of bronze for the manufacture of

---

[42] We find on business documents of Assyria and Babylonia from
the eighth to the fourth century endorsements in Aramaic. See
Clay, *Some Aramaic Endorsements on Documents of Murashu Sons*
in *Harper Memorial Studies*, vol. i, pp. 285–322.

PLATE LXVIII

FIGS. I AND 2, BRONZE COVERINGS ON PALACE GATES AT BALAWAT

PLATE LXIX

FIGS. I AND 2, BRONZE COVERINGS ON PALACE GATES AT BALAWAT

ornaments such as rings, bracelets, trinkets and amulets or talismans is illustrated by many specimens, though it cannot be said on the basis of what has been found that a high degree of artistic perfection was reached until we come to the Persian period when new influences found their way into Mesopotamia.

Gold and silver were also largely used for ear-rings, necklaces,[43] for inlaid work and as coverings for ceilings and walls in part or for royal thrones, while it did not appear to be even unusual for statues of gods to be made entirely of gold. A Babylonian ruler of the middle of the ninth century, Nabupaliddin, tells us that he prepared a statue of Shamash, the sun-god, made of gold and lapis lazuli, and there are good reasons for believing that the image of the chief god Marduk which stood in his temple at Babylon was entirely of gold. At Ashur the explorers found the remains of a gold lightning fork which had been placed in the hands of the life-size statue of the storm god Adad.

We are fortunate in possessing a specimen of the silversmith's art, all the more remarkable because of its antiquity (Plate LXXI). It was found at Lagash and was a dedicatory offering of Entemena (c. 2850 B.C.). Resting on a copper base, supported by four lions' feet, the vase stands 28 inches above the base. The shape is most graceful, but what adds to its artistic merit is the delicate engraving running around the centre of crouching heifers and of four fantastic eagles with human heads, clutching lions and ibexes alternately. The upper row of seven heifers is particularly well executed, in contrast to the grotesqueness of the lions and to the stiff conventionalism of the ibexes. On the other hand,

---

[43] A particularly fine specimen of an early Babylonian gold necklace in private possession is pictured in Meissner, *Grundzuege der altbabylonischen Plastik*, p. 64 (*Alte Orient*, xv, Heft 1 and 2). See also Botta et Flandin, *Monument de Ninive*, Vol. II, Pl. 161 and Handcock, *Mesopotamian Archæology*, p. 348.

there is a certain dignity in the eagle with the human face, the symbolism of which is of the same general character as in the case of the winged creatures standing before the sacred tree. Significant, however, in the case of all the figures on the silver vase is the delicacy of the work, in which respect it has rarely been excelled in works of art coming down to us from antiquity.

XV

A special class of Babylonian monuments which enter into the subject of the art because of the symbolical designs engraved on them are the so-called "boundary stones" which, recording either certain land privileges granted to individuals by royal decree or the transfer of property made by a legal procedure, were set up at the boundary of the property in question as memorials of the gift or transfer. A large number of such boundary stones have been found in the course of excavations,[44] dating from the fourteenth to the twelfth centuries—coincident with the period of the Cassite control of Babylonia.

At the close of the inscription on the monument describing the property in detail and the terms of gift or transfer, there were added long series of curses, in the names of the various gods, hurled against those who interfered with the rights recorded or who injured in any way the monument itself. As a further warning against transgressors the symbols of the gods were engraved on these monuments, and it is from this point of view that they are of interest to the student of Babylonian art. The symbols themselves are very numerous, consisting of symbols of the heavens, thrones, and animals of various kinds. Three symbols which are never missing are the moon's crescent, the symbol of the

[44] See L. W. King's Introduction to *Memorials and Boundary Stones in the British Museum* (London, 1912), and Morgan and Scheil, *Délégation en Perse, Mémoires I*, pp. 165–182.

PLATE LXX

FIGS. I AND 2, ASSYRIAN BRONZE BOWLS (8TH CENTURY, B. C.)

PLATE LXXI

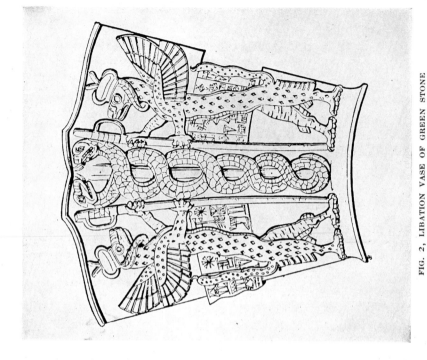

FIG. 2, LIBRATION VASE OF GREEN STONE

FIG. I, SILVER VASE OF ENTEMENA, RULER OF LAGASH
(c. 2850 B.C.)

moon-god Sin; the solar disc and the rays of light, symbolizing Shamash the sun-god; and the sixteen-rayed star, symbolizing the goddess Ishtar, who was identified in the astrological system with the planet Venus. The three thrones, often surmounted by royal caps, are the symbols of the great triad, Anu, Enlil and Ea, while among the animals portrayed on these monuments we encounter the scorpion, the symbol of the goddess Ishkhara, the tortoise, the crouching lion, the symbol of Nergal, and the lion-headed mace, the symbol of Ninib (see Plates LXXII and LXXIII).

These and other animals are frequently drawn with great skill confirming the characteristics of Babylonian art in the portrayal of animals as we have had occasion to set them forth. The same applies to a remarkable drawing of a wolf on one of these monuments,[45] and even the fantastic figures on these monuments such as winged lions, bulls and sphinxes, show remarkable vigor as well as considerable skill. Occasionally the portrait of a king is added. A particularly good specimen showing a remarkable attention to minute details is to be found in the case of a boundary stone of the time of Marduk-nadin-akhe in which the royal chief of the country is thus portrayed.[46] There is, to be sure, a conventional stiffness about the face which applies also to the picture of the goddess Gula, who is not infrequently represented by the image of herself on the boundary stone, accompanied by a dog (Plate LXXII, Fig. 2). The combination of these symbols, which are arranged in rows or in circles, gives a weird yet at the same time impressive appearance to the monument. The order in which the symbols are arranged varies somewhat. The moon, the eight- or sixteen-rayed star and the sun-disc are invariably found at the head of the monument, followed usually by the thrones representing

[45] King, Plate 91.
[46] See above, Plate XXIV, Fig. 2.

27

Anu, Enlil and Ea, though at times the latter god is replaced by his more specific symbol, a combination of goat and fish, holding on his back a throne with a ram's head. Among the animals, attention might also be directed to the dog of the goddess Gula which is generally exceedingly well drawn. Among smaller animals there is the falcon on a pole, the symbol of the goddess Bau, and another bird generally represented as marching, and which may be an eagle. The lamp (Plate LXXIII, Fig. 2) is the symbol of the fire-god Nusku.

XVI

We have still to consider a phase of the engraver's art represented by the thousands of so-called seal cylinders, ranging from the earliest to the latest period of Babylonian-Asyrian history. These seals, serving as seals still do in the modern Orient as a means of identifying property or as an attest to a legal document, vary in shape and size from that of a large, thick, and clumsy spool to a graceful and elongated cylinder, with the tendency to become smaller as we pass down the ages until in the Persian period they become cone shaped. The feature common to the Babylonian-Assyrian seals of all ages is the perforation through which a thread or wire was passed, so that the seal might be worn around the neck or carried on the wrist. Herodotus is our witness [46a] that in his days a seal and a walking stick still formed part of the outfit of a Babylonian man of affairs. The materials of which the seals were made cover likewise a large variety of materials, shell being the earliest known material, and hematite the most common, but chalcedony, obsidian, agate, jasper, lapis lazuli, marble, serpentine, quartz, carnelian, crystal and other mineral substances were also largely used. In the case of soft stones, the engraver's tool was probably made of flint, for the harder ones probably of corundum.

[46a] Book I, § 195.

PLATE LXXII

FIGS. I AND 2, SYMBOLS OF THE GODS ON BABYLONIAN BOUNDARY
STONES

PLATE LXXIII

FIGS. 1 AND 2, WINGED AND NON-WINGED HIPPOCENTAURS ON BABYLONIAN
BOUNDARY STONES

Dr. Ward [47] has shown that in the earlier periods the seals were entirely made by hand, and that drilling was not introduced till the later periods, though exactly when it is impossible to say.

In addition to mythological designs, the seal cylinders frequently contain the name of the owner or a dedicatory inscription to some deity. Through the character of the writing, and in the case of royal seals or those of high officials through the names a means can be found of dating some of the seals, while through the occurrence of certain designs impressed on clay tablets bearing a date, a further control is secured for the age of these designs. The art in the earliest seals is exceedingly crude, so crude as frequently to border on grotesqueness, but in the course of centuries the progress made was considerable until we reach a time when the delicacy of the execution reaches a truly remarkable degree of perfection. By way of illustration we may choose the representation of two deities facing one another, each reaching out a hand to grasp a tube through which to drink a liquid placed in a bowl standing on a high table. The scene is presumably a sacrificial one, though it may also represent an episode in some myth. The faces are indicated in bare outline. The drawing throughout is rough and irregular, and the artist found difficulty even in representing the two figures as actually seated on the stools beneath them. The crescent as a symbol of the moon suggests that the two deities are Sin and his consort Ningal. Contrast with this the design on a cylinder also belonging to an early period,[48] representing a mythical figure, Enkidu, fighting with a lion. The design is repeated,

---

[47] *Seal Cylinders of Western Asia*, p. 9. This is the most comprehensive investigation of the subject, and one that will for many years retain its place as the authoritative work.

[48] Ward, *Cylinders and Other Ancient Oriental Seals* in the library of J. Pierpont Morgan (N. Y., 1909), No. 60.

as is frequently the case on cylinders. While the attitude of both man and lion leaves much to be desired,
the drawing of both figures is remarkably good. Note
particularly the shaggy mane of the lion and the carefully drawn strands of Enkidu's beard. The roar of
the lion as Enkidu plunges the weapon into the lion's
breast is admirably suggested by the open mouth. In
the case of both man and animal the attempt at least
is made to indicate the muscles of the body. Even finer
in execution is the representation of the sun-god
Shamash with streams of water issuing from his
shoulders, into whose presence a two-headed figure is
introducing two others, the one carrying a bunch of
dates on a staff slung over his shoulder, the other carrying a bound man strung up by the heel on the club, likewise slung over his shoulder. The three figures move
towards the god in a most graceful fashion, the position
is easy, the garments fit admirably to the bodies, while
in the case of Shamash, there is, despite the conventionality in the drawing of the flounced skirt and upper
garment, a certain dignity about the figure as a whole
which suggests a superior being (Plate LXXV, Fig. 3).

The most striking feature of these seal cylinders
is the variety of the designs. Through them we obtain
an insight into the manner in which Babylonians and
Assyrians represented their gods and goddesses. The
rich symbolism of the cult also finds an illustration in
the various designs, and lastly the current myths and
popular tales are revealed to us in a most graphic manner through the engravings on the seal cylinders. Episodes in popular tales formed a favorite subject for the
artists who, while bound to certain conventionalism,
yet astonish us by the variations which they introduce
in the portrayal of one and the same subject. A large
number of seal cylinders of the earliest periods show a
contest among wild beasts—lions, ibexes, bulls, ante-
lopes. No two are exactly alike, and it is interesting to
note even in this early age the endeavor to reproduce

PLATE LXXIV

FIGS. 1, 2 AND 3, ENGRAVING ON BONE AND SHELL

a continuous story by a division into registers [49] as in the case of sculptured plaques, though at times the two divisions are not even separated by a dividing line. An example which illustrates the thoroughly archaic character of the art shows in the upper portion an eagle, the heraldic standard of the city of Lagash,[50] clutching with one of his claws a bull lying prostrate. The bull has evidently been killed and a vulture is seen feeding on his body. In the lower section a hunter appears in the midst of lions and ibexes fighting with one another. The star and the scorpion to one side are symbols of gods.

Closely allied with these episodes in some popular tale are the numerous variations on seal cylinders of the episode in the adventures of the great hero Gilgamesh who with his companion Enkidu engages in a contest with wild beasts.[51] In the earliest specimens both figures appear entirely nude. Gilgamesh is always distinguished by his abundant and usually carefully arranged hair and beard, while Enkidu has horns on his head as a symbol of his divine character. The variations of the scene are again numerous, though not to the same extent as in the case of the contests of wild beasts.

Another favorite scene was the representation of the semi-divine beings in front of the sacred tree,[52] appearing again in many variations.[53] In archaic examples the two figures are without wings, and it is a distinguishing mark of cylinders of Assyrian origin to attach the wings. As on the sculptured bas-reliefs we also find the king before the tree, accompanied by the eagle-headed winged creature with the standard of

---

[49] See the illustrations in Ward, *Seal Cylinders of Western Asia,* Chapter IV.

[50] Above p. 389 and Plate XLIX, Fig. 1.

[51] *Seal Cylinders of Western Asia,* Chapter X.

[52] Above Plate XXXIII.

[53] Ward, *Seal Cylinders of Western Asia,* Chapter XXXVIII.

Ashur over the tree. Among the variations two call
for special mention, the winged figures standing on
winged sphinxes and the priest of the water deity Ea
clad in fish scales in place of the winged being,[54] of
which we again have quite a number of variations according as a king is added to the scene or not. The
conventionalism of the art obtrudes itself in these scenes
in a more pronounced degree than usual so as to give
to the tree more particularly most fantastic forms. The
pose of the kings and of the winged or wingless beings
plucking the fruit of the tree of life is always the same,
and generally very stiff and void of all grace. On the
other hand the dress is commonly most carefully worked
out to smallest details, the execution being delicate as
well as accurate (see Plate LXXVI, Figs. 2 and 3).

Of the gods represented on the seal cylinders, the
moon-god Sin and the sun-god Shamash are the ones
most frequently selected. While it is certain that the
appearance of the moon's crescent on or near the figure
of a seated deity into whose presence a worshipper is
being led is not always intended as the moon-god, in
many instances Sin is certainly intended. A good specimen of an early period is the seal cylinder of Ur-Engur
of the Ur dynasty who is being led by a female—perhaps the consort of Sin—followed by another goddess
with uplifted hands, the gesture of intercession. The
human figure is no doubt intended for the king himself
who is represented, in accordance with early religious
usage in approaching a god, as shaven and beardless.
Despite its crudity, the figure of the seated god in an
easy posture conveys the impression of a certain dignity. The throne on which the god sits is a graceful
piece of work, and the artist has not stopped short of
such a detail as the carving of one of the legs of the
throne in imitation of an ox's leg. In a most skilful
manner he has also succeeded in conveying the femi-

---

[54] Ward, *l.c.*, No. 679 and 687.

PLATE LXXV. SEAL CYLINDERS

FIG. I, MAN AND WOMAN, DRINKING THROUGH TUBES

FIG. 2, MONSTROUS BEING, FIGHTING LION—SYMMETRICALLY REPEATED

FIG. 3, THE SUN-GOD SHAMASH, WITH DIVINE ATTENDANTS

FIG. 4, GILGAMESH, FIGHTING LION—SYMMETRICALLY REPEATED

ninity in the expression of the two goddesses—especially of the first one—in contrast to the greater strength of the face of the god and of the worshipper (see Plate LXXVII, Fig. 2).

A favorite manner of representing the sun-god was in the act of rising over the mountains. The god is naïvely portrayed as stepping on a mountain peak and about to pass through a gate symbolizing sunrise, while the other gate is the one through which, after having run his course, he enters the heavens at evening. In this case again we find the design with many variations [55] used from the oldest to the latest period—an interesting proof of the continuity of artistic tradition in the Euphrates Valley. The art, to be sure, does not rise beyond a very primitive level in the specimens preserved, though in some instances the influence of conventionalism is not so marked as, for example, in those where the mountain has been reduced to a mere footstool on which the one foot of the god rests, while instead of the gate we find a worshipper led into the presence of Shamash by the god's consort, Â, whose uplifted hands portray her in the usual rôle of interceding on behalf of the worshipper who approaches his god with a sacrificial offering.

Superior from an artistic standpoint are some of the representations of the seated sun-god with a worshipper before him. The distinguishing marks of Shamash in these designs are the rays issuing from his shoulders or streams flowing from his shoulders. This combination of rays and streams is also found attached to the solar disc which is the common symbol of the god Ashur, the rays symbolizing the beneficent warmth of the sun, and the water the fertility which is within the province of the great orb, whose favor is so essential to the well-being of the agriculturist.

Another interesting group of seal cylinders—chiefly Babylonian—is formed by those showing a deity in

---

[55] Ward, l.c., Chapter XIII.

a conflict with a dragon. The underlying tale appears to be the myth of the sun-god driving away the storms and rains of the winter season. This season was depicted as a time of lawlessness and utter confusion for which a monstrous being in control of the wild elements of nature seemed to be the appropriate symbol. This myth became the basis of the scheme of world creation in Babylonia, the rôle of creator being assigned in each of the large centres to the chief deity—Ea in Eridu, Enlil in Nippur, and Marduk in Babylon. When through the political supremacy of Babylon, the god Marduk became the head of the pantheon, the functions of other gods were assigned to him. He thus becomes in the later forms of the myth the vanquisher of primitive chaos, known as Tiamat.[56] The springtime when nature celebrates a revival was appropriately regarded as the time of the creation of the world. Crude as most of the representations of this conflict are,[57] there is nevertheless in some of them much force and vigor in the attitude of the god pursuing the monster with bow and arrow or despatching him with a powerful weapon. It is particularly interesting to see how in the course of the endeavor to vary the scene, elements of other myths are introduced—particularly of the one illustrating the contest with wild beasts,[58] which may at bottom indeed represent the same idea—the portrayal of a time of chaos and confusion, preceding the reign of law and order in the world (see Plate LXXVI, Figs. 1 and 4).

Of special interest is a physician's seal, containing the name of the owner Ur-Lugal-Edina (*i.e.*, the man of the god Lugal-Edina), with a dedicatory inscription

[56] See the translation of the tale of Marduk's conquest of Tiamat pp. 428–443. See also Plate XXVIII, Fig. 1.

[57] Ward, *l.c.*, Chapter VIII.

[58] Ward, *l.c.*, Chapter VII.

PLATE LXXVI. SEAL CYLINDERS

FIG. 1, CONTESTS WITH WILD BEASTS

FIG. 2, WINGED BEING BEFORE THE TREE OF LIFE—SYMMETRICALLY REPEATED

FIG. 3, WINGED BEING, PLUCKING THE FRUIT OF THE TREE OF LIFE

FIG. 4, CONFLICT WITH THE DRAGON TIAMAT

to a deity, Edina-mugi,[59] and shows, as the symbols of
his profession, a physician's scalpel and lancets (or
knives) and cups. These instruments are exceedingly
well drawn, while the picture of the deity—no doubt
the one mentioned in the inscription—despite the
archaic delineation of the feet, is a good specimen of the
delicacy of the engravers' art at the early period to
which the seal reverts (see Plate LXXVII, Fig. 3).

As the last specimen, a curious design may be given
representing a male and female figure sitting opposite
one another with a tree between them, while behind
the female figure is an upright serpent. The resemblance of the scene to the famous story in the third
chapter of Genesis has aroused considerable discussion.
We have the same elements in both cases, the man, the
woman, the serpent and the tree. The horns, however,
with which both figures on the seal cylinder are provided show that they are intended to represent deities.
The tree is no doubt the tree of life as in the case of
the designs above discussed.   According to Babylonian beliefs, the gods alone can pluck the fruit of the
tree of life. The serpent is a very common symbol,[60]
constantly appearing on the so-called boundary stones.
Its particular significance on the seal cylinder in question escapes us, but it may well be that the myth of
which the entire scene is an illustration is the prototype
of the story in Genesis. It would be quite natural in
the course of the adaptation of old folk-tales to later
aspects of religious beliefs, for the deities to become

---

[59] The deity is designated as the messenger of Gir, one of the
designations of the god of pestilence—Nergal—which suggests a
grim sense of humor on the part of the physician who thus chooses
as his protecting deity the "messenger of death," against whom the
healer of disease is supposed to direct his efforts.

[60] See an elaborate monograph on the serpent as a symbol by
Paul Toscanne, "Etudes sur le Serpent, figure et symbole dans
l'Antiquitè Élamite" in Délégation en Perse, Mémoires, Vol. xiii,
pp. 153–226.

human figures, and the primitive myth, whatever its original significance may have been, to become a tale intended to illustrate that man forfeited immortality —the prerogative of the gods—by an act of disobedience.[61] Man, according to the earlier form of the story, would thus be regarded as a god fallen from his high estate. From this as a starting point, the step would be a natural one to make the real fall of man consist in his having disobeyed a divine command.

---

[61] See Frazer, *Belief in Immortality* i, p. 73, *seq.*, for many other illustrations among primitive peoples of stories intended to explain the presence of death in the world, due either to eating of a forbidden fruit, or to the failure to eat it. Both *motifs* are found in these primitive tales.

PLATE LXXVII. SEAL CYLINDERS

FIG. I, SHAMASH, THE RISING SUN-GOD, STEPPING OVER THE MOUNTAIN

FIG. 2, SIN, THE MOON-GOD, RECEIVING A WORSHIPPER

FIG. 3, SEAL OF A BABYLONIAN PHYSICIAN

FIG. 4, DIVINE BEINGS, SEATED BEFORE THE TREE OF LIFE

CHAPTER VIII

SPECIMENS OF BABYLONIAN-ASSYRIAN LITERATURE.

I

The Later Babylonian Poem of Creation

THE story of Creation among Babylonians assumed the form of a nature myth, based upon the transition of winter and the rainy season to the spring and dry season. The stormy and rainy winter was pictured as a time of chaos and was symbolized by a monster Tiamat, who with a large body of attendants, likewise monstrous in form, is represented as in control of things. The spring sun driving away the winter becomes the vanquisher of Tiamat; and after chaos has been overcome, law and order prevail.

Various versions of this nature myth were produced in ancient Babylonia, both in Sumerian and in Akkadian. The one here given celebrating the triumph of Marduk over Tiamat is the form assumed by the story after Marduk as the patron deity of the city of Babylon [1] had become the head of the pantheon. To Marduk, therefore, as a solar deity the distinction is assigned of being the one strong enough among the gods to dispatch Tiamat and her followers. The poem is a composite production, and gives evidence of containing elements of a number of independent tales that have been combined to add to the glory of Marduk.[2]

---

[1] See above, p. 211 seq.

[2] See an article by the writer on "The Composite Character of the Babylonian Creation Story" in the Nöldeke Festschrift II, pp. 969–982. For a complete edition of the text together with an English translation and commentary, see L. W. King, *The Seven Tablets of Creation* (2 vols. London, 1902); also *Cuneiform Texts*, Part XIII, Plates 1–41. For the relationship of the Babylonian versions of Creation to the Biblical tale, see Jastrow, "*Hebrew and Babylonian Views of Creation*," being chapter II of the author's *Hebrew and Babylonian Traditions* (New York, 1914).

The text in its complete form covered seven tablets. Of these only the fourth has been preserved in full, while of the remaining tablets we have merely larger or smaller fragments.

TABLET I

The poem begins as follows:

"When on high, heaven was not named,
Below, dry land was not named.[3]
Apsu, their first begetter,
Mummu (and) Tiamat, the mother of all of them,[4]
Their waters combined together.
Field was not marked off, sprout had not come forth.
When none of the gods had yet come forth,
Had not borne a name,
No destinies had been fixed[5];
Then gods were created in the midst of heaven.[6]
Lakhmu and Lakhamu came forth
Ages increased[7] . . .
Anshar and Kishar were created.[8]

[3] "To have a name," according to ideas widely prevalent in antiquity, was to exist. Hence, to express the idea of non-existence of heaven and earth it was said that they were not named.

[4] These three terms, Apsu (deep), Mummu (water), and Tiamat (sea), are synonymous, each one representing the name of the Being symbolizing primeval chaos in some version. The combination of the three names and the endeavor to establish a relationship between them are indications of the composite character of the poem.

[5] One of the functions of the gods is to determine the fate of individuals, as well as the future in general. See p. 217 and p. 278.

[6] The late origin of this form of the poem is shown by the transfer of all the gods to the heavens—a reflection of astrological views. See above, p. 209.

[7] Defective lines are indicated by leaders, (. . .).

[8] An-Shar (the totality of what is above) and Ki-Shar (the totality of what is below) are " theological " abstractions, rather than popular figures of deities in the system of the pantheon as perfected by the priests of Babylonia. Anshar and Kishar are, according to this system, the ancestors of all the gods.

After many days had passed by there came forth . . .
Anu, their son . . .
Anshar and Anu . . .
Anu . . .
Nudimmud [9] whom his father, his mother, . . .
Of large intelligence, knowing (wise),
Exceeding strong . . .
Without a rival . . .
Then were established.''

The following seven lines are too fragmentarily preserved to permit of translation, but it would appear that at this point a description is given of the confusion and disturbance aroused among the monsters of the deep through the creation of the gods, who saw in this rise of the gods a foreshadowing of the end of their own rule. Apsu and Mummu together go to Tiamat in order to consult with her regarding the plan to keep the gods in restraint.

''Then Apsu, the begetter of the great gods,
Cried out, to Mummu, to his messenger, he spoke:
'Oh Mummu, joy of my liver,
Come, unto Tiamat let us go.'
They went, and before Tiamat they crouched,
Hatching a plan with regard to the gods . . .
Apsu opened his mouth and spoke,
Unto Tiamat, the splendid one addressed a word:
'. . . their course against me
By day I have no rest, at night I cannot lie down, I wish to destroy
    their course,
So that clamor cease and we may again lie down to sleep.'
When Tiamat (heard) this,
She raged and shrieked for (revenge?),
She herself became furiously enraged.
Evil she conceived in her heart.
'All that we have made let us destroy,
That their course may be full of misery so that we may have
    release.'

---

[9] A designation of Ea, the god of the deep.

Mummu answered and counselled Apsu,
Hostile was the counsel of Mummu.
'Come, their course is strong, destroy it!
Then by day thou wilt have rest,
At night thou wilt lie down.'
Apsu(hearkened), and his face shone;
Evil he planned against the gods, his sons.''

The following fifty lines tell of the conflict of
Mummu and Apsu against the gods which ends in the
capture of the two; it appears that they are overcome
through the agency of Ea, the god of the deep and who,
it will be recalled,[10] is pictured as the god of humanity,
teaching mankind knowledge and saving them in
distress. It is natural, therefore, to find Ea also in the
rôle of the saviour of the gods, and we may conjecture
that we have in this part of the story the old version of
the overcoming of chaos through Ea, the patron god of
Eridu—a version, therefore, which had its rise in the old
city that lay at or close to the Persian Gulf. But Tiamat
still remains at large. Realizing that she, too, will
have to face the conflict with the gods, Tiamat gathers
a new army of followers, described as monstrous serpents of various kinds, fierce and merciless. With
these she associates other monsters, and places the entire army under the generalship of Kingu. The gaps
in the first tablet at this point can be supplied from
Tablets II and III in which the description of Tiamat's
army is repeated.

''They uttered curses and at the side of Tiamat advanced.
In fury and rage they devised plans ceaselessly night and day.
They rushed to the conflict, raging and furious.
They grouped themselves and ranged the battle array.
Ummu-Khubur,[11] creator of all things,
Gathering invincible weapons, she brought forth huge monsters,

---

[10] Above, p. 210.

[11] A title of Tiamat, signifying probably ' mother of totality.'
The name points to another version, combined with our tale.

FIG. 1, THIRD TABLET OF THE BABYLONIAN STORY
OF CREATION

FIG. 2, PORTION OF THE BABYLONIAN STORY OF THE DELUGE

PLATE LXXVIII

Sharp of tooth and merciless of fang.
With poison instead of blood she filled their bodies.
She clothed with terror the terrible dragons,
Decking them with brilliancy, giving them a lofty stature,
So that whoever beheld them would be overcome with terror.
With their bodies reared up, none could withstand their attack.
She brought forth great serpents, dragons and the Lakhami,[12]
Hurricanes, raging dogs and scorpion men,
Mighty tempests, fish men, and rams,
Bearing cruel weapons, fearless in combat,
Mighty in command, irresistible.
In all eleven monsters of this kind she made.
Among the gods, the first born who formed the assembly,
She exalted Kingu, giving him high rank in their midst;
To march in advance and to direct the host;
To be foremost in arming for the attack,
To direct the fight in supreme control,
To his [13] hand she confided. She decked him out in costly gar-
     ments:
'I have uttered thy magic formula, in the assembly of the gods I
     have exalted thee '
The dominion over all the gods was entrusted unto his hands:
'Be thou exalted, my one and only husband;
May the Anunnaki exalt thy name above all the gods!'
She gave him the tablets of fate, to his breast she attached them.
'Oh, thou, thy command will be irresistible!
Firmly established be the utterance of thy mouth!
Now Kingu is exalted, endowed with the power of Anu;
Among the gods, his children, he fixes destinies.
By the word of thy mouth fire will be quenched;
The strong in battle will be increased in strength.' "

TABLET II

In the second tablet the gods learn of the plans of
Tiamat and hear the description of the mighty army
which she has gathered.

---

[12] Here a collective name for a group of monsters.
[13] That is, unto Kingu she entrusted the destinies of the army,
forming in part, at least, descriptions of constellations in the heavens.

"Tiamat finished her work.
(The evil that) she contrived against the gods her offspring,
To avenge Apsu, Tiamat planned evil.
When she had equipped her army, it was revealed to Ea;
Ea heard the words,
And was grievously afflicted, and overwhelmed with grief.
Days passed by and his anger was appeased.
To Anshar, his father, he took the way.
To Father Anshar who begot him he went.
All that Tiamat had planned he repeated to him.
'Tiamat our mother has taken a dislike for us,
She has assembled a host, she rages furiously.
All the gods are gathered to her,
Aye, even those whom thou hast created, march at her side.' "

It would appear from these words that Tiamat had stirred up a rebellion also among the gods descended from Anshar and Kishar, and succeeded in gathering many of them to her side to proceed with the host of monsters against the gods represented as her own offspring, though this is in contradiction to the other point of view brought forward in the poem according to which Anshar and Kishar are the ancestors of all the gods.

Anshar, upon hearing the description of the terror-inspiring army, is dismayed. He calls upon Ea, who has smitten Mummu and captured Apsu to proceed against Tiamat. Unfortunately the text at this point is again defective, but it is evident that Ea declines the task. Anshar then calls upon another son, Anu, to fight the cause of the gods which is the cause of law and order against choas and lawlessness, represented by Tiamat and her followers. But this son declines or is unable to carry out the task, and accordingly we find Anshar addressing a third, this time Marduk, who will succeed where others fail.

" 'Thou art my son of strong courage,
    . . . draw nigh to the battle!
    . . . at sight of thee there shall be peace.'
The Lord rejoiced at the word of his father.

He drew nigh and stood in front of Anshar;
Anshar saw him and his heart was full of joy.
He kissed him on the mouth, and fear departed from him.
'(Oh my father), may the words of thy lips not be taken back,
May I go and accomplish the desire of thy heart!'

Marduk repeats these two lines, after which begins another address of Anshar to his son [14] in which he calls upon Marduk to 'trample swiftly on the neck of Tiamat.' The text then continues.

'Oh my son, full of all knowledge,
Quiet Tiamat with thy supreme incantation;
Quickly proceed (on thy way)!
Thy blood will not be poured out, thou shalt surely return.'
The lord rejoiced at the word of his father,
His heart exulted and he spoke to his father.
'Oh Lord of the gods, (who fixes) the fate of the great gods,
If I become thy avenger,
Conquering Tiamat, and giving life to thee,
Call an assembly and proclaim the preëminence of my lot!
That when in Upshukkinaku [15] thou joyfully seatest thyself,
My command in place of thine should fix fates.
What I do should be unaltered,
The word of my lips be never changed or annulled.' "

TABLET III

The third tablet opens with an address of Anshar unto Gaga his messenger, asking the latter to go to the gods that they gather together for a banquet and listen to the message which Anshar sends them. The message itself recounts the rebellious purpose of Tiamat and her brood of monsters, repeats the detailed description of the vipers, dragons, hurricanes, raging hounds, fish-men and the strange host with Kingu at the head which we have already encountered in the epic.

[14] Indication of another version.
[15] The "Walhalla" of the gods where they assemble to determine destinies.

28

"Then they gathered and went,
The great gods, all of them, who fix fates,
Came into the presence of Anshar, they filled (the assembly hall),
Embracing one another in the assembly (hall),
They prepared themselves to feast at the banquet.
They ate bread, they mixed the wine,
The sweet mead confused (their senses).
Drunk, their bodies filled with drink,
They shouted aloud, with their spirits [16] exalted,
For Marduk, their avenger, they fixed the destiny."

TABLET IV

"They prepared for him a royal chamber,
In the presence of his fathers as ruler he stood.
'Thou art the weightiest among the great gods.
Thy (power of decreeing) fate is unrivalled, thy command is
    (like that of) Anu.
Oh Marduk, thou art mightiest among the great gods!
Thy power of decreeing fate unrivalled, thy word is like that of
    Anu! [17]
From now on thy decree will not be altered,
Thine it shall be to raise up and to bring low,
Thy utterance be established, against thy command no rebellion!
None among the gods will transgress the limit (set by thee).
Abundance is pleasing to the shrines of the gods,
The place of their worship will be established as thy place.
Oh Marduk, thou art our avenger!
We give thee kingship over the entire universe,
Take thy seat in the assembly, thy word be exalted;
Thy weapon be not overcome, may it crush thy enemies.
Oh lord, the life of him who trusts in thee will be spared,
But pour out the life of the god who has planned evil.' [18]
Then they placed in their midst a garment.
To Marduk, their first born, they spoke:
'Thy fate, O lord, be supreme among the gods!

[16] Literally, "liver."

[17] This trait of repeating certain particularly emphatic lines is, as we have seen above, p. 433, characteristic of this composition.

[18] I.e., Tiamat, who organized the rebellion against the highest gods.

For destruction and creation speak, and it shall be done;
Declare that the garment vanish,
And speak the word again that the garment be intact.'
Then he gave the command, and the garment vanished;
He commanded again, and the garment appeared.
When the gods, his fathers, thus beheld (the power of) his utter-
    ance [19]
They rejoiced and paid homage to Marduk, King;
They bestowed on him scepter, throne and *palu* [20];
They gave him an invincible weapon ' overcoming the enemy.' [21]
'Go and cut off the life of Tiamat,
That the wind may carry her blood to hidden spots.'
When the gods, his fathers, had decreed the fate of the lord,
They brought him on the road leading to peace and success.
He made a bow and took it as his weapon,
He took a spear and fastened it with a cord (?),
He raised the club (?), taking hold of it with his right hand,
The bow and quiver he hung at his side,
Placed the lightning on his face,
With a burning flame he filled his body,
He made a net to enclose Tiamat therein.
The four winds he took hold of, that nothing whatsoever should
    escape.
The South Wind, North Wind, East Wind, West Wind,
He brought to the side of the net, the gift of his father Anu.
He created the hostile wind, the tempest and the hurricane,
The fourfold wind and the sevenfold wind, [22] the whirlwind, and
    the wind without rival.
He sent forth the winds which he had created, the seven of them;
To trouble the spirit of Tiamat, they followed behind him.
Then the lord raised on high the Deluge, [23] his mighty weapon.
He mounted the storm chariot, unequalled in power,

---

[19] Meaning, of course, the result of his utterance.

[20] Some symbol of royal power, perhaps a crown.

[21] We know from other sources that the weapons of the gods bore symbolical names, just as did the blades among the Arabs of the Middle Ages.

[22] *I.e.*, the wind blowing four and seven days, respectively.

[23] One of the terms for an inundating rain-storm, and used in the description of the deluge. See below, p. 446, *seq.*

He harnessed and attached to it four horses,
Merciless, overwhelming, swiftly flying.
 (Sharp of) teeth, bearing poison.

.   .   .   .

Then the lord drew nigh, piercing Tiamat with his glance;
He saw the purpose of Kingu, her spouse,
As he (*i.e.*, Marduk) gazed, he (*i.e.*, Kingu) tottered in his gait.[24]
His mind was destroyed, his action upset,
And the gods, his helpers, marching at his side,[25]
Saw (the terror of) the hero and leader.
But Tiamat (uttered a cry) and did not turn her back,
From her lips there gushed forth rebellious words [26]
 . . . ' coming to thee as lord of the gods,
As in their own sanctuaries they are gathered in thy sanctuary.'[27]
Then the lord raised on high the Deluge, the great weapon,
And against Tiamat, who was foaming with wrath, thus sent forth
    (his answer).
'Great art thou! Thou hast exalted thyself greatly.
Thy heart hath prompted thee to arrange for battle

.   .   .   .

Thou hast (exalted) Kingu to be thy husband,
(Thou hast given him power to issue) the decrees of Anu.[28]
(Against the gods, my fathers), thou hast planned evil,
 Against the gods, my fathers, thou hast planned evil.
Let thy army be equipped, thy weapons be girded on;
Stand; I and thou, let us join in battle.'
When Tiamat heard this,
She was beside herself, she lost her reason.
Tiamat shouted in a paroxysm of fury,
Trembling to the root, shaking in her foundations.

---

[24] The mere sight of Marduk terrifies Kingu and bewilders Tiamat.

[25] *I.e.*, the whole army of Tiamat and Kingu.

[26] No doubt curses hurled against Marduk.

[27] These two lines, obscure because of the break in the first part of line 73, evidently represent the curse intended to annihilate Marduk. The god, however, is undismayed.

[28] *I.e.*, To Kingu had been assigned by Tiamat the right belonging to Anu as supreme arbiter.

She uttered an incantation, she pronounced a magic formula.[29]
The gods of battle, appeal [30] to their weapons.
Then stepped forth Tiamat and the leader of the gods, Marduk.
To the fight they advanced, to the battle they drew nigh.
The lord spread his net and encompassed her,
The evil wind stationed behind him he drove into her face.
Tiamat opened her mouth to its full extent.
He drove in the evil wind before she could close her lips.
The terrible winds filled her belly,
Her heart was seized, and she held her mouth wide open.
He drove in the spear and burst open her belly,
Cutting into her entrails, he slit her heart.
He overcame her and destroyed her life;
He cast down her carcass and stood upon it.
When he had thus subjected Tiamat, the leader,
Her host was scattered, her assembly was dissolved;
And the gods, her helpers, who marched beside her,
In fear and trembling turned about,
Taking to flight to save their lives.
But they were surrounded and could not escape.
He captured them and smashed their weapons,
They were cast into the net, and brought into the snare;

.   .   .   .

After he (*i.e.,* Marduk) had bound and cast down his enemies,
Had battered down the arrogant foe,
Had completely gained the victory of Anshar over the enemy,
The hero Marduk had attained the aim of Nudimmud,[31]
He strengthened his hold over the captive gods.[32]
To Tiamat, whom he had bound, he came back,
And the lord trampled under foot the foundation of Tiamat.
With his merciless weapon he smashed her skull,
He cut the channels of her blood,

---

[29] As a last resort to overwhelm Marduk, to bring him within her power through the force of her magic formula. See above, p. 244, *seq.*

[30] Literally, *ask,* which suggests that possibly some oracles were sought through their weapons.

[31] Which Nudimmud (or Ea) was unable to carry out.

[32] *I.e.,* he made sure of their being unable to get away.

And made the north wind carry them to secret places.[33]
His fathers beheld and rejoiced exceeding glad,
Presents and gifts they brought to him.
Then the lord rested and looked at the carcass.
He divided the flesh of the monster, and created marvellous things.
He split her like a fish flattened into two halves;
One half he took and made it a covering for heaven.
He drew a bolt, he stationed a watchman,
Enjoining that the waters be not permitted to flow out.
He passed over the heavens, inspecting the regions (thereof),
And over against the Apsu,[34] he set the dwelling of Nudimmud.[35]
The lord measured the structure of the Deep.
He established E-sharra as a palace corresponding to it.
The palace E-sharra which he created as heaven,
He caused Anu, Enlil and Ea to inhabit their districts."

The creation of the Universe, which thus begins after the overthrow of Tiamat by the formation of the heavens, is continued in the fifth tablet which describes the constellations and the fixing of seasons, the division of the year into months, and of days into night and day. All this is done at the instance of Marduk whose work is essentially that of one who establishes order in place of chaos, rather than that of a creator.

TABLET V

"He made stations for the great gods,
The stars, their counterparts, the twin stars he fixed.
He fixed the year and divided it into divisions.
For the twelve months he fixed three stars.[36]
Also for the days of the year (he had fashioned) pictures[37]

---

[33] Apparently we have in these lines a second description of the way in which Marduk overcame Tiamat. They may be taken, therefore, as another proof of the dovetailing of several originally distinct versions into our story.

[34] I.e., personification of the deep.

[35] I.e., Ea, the god of waters.

[36] Each star presiding over four months.

[37] I.e., the constellations.

He founded the station of Nibir [38] to regulate their limits,
That none might err or go astray.
He placed the station of Enlil and Ea [39] with him.[40]
He opened great gates to both sides,
He supplied a strong bolt to the left and the right.
In the midst (of the heavens) he fixed the zenith,
He caused Sin [41] to shine forth, entrusting to him the night;
He assigned to him the control of the night for counting the days;
Each month without interruption he covered him with a crown.[42]"

Marduk thereupon addresses the moon-god, though
it is evident that the original address was made by Anu,
god of the heavens and as such the one in supreme
control of everything above.

" 'At the beginning of the month in rising over the land
Thou wilt show a horn for a period of six days.
On the seventh day the crown will be divided (?).
On the fourteenth day thou shalt stand opposite, it being the
half (of the month).
When the sun-god in the foundation of heaven (is opposite)
thee.' "

At this point unfortunately the tablet again becomes
defective, and there is little of it remaining until we
reach the end. We can only conjecture that the chief
constellations were included in the description of the
heavens, and all the courses fixed for the planets, as
well as the positions for the stars. At the close of the
tablet the gods gather around Marduk and formulate
the complaint that, while order has been established and
the position of the gods represented by the stars fixed
in the heavens, the universe was empty. There was no
one to do homage to the gods. Curiously enough this
complaint of the gods is assigned in the sixth tablet as

[38] *I.e.*, Jupiter, who as the brightest planet is the leader.
[39] Variant, Anu.
[40] Anu, Enlil and Ea represent three divisions of the ecliptic.
[41] The moon-god.
[42] The crescent of the new moon.

the reason for the creation of man, which Marduk undertakes in order to satisfy the craving of the gods for worship. It is most unfortunate that this tablet also is badly mutilated, so that only the first ten lines and a few of the closing lines furnish an intelligible sequence. It begins as follows:

TABLET VI

"Upon (Marduk's) hearing the word of the gods,
His heart led him to create (marvellous things) [43]
He opened his mouth and (spoke) to Ea [44]
(What) he had conceived in his heart he imparted to him;
'My blood I will take and bone I will (form).
I will set up man that man . . .
I will create man to inhabit (the earth),
That the worship of the gods be fixed, that they may have shrines.
But I will alter the ways of the gods, I will change . . .
They shall be joined in concert, unto evil shall they' . . .
Ea answered him and spoke.''

The answer of Ea is too imperfectly preserved to warrant even a conjecture. If the last two lines of Marduk's address to Ea indicate his intention to punish the gods because of their complaint, while granting what they desire, it may be, as has been suggested, that Ea dissuaded Marduk from this purpose; but until some fortunate chance may enable us to fill the gap in this important tablet it is idle to indulge in conjectures. Nor is it certain that this Babylonian version of creation contained any account of the actual formation of the

---

[43] Conjectural restoration *niklâti*, proposed by King on the basis of Tablet IV, 136.

[44] Ea is always introduced as the god of humanity who loves and protects mankind; and in the version of creation which arose in Eridu, the seat of which Ea was the patron, it is Ea who is also the creator of man. All other gods, however, must yield to Marduk, though there is a trace of the older version where Marduk is introduced as telling Ea of his purpose.

earth, of verdure, trees and mountains and of animals. The main purpose of the poem was to celebrate the triumph of Marduk over Tiamat; everything else is incidental, and even in describing the establishment of order in the heavens the chief thought was to emphasize the control of Marduk over the gods. At the same time, from other fragments of creation tales, we know that to Marduk (and in other versions to other gods) the detailed creation of everything on earth, including verdure and animals, was ascribed.[45]

At the close of the sixth tablet there is a description of the return of Marduk after his labors to the assembly hall of the gods in Upshukkinnaku. They rejoice at his return and gather to do him honor.

TABLET VII

The seventh tablet is entirely taken up with the names bestowed upon Marduk by the gods. The names themselves constitute attributes of Marduk, though no doubt designating originally local gods whose cult was absorbed by that of Marduk. In this way by assigning to Marduk the power of all the other gods he becomes supreme; and as we have seen, views about Marduk in Babylonia and about Ashur in Assyria form the closest approach to be found in Babylonian-Assyrian religion to a monotheistic conception of divine government.[46]

"Asari, the source of planting (the founder of sowing),
Creator of grain and flour, (causing the verdure to spring forth).
Asaru-alim, honored in the house of counsel (abounding in counsel).
To him the gods pay homage, (and of him they stand in dread).
Asaru-alim-nunna, the mighty, the light (of his father who begat him),
Who prescribes the laws for Anu, Enlil (and Ea),

---

[45] See Jastrow, *Hebrew and Babylonian Traditions*, p. 92.
[46] See above, p. 217 and 229, *seq.*

Who provides for them, who fixes (their bounds),
Who provides abundance, brings out . . .
Tutu, 'the creator who renews them,'
May their sanctuaries be purified, may (they be pacified).
May he bring about an incantation, that the gods (may be
    calmed).
When they attack in fury may he repulse (their advance)!
Be he exalted even in the assembly of the gods.
None among the gods is like to him.''

In this way the text proceeds somewhat monoto-
nously, describing the manifold attributes and powers
of Marduk. Towards the close of the tablet an interesting reference is made to the manner in which, after all
the other gods had paid homage, Enlil and Ea stepped
forward and bestowed their names, and with their
names their power, upon the favorite Marduk.

''Nibiru [47] be his name, the one who seized the inside; [48]
May he maintain the stars of heaven in their path,
Shepherding all the gods like sheep!
May he keep Tiamat enchained,
Crushing and putting an end to her life.
In the future of mankind, when the days grow old,
May one hear this without ceasing, may it survive forever! [49]
Since he created the region (of heaven), and formed the earth,
Lord of the worlds, father Enlil [50] called him,
The name which all the Igigi proclaimed.
Ea heard and his liver rejoiced,
'He whose name his fathers have made glorious,
Be he like I am, Ea be his name!
All my commands be in his control,
All my decrees let him pronounce!'

---

[47] *I.e.*, Jupiter.
[48] *Sc* of Tiamat.
[49] *I.e.*, the story of Marduk's conquest of Tiamat.
[50] Enlil, the old god of Nippur, confers his own name upon
Marduk.

By the name 'fifty' [51] did the great gods
Confer upon him fifty names to make his path supreme.''

The poem closes with an epilogue, calling upon all
mankind ever to bear in mind the great deeds of Marduk, and to hand down the memory thereof from father
to son to the end of days.

"Let them be remembered, let the older (man) speak of them! [52]
  Let the wise and the intelligent reflect on them together,
  Let father repeat and teach them to his son!
  Let pastor and shepherd open their ears,
  To rejoice in Marduk, the lord of the gods,
  That his land may be fertile and prosper.
  His word (*i.e.*, Marduk's) is firm, his command unchangeable.
  What he utters no god annuls,
  He casts a glance and turns not his neck.
  In his wrath no god can withstand him,
  But wide is his heart, broad is his mind;
  The sinner and evil-doer before him . . . ''

The remaining six lines are again too fragmentary
for translation, but it is evident that the epilogue closed
with the glorification of Marduk's justice tempered with
mercy.

II

The Babylonian Story of the Deluge

As of the Creation story, so of an account of a great
flood that destroyed the world and mankind we have a
number of versions in Babylonian literature. The
oldest of these versions is in Sumerian and is told as
part of a story of the beginnings of things leading from

[51] As the last of fifty names, they called Marduk "fifty" which
was transferred presumably from the god Ninib or Ningorsin, who
was symbolized as "fifty," and whose temple at Lagash was known
as E-ninnu, *i.e.*, "house of fifty." See above, p. 200.

[52] *I.e.*, hand the memory of Marduk's deeds down to the younger
generation.

creation to flood myths and thence to the oldest traditions of the earliest dynasties of the states of the Euphrates Valley,[53] while the latest version is embodied
in the great Babylonian epic, recounting the adventures
of a semi-mythical hero Gilgamesh.[54] This epic, known
to us from numerous fragments in the library of Ashurbanapal, is a composite production containing a number
of independent tales, loosely strung together, and all
brought into connection with the favorite hero Gilgamesh. Some of the tales embody dimmed historical
traditions centring around the ancient centre Uruk,
while others are nature myths, associated with occurrences in nature and in which the gods appear as the
actors. The epic in its final form comprised twelve
tablets, corresponding to the months of the year, with at
least some of the episodes told on tablets the number of
which in the series is correlated to the season of the year
to which the myth belongs. Thus on the sixth tablet
marking the end of the summer season,[55] there is told the
story of Gilgamesh's rejection of the marriage offer
of the goddess Ishtar—symbolizing the loss of nature's
charms. In the same way, the Deluge story is recounted
in the eleventh tablet, corresponding to the month when
the rainy season is at its height and the winter storms
reach their climax. Gilgamesh himself, however, has
nothing to do with the Deluge. He is somewhat artificially introduced into it by the accident of his encounter-
ing the hero who has escaped the general destruction of
mankind. Gilgamesh, smitten with painful disease as

---

[53] See Poebel, *Historical and Grammatical Texts* (University of
Pennsylvania Museum Publications, Philadelphia, 1914), Plate I
and pp. 9–24). On this and other versions, see Jastrow, *Hebrew and
Babylonian Traditions* (Philadelphia, 1914), pp. 335–348.

[54] See for a summary of the epic, with copious extracts, Jastrow,
Religion of Babylonia and Assyria (Boston 1898), Chapter XXIII;
and for a complete translation of all the fragments, Ungnad-Gress-
mann, *Das Gilgamesch-Epos* (Goettingen, 1911).

[55] The Babylonian year began in the spring.

a punishment for the insult offered to the goddess Ishtar,
and fearing death, wanders about in search of healing
and to secure immortality. He learns of a remote ancestor Ut-napishtim, who has been granted the boon of
immortal life. After long and weary wanderings with
many adventures he at last finds himself face to face
with Utnapishtim, whose name signifies "He who has
experienced life." Amazed to find Utnapishtim looking like an ordinary mortal, Gilgamesh asks Utnapishtim how he came to secure immortality. In reply, Utnapishtim tells him the story of a great deluge which
destroyed mankind, and from which he and his family
were rescued through the contrivance of Ea, the god of
humanity. The Deluge was suggested, as was the picture of primeval chaos,[56] by the climatic conditions prevailing in the Euphrates Valley, which before the perfection of an elaborate canal system experienced a destructive overflow at each recurring rainy and stormy
season. The tradition of a particularly destructive
flood entailing much loss of life may have been an additional factor in giving to the deluge myth its definite
form. The eleventh tablet of the Gilgamesh epic [57] begins as follows:

"Gilgamesh speaks to him, to Utnapishtim, the far-removed:
'I gaze at thee, Utnapshtim!
Thy appearance is not different. As I am, so art thou.
And thou are not different. As I am, so art thou.
Thou art completely ready for the fray.
. . . thou hast placed upon thee.
(Tell me) how thou didst enter into the assembly of the gods and
secure life."

---

[56] See above, p. 427.

[57] The text of this tablet will be found in Rawlinson IV. (2d,
ed.), Pl. 43–44; the full text of the Gilgamesh Epic in Haupt's *Das
Babylonische Nimrodepos* (Leipzig, 1891), supplemented by Haupt,
"Die Zwölfte Tafel des Babylonischen Nimrodepos" in Beitrage
zur Assyriologie, I, pp. 48–80.

In reply Utnapishtim tells the following story:

"I will reveal to thee, Gilgamesh, a secret story,
And the decision of the gods I will tell thee.
The city Shuruppak,[58] a city which thou knowest,
(The one that) lies on the Euphrates,
That city was old, and the gods thereof
Induced the great gods to bring a cyclone over it;
It was planned (?) by their father Anu,
(By) their counsellor, the warrior Enlil,
(By) their herald Ninib,
(By) their leader En-nugi.
The lord of brilliant vision, Ea, was with them.
He repeated their decision to the reed-hut.[59]
'Reed-hut, reed-hut, wall, wall,
Reed-hut, hear! Wall, give ear!
O man of Shuruppak, son of Ubara-Tutu,
Break up the house, build a ship,
Abandon your property, seek life!
Throw aside your possession and preserve life!
Bring into the ship seed of all living things!
The ship that thou shalt build,
Let its dimensions be measured, (so that)
Its breadth and length be made to correspond.
On a level with the deep, provide it with a covering.''[60]

In another version the name of the hero of the Deluge is given as Atrakhasis, signifying "the very clever one.' This alternate name is introduced also at the end of our version of the tale, where Ea says that he sent Atrakhasis a dream which the latter correctly understood. Evidently two traditions of the manner in which the hero of the deluge was warned of the coming destruction were current. Both were embodied in our

---

[58] Now identified as the site of the mound Fara. The name also appears as Shurippak, but the spelling with *u* is more correct.

[59] In which Utnapishtim dwells. The reed hut points to the primitive conditions in which man lived when the Deluge came on.

[60] The first part of the line is obscure. I believe that the covering here meant is the deck of the framework.

tale, which thus is revealed as itself a composite production. Utnapishtim continues his narative:

"I understood [61] and spoke to Ea, my lord:
  (The command) of my lord which thou hast commanded,
  As I have understood (it), I will carry out.
  (But what) shall I answer the city, the people, and the elders?
  Ea opened his mouth and spoke:
  Spoke to me, his servant.
 '(As answer) thus speak to them:
  (Know that) Enlil has conceived hatred towards me,
  So that I can no longer dwell (in your city).
  (On) Enlil's territory I dare no longer set my face.
  Therefore, I go to the "deep" to dwell with Ea, my lord.
  Over you he will cause blessing to rain down.
  (Catch of) bird, catch of fish,'
  And . . . rich crops."

At this point the tablet is defective. Utnapishtim must have told Gilgamesh how he completed the ship, first drawing a plan and building according to it. Thereupon the text proceeds:

"On the fifth day, I designed its outline.
  According to the plan (?), the walls were to be ten Gar [62] high.
  Correspondingly, ten Gar the measure of its width.
  I determined upon its shape (and) drew it.
  I weighted it six-fold.[63]
  I divided (the superstructure?) into seven parts.
  Its interior I divided into nine parts.
  Water-plugs I constructed in the interior.
  I selected a pole and added accessories.
  Six [64] Sar of asphalt I poured on the outer wall.

---

[61] Referring, evidently, to the mysterious dream, and not to the explicit command, which is so clear that it could not be misunderstood.

[62] A Gar is 12 cubits.

[63] A somewhat obscure line to indicate, perhaps, the strong substructure so as to be capable of holding seven stories.

[64] A variant text has "three."

Three Sar of pitch (I poured) on the inner wall.
Three Sar the workmen carried away in their baskets.[65]   Of oil,
Beside one Sar of oil which was used for the sacrifices,
The boatman secreted two Sar of oil."[66]

Utnapishtim then proceeds:

"All that I had I loaded on her.
All that I had of silver I loaded on her.
All that I had of gold I loaded on her.
All that I had of living beings of all kinds I loaded on her.
I brought to the ship all my family and household;
Cattle of the field, beasts of the field, all the workmen I brought
    on board."

The ship draws water to two-thirds of its bulk.

The description of the storm which now follows is
one of the finest passages in the narrative.

"Shamash had fixed the time,
'When the rulers of darkness (?) at evening time shall cause
    a terrific rain-storm,
Step into the ship and close the door! '
The fixed time approached,
When the rulers of darkness (?) at evening time were to cause
    a terrific rain-storm.
I recognized the symptoms of (such) a day,
A day, for the appearance of which I was in terror.
I entered the ship and closed the door.
To steer the ship, to Puzur-Kurgal, the boatman,
I entrusted the palace [67] together with its cargo.
As morning dawned,
There arose on the firmament of heaven black clouds,
Adad thundered therein;
Nabu and Lugal marched in advance,
Ira [68] tears out the ship's pole.

---

[65] *I.e.,* "graft" taken by the workman.

[66] More "graft."

[67] Note this designation given to the structure—an indication
of its large size, with its many stories and compartments.

[68] God of pestilence.

Ninib marches, commanding the attack,
The Anunnaki [69] lift torches,
Illuminating the land with their sheen,
Adad's roar reaches to heaven,
All light is changed to darkness.

.   .   .   .

One day the hurricane raged . .. .
Storming furiously. . .
Coming like a combat over men.
Brother sees not brother:
Those in heaven [70] do not know one another.
The gods are terrified at the cyclone,
They flee and mount to the heaven of Anu [71];
The gods crouch like dogs in an enclosure.
Ishtar cries aloud like one in birth throes,
The mistress of the gods howls aloud:
'That day be turned to clay,[72]
When I in the assembly of the gods decreed evil;
That I should have decreed evil in the assembly of the gods!
For the destruction of my people should have ordered a combat!
Did I bring forth my people,
That like fish they should fill the sea?'
All of the Anunnaki weep with her.
The gods sit down, depressed and weeping.
Their lips are closed . . .
Six days and nights
The storm, cyclone (and) hurricane continued to sweep over
    the land.
When the seventh day approached, the hurricane and cyclone
    ceased the combat,
After having fought like warriors (?).
The sea grew quiet, the evil storm abated, the cyclone was re-
    strained.
I looked at the day and the roar had quieted down.
And all mankind had turned to clay.
Like an enclosure . . . had become.

---

[69] A collective name for the minor gods.
[70] *I.e.*, the gods in general.
[71] The highest part of heaven.
[72] *I.e.*, be cursed with destruction.

29

I opened a window and light fell on my face,
I bowed down and sat down (and) wept,
Tears flowed over my face.
I looked in all directions of the sea.
At a distance of twelve (miles) [73] an island appeared.
At mount Nisir the ship stood still.
Mount Nisir took hold of the ship so that it could not move.
One day, two days, Mount Nisir etc.[74]
Three days, four days, Mount Nisir, etc.
Five days, six days, Mount Nisir, etc.
When the seventh day arrived,
I sent forth a dove letting it free.
The dove went hither and thither;
Not finding a resting-place, it came back.
I sent forth a swallow, letting it free.
The swallow went hither and thither.
Not finding a resting-place, it came back.
I sent forth a raven, letting it free.
The raven went and saw the decrease of the waters.
It ate, croaked (?), but did not turn back.
Then I let (all) out to the four regions (and) brought an offering.
I brought a sacrifice on the mountain top.
Seven and seven *adagur* jars I arranged.
Beneath them I strewed reeds, cedarwood and myrtle.
The gods smelled the odor,
The gods smelled the sweet odor.
The gods like flies gathered around the sacrificer."

The gods now realize what havoc had been wrought by their decision and begin to regret it. Ishtar, more particularly as the mother goddess, bitterly laments the destruction of mankind.

---

[73] Or "after a space of twelve double hours."

[74] Sign of reduplication, *i.e.*, "Mount Nisir took hold of the ship so that it could not move." Nisir means "salvation"—a symbolical name therefore.

"As soon as the mistress of the gods [75] arrived,
She raised on high the large necklace (?) which Anu had made
   according to his art.
'Ye gods, as surely as I will not forget these precious stones at
   my neck,
So I will remember these days—never to forget them.
Let the gods come to the sacrifice,
But let Enlil not come to the sacrifice.
Because without reflection he brought on the cyclone,
And decreed destruction for my people.'
As soon as Enlil arrived,
He saw the ship, and Enlil was enraged.
Filled with anger at the Igigi.[76]
'Who now has escaped with his life?
No man was to survive the destruction!'
Ninib opened his mouth and spoke,
Spoke to the warrior Enlil,
'Who except Ea can plan any affair?
Ea indeed knows every order.'
Ea opened his mouth and spoke,
Spoke to the warrior Enlil:
'Thou art the leader (and) warrior of the gods.
But why didst thou, without reflection, bring on the cyclone?
On the sinner impose his sin,
On the evil-doer impose his evil,
But be merciful not to root out completely, be considerate not
   (to destroy altogether)!
Instead of bringing on a cyclone,
Lions might have come and diminished mankind.
Instead of bringing on a cyclone,
Jackals might have come and diminished mankind.
Instead of bringing on a cyclone,
Famine might have come and overwhelmed the land.
Instead of bringing on a cyclone,
Ira [77] might have come and destroyed the land.

---

[75] Ishtar.

[76] Here a collective name for the gods, though generally designating, like Anunnaki, a lower group of divine beings; see above,
pp. 331 *seq*.

[77] God of pestilence.

I did not reveal the oracle of the great gods,
I sent Atrakhasis a dream and he understood the oracle of the
    gods.
Now take counsel for him.' "

Enlil is moved by this eloquent appeal and is reconciled. He himself accords immortal life to Utnapishtim
and his wife, and with this act the story ends.

"Enlil mounted the ship,
  Took hold of my hand and led me up,[78]
  Led me up and caused my wife to kneel at my side,
  Touched our foreheads, stepped between us (and) blessed us.
  'Hitherto Utnapishtim was a man;
  Now Utnapishtim and his wife shall be on a level with the gods.
  Utnapishtim shall dwell in the distance, at the confluence of the
    streams.'
  Then they took me and settled me at the confluence of the
    streams."

The remainder of the tablet is taken up with Gilgamesh's sojourn with Utnapishtim and his wife who care
for the weary wanderer. He is refreshed by a deep
sleep, is given guidance for a safe return across the
waters of death which he had to pass in order to reach
the dwelling place of Utnapishtim, but the hero returns
without having secured from his remote ancestor any
hint of how to attain the boon of immortal life. The
story merely shows that some favorite of the gods *may*
escape the general fate of mankind, but that is all. Immortality is the privilege of the gods. Man must be
resigned to his fate, to pass to Aralû, the general gathering place of the dead after life has fled, and there to lie
inactive but conscious, imprisoned in a dark and gloomy
prison, time without end.

---

[78] *I.e.,* brought me on land.

III

STORY OF THE DESCENT OF THE GODDESS ISHTAR INTO THE LOWER
WORLD.

The goddess Ishtar, as the great mother goddess,[79]
is the goddess of vegetation in nature, as of fertility
among mankind and animals. She is pictured as spending half the year on earth, when nature is in bloom and
animals throw off their young, while during the remaining half, when nature seems dead, she is imprisoned in
the lower world known as *Aralû.* The story of her descent to Aralû is, therefore, a nature myth, symbolizing
the change from the summer to the winter season, while
her release is the corresponding change from winter to
summer. The story, as related in the following poem,[80]
appears to have had attached to it as a moral the faint
possibility of a revivification of the dead; it may have
been composed in connection with a ritual in honor of
the old Sumerian god Tammuz or Dumu-Zi-Apsu "the
child of the spirit (or life) of the Deep," [81] the sun-god
of the springtime whose departure was mourned and
whose return was hailed with appropriate ceremonies.
In other tales Tammuz is pictured as the lover of Ishtar,
slain by the goddess because of his rejection of her love.

"To the land of no return, the land of (darkness [?])
   Ishtar, the daughter of Sin [82] (directed) her thought,[83]

---

[79] Above, p. 232.

[80] Cuneiform Texts, XV, Pl. 45–48. See further, Jastrow, *Religion of Babylonia and Assyria* (Boston, 1898), chap. XXV. The
poem consists of lines of two hemistichs, with three beats to each
hemistich.

[81] Tammuz is the Hebrew form of the Sumerian Dumuzi, "child
of life," which is itself an abbreviation of the fuller name "Dumu-
Zi-Apsu." This name is an allusion to the sun's rising every
morning out of the ocean, on which the earth, according to Babylonian notions, floats.

[82] The moon-god.

[83] Literally "fixed her ear."

Directed her thought,[34] Ishtar, the daughter of Sin,
To the house of shadows, the dwelling of Irkalla,[35]
To the house without exit for him who enters therein,
To the road whence there is no turning,
To the house without light for him who enters therein,
The place where dust is their nourishment, clay their food.[36]
They have no light, in darkness they dwell.
Clothed like birds, with wings as garments,
Over door and bolt, dust has gathered.[37]
Ishtar on arriving at the gate of the land of no return,
To the gate-keeper thus addressed herself:
'Gate-keeper, ho, open thy gate!
Open thy gate that I may enter!
If thou openest not the gate to let me enter,
I will break the door, I will wrench the lock,
I will smash the door-posts, I will force the doors.
I will bring up the dead to eat the living.[38]
(And) the dead will outnumber the living.'
The gate-keeper opened his mouth and spoke,
Spoke to the lady Ishtar:
'Desist, O lady, do not destroy it.
I will go and announce thy name to my queen Ereshkigal.'[39]
The gate-keeper entered and spoke (to Ereshkigal):
'Ho! here is thy sister, Ishtar . . .
Hostility of the great powers (?) . . .'
When Ereshkigal heard this,
As when one hews down a tamarisk (she trembled [?])

---

[34] Note the characteristic repetition of the lines as above pointed out p. 434, note 17.

[35] Another name for the nether world.

[36] i.e., of the inhabitants.

[37] The nether world is pictured as a plane filled with dust, and guarded by seven gates through which one must pass before reaching it.

[38] Based on the belief in vampires and other monsters, who as spirits of the dead return to earth to destroy the living.

[39] The goddess of the nether world, pictured as Ishtar's sister, just as life and death are frequently pictured as brothers in popular poetry. The name signifies "lady of the great palace," i.e., of Aralû.

'As when one cuts a reed, (she shook [?]) :
'What has moved her heart, what has (stirred) her liver ?[90]
Ho there, (does) this one (wish to dwell [?]) with me?
To eat clay as food, to drink (dust [?]) as wine?
I weep for the men who have left their wives.
I weep for the wives (torn) from the embrace of their husbands;
For the little ones (cut off) before their time.[91]
Go, gate-keeper, open thy gate for her,
Deal with her according to the ancient decree.[92]
The gate-keeper went and opened his gate to her:
'Enter, O lady, let Cuthah [93] greet thee.
Let the palace of the land of no return rejoice at thy presence! '
He bade her enter the first gate which he opened wide, and took
    the large crown off her head:
'Why, O gate-keeper, dost thou remove the large crown off my
    head?'
'Enter, O lady, such are the decrees of Ereshkigal.'
The second gate he bade her enter, opening it wide and removed
    her earrings:
'Why, O gate-keeper, dost thou remove my ear-rings?'
'Enter, O lady, for such are the decrees of Ereshkigal.'
The third gate he bade her enter, opened it wide and removed
    her necklace:
'Why, O gate-keeper, dost thou remove my necklace?'
'Enter, O lady, for such are the decrees of Ereshkigal.'
The fourth gate he bade her enter, opened it wide and removed
    the ornaments of her breast:
'Why, O gate-keeper, dost thou remove the ornaments of my
    breast?'
'Enter, O lady, for such are the decrees of Ereshkigal.'

---

[90] Heart and liver as the seat of the intellect and of the emotions
respectively. See above, p. 215.

[91] With Ishtar in the nether world, the living are without protection; they die, as does all nature, and Ereshkigal is moved with pity
for their fate.

[92] *i.e.*, treat her as the dead are dealt with.

[93] The old city of which Nergal, the god of pestilence, was the
patron becomes a poetical name for Aralû. See above p. 206, *seq.*

The fifth gate he bade her enter, opened it wide and removed the
girdle of her body studded with birth-stones.[94]

'Why, O gate-keeper, dost thou remove the girdle of my body,
studded with birth-stones?'

'Enter, O lady, for such are the decrees of Erishkigal.'

The sixth gate, he bade her enter, opened it wide and removed
the spangles off her hands and feet.

'Why, O gate-keeper, dost thou remove the spangles off my hands
and feet?'

'Enter, O lady, for thus are the decrees of Ereshkigal.'

The seventh gate he bade her enter, opened it wide and removed
her loin-cloth.[95]

'Why, O gate-keeper, dost thou remove my loin-cloth?'

'Enter, O lady, for such are the decrees of Ereshkigal.'

Now when Ishtar had gone down into the land of no return,

Ereshkigal saw her and was angered at her presence.

Ishtar without reflection threw herself at her.[96]

Ereshkigal opened her mouth and spoke,

To Namtar, her messenger, she addressed herself:

'Go Namtar,[97] (imprison her) in my palace.

Send against her sixty diseases,[98] (to punish [?] Ishtar.)

Eye disease against her eyes,

Disease of the side against her side,

Foot-disease [99] against her foot,

Heart disease against her heart,

Head-disease [100] against her head,

Against her whole being, against (her entire body [?]).'

After the lady Ishtar had gone down into the land of no return,

---

[94] It is appropriate for Ishtar, as the goddess who presides over
the new life, to have her girdle studded with birth-stones, *i.e.*, stones
that have the power to secure an easy delivery for women. The
"birth-girdle" appears elsewhere in folk customs.

[95] Literally "the garment of the *pudenda* of the body."

[96] The two sisters fly at each other in a rage.

[97] The god or demon of pestilence.

[98] The diseases are personified through demons supposed to be
their cause.

[99] Rheumatism.

[100] Fevers and headaches.

The bull did not mount the cow, the ass approached not the
    she-ass,
To the maid in the street, no man drew near,
The man slept in his apartment,
The maid slept by herself.''

The gradual disrobing of Ishtar, her ornaments and
garments being taken away as she passes from one gate
to the other, symbolizes the gradual decay of nature
after the summer has waned until at last Ishtar enters
the lower world naked, and cold, bare winter has set in.
It is a time when not only nature seems dead, but when
among animals and men all desire for new life ceases.
Copulation among animals has stopped, and even the
sexual passion among men is stilled—to symbolize the
interruption in the course of things on earth. The gods
mourn the departure of Ishtar from the surface of the
earth and devise plans for her return that life may not
perish altogether. The second half of the poem continues as follows:

"The countenance of Papsukal, the messenger of the great gods
    fell, his face (was troubled).
In mourning garbs he was clothed, in soiled garments clad.
Shamash [101] went to Sin, his father, weeping,
In the presence of Ea, the king, he went with flowing tears.
'Ishtar has descended into the earth and has not come up.
The bull does not mount the cow, the ass does not approach the
    she-ass.
The man does not approach the maid in the street,
The man sleeps in his apartment,
The maid sleeps by herself.'
Ea in the wisdom of his heart formed a being,[102]
He formed Asu-shu-namir,[103] the eunuch.
'Go, Asu-shu-namir, to the land of no return direct thy face!
The seven gates of the land without return be opened before thee,

---

[101] *i.e.*, the sun-god.

[102] *Zikru,* "a male.''

[103] The name signifies "His exit is resplendent"—clearly a
symbolical allusion to the rising sun of the springtime.

May Ereshkigal at sight of thee rejoice!
After her heart has been assuaged, her liver quieted,
Invoke against her the name of the great gods,
Raise thy head, direct (thy) attention to the *khalziku* skin.' [104]
'Come, lady, let them give me the *khalziku* skin, that I may drink
    water out of it.'
When Ereshkigal heard this, she struck her side, bit her finger,
'Thou hast expressed a wish that cannot be granted.
Go, Asu-shu-namir, I curse thee with a great curse,
The sweepings of the gutters of the city be thy food,
The drains of the city be thy drink,
The shadow of the wall be thy abode,
The thresholds be thy dwelling-place;
Drunkard and sot strike thy cheek!' [105]
Ereshkigal opened her mouth and spoke,
To Namtar, her messenger, she addressed herself.
'Go, Namtar, knock at the strong palace,[106]
Strike the threshold of precious stones,
Bring out the Anunnaki, seat (them) on golden thrones.
Sprinkle Ishtar with the waters of life and take her out of my
    presence.' "

The gods at the instance of Ea thus form a plan to release Ishtar, demanding of Ereshkigal to give the messenger of Ea, the eunuch Asu-shu-namir, the skin (?)
out of which he is to drink, and thus to secure the power
to fetch Ishtar out of the nether world. Ereshkigal sees
through the strategy, and in her rage curses Asu-shu-
namir, but, nevertheless, realizing that Ishtar must be
released proceeds to do so of her own free will and in
her own way, by asking the messenger Namtar to
sprinkle the goddess with water of life, that when thus
filled with new vigor, Ishtar may pass through the
seven gates encompassing the palace of the nether world

---

[104] An obscure word—perhaps the name of some kind of a bag,
made of skin, containing the waters of life.

[105] *i.e.*, the lowest of the low show their contempt for thee.

[106] Or "the just palace" where the Anunnaki, the minor group
of gods, dwell, acting as judges of the dead.

and at each gate receive back the ornaments and garments that she was obliged to leave there. The gradual resuscitation of nature after the imprisonment is thus symbolized, until when the last gate is passed, Ishtar emerges into the world in all her beauty and glory. The poem continues as follows:

"Namtar went, knocked at the strong palace,
Tapped on the threshold of precious stones.
He brought out the Anunnaki and placed them on golden thrones,
He sprinkled Ishtar with the waters of life and took hold of her.
Through the first gate he led her out and returned to her her loin cloth.
Through the second gate he led her out and returned to her the spangles of her hands and feet.
Through the third gate he led her out and returned to her the girdle of her body, studded with birth-stones.
Through the fourth gate he led her out and returned to her the ornaments of her breast.
Through the fifth gate he led her out and returned to her her necklace.
Through the sixth gate he led her out and returned to her her ear-rings.
Through the seventh gate he led her out and returned to her the large crown for her head."

The following lines are in the form of an address—apparently to some one who has sought release for a dear one from the portals of the lower world.

" 'If she (sc. Ishtar) will not grant thee her release,[107]
To Tammuz, the lover of her youth,[108]
Pour out pure waters, (pour out) fine oil;
With a festival garment deck him [109] that he may play on the flute of lapis lazuli,

---

[107] i.e., the release of the loved one through the mediation of Ishtar.

[108] i.e., Ishtar's lover.

[109] i.e., deck Tammuz's statue with a festival garment.

That the votaries [110] (may cheer) his liver.[111] '

Belili [112] had (gathered) the treasure,

With precious stones filled her bosom(?).

When Belili heard the lament of her brother, (she dropped [?]) her treasure,

She scattered the precious stones (before her[?]).

'O my only brother do not let me perish!

On the day when Tammuz plays for me on the flute of lapis lazuli, playing it for me with the porphyry ring.

Together with him, play ye for me, ye weepers and lamenting women! [113]

That the dead may rise up and inhale the incense.' "

The closing lines are obscure. We lack the key to their interpretation, but it is a plausible conjecture that the poem, composed for and perhaps sung at the festival of Tammuz, when, as the prophet Ezekiel (8, 14) tells us, it was the custom of women to wail for the lost Tammuz, closed with instructions to those who in commemorating the departure of Tammuz thought of their own dead, who like Ishtar "had gone to the land of no return," to turn in prayer to Tammuz, pour out libations of pure water and oil to him, honor him that he may at least regale the dead by letting them hear the sound of his magic flute. There is a reference here to some rite on Tammuz day—which was also a time of commemorating the dead in general. Perhaps the six lines beginning with "Belili" represent a Tammuz lamentation of which we have quite a number,[114] to be sung at the Tammuz festival, with the last line as expressing the hope that the dead will be for a time at least re-

[110] *Shamkhâte*, one of the class of votaries, attached to the Ishtar cult. See above, p. 307.

[111] *i.e.*, his spirit.

[112] Sister of Tammuz.

[113] The professional mourners who sing the lament for the dead, to the accompaniment of musical instruments.

[114] See Zimmern, *Sumerisch-Babylonische Tammuzlieder* (*Berichte der Phil. Hist. Klasse der Kgl. Saechs. Akad., d. Wiss.*, vol. lix, pp 201–252).

vivified by the song and by the incense. If this interpretation is justified, the poem would thus hold out a faint hope for some joys for the unhappy dead in their dark and gloomy prison.

IV

"Eat, Drink and be Merry"

Gilgamesh in the course of his wanderings to seek healing from a fatal disease with which he has been smitten by the goddess Ishtar [115] comes to a maiden, Sabitu,[116] pictured as dwelling by the sea. In the tenth tablet of the Epic he is described as arriving at the sea with "his strength exhausted and his countenance fallen." Sabitu asks him as to the cause of his dejection, and in reply Gilgamesh speaks of his exploits with Enkidu, how they together overcame the tyrant Khumbaba, and how they offended Ishtar by killing the divine bull,[117] and how in revenge Enkidu had been snatched away, while Gilgamesh himself is obliged to go in search of life, which he feels to be ebbing away. According to one version, Gilgamesh addresses Sabitu as follows: [118]

---

[115] See above, p. 444, *seq.* It is Gilgamesh, the personification of the sun-god, who thus appears in the rôle of Tammuz stricken by Ishtar, the goddess of vegetation; he is the waning sun, approaching the period when nature lies down to winter's sleep.

[116] Sabitu appears to be an appellative, perhaps "the maid of Sabu"; another name is Siduri, which likewise has the force of "maid." The locality described in Sabitu is regarded by some scholars as southern Arabia.

[118] This address and Sabitu's answer are found in a fragment, of Mithraism. See Cumont, *Mysteries of Mithra* (Chicago, 1910).

[118] This address and Sabitu's answer is found in a fragment, dating from the Hammurapi period (c. 2100 B. C.) published by Meissner, *Ein Altbabylonisches Fragment des Gilgameschepos* (Mitteilungen der Vorderasiatischen Gessellschaft VII, No. 1, Leipzig, 1902). In this version both the name of Gilgamesh and of his companion are written in different fashion from the forms in which they appear in the main version.

"Enkidu [119] whom I deeply loved,
Who with me undertook all kinds of different (tasks),
Has gone to the fate of mankind,
Day and night I weep for him,
I did not (want to) destine him for the grave.
A god saw (him) and came at my cry.[120]
Seven days and seven nights,
Like a worm he lay on his face,
After which he was no more,
(And) I like a vagabond wander about in the wilderness.
Now that I see thy face, O Sabitu,
The death that I feared I do not see." [121]

Gilgamesh's hope is revived for the moment, now that he has at last reached the dwelling-place of Sabitu, from whom he expects aid and consolation. He is doomed to disappointment.

"Sabitu speaks to him, to Gilgamesh.
'O Gilgamesh, why dost thou run in all directions?
The life that thou seekest thou wilt not find.
When the gods created mankind,
They determined death for mankind;
Life they kept in their hands.
Thou, O Gilgamesh, fill thy belly,
Day and night be thou merry.
Daily arrange a merry-making,
Day and night be joyous and content!
Let thy garments be pure,[122]

---

[119] Enkidu is stricken, and despite Gilgamesh's hope that his friend may not be taken away and his appeal to a god, the friend languishes for a week and then dies.

[120] *i.e.*, "at my appeal," but though the god comes, he affords no help.

[121] According to the main version of the Epic in the form as found in the fragments of Ashurbanapal's library, Gilgamesh asks Sabitu to help him sail across the sea in order to reach Utnapishtim.

[122] Clean garments are a sign of joy, as soiled garments (above, p. 457) are a symbol of mourning.

Thy head be washed, wash thyself with water!
Regard the little one [123] who takes hold of thy hand,
Enjoy the wife (lying) in thy bosom.' ''

The advice is not unlike some of the utterances in
the Biblical book of Ecclesiastes, the resemblance extending even to a similarity of phrases, as, for
example,[124]

"Go thy way, eat thy bread with joy, and drink thy wine with a
merry heart. Let thy garments be always white, let thy head not
lack ointment. Live joyfully with the wife whom thou lovest."

It was a natural philosophy of life for a people who
looked forward not to extinction of life as the Nirvana
of Buddha, but to a continuation of consciousness after
death under most depressing conditions—imprisoned
in a dark and gloomy cave, there to lie forever deprived
of all activity and of all joys. Despite this materialistic view—or perhaps in consequence of it—the Babylonians and Assyrians did not fail to emphasize also the
higher aspects of life, duties towards one's fellows, a
proper consideration for the weak and helpless; and
from this level they rose still higher to an appreciation
of such virtues as purity of heart, self-restraint in
anger, and the obligations of piety.[125] It may be proper
to add, by way of illustration, a specimen from a collection of moral maxims of which we have a number in
the library of Ashurbanapal.

[123] *i.e.*, your child.
[124] Ecc. 9, 7–9.
[125] See further Jastrow, *Aspects of Religious Belief and Practice
in Babylonia and Assyria* (New York, 1911), p. 375 *seq;* and on
the relation between Hebrew and Babylonian Ethics, the author's
Hebrew and Babylonian Traditions (New York, 1914), Chapter V.

V

MAXIMS OF CONDUCT

In a text of this character we read: [126]

"Thou shalt not slander—speak what is pure!
Thou shalt not speak evil—speak kindly!
He who slanders and speaks evil,
Shamash [127] will visit it on thy head.
Do not speak boastfully—guard thy lip;
If in anger—do not speak out.
Speaking in anger, thou shalt regret it later;
And in silence nurse thy sadness.
Approach thy god daily,
(Offering) sacrifice and prayer with pure incense,
Before thy god have a pure heart!
Prayer, request and prostration,
Render him each morning,
So that with the help of (thy) god thou wilt flourish.
Learn wisdom from the tablet.[128]
Fear (of god) begets favor,
Offering increases life,
Prayer brings forgiveness of sin.
He who fears the gods will not cry (in vain [?]).
He who fears the Anunnaki [129] will lengthen his days.
Speak not evil of thy friend and companion,
Do not speak meanly—speak what is kindly!
If thou promisest (give what thou hast promised [?])
. . . .
Do not oppress them [130] tyranically;
His god will be angry with one for this;

---

[126] Cuneiform Texts, XIII, Pl. 29–30, and Macmillan, *Some Cuneiform Tablets Bearing on the Religion of Babylonia and Assyria*, No. II (Beitrage zür Assyriologie, Vol. V, pp. 531–712).

[127] The god of Justice. Above, p. 204, *seq.*

[128] As we would say "learn from books."

[129] Here used as a synonym for the gods in general, though more commonly designating a group of minor deities. See p. 451, note 76.

[130] Perhaps the members of the household are meant. The preceding lines being defective, the context naturally is not altogether clear.

It is not pleasing to Shamash—he will requite with evil.
Give food to eat, wine to drink,
Seek what is right, avoid (what is wrong [?])
This is pleasing to one's god,
Pleasing to Shamash—he will requite it.
Be helpful and kind (to the servant [?])
The maid in the house (do thou protect [?])."

VI

BABYLONIAN-ASSYRIAN PRAYERS

The same spirit is to be found in the prayers embodied in inscriptions of Babylonian-Assyrian rulers,[131] even if the same high ethical plane is not always reached. For the older period we have a prayer addressed by Gudea,[132] the ruler of Lagash (c. 2450 B.C.), on the occasion of his decision to build a temple in honor of Ningirsu, the chief god of Lagash, in response to a dream in which he is called upon to erect a sacred edifice.[133]

"O Warrior, powerful lion, without a rival,
O Ningirsu, (ruling?) the deep,
Thou who art ruler of Nippur,
O Warrior, whose orders whatever they may be, may I carry out;
O Ningirsu, thy temple I wish to build,
Thy decrees I propose to carry out.
May thy sister [134] the child of Eridu,[135]
Who gives proper counsel,
The queen who interprets the oracles of the gods,
May thy goddess Ninâ, the sister of Sirara-shum-ta,[136] place her
    foot in her bark." [137]

---

[131] A translation of most of such prayers will be found in the author's *Religion Babyloniens und Assyriens*, I, pp. 394–420.

[132] Above, p. 137, *seq.*

[133] Thureau-Dangin, *Sumerisch-Akkadische Königsinschriften*, p. 90–91.

[134] The goddess Ninâ.

[135] *I.e.*, the daughter of Ea, the god of Eridu. See above, p. 210

[136] An epithet of Ningirsu.

[137] *I.e.*, be favorable to me.

30

The same Gudea prays to Bau,[138] the consort of Ningirsu, as follows: [139]

"O my queen, daughter of the shining heaven,[140]
Who gives proper counsel, who occupies the first rank in heaven,
Who grants life to the land,

   .   .   .   .

Thou art the queen, the mother who has established Lagash;
The people on whom thou lookest is rich in power,
The worshipper on whom thou lookest—his life is prolonged.
I have no mother—thou art my mother;
I have no father—thou art my father.
My father . . . in a holy place thou hast produced me,
My goddess Bau thou knowest what is good.

   .   .   .   .

Thou hast given me the breath of life,
Under the protection of my mother, in thy shadow I will reverently dwell."

Particularly impressive are the prayers attached to the inscriptions of the Neo-Babylonian rulers, Nebopolassar and his son Nebuchadnezzar. On the completion of his palace in Babylon the latter prays to Marduk, god of Babylon and head of the pantheon, as follows:[141]

"As my precious life, do I love thy sublime appearance! Outside of thy city Babylon, I have not selected among all settlements any dwelling. Since I love the fear of thy divinity, and am zealous for thy rule, be gracious to my prayer, hear my appeal, for I am the King who adorns thee (i.e., thy temple), who rejoices thy heart, the thoughtful governor who beautifies all thy settlements. At thy command, O merciful Marduk, may the house that I have built endure forever, may I be satiated with its splendor, attain old age therein, with abundant offspring, and receive therein tribute of the kings of all regions, from all mankind.

   .   .   .   .

---

[138] He addresses her as Ga-tum-dug. See above, p. 466, and Pl. XLII, Fig. 3.

[139] Thureau-Dangin ib, p. 92–93.

[140] i.e., as the consort of the sun-god, Bau is also the daughter of Anu, the god of heaven.

[141] Rawlinson, I, Pl. 58, Col. IX, 47–X, 19. The opening lines are similar to the prayer translated above, p. 216.

On his completion of the temple at Sippar, the same king dedicates the edifice by a prayer to Shamash, the sun-god,[142] who, it will be recalled,[143] is preëminently the god of justice and righteousness.

"O Shamash, great lord, on entering joyfully thy brilliant [144] temple, E-barra, look on my precious handiwork! Thy lips proclaim grace for me! By thy just [145] command, may I have plenty of offspring. Grant me a life of long days and a firm throne. May my rule [146] stretch out into eternity, with a just sceptre, with good rule. Adorn my kingdom forever with a legitimate staff of authority, bringing salvation to mankind. Protect my troops with strong weapons against the attack. Answer me aright, O Shamash, through thy judicial decision and oracle. At thy supreme, unchangeable command, may my sharp weapons advance and overcome the weapons of my enemies."

It was usually at the close of their inscriptions that the rulers added these appeals to grant long life, happiness and plenty of offspring; and the custom was continued by the Persian and Greek rulers whose prayers are modelled on those of the Neo-Babylonian rulers, with merely slight variations. Somewhat more original are the prayers of Assyrian rulers, though here, too, conventionality leads to certain phrases which one ruler copies from the other.

Esarhaddon, the king of Assyria (680–669 B.C.), towards the close of a long inscription setting forth his activity as a builder and restorer of temples and palaces in Babylonia and Assyria, inserts a long prayer addressed to all his gods: [147]

---

[142] Ball, Proceedings of the Society of Biblical Archæology, Vol. xi, p. 127, Col. II; 32–111, 30.

[143] Above, p. 203.

[144] With a play on E-barra, which signifies the "brilliant house."

[145] Note the constant play throughout the prayer on "justice," "right" etc. as the attributes of Shamash.

[146] *i.e.*, my dynasty.

[147] Meissner-Rost, *Bauinschriften Asarhaddon's* (Beiträge zur Assyriologie, III, p. 253.)

"May the gods, my helpers, look joyfully on my pious works and in the fidelity of their heart bless the kingdom. May my priestly seed [148] prevail forever as the foundation of E-sagila and of Babylon. May the kingdom be beneficial to mankind like the plant of life! [149] May I rule the people according to law and justice! May I attain a ripe old age, have offspring, be satiated with a fulness of life, with days well filled! May I extend my family, gather a large household and spread my posterity, may the offshoot flourish! May the foundation of my priestly throne be as firm as a rock! May my rule stand like heaven and earth! In joy and jubilation, in happiness, with beaming countenance and in cheerfulness may I daily wander! A kind fate, a favorable fortune accompany me during my rule, protecting my priestly rank!" [150]

Of a more direct and specific character is a prayer of his successor, King Ashurbanapal (668–626 B.C.), who in the course of his campaign against an inveterate enemy, Teumman, king of Elam, who gave Assyria a great deal of trouble, [151] appeals to the goddess Ishtar for victory over Teumman. The mighty king humbles himself before his gods, realizing that without their help no battle can be won, no victory gained. At the same time the king voices his bitterness against his enemy and makes the direct appeal to the goddess to crush Teumman. [152]

"O lady of Arbela! [153] I am Ashurbanapal, the king of Assyria, the creature of thy hands, (called by) the father who produced

---

[148] i.e., his family. The kings of Assyria originally were priests of Ashur and retain priestly functions through all periods of the kingdom.

[149] A play upon Babylon which is often designated as the "abode of life."

[150] The king thus indicates his double status as secular chief and as priest.

[151] See above, p. 179 and p. 406, seq., and the illustration, Plate LXI, Fig. 2.

[152] Cylinder B. Col. V, 30–49 (Geo. Smith, *History of Assurbanapal*, pp. 120–122).

[153] One of the titles of Ishtar.

thee,[154] to renew the temples of Assyria and to build up the cities of Babylonia. (In humility [?]) have I directed my thoughts towards thy holy sites, concerned for the honor (of thy divinity), whereas this Teumman, the king of Elam, who does not honor the gods (vilifies me [?]).[155] But I (appeal to thee), thou goddess of goddesses, queen of battle, lady of battles, princess of the gods . . . to intercede for me with Ashur, the father who produced thee, (for Teumman) has put his host in array for battle, has gathered his weapons to proceed to Assyria. Thou, warrior among the gods like a . . . drive against him in the midst of battle and destroy him by a mighty storm, an evil wind."

VII

PENITENTIAL PSALMS

The deep emotions aroused through the current beliefs regarding the relationship between gods and worshippers receive an impressive illustration in a class of prayers in which the sense of human weakness and the confession of guilt find an expression. While the conception of sin never rose beyond the point of one's becoming conscious of a wrong committed through some misfortune, affecting the country or the individual, yet within this limit we find the spirit of contriteness touchingly brought out, and the appeal to the angered god or goddess as eloquently made as in the finest of the Biblical Psalms. While the penitent in the specimens at our disposal [156] is in most if not in all cases the king speaking at times for himself and at times for the whole people of which he is the representative, standing close to the gods by virtue of his august position, this is due in part to the accident of the provenance of

[154] The god Ashur.

[155] Text defective. From another passage we know that Teumman called Ashurbanapal "insane," i.e., one possessed by a demon, which was a bitter insult.

[156] See translations of most of them in Jastrow, *Religion Babyloniens und Assyriens*, II, pp. 75–116. See also above, p. 194, *seq.*, and 234 *seq.*

the material from the official archives of the temple or
the palace. To be sure, worship in Babylonia and Assyria always partook largely of an official state character, but on the other hand, there is plenty of evidence
that the needs of the individual were also considered.
In general, it was in the case of public misfortune—a
defeat, a pestilence, the failure of crops or devastation
through storms—that the anger of the gods was felt.
For all that, the form of expression even on such occasions is often distinctly personal, and we are permitted to conclude that the individual likewise, when
through illness or through some misfortune he became
conscious of the divine anger, repaired to the temple
to ascertain, perhaps through some form of divination, what god he had offended. There with the aid of
the priest and with appropriate ceremonies he would
seek to purify himself from sin and secure divine forgiveness. The sin itself may have been a real transgression or a ceremonial omission or mishap. No distinction was drawn down to the latest periods between
the two kinds of guilt, but with due recognition, likewise, of this limitation, the intensity of the emotions
aroused by the sense of guilt is in no way affected. The
priest acts in these outpourings of the penitents as the
mediator, bringing the appeal to the gods and emphasizing it by his own endorsement of it. In most of the
specimens, therefore, the penitent and priest are introduced alternately. So, for example, in the following
psalm addressed to a goddess.[157]

Penitent.
"(Look graciously) on the prostration of living beings!
    (I), thy servant, full of sighs cry to thee.
    The appeal of him who has sinned, do thou accept!
    If thou lookest on a man, that man lives,
    O almighty lady of mankind,
    Merciful one to whom it is good to turn, accept my petition!"

---

[157] Rawlinson, IV², 29**, No. 5.

Priest.

"Because his god and his goddess [158] are
'Angry with him, he cries to thee.
(Turn thy countenance to him), take hold of his hand!"

Penitent.

"Except thee, there is no guiding deity,
Faithfully look on me, accept my petition,
Speak 'Atonement is granted,' may thy liver be assuaged!
How long yet, O my lady! Turn thy countenance to me!
As a dove I moan, satiated with sighs."

Priest.

"With woe and pain, his spirit is full of sighs,
Tears he weeps, he breaks forth in lament."

In another composition of this character, the priest
as mediator sets forth in detail the sufferings of the
penitent, who appears to have been stricken with a painful disease. [159]

Priest.

"(Loosen) his fetters, release his bonds,
(In mercy[?]) look on the one bound!

. . . .

(His heart is full of) misery and (woe).
Sickness, suffering, misery and distress,
Which have befallen him have weakened his sighing.
Those [160] who have overcome him have silenced his plaint.
He has sinned and weeps bitterly before thee.
His spirit [161] is depressed, he is consumed before thee.

---

[158] The priest often refers thus indefinitely to a god or goddess
who has shown his or her disfavor. Usually the special protecting
deity of the individual is meant. At times, however, the indefinite-
ness indicates an uncertainty as to which one of the deities has been
offended.

[159] Rawlinson, IV², Pl. 54, No. 1.

[160] The demons of sickness, etc., have so weakened him that he is
no longer able to voice his complaint.

[161] Literally "his liver."

Overpowered by tears that stream like a rainstorm,
Entirely overcome he sits as one no longer living.
Like a mourner he breaks forth in lamentation,
By imploring he manifests his misery.
What has my lord decided and planned in regard to his servant?
May his [162] mouth proclaim what I do not know."

Penitent.
"Many are my sins which I have committed,
    May I escape this (misfortune), may I be rescued from this dis-
        tress!"

Priest.
"May the (sin and) misdeed be covered up . . .
    With distorted countenance, robbed of light, he is utterly crushed.
    Because of thy misdeed thy hands are tied,
    Whether he will release thee, I do not know."

The penitent sinner is compared to one languishing in prison, tied hand and foot, deprived of light.
We may assume that accompanying the prayer were
some exorcising rites to drive out the evil demons that
had taken possession of him. The inquiry of the god,
through some process of divination, to ascertain
whether the sufferer will be relieved, appears to have
led to a doubtful answer; and, accordingly, we find the
priest proceeding to a second appeal, again with certain
rites and accompanied presumably by a further inquiry.
Not infrequently the penitent asserts that he is not
aware of the deed for which he has been punished, nor
what god or goddess he has offended. Misfortune or
sickness, however, has come, with the inevitable conclusion that some god is angry for some wrong—ceremonial or ethical—committed. So in the course of a
lamentation psalm,[163] too long to quote in full, the penitent exclaims:

---

[162] *I.e.*, the god's.
[163] Rawlinson, IV², Pl. 10.

"The transgression that I have committed, I know not,
The sin that I have committed I know not,
The unclean that I have eaten I know not,
The impure on which I have trodden I know not;
The lord in the anger of his heart has looked on me,
The god in the wrath of his heart has encircled me;
The goddess who is angry against me has made me like one diseased.[164]
A god, whoever he may be,[165] has oppressed me,
A goddess, whoever she may be, has brought misery on me.
I sought for help, but no one took me by the hand;
I cried but no one approached my side;
I broke forth in cries, but no one heard me.
Full of grief I am overpowered, I dare not look up.
To my merciful god,[166] I turn, imploringly,
The feet of my goddess I kiss, I touch;
To the god, whoever he may be, (I turn imploringly).
O lord, (turn thy countenance to me, accept my petition)!
O goddess, (look in mercy on me, accept my petition)!
God, whoever he may be, (turn thy countenance to me, accept my
    petition)!
Goddess, (whoever she may be), look in mercy on me, accept my
    petition!
How long yet, O my god!—may thy heart be assuaged!
How long yet, O my goddess—may thy liver be quieted!
God, whoever he may be,—may the wrath of thy heart return to
    its place!
Goddess, whoever she may be,—may thy hostile heart return to
    its place!"

The penitent closes with some general reflections on
the stubbornness and senselessness of mankind.

"Mankind is stubborn, no one has understanding,
As many as there are—who knows anything?
Whether they do shameful acts or good ones—no one has understanding.
O lord, do not cast thy servant

---

[164] *I.e.*, like one possessed by a demon of sickness.
[165] Literally "known or unknown."
[166] The penitent turns to his special protecting god and goddess.

Into the waters of the marsh! Take hold of his hand!
The sin that I may have committed, turn to grace!
The transgression that I may have committed,
May the wind carry off.
Tear assunder my many misdeeds like a garment!
O my god, my transgressions are seven times seven,[167] forgive my transgressions.
O my goddess, my transgressions are seven times seven, forgive my transgressions!
O god, whoever he may be, my transgressions are seven times seven, forgive me my transgressions!
O goddess, whoever she may be, my transgressions are seven times seven, forgive me my transgressions!
Forgive my transgressions that I may in humility serve thee!
May thy heart like the heart of a mother return to its place![168]
Like the heart of a mother who has given birth, (the heart of) a father who has begotten—return to its place!"

VIII

THE PIOUS SUFFERER

The sense of guilt as expressed in the penitential laments leads naturally to the problem as to the cause of suffering in this world endured by those who are not conscious of any wrong-doing. We have seen how the penitent himself confesses at times that he does not know what deity he has offended, which implies that he also does not know wherein his guilt consists. The impossibility of fathoming the ways of the gods is suggested in the frequent outburst of despair "how long, how long yet, O lord," introduced at times like a refrain in the appeal for forgiveness and release, as well as in such utterances that no one really has certain knowledge—"no one has understanding."[169] This thought carried further leads to a doubt whether the gods have the same standards as prevail in human society. At

---

[167] *i.e.,* are very many.
[168] *i.e.,* be as before, reconciled and gracious.
[169] Above, p. 473.

least the question is raised, and in the face of the fact, too evident to be concealed, that the wicked often flourish in this world, whereas those who lead blameless lives are weighed down with sickness, distress, and misfortune of all kinds, there must have been many a thinker who struggled with the problem that lies at the basis of the Biblical Book of Job—the reason for the existence of evil in a world controlled by powers who are supposed to be kindly disposed. The pious Babylonian had an answer ready at hand. The gods were kind and gracious as long as one did not offend them, but there were the demons lurking everywhere, ready to pounce on their victims unawares—particularly the demons of the various diseases that destroy one's vitality. But the further question would still arise—why do the gods, superior to the demons, allow the latter to maim at will and strike the guilty and guiltless alike, and why are those whose wickedness is apparent permitted to escape?

The tragedy of life, with its woes and hardships, and the impossibility of penetrating the mysteries of the universe, are brought out with considerable force in a composition, Babylonian in origin, which has come down to us in several fragments from the library of Ashurbanapal and from the literary section of the temple at Sippar.[170] The poem, for such it is, is in the form of a lament of an individual Tabi-utul-Enlil, whose home is Nippur and who appears to have been a ruler in

---

[170] The popularity of this valuable composition is indicated by portions of no less than three copies that we have of the text among the fragments of Ashurbanapal's library published, Rawlinson, IV (2d ed.), Pl. 60, as well as a commentary to the text, Rawlinson, V, Pl. 47, explaining certain terms and phrases. Two fragments were also found at Sippar for the publication of which, as well as for further details, see Jastrow, "A Babylonian Parallel to Story of Job" (*Journal of Biblical Literature*, Vol. XXV, pp. 135–191); Martin, "Le Juste Souffrant Babylonien" (*Journal Asiatique*, July–August, 1910) and Landersdorffer, *Eine Babylonische Quelle für das Buch Hiob?* (Freiburg, 1911).

that place.[171] He speaks of himself as obedient to the
gods, concerned for his salvation, careful in his doings,
and yet, despite all this, he has been smitten with painful
disease affecting every part of his body, for which he
can find no relief, and the cause of which he has been unable to ascertain. He is not conscious of guilt, and the
priests to whom he applied offered neither help nor
consolation. The story is made the occasion of philo-
sophical reflections on the fate of man, on his helpless-
ness in suffering and his weakness in combating the ills
to which human flesh is heir. These reflections constitute the value of the composition, and give it an exceptional place among the productions of Babylonian
literature. Unfortunately it is only preserved in part.
It consisted of four tablets of approximately 120 lines
each, but of the total only about one-third are preserved
and many of these lines are imperfect. Fortunately,
by a careful study it is possible to follow the general
course of the composition. The preserved portions,
moreover, include two passages which belong to the
finest specimen of Babylonian literature, noteworthy
both in thought and in eloquent diction.

In the first tablet,[172] beginning with the praise of
"lord of wisdom"—originally no doubt Enlil of Nippur,
but transferred in the course of further redaction to
Marduk, the head of the later Babylonian pantheon,
we have a description of the evil that has overwhelmed
Tabi-utul-Enlil which reads, so far as preserved, as
follows: [173]

---

[171] The name signifies "good is the loin (*i.e.*, protection) of
Enlil."

[172] Only 10 intelligible lines of the first tablet are preserved
through the commentary (V. Rawlinson, Pl. 47, to which we can
add as an eleventh the opening line "I will praise the lord of
wisdom," derived from the colophon to a copy of a portion of the
2nd tablet.

[173] Conjectural restrictions of the text are placed in parentheses.

"(My eyeballs he obscured, bolting them as with) a lock
  (My ears he bolted), like those of a deaf person.
  A king—I have been changed into a slave,
  As a madman (my) companions maltreat me.
  Send me help from the pit dug (for me)!
  At the cry of my lament, open a hole for him (?),[174]
  By day—deep sighs, at night—weeping,
  The month—cries, the year—distress."

The second tablet opens with a reflection on the sadness of life's experiences and the difficulty of penetrating the ways of the gods to ascertain how to please them; and as in the case of Job, the reflections are interspersed with laments about his own forlorn condition.

"I had reached and passed the allotted time of life;
  Whithersoever I turned—evil upon evil.
  Misery had increased, justice was gone,
  I cried to my god, but he did not show me his countenance;
  I prayed to my goddess, but she did not raise her head.
  The diviner-priest could not determine the future by an inspection,
  The necromancer did not through an offering justify my suit,
  The zakiku-priest[175] I appealed to, but he revealed nothing,
  The chief exorciser did not by (his) rites release me from the ban.
  The like of this had never been seen;
  Whithersoever I turned, trouble was in pursuit."

His punishment seems inexplicable to him, as he proceeds to set forth how he always endeavored to perform his duties towards the gods and men punctiliously.

"As though I had not always set aside the portion for the god,
  And had not invoked the goddess at the meal,
  Had not bowed my face, and brought my tribute,
  As though I were one in whose mouth supplication and prayer
    were not constant,

[174] Meaning "himself."
[175] An oracle priest.

Who had set aside the day of the god,[176] neglected the new-moon
    festival,
Been negligent, spurned their images,
Not taught his people fear and reverence,
Not invoked his god, eaten of his (*sc.* the god's) food;[177]
Neglected his goddess, and did not offer to her a libation.
With the oppressor who has forgotten his lord,
Who has profaned the sacred name of his god, am I rated.
(Whereas) I thought only of supplication and prayer;
Prayer was my practice, sacrificing my law,
The day of worship of the gods the joy of my heart,
The day of devotion to the goddess more (to me) than riches;
Royal prayer,—that was my joy;
Its celebration,—my delight.
I taught my country to guard the name of the god,
To honor the name of the goddess I accustomed my people.
The glorification of the king I made like unto that of a god,[178]
And in the fear of the palace I instructed the people.
I thought that such things were pleasing to a god.''

Despite all this, the pious ruler was smitten with disease and accordingly he indulges in the gloomy thought
that the ways of the gods are mysterious. One can
never be certain of pleasing them. The fate of man is
uncertain. Joy changes to grief suddenly, and apparently without cause or reason.

''What, however, seems good to oneself, to a god is displeasing,
What is spurned by oneself finds favor with a god;
Who is there that can grasp the will of the gods in heaven?
The plan of a god full of mystery (?)—who can understand it?
How can mortals learn the way of a god?
He who was alive yesterday is dead to-day;
In an instant he is cast into grief, of a sudden he is crushed;
For a moment he sings and plays,

---

[176] *i.e.*, the festival.

[177] Tabooed food.

[178] Note the characteristically Babylonian view of the king as
demanding homage, only second to that accorded to the gods.

In a twinkling he wails like a mourner.
Like opening and closing,[179] their (sc. mankind's) spirit changes;
If they are hungry they are like a corpse,
Have they had enough, they consider themselves equal to their
    god;
If things go well, they prate of mounting to heaven,
If they are in distress, they speak of descending into Irkalla." [180]

The sufferer reverts to his sufferings and describes
how the demons of disease have laid him low.

"An evil demon has come out of his (lair);
From yellowish, the sickness became white.[181]
It [182] struck my neck and crushed my back,
It bent my high stature like a poplar;
Like a plant of the marsh, I was uprooted, thrown on my back.
Food became bitter and putrid,
The malady dragged on its course.
Though without food, hunger diminished (?);
The sap of my blood (he [183] drained).
Nourishment was withheld . . .
My flesh was wasted, my body grew wan.
I took to my bed, unable to leave the couch.
The house became my prison;
As fetters for my body, my hands were powerless,
As pinions for my person, my feet were stretched out,
My discomfiture was painful, the pain severe.
A strap of many twists has struck me,
A sharply-pointed spear pierced me.
All day the pursuer followed me,
At night he granted me no respite whatever,
As though wrenched, my joints were torn apart,
My limbs were shattered and rendered helpless.
In my stall I passed the night like an ox,
I was saturated like a sheep in my excrements;

---

[179] Explained in the commentary "like day and night."
[180] One of the names of the nether world. See above, p. 454.
[181] The color of his skin at first yellow becomes pale.
[182] i.e., the sickness.
[183] i.e., the demon of disease.

The disease of my joints baffled the chief exorciser,
And my omens were obscure to the diviner,
The exorciser could not interpret the character of my disease,
And the limit of my malady the diviner could not fix.
No god came to my aid, taking me by the hand,
No goddess had compassion for me, coming to my side.
The grave was open, my burial prepared,
Though not yet dead, the lamentation was over.
The people of my land had already said 'alas' over me.[184]
My enemy heard it and his face shone;
As the joyful tidings were announced to him his liver rejoiced,
I knew it was the day when my whole family,
Resting under the protection of their deity would be in distress." [185]

The sufferer, paralyzed, bed-ridden, totally helpless, blind, deaf, unable to take food, racked with unceasing pain, was thus brought to the brink of despair.[186] All hope had fled and his friends and family already mourned him as dead.

The third tablet beginning

"His hand is heavy, I can no longer endure it," [187]

evidently continued the plaint but soon passed on to an account of a dream sent to the sufferer in which Ur-Bau, described as "a strong hero decked with a crown" appears and apparently gives him a reassuring message from Marduk [188] that he will be released from his sufferings. It is to be regretted that this portion of the composition is so badly preserved, for it must have contained the reason why Marduk decided to come to the relief of the pious sufferer. We are left to conjecture why, but it is plausible to assume that Marduk is seized

---

[184] As over a dead person.

[185] Two obscure lines, the general sense of which is that he felt the end to be near.

[186] He is suffering from a variety of diseases—in fact from almost every ill that can affect a human being.

[187] Furnished by the colophon of the 2d tablet.

[188] Originally, no doubt, Enlil again.

with pity and recognizes that Ṭabi-utul-Enlil did not merit the punishment sent to him. Perhaps it was even suggested that the sufferings were sent as a trial of his piety, though this in default of direct evidence must not be regarded as more than a conjecture. At all events, Ṭabi-utul-Enlil is healed, and we are given a vivid picture of how, as a result of his final appeal to Marduk, the demons of disease are driven away by a mighty storm.

.   .   .   .

"He sent a mighty storm to the foundation of heaven,
  To the depths of the earth he drove it.
  He drove back the evil demon into the abyss.[189]
  The nameless Utukku he drove into his mountain house.[190]
  He confounded Labartu,[191] forcing him back into the mountain.
  On the tide of the sea he swept away the ague.[192]
  He tore out the root of my disease like a plant.
  The bad sleep,[193] (disturbing?) my rest, filled and darkening the
    heavens as with smoke.
  The aches and groans like (those of) a lion (?),
  He stirred up as in a storm and filled the earth,
  The violent headache [194] which overthrows (the strong [?]),
  He tore out . . . and bathed me with the dew of the night.
  My eyeballs which were covered with a veil of night,[195]
  Through a mighty wind he drove away (sc. the veil) and made
    them shine brilliantly.
  My ears which had been closed and bolted as those of a deaf
    person,

---

[189] Apsu—here perhaps intended as a designation of the depths of the earth whence the demons rise up.

[190] Literally "his E-Kur"—here a designation of the dwelling-place of the demons in the mountains.

[191] On the demons Utukku and Labartu see above, p. 242.

[192] *Shuruppû* "chills and fever" here personified, as were all diseases.

[193] *i.e.*, the nightmare, also personified as a demon.

[194] Again personified as in the medical texts. See above, p. 250, *seq.*

[195] Cataract is meant.

31

He removed their deafness and opened their hearing.
My nose which through the force of the fever was choked up,
He healed the hurt so that I could breathe again.
My lips which had been closed through exhausted strength,[196]
He reduced their swelling (?) and loosened their bonds.
My mouth which had been covered, so that with difficulty (?)
(I uttered sounds),
He purified, like copper he made it shine.
My teeth which had been seized so that they were (pressed)
together,[197]
He opened a space between them and strengthened their base.[198]
The tongue which was swollen so that I could not move it,
He took away its coating (?) so that speech returned.
The throat which was compressed, closed up like that of a corpse,
He healed so that my breast resounded like a flute.
My spittle which had been shut off so that it could not come
forth,[199]
He loosened the bonds, opening them like a door.

.   .   .   .

To the opulent [200] who had been reduced to starvation, enchained
like a guilty one,
He brought food and provided drink.
My neck which had been twisted and bent low,
He made erect and like a cedar raised up.
He made my stature like one of perfect strength,
Like one released from a demon, he polished my nails.
He cured me of scurvy, healed me of the itch (?).
My knees that had been fettered like those of a bird of the
gorge,[201]

.   .   .   .

My entire body he restored,
He wiped away the blemish, making it [202] resplendent,

---

[196] He was no longer able to open his mouth.
[197] The teeth were pressed together as in lockjaw.
[198] *i.e.*, fixed them firm in their sockets.
[199] Like Job he was unable to swallow or spit out the saliva.
[200] Though a king with all things at his command, he is wasted
like one dying of famine, since he could not eat nor drink.
[201] *i.e.*, he could not walk.
[202] *i.e.*, the body.

The oppressed stature regained its splendor,
On the banks of the stream where judgment is held over men [203]
The brand of slavery was removed, the fetters taken off.''

Thus one trace after the other of the complicated series of diseases from which he was suffering was removed till he was entirely restored to his former vigor. The composition closes with the enforcement of the lesson never to despair of divine help.

"Let him who sins against E-sagila,[204] let him learn from me,
Into the jaw of the lion, about to devour me, Marduk inserted a bit.
Marduk has seized the snare (?) of my pursuer, has encompassed his lair.''

In this strain no doubt the poem continued to the close—in illustration of the lesson to be derived from Tabi-utul-Enlil's terrible yet marvellous experience. Like the Biblical poem, detailing Job's sufferings and the discourse of the problem involved, our composition ends in a kind of *non sequitur*. The problem is not solved, at least not to our satisfaction, for the just and innocent continue to suffer. The consolation, however, remains that the mercy of the gods in the end never fails. Even though one may be already in the jaws of death, a god if he be so inclined as was Marduk or as was Enlil, the god of Nippur, in the original form of the story, can still save one. Though diviners and exorcisers fail, Marduk can intervene directly and restore the wasted body to perfect vigor. So all ends happily—at least for Tabi-utul-Enlil.

---

[203] Referring to a ceremony of cleansing from sin by immersion into a stream.

[204] The name of Marduk's temple at Babylon, here used for the god.

IX

BUSINESS AND PERSONAL LETTERS

I.[205] Request for a loan.

"Letter[206] of Gula-balatsu-ikbi[207] to Kurbanni-Marduk, my brother. May Nabu and Marduk bless my brother! Shaddinnu has no grain for seed. Let my lord[208] give him one Gur of grain and let my lord take from him a promissory note. In urgent need I am sending to my brother. Let my lord not refuse it, and let my lord give him[209] grain for seed."

II.[210] An inquiry regarding the welfare of relatives and friends.

"Letter of Iddina to the lady Kudashu.
My Lady! Daily I implore Bel[211] and Nabu to grant long life and happiness to my lady. Through the protection of the gods I am well and all with me (are well). Do not worry on my account that you have not received word. Since the month of Siwan[212] I have removed to the land of Paniragana under the guidance of Bel and Nabu.

"Iddina[213] has asked for news about Ina-Marduk, his father, and Ina-E-sagila-ramat, his mother. Iddina has asked for news about

---

[205] Cuneiform Texts XXII, No. 75.

[206] The word used is *duppu*, meaning tablet.

[207] Signifying "the goddess Gula has commanded his life."

[208] The writer addresses his brother in this formal way—perhaps in order to flatter him. Perhaps, however, "brother" is not used literally here. See below, p. 486, note 221.

[209] Namely, Shaddinnu.

[210] Cuneiform Texts, XXII, No. 6.

[211] Here an epithet of Marduk.

[212] Third month.

[213] The writer from here on speaks of himself in the third person, perhaps playfully or perhaps because he is dictating the letter to a scribe.

Shullumu, his father, and Damka, his mother. Iddina has asked for news about Dumuk, his brother.
"By the life of the gods, why do not I get any news from them?

. . . .

Iddina has asked for news about Khabasiru, about Shaddinnu and the lady Ilat-akhe-shu. Iddina has asked [214] for news about Itti-Nabu-balatu, his brother. Why do I not hear from you? And to all the messages which I have sent you I have not seen any response. I have sent you (a message) as follows:
'Since the day that I left, what has happened in the house . . . Why do I not receive any news? Let me know whether Burkû has fallen into the lap [215] of the goddess Tashmetum. Iddina has asked news about the lady Tashmetum-tabni, about Ina-Esagila-Belit, about Shirku, about Lublut, about Burkû . . . and concerning the entire household. For an entire month I have not received any message from you regarding Bel-supê-mukhur.''

III. Letter from a husband to his wife, telling her to take good care of the house.[216]

"Nabu-zer-ushabshi to Sikku, my wife. May Bel and Nabu proclaim good health and long life to my wife! Through the protection of the gods I am well, and Bel-iddin also is well.
"Now I have sent a message to Iddin-Marduk, the son of Ikisha, that he should give thee 10 Gur of grain. Do not neglect the house. Have a look to things. Pray to the gods on my behalf. Let me hear through some message what you are thinking of.'' [217]

---

[214] These various inquiries repeated in this way have reference to a number of separate messages sent by the writer and to which he had not received reply.

[215] The word for lap, *burku,* is here introduced as a play upon the name Burkû. "To place in the lap of a god" is an expression occurring frequently in business documents meaning to deposit in the treasury of the temple. Iddina jokingly asks whether Burkû has lifted something out of the lap,—*i.e.,* whether he has made any money, as we would say.

[216] Cuneiform Texts XXII, No. 151.

[217] The phrase seems to imply the husband's desire to find out what his wife is doing, but perhaps the words mean merely that he wishes to have news of her.

IV.[218] An urgent request for money to settle a promissory note.

"To Ibi-Nin-Shubur speaks as follows Yaum-iluma.
May Shamash and Marduk grant you life!
"I am responsible for a note for (the purchase of) a female slave. Now that the time of the payment of that note has arrived the agent is pressing me. Therefore, I am sending Arad-Innanna to thee. Give him three shekels of silver due from you and two shekels of your own money to be charged against me and properly attested in Babylon. Be sure to give Arad-Innanna the correct amount. Do not detain Arad-Innanna [219] and please fix up the transaction with him correctly."

V.[220] Letter addressed to four friends, urging them not to pay any attention to slanderous reports about the writer's brother.

"Letter of Nabu-zer-ibni to Akar-apli, Balatu, Nabu-bêl-shumâte and to Shamash-udammik his brothers.[221]
"Ever to Nabu and Nanâ for the life of my brothers I pray. Bel-epush who is with you is indeed my brother. Whatever evil reports may be spread about him, may it please my brothers (i.e., my friends) to be deaf to them. From the beginning to the end we have been brothers to one another.[222] Because of distress I am sending this message to my brothers. May my brothers kindly do this. I look forward to the answer to this message from my brothers."

VI. A peremptory request to send on money due or promised.[223]

---

[218] Cuneiform Texts IV, Plate 27 ª.

[219] i.e., send him back as soon as possible.

[220] Cuneiform Texts XXII, No. 155.

[221] The word "brother" is frequently used in the tablets as we would say "friend."

[222] i.e., at all times we have been in perfect harmony with one another.

[223] Cuneiform Texts, XXXIII, Pl. 25 (Hammurapi period).

"To Adaiatum speaks as follows Ili-ishmeanni. May Shamash and
Marduk grant you life! Send on the money which you spoke of. As
I told thee, I need it. In any case, by all means send (it) to me."

VII. A letter with three commissions.[224]

"To Etiatim speaks as follows, Ili'u-Shamash.
"May Shamash and Marduk grant you life! I am well. (1) It
is impossible (for me) to come to see you. I am obliged to go
to Gatana.[225] (2) The she-ass and a young one of good breed, let
the butcher kill for me.[226] The young one I got from Belânu, son
of Sin-turrim, for 5½ shekels of silver. Two shekels of silver
I gave him. Three and one half shekels of silver give him. Do
not give him more or less. Let him weigh the silver for me.[227]
(3) As to the one female slave which I left with you, do not
put her to service.[228] Sell her for silver on my account. Hand
over 7½ Ka of sesame and take a receipt for 2 Gur. One Gur you
have received, and this leaves one Gur."

X

Official Letters and Reports

I. An order of King Hammurapi to clear out a canal.[229]

"To Sin-idinnam, Hammurapi speaks as follows:
"Gather the men who have fields along the Damanum canal to
dig [230] the Damanum canal. Within this month, let them complete
the digging of the Damanum canal."

---

[224] Cuneiform Texts, Pl. 22 (Hammurapi period).

[225] Or possibly Bitana—in any case the name of some place.

[226] *ush-ta-zi-ba-an-ni.*

[227] To make sure that the exact amount is given.

[228] Literally "do not subdue her," evidently in the sense of not
to use her for slave service, but to sell her.

[229] King, *Letters and Inscriptions of Hammurabi* (London,
1900), No. V.

[230] *i.e.,* in the sense of clearing out.

II. A royal order to investigate a charge of graft against an official.[231]

"To Sin-idinnam, Hammurapi speaks as follows:

" Shummanlailu has reported as follows: Bribery has taken place in Dur-Gurgurri. The man who took the bribe and the witness to these matters are here. Thus he (*i.e.*, Shummanlailu) has reported. Now this Shummanlailu and a watchman (?) and one . . . I am sending down to thee. When you receive this tablet, investigate it and if bribery has taken place, send me an official report [232] of the silver and whatever is (involved) in the bribe, and (send) to me the men who took the bribe and the witnesses to these matters."

III. It is interesting to see the king who compiled the great code thus actively engaged in seeking out and punishing miscreants. Another letter to the same Sin-idinnam shows us the king in the same capacity of a rightful judge ordering the restoration of grain to its owner.[233]

"To Sin-idinnam, Hammurapi speaks as follows:

"Amêl-tummumu, a Nippurian, thus has reported to me. 'I stored up 70 Gur of grain [234] in a granary. Apil-ili opened the granary and (took the) grain. Thus he reported to me. Herewith I am sending this Amêl-tummumu to thee. Send for Apil-ili and let them confirm their statements to thee. See to it that Apil-ili takes the grain and returns it to Amêl-tummumu.' "

IV. Military report to an Assyrian king of the submission of certain places in a mountainous region, and a request for further orders.[235]

---

[231] King, *Letters and Inscriptions of Hammurabi* (London, 1900), No. VIII.

[232] Literally "seal," *i.e.*, an official document with witnesses and seals.

[233] King, *ib.* No. XII. The case was probably one covered by § 113 of the Code according to which a creditor has no right to seize the granary of a debtor without an order of the court. See above, p. 300.

[234] About 8,400 litres.

[235] K. 669 (Harper, *Assyrian and Babylonian Letters*, No. 246.)

"To the king my lord, thy servant Ashur-bel-danin, greeting to the king, my lord! The people of Ushkha and the people of Kudâ against whom the king my lord sent me have submitted to the authority of the king my lord. Cities which since the days of Shamash and Â [236] have never been subjected, now with the aid of the guard at my disposal I subdued completely. Those once dependent remain dependent, those (once,) troops remain **troops** of the king.[237] The entire mountain district now recognizes (the authority [?]) of the king. May the heart of the king my lord rejoice! The troops at my disposal I shall retain that they may act as a guard.

"Regarding the people of Mumâ who have not (yet) submitted themselves, (and) have not accepted the authority of the king and with whom there has been no intercourse,[238] let the king send me his orders."

V. A report from the official astrologer regarding the time of full moon.[239]

"To the king my lord, thy servant Nabû'a. May Ashur, Shamash, Bel and Nabu bless the king my lord! May my wishes for the king my lord be fulfilled! We held watch on the 14th day—moon and sun were seen together." [240]

VI. A careful watch was held for the appearance of the new moon,[241] the exact time of which in default of accurate calculation could not be determined before hand; the lunar months varied in this way between 29

---

[236] *i.e.*, never.

[237] A characteristic Assyrian boast, voicing the confidence in the military supremacy of Assyria. As a matter of fact, however, rebellions against Assyrian authority were constantly taking place. See above, p. 173, 176, etc.

[238] *i.e.*, no negotiations for terms of submission have been as yet opened.

[239] Rawlinson III, Pl. 51, No. 2. See above, p. 260, *seq.*

[240] *i.e.*, were in opposition.

[241] This primitive method of fixing the beginning of the month through personal observation of officials was continued among the Jews of Palestine beyond the threshold of our era.

and 30 days. A report of this order to the Assyrian king, who in accordance with the announcement officially declared the time of the beginning of each month, reads: [242]

"To the king [243] my lord, thy servant, Ishtar-nadinapal, the chief astrologer of Arbela.[244] Greeting to the king, my lord. May Nabu and Marduk and Ishtar of Arbela bless the king my lord. On the 29th we kept watch. The place of its appearance was clouded. We did not see the moon. Month of Shebat,[245] first day, in the eponymate [246] of Bel-kharranu'a.''

It follows from the report that the length of the month in question was fixed at 30 days.

VII. Usually, extracts were attached to the reports from the astrological hand-books furnishing the omens for the phenomena reported, the day of the appearance of the new moon, of full moon, of the day of disappearance at the end of the month, of an eclipse and so on *ad infinitum*. A full report of this kind accompanied by three extracts reads: [247]

"On the 1st day I reported to the king as follows: On the 14th day moon and sun were seen together.[248]

---

[242] Rawlinson, III, Pl. 51, No. 6; Harper, *ib.*, No. 829.

[243] The king addressed in these reports is always either Sennacherib, Esarhaddon or Ashurbanapal.

[244] Near Nineveh.

[245] 11th month.

[246] See above, p. 351.

[247] Thompson, *Reports of the Magicians and Astrologers of Nineveh and Babylon* (London, 1900), No. 154.

[248] *i.e.*, full moon appeared on the 14th day of the month. Like the day of the appearance of the new moon, the day of full moon could not be calculated in advance. According to observation it fell on the 13th, 14th or 15th of the month; and in case the new moon day was not certain owing to the cloudy conditions of the sky but would have to be guessed at, the variation might be even greater.

"(*a*) If moon and sun are seen together on the 14th day, order and prosperity in the land. The gods will be gracious to Akkad,[249] joy among men. The cattle of Akkad will graze in security.

"(*b*) 'If the moon reaches the sun [250] with faint illumination, one horn shading the other,[251] justice will prevail in the land. The son will be faithful to the father.' [252]

"(*c*) If on the 14th day the moon was seen with the sun,[253] the king of the land will be (filled with) wisdom.

" 'On the 14th day sun and moon were seen together.' "

VIII. Report of an eclipse of the moon.[254]

"To the gardener,[255] my lord, thy servant Nabu-shumiddin, the chief astrologer of Nineveh. May Nabu and Marduk bless the gardener my lord! On the 14th day we held a watch for the moon. An eclipse of the moon took place."

IX. An eclipse [256] was always looked upon with a certain amount of terror. The evil omen varied, however, according to the direction in which the shadow passed over the moon or a portion thereof. For this purpose the face of the moon was divided into four sections, one represented Akkad or Babylonia, another Assyria, a third Elam—a general term for the East—and a fourth Amurru—a general term for the West. A report of this character reads.[257]

---

[249] *I.e.*, Babylonia where the hand-books were compiled, though the good omen was applicable also to Assyria.

[250] Another phrase to describe full moon.

[251] A shadow on one-half of the moon.

[252] *I.e.*, no rebellion of the crown prince against his father.

[253] *I.e.*, full moon.

[254] Rawlinson, III Pl. 51, No. 7; Harper, *ib.*, No. 816.

[255] A high official—a kind of *major-domo*.

[256] The Babylonians and Assyrians used a term for eclipse, *atatû*, literally "darkening," which was applied to any kind of obscuration of the moon or sun—often not an eclipse at all, but some obscuration due to atmospheric phenomena.

[257] Harper, *ib.*, No. 407.

"To the king my lord, thy servant Nabu-akhe-irba. Greeting to the king my lord. It is a day of terror. I cannot report favorably. The eclipse began in the east [258] and moved to the west. The planets Jupiter and Venus stood therein [259] till they were released. Greeting to the king my lord. It is an evil sign for Amurru.[260] In the morning the evil portent of the moon eclipse shall have passed away from the king my lord." [261]

X. A report regarding favorable days for certain undertakings.[262]

"To the king, my lord, thy servant Nabu-akhe-irba. Greeting to the king my lord! May Nabu and Marduk bless the king my lord! Regarding the carrying out of a building operation about which the king has made inquiry, this month is favorable for the sacred service [263]—favorable, therefore, for carrying out the operation. On the 13th, 15th or 17th day let him carry it out.

"In regard to sacrifices about which the king, my lord, has inquired, this month is favorable for bringing them. To-morrow or the morning after as it pleases the king, my lord, let him bring them.

"In regard to Ashur-mukin-palû'a,[264] about whom the king my lord has made inquiries—let him go. It is a favorable time for going.

"May the king, my lord, raise his grandchild on his knees.[265] Let him, i.e., the grandchild) go at once to present himself."

---

[258] That is, the shadow began on the eastern side of the moon. The orientation in Babylonia for astrological purposes was towards the south. The east side of the moon was therefore to the left.

[259] i.e., were affected by the shadow.

[260] i.e., for the western districts.

[261] i.e., if by morning no evil had set in, the danger was past.

[262] Harper, ib., No. 406.

[263] Some ceremony connected with the building operation to ensure the favor of the gods for the work.

[264] A younger brother of Ashurbanapal, king of Assyria. If Ashur-mukin-palû'a is identical with the "grandson" mentioned in this letter, then the report must have been made to Sennacherib (705–681 B. C.), the grandfather of Ashurbanapal and of Ashur-mukin-palû'a.

[265] A somewhat obscure phrase, indicating perhaps a formal presentation at the court.

XI. A report regarding a storm and a rainbow.[266]

"If a heavy storm breaks forth in the month of Adar, the land will
suffer injury.[267]

"A rainbow (appeared), extending from the zenith to the horizon
of heaven without rain.

" 'If a rainbow extends through the city, things will go well with the
city, with the king and with the princes.' [268]   From Akhesha,
of Uruk."

XII. A report of the birth of a monstrosity.[269]   The report begins with an extract from a hand-book, giving the interpretation of the omen involved in such an occurrence.

"If a fœtus has eight feet and two tails, the ruler will acquire world-
sovereignty." [270]

"A certain butcher, named Uddanu, reported as follows: A sow
in throwing off gave birth to a fœtus that had eight feet and two
tails. I preserved it in salt [271] and have kept it in the house."
From Nergal-eṭir.

XIII. Report of the defilement of a most sacred portion of the temple of Nabu in Nineveh.[272]

"To the king my lord, thy servant Nergal-sharrâni. Greeting to
the king my lord! May Nabu and Marduk bless the king, my

---

[266] Thompson, *ib.*, No. 252.

[267] This is the extract from the hand-book which the astrologer
sends the king in answer to an inquiry as to the meaning of a severe
storm in the month of Adar—the 12th month.

[268] Again an extract.

[269] Cuneiform Texts, XXVII Pl. 45. On the significance attached to monstrosities and all kinds of abnormal marks on infants
and the young of animals, see Jastrow, *Babylonian-Assyrian Birth-
Omens and their Cultural Significance* (Giessen, 1914), and above,
p. 263, *seq.*

[270] A favorable omen, therefore.

[271] As we preserve a monstrosity in alcohol, and send it to an
anatomical museum.

[272] Harper, *ib.*, No. 367.

lord. A mouse was seen in the court of the *bitanu* [273] of the Nabu temple, and a rat on the wall of the inner chamber.[274] The purification rites have already been arranged for. The ceremony will be carried out to-morrow without delay by Adad-shumuṣur.''

XI

Medical Letters

I. Letter of the court physician to the king reporting progress in the treatment of an injury to the eye of a young prince.[275]

''Arad-Nanâ to the king my Lord, thy servant Arad-Nanâ. Hearty greetings to the king, my Lord. May Ninib and Gula [276] grant happiness and health to the king my Lord!

''Hearty greetings to the little chap whose eye causes him trouble. I put a bandage [277] on his face. Yesterday, towards evening, I

---

[273] Probably near the ''holy of holies'' where the statue of the god stood.

[274] The inner division of the temple, leading to the sacred chamber of the god. See further for translations of several hundreds of such official reports of all kinds, astrological, divinatory, dreams, portents, etc. etc., Jastrow, *Religion Babyloniens und Assyriens* II, pp. 213–445 (liver omens or hepatoscopy), pp. 457–741, (astrological and atmospheric) pp. 749–775 (oil and water divination); pp. 843–946 (birth omens); pp. 946–969 (dreams, miscellaneous portents).

[275] Harper, *Assyrian and Babylonian Letters,* No. 392. For a general survey of Babylonian and Assyrian medicine, with copious extracts from medical texts, see Jastrow, *Medicine of the Babylonians and Assyrians* (Proceedings of the Royal Society of Medicine, 1914, Vol. vii, Section of the History of Medicine, pages 109–176).

[276] In these medical letters the gods invoked in the greeting, with which a letter invariably begins, are Ninib, the god of healing, and his consort Gula. In other letters the gods most commonly invoked are Marduk and Nabu (or in reversed order), though the moon-god, Sin, and his consort Nin-gal are sometimes substituted for Marduk and Nabu. Frequently, however, a longer list of deities is introduced in the greeting.

[277] The word used is *ta'alitu,* literally ''a covering.''

took off the bandage that had been applied, removing also the dressing below, and there was blood on the dressing as much as the point of the little finger. To which ever one of thy gods this is due, his command has surely been heeded.

"Hearty greetings. Let the king my Lord rest assured; in seven or eight days he will be well."

II. Letter of the same court physician to the king, replying to a complaint of the king that his physician has failed to cure him.[278]

"The king my Lord continues to declare 'the state of this sickness of mine thou dost not recognize, thou dost not bring about a cure.' Now I confess that hitherto I did not understand this rheumatism,[279] but now I seal this letter to send it to the king my Lord. Let it be read to the king my Lord and properly understood. When it reaches the king my Lord let a physician . . . carry out the accompanying directions. Let the king apply this liniment.[280] If the king does this, this fever will soon leave the king my Lord. A second and a third time this liniment should be applied to the king my Lord. The king must see to this. If it please the king, let it be done in the morning. This disease is in the blood. Let them bring the king *silbani*,[281] as was twice done already, and let it be vigorously done. I shall come to inform myself, and as soon as the perspiration flows freely from the king, my Lord, I will send to the king, my Lord, something to apply to the king's neck. With a salve which I shall send the king let the king be rubbed at the appointed time."

III. Letter of Arad-Nanâ, the court physician, regarding a case of hemorrhages of the nose from which the king's son is suffering.[282]

---

[278] Harper, *ib.*, No. 391.

[279] Literally "sickness of the muscles."

[280] *markhushu;* evidently the wash or liniment was sent with the letter.

[281] *silbanu* is "dried liquorice root," but in this passage a liniment or a massage treatment appears to be intended.

[282] Harper, *ib.*, No. 108.

"To the king my Lord, thy servant Arad-Nanâ. Hearty greetings to the king, my Lord. May Ninib and Gula grant the king, my Lord, happiness and health.

"Hearty greetings to the king's son. The treatment which we prescribe for him is to be given every two-thirds of a double hour during the day.[283] . . .

"In regard to the bleeding of the nose about which the Rab-Mugi [a high official] has reported to me that yesterday toward evening there was much bleeding, those dressings are not properly applied; they have been placed upon the alae of the nose, obstructing the breathing, while at the same time the blood flows into the mouth. Let the nose be plugged up to the back so that air will be held off, and the bleeding will cease. If it please the king I will come to look at it to-morrow. Meanwhile may I hear good news."

---

[283] The Babylonians and Assyrians divided the full day into twelve double hours. As a survival of this method based on the sexagesimal system, we still have only twelve numerals on our watch dials and divide day and night each into twelve hours, instead of counting the hours of a full day consecutively from one to twenty-four, as indeed is now done in the time-tables of some European railways. Every two-thirds of a double hour would therefore be every eighty minutes. The following four lines are obscure.

INDEX

Hunting, 168, 199, 201, 400 *seq.*
Hyde, Thomas, 63
Hymns, 22, 46, 104, 203. See also Incantation
Hystaspes, 74, 77, 78, 81, 111

I

Ib, in oath formula, 357
Ibi-Sin, King of Ur, 140
Idiklat = Tigris, *q. v.*
Igigi, 198, 213, 227, 229, 235, 442, 451
Ilumailu, King of "Sea Land," 150, 151
Ilushuma, patesi of Ashur, 145
Imgur-Enlil (Balawat), 35, 413
Immersion, 483
Immortality, 211, 281, 425 *seq.*, 445, 452. See also Life after death. Nether world
Incantation (*shiptu*), 22, 46, 104, 198, 211, 226, 239 *seq.*, 411 *seq.*, 433, 437, 442
Incest, 286, 312 *seq.*
Indenture, 285, 301
India, 2, 6
Inheritance, 305 *seq.*, 308, 362 *seq.*
Injuries, 285 *seq.*
Innina, or Innanna (goddess), 202, 232, 340
Inscriptions, votive, 49, 113, 143, 189, 197, 202, 208, 210, 222; bilingual, 69; trilingual, 65 *seq.*, 82, 87; Elamitic, 110 *seq.*, 114; Hittite, 115 *seq.* See also Cuneiform, Offerings
Interest, rate of, 326, 338, 339, 340 *seq.*
Inundation, in Babylonia, 7, 8, 9, 128, 297, 367; suggests deluge story, 445
Ira, god of pestilence, 448, 451
Irkalla (nether world), 454, 479
Irnina (goddess), 232, 235
Iron, 17, 41
Irrigation, 7, 9, 10, 128, 367. See also Canals
Ishkhara (goddess), symbol, 417
Ishme-Dagan, ruler of Assyria, 158
Ishtar (goddess), 26, 238 *seq.*, 270, 468; Gate of, Babylon, 60, 370; associated with triad, 232; consort of

Ashur, 232; various names, 232; as Mother goddess, 233; as goddess of love, 233 *seq.*; as goddess of war, 234; identified with Venus, 234, 261; symbol, 411, 417; in Gilgamesh epic, 444 *seq.*, 461; descent into nether world, 453 *seq.*
Ishum, fire-god, 226
Isin (City), 124, 146, 149, 150, 151, 153; dynasty, 141 *seq.*, 170 *seq.*, 329
Izdubar, 34, see Gilgamesh

J

Jacob, 309
Jamutbal, see Emutbal
Japan, 2
Japhet, 96
Jastrow, Morris, Jr., 4, 5, 22, 74, 216, 227, 235, 242, 251, 254, 257, 262, 264, 265, 266, 267, 279, 280, 281, 308, 380, 389, 427, 441, 444, 453, 463, 465, 469, 475, 493, 494
Jensen, Peter, 198
Jeremias, Johannes, 38
Jerusalem, 135, 196; fall of, 183
Jewelry, 410, 415
Jews, burial, 48, 196
Job, 475, 477, 482, 483
Johns, C. H. W., 284, 315, 344, 345
Jonah, 12
Josephus, 9
Judaea, 176, 183
Judges, 288, 365. See also Courts, Priests
Jupiter, identified with Marduk, 261, 439, 442, 491
Jurisprudence, see Courts, Dating, Law codes, Legal documents, Judges, Priests

K

Ka, a measure, 326
Kadesh, male votary, 308
Kadishtu, "holy woman," 308. See also Votaries, Prostitution
Kaempfer, Engelbert, 65
Kalah, see Calah and Nimrud
Kaleh-Shergat, 35, 55, 86, 157, 158, 379 *seq.* See also Ashur
Kalû, "musician," 272, 325